Contents

CD-ROM contents

Introduction

Welcome to the Level 3 Candidate Handbook for the Diploma in Health and Social Care (Adults) award.

How is the book organised?

Each chapter of the book covers a specific level 3 unit. You will see that the chapters are divided into different sections, which are exactly matched to the specifications for the level 3 qualification. Each section provides you with a focused and manageable chunk of learning and covers all of the content areas that you need to know about in a particular unit.

There is a strong work-related focus to the materials in this book, using case studies, a range of practice-focused activities and realistic examples to develop your interest in and understanding of professional practice within the Adult health and social care workplace.

How is assessment covered?

In order to achieve your level 3 award, you will need to provide evidence of your knowledge and understanding as well as your practical competence in the real work environment. Each chapter of this handbook begins with a summary of 'What you need to know' and 'What you need to do' in order to successfully complete the unit. The checklist at the end of the each chapter will help you to keep track of your progress.

The suggested assessment tasks in each chapter will help you to gather the evidence you need for each unit. Your tutor or assessor will help you to plan your work in order to meet the assessment requirements.

Which units should I choose?

The material in this book covers all 9 mandatory units of the level 3 diploma, together with a range of optional units. You must achieve a minimum of 58 credits to gain the Level 3 Diploma in Health and Social Care (Adults) award. To do this you must achieve:

▶ 28 credits from the mandatory units (chapters 1 to 9)

▶ a minimum of 2 and a maximum of 7 credits from the optional context / specialist knowledge units (chapters 10, 11, 14 and 15)

▶ at least 23 credits from the optional competence units (chapters 12, 13 and 16 to 20).

If you wish to claim a specialist dementia pathway award you must complete chapter 15 which is the mandatory dementia knowledge unit for this pathway. In addition, you must complete either chapter 10, 11 or 14 (optional context / specialist knowledge units) and either chapter 16 or 17 (mandatory dementia competence units). You must also obtain 19 credits from chapters 12, 13, 18, 19 and 20 (optional competence units). Social care workers in Wales must complete chapter 14 to gain their award. Other candidates in Wales, Northern Ireland and England have a free choice of optional units.

We hope that the material in this book is accessible, interesting and inspires you to pursue a rewarding career caring for and supporting adults in health and social care settings. Good luck with your course and your future career!

Mark Walsh

1 | Promote communication in health and social care settings (SHC 31)

Assessment of this unit

This unit highlights the central importance of communication in working with service users. It focuses on the reasons why people communicate in health and social care settings, the methods they use and the importance of ensuring that communication is effective. You will need to:

1. Understand why effective communication is important in the work setting.

2. Be able to meet the communication and language needs, wishes and preferences of individuals.

3. Be able to overcome barriers to communication.

4. Be able to apply principles and practices relating to confidentiality.

You will be assessed on both your knowledge of effective communication and your ability to apply this in practical work with service users. To complete this unit successfully, you will need to produce evidence of your knowledge, as shown in the 'What you need to know' chart opposite, and evidence of your practical competence, as shown in the 'What you need to do' chart. The 'What you need to do' criteria must be assessed in a real work environment by a vocationally competent assessor. Your tutor or assessor will help you to prepare for your assessment and the tasks suggested in the chapter will help you to create the evidence that you need.

CHAPTER 1

AC What you need to know

1.1 Identify the different reasons people communicate

1.2 Explain how communication affects relationships in the work setting

AC What you need to do

2.1 Demonstrate how to establish the communication and language needs, wishes and preferences of individuals

2.2 Describe the factors to consider when promoting effective communication

2.3 Demonstrate a range of communication methods and styles to meet individual needs

2.4 Demonstrate how to respond to an individual's reactions when communicating

3.1 Explain how people from different backgrounds may use and/or interpret communication methods in different ways

3.2 Identify barriers to effective communication

3.3 Demonstrate ways to overcome barriers to communication

3.4 Demonstrate strategies that can be used to clarify misunderstandings

3.5 Explain how to access extra support or services to enable individuals to communicate effectively

4.1 Explain the meaning of the term confidentiality

4.2 Demonstrate ways to maintain confidentiality in day to day communication

4.3 Describe the potential tension between maintaining an individual's confidentiality and disclosing concerns

This unit also links to some of the other mandatory units:

HSC 025 The role of the health and social care worker

DEM 312 Understand and enable interaction and communication with individuals who have dementia

SS MU 3.1 Understand sensory loss

Some of your learning will be repeated in these units and will give you the chance to review your knowledge and understanding.

Why do people communicate?

Communication is a central part of everyday life for most people and is particularly important when you work with service users and their families in a health and social care setting. You must understand:

- what communication involves
- the different reasons for communication
- the way communication affects how practitioners work.

Communication is about making contact with others and being understood. We all communicate continuously, involving a two-way process of sending and receiving messages. These messages can be:

- **verbal communication**, using spoken or written words
- **non-verbal communication**, using body language such as gestures, eye-contact and touch.

When you work in a health and social care setting as well as communicating with service users you will also need to communicate with their relatives and other visitors, with your colleagues and with practitioners from other care agencies. You will need to communicate for a variety of different reasons, as shown in Figure 1.1.

Making and developing relationships

People communicate to make new relationships. The way you first speak and listen to a newcomer can make them feel welcome or overlooked. As you speak and comment, listen and watch, take an interest, smile and nod, whether to a service user, a member of their family, a colleague or a visiting practitioner you are building and developing your relationship with them. Communication will continue to be the main way you nurture and develop your relationships at work.

Giving and receiving information

At work you will be expected to give and receive different types of information. Perhaps a service user confides in you, or a member of their family asks you a question. A colleague could give you instructions or a visiting practitioner might make an observation. The information you give, receive and pass on will help you to carry out your work effectively.

Key terms

Non-verbal communication: ways of communicating without using words (for example, through body language such as gestures, eye-contact and touch)

Verbal communication: forms of communication that use (spoken or written) words

Figure 1.1 Why people communicate

People communicate to ...
- Affirm one another
- Make and develop relationships
- Give and receive information
- Express needs and feelings
- Share thoughts and ideas

Expressing needs and feelings

Expressing needs and feelings is part of being human and these are communicated through behaviour as well as speech. Most people need to share needs and feelings with each other and in this way build up a sense of trust with the person they confide in.

Sharing thoughts and ideas

Humans process many of their thoughts by discussing them. If you have ideas, questions and opinions about your work, sharing them with colleagues helps to clarify, develop and even change the way you think and act. The way in which you respond to the thought processes of service users could encourage or discourage their sharing with you.

Affirming one another

Affirmation is about acknowledging and encouraging each other and reassuring individuals of their worth and value. Affirmation is communicated through positive words, praise and gestures. Some care settings use support groups, staff meetings and appraisals as ways of affirming practitioners about their work performance.

Investigate

Carry out a piece of personal research during an hour to analyse the different reasons you communicate during that time. Jot down each time you communicate to make and develop relationships; give and receive information; express needs and feelings; share thoughts and ideas and affirm another person.

Key terms

Affirmation: a positive statement declaring a quality about something or someone

Case study

Deshan is visiting his wife in hospital following a minor operation. She has dementia and cannot fully understand what is happening to her, which makes both of them feel anxious. He wants to speak to someone about her progress and tries to catch the attention of passing nurses, but they all seem so busy. He hovers around the nurses' station, where he is asked brusquely if he needs any help. The nurse answers his questions in a vague way, saying his wife is 'doing as well as can be expected' and when he asks if she is being given a vegetarian diet he is told, 'I expect so – if that's what she requested.'

1. What are the different reasons why Deshan needs to communicate?
2. How well do you think the nurse has responded to these needs?
3. How do you suggest she improves the communication?

Knowledge Assessment Task   1.1

Communication is a vital skill in health and social care settings as you communicate with service users and their relatives and with members of the staff team. For this task you will need to read the statements and match each one to the relevant reasons for communicating, which appear below.

1. The health care assistant praised Sylvie because of her effort in the physiotherapy session.
2. Tanya confides to the social worker that she finds it a strain dealing with her husband's dementia and doesn't know how long she can carry on caring for him.
3. Lisbet and Matthew discuss different ways to record staff meetings.
4. Ken asks the new carer, Ghalib what his name means in African.
5. The senior care worker told all the staff at handover that Mrs Watts is now on a diabetic diet.

   Reasons for communicating: a. To give or receive information; **b.** To make and maintain relationships; **c.** To express needs and feelings; **d.** To share thoughts and ideas; **e.** To affirm a person

How does communication affect relationships in care settings?

The ability to communicate well is a key skill that enables you to work effectively with others. Always remember that the communication process is as much about listening and receiving messages as it is about talking and giving messages. As a care worker you need to be skilled in both aspects. In general, you will use communication effectively as part of your work role if you:

▶ get the other person's attention before you begin communicating with them

▶ communicate clearly and directly so that you get your message across

▶ adapt the way you communicate to a service user's needs so that they are able to understand you

▶ use **empathy** to try and understand the other person's needs, point of view or the way they might be affected by what you are saying to them

▶ listen carefully to what service users communicate to you

▶ use your own non-verbal communication skills effectively

▶ summarise what the other person has said as a way of checking and confirming your understanding of what they mean.

Your communication skills will develop and become more effective as you gain experience in your work role, learning from observing more experienced colleagues. Learning from others, seeking advice and using support are all part of this process.

During your work with service users there will be specific situations where good communication skills are particularly necessary. Some of these are illustrated in Figure 1.2.

Your assessment criteria:

1.2 Explain how communication affects relationships in the work setting.

Key terms

Empathy: understanding another person's feelings as if they are your own

Investigate

Using library or internet resources find out as much as you can about the term empathy. Ask colleagues what they understand by the term and consider how better to demonstrate your empathy at work.

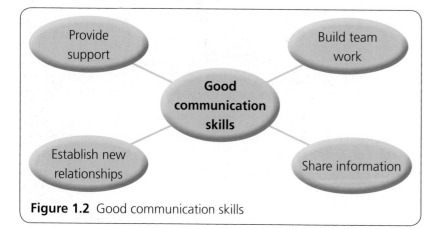

Figure 1.2 Good communication skills

Building team work

Working in a health and social care setting usually means working in a team. Members of the team may have different roles, but the wellbeing of the service users you care for is a common focus for all. A team with members who communicate well with each other is a strong team.

Sharing information

In a care setting it is vital that information is shared appropriately between workers to enable each member of the team to carry out his or her role effectively. You will also need to share information with service users and their relatives. Sometimes the information might be of a sensitive nature, such as when breaking bad news or dealing with private information, and you will need to be especially sensitive. In the course of your work you will need to find out information, pass on information and listen to information.

Establishing new relationships

When a service user arrives in a new environment, he or she may feel apprehensive. The ability to empathise, that is, to imagine how the person is feeling, is a key communication skill. It helps you understand what the person needs in order to feel at ease, such as a warm welcome, information and reassurance.

Providing support

Communication is the main way in which you continue to sustain relationships and build these up. As a health and social care worker you will need to offer support to service users and their families and this is enabled through both verbal and non-verbal communication. You will need to listen, as much as speak and the use of appropriate and non intrusive touch can add to the sense of being supportive.

You may need to allow more time and additional methods to communicate with people with special needs

Effective communication with relatives and visitors

Service users and their relatives need to be able to trust you and have confidence in your ability to support and care for them. Communication with relatives and visitors is more likely to be effective if you:

▶ establish a good rapport with each individual

▶ show people respect by using their preferred names (e.g 'Mrs Griffiths' not 'Jenny', if preferred) and recognise that they should always be consulted about anything that affects them

▶ speak directly and clearly, using positive body language and good eye contact when interacting

▶ give each individual enough time to understand what you are saying and listen carefully to what they say to you

▶ respond quickly and in an appropriate way to an individual's communication by phone, email or in person

▶ respect **confidentiality** by communicating personal, sensitive or private information about individuals in an appropriate, private area of the care setting

▶ adapt your communication skills to meet the needs of a people who have hearing or visual impairments or whose first language is not English.

Effective communication with colleagues

Effective communication with colleagues is an essential part of your work role when you work in a team. It is based on establishing a friendly but professional working relationship where you can give and receive support and should focus on your shared goal

Your assessment criteria:

1.2 Explain how communication affects relationships in the work setting.

Key terms

Confidentiality: ensuring information is only accessible to people who are authorised to know about it

Discuss

Share with a colleague any experiences you have had of needing to discuss sensitive or confidential information with a service user or their relatives.

▶ What was it you found most difficult?

▶ What was positive about the experience?

of promoting the health and wellbeing of the service users. Communication is more likely to positively affect relationships with colleagues in the work setting if you:

▶ establish an appropriate work-related rapport

▶ show that you respect your colleagues' skills, abilities and professional approach towards their work role

▶ talk to your colleagues clearly and directly, using positive body language and allowing enough time

▶ always listen to your colleagues' point of view, making sure you are polite and constructive where you disagree

▶ check that colleagues understand any important information you pass on

▶ clarify any points or ask questions if you don't understand

▶ respect confidentiality by communicating about sensitive, personal or private issues in an appropriately private place

▶ when writing emails, letters or notes, ask someone to check that your language and presentation are professional.

Reflect

Think of an example of communication that regularly takes place with colleagues at your place of work, such as a handover report or a team meeting.

▶ What enables good communication on these occasions?

▶ What interferes with or interrupts the communication process?

Case study

Kimberley has worked as a carer at a care home for older people with dementia for many years. She advises the new care worker, Tilly that it's easy to make relationships with the residents if she just thinks of them as children. After all, they need everything doing for them and they're often a bit naughty, calling out, spilling food and being incontinent. When Tilly tries to remember the residents' names, Kimberley tells her not to worry and just call them 'darling' or 'sweetheart'. She laughs when Tilly knocks on the bedroom doors before entering and says she'll never get to know the residents at that rate – better to walk straight in and give them all a big hug so they feel loved.

1. What do you think about Kimberley's advice to Tilly about communicating with the residents?

2. In what ways do you think Kimberley's communication with Tilly has helped or hindered welcoming and supporting her as a new member of staff?

3. How would you suggest Tilly uses communication to build a relationship with the residents?

Knowledge Assessment Task   1.2

Communication is the way that relationships are established and built up and is also at the root of most relationship break-downs.

1. Think of two practical examples from your work setting or placement that illustrate how you have used communication to affect relationships positively.

2. Describe both scenarios.

3. Explain how you used different types of communication to build team work successfully, or to share information, establish new relationships and to provide support.

Keep the written work that you produce as evidence for your assessment.

How do you establish communication needs?

When you work in a health or social care setting an important part of your role is to **facilitate** communication. This means enabling individuals to express themselves and understand the communication of others. To be effective in this role you must first recognise that each person is unique, meaning there will be differences in the way each person communicates.

Different influences affecting communication

Communication is a particularly individual activity which can be affected by a number of different influences.

Cultural differences

Acknowledging and responding to the cultural aspects of a person's identity and care needs are strategies that are likely to enhance communication. Avoid general assumptions that beliefs about issues such as diet, personal care practices, sleeping arrangements and 'health' are shared by all service users. The danger of imposing dominant cultural assumptions is that both the identities and care needs of service users who don't belong to the dominant culture are neglected. This obviously makes interaction and communication less effective. Finding out about another person's cultural background will give you insights as to the best way to communicate with them.

Language differences

Language is a central feature of any communication process. There is often an assumption in care settings that the language of the dominant culture should be used, which in most cases is English. Where care professionals are involved, this may also include use of technical health or social care jargon. Avoid using jargon where possible as it can confuse service users who are unfamiliar with the specialist terms.

The issue of language is even more problematic for people whose first language is not English. Don't assume that all service users can understand English. You could use multi-lingual signs in the care setting, and letters and leaflets translated into other languages used by members of various local communities, alongside access to interpreter services and multilingual care staff. All these strategies can help service users whose choice of language is not English, to understand and communicate more effectively.

Your assessment criteria:

2.1 Demonstrate how to establish the communication and language needs, wishes and preferences of individuals.

Key terms

Facilitate: to encourage and enable

Reflect

Think about cultural influences on your communication. Do you have an accent and do you use particular words or expressions associated with your upbringing, or the friends you have? How does the way you use language add to your identity and sense of self?

Specific needs

Physical difficulties influence the way individuals are able to communicate. This is discussed further on page 22 in terms of barriers to communication. You need to be sensitive to the specific needs of individuals so communication is facilitated from the start. For example, if a person has difficulty enunciating (speaking clearly) following a stroke, allow enough time for a conversation to take place, check frequently that you are receiving their message correctly and reassure the person that they don't need to rush.

Facilitating good communication

As well as different influences affecting the communication of individuals, there will be different conditions in the environment of a care setting, for example to do with levels of noise or different types of activity going on. You will need to modify your methods of communication according to whom you are speaking with and the conditions you are in, which requires a flexible approach.

Working with adults

When working with adults (service users and their relatives, colleagues, practitioners) you can usually ask directly about language and communication needs and preferences. For example, how to address a person: whether by their first name, or more formally; and whether a woman wishes to be called Miss, Mrs or Ms. Remember it is not possible to tell just by outward appearances whether a person has literacy needs to do with reading and writing. You may need to question directly how a person wishes to receive information to enable them to understand, for example, via a leaflet translated into their first language.

Working with people who are hearing impaired or visually impaired

If you are working with service users who are hearing or visually impaired it needn't be a barrier to communication if you ensure you follow the advice set out in Figure 1.3.

Key terms

Non-verbal: communicating without using words

Figure 1.3 Communicating with hearing or visually impaired people

Hearing impaired	Visually impaired
Check hearing aid is in and working	Introduce yourself and anyone with you before launching into conversation
Use available aids, such as a loop system	Can use a light touch on the arm to indicate where you are
Face the person you are speaking to at all times	Explain if anything arises that might affect the communication, such as people joining or leaving
Speak slowly and clearly	End the conversation clearly so the person knows you are leaving
Use your eyes, facial expressions and gestures to give **non-verbal** support for your words	
Do not be tempted to shout into a person's ear or hearing aid	

What factors promote effective communication?

When communicating with others the content of the message needs to be clear, but it also needs to be said in a clear way. When receiving messages it is necessary to be alert to both verbal (spoken) and non-verbal (body language) messages.

To communicate effectively keep in mind the factors illustrated in the table in Figure 1.4. There is no one combination of factors which provides the ideal way to communicate a message. It will differ according to the message, the recipient and the situation.

Your assessment criteria:

2.2 Describe the factors to consider when promoting effective communication.

Key terms

Body space: the physical space between two people that feels comfortable

Safeguarding: the protection of adults who are more vulnerable to harm and abuse

Figure 1.4 Factors that affect communication

Environment: location	Proximity: physical distance	Orientation: body positioning	Posture: behaviour	Touch: type and appropriateness
Are noise and activity levels too high? Do you need privacy? Would it be easier to have this conversation while carrying out an activity together? Walking or working side by side can ease the flow of conversation.	The better you know a person the closer you are likely to be physically. Closeness can encourage sharing. Positioning chairs at an angle rather than side by side makes it physically easier to talk to another person. Sitting directly opposite is more formal and can feel confrontational. Sometimes a table between you helps a person feel protected. Yelling from one room to another doesn't aid communication!	Leaning forward can communicate that you are interested, but too close might invade 'body space'. Turning away can show lack of interest, but standing directly opposite a person can be too direct, where being at an angle can provide a helpful space.	Folded arms can look defensive and discourage communication. Friends and family without realising, often mirror the other person's posture during conversation, which is thought to increase a sense of familiarity. Standing over a person who is seated might feel patronising or threatening.	A light touch on a person's arm or hand can communicate caring and understanding, but sometimes touch can feel intrusive, even threatening. Touch is a **safeguarding** issue and you must never impose yourself physically on a vulnerable adult. (See chapter 5 for more about this)

Case study

20-year-old Shihong, who is Chinese and a healthcare assistant, needs to complete the menu cards for the ward. Mr Menzie, who is Scottish, has not filled his in and moans, saying his leg hurts too much for him to think properly. Shihong offers to complete it, but Mr Menzies replies that he's not some useless old geezer. A nurse administers a painkiller to Mr Menzies and Shihong tries again, but Mr Menzies is getting sleepy. Anxious to complete her task, Shihong wakes him. He answers in a slurred voice she can hardly hear, 'Put down anything, hen – I dinnae care, so long as it's plain, plenty tatties, but nae neeps as I cannae stand them.' Shihong has no idea what he means and fills his menu in with her choices.

1. What cultural factors might be influencing the communication between Shihong and Mr Menzies?
2. What factors might promote better communication between Shihong and Mr Menzies?
3. What would you have done in this situation?

Reflect

Think about the last time you felt you were really listened to. What did the person do and say to make you feel heard? Now think about the last time you felt overlooked and not listened to. What did the person do and say to make you feel dismissed?

Active listening

Communication is as much about listening and observing as it is about talking. **Active listening** means more than just hearing a message – it is about really tuning in and taking in what is being communicated. Active listening requires you to understand non-verbal communication, which is explored further on page 16.

Allowing time to communicate

When working in health and social care it is important to allow time for communication to take place. Service users may need you to repeat, explain and give examples in order to fully understand your message. They may need to question, challenge and negotiate. Each individual needs time to take in what has been said and to formulate an answer. In a busy care setting you may have to respond quickly to a range of communications and at times these might be urgent. Try to find some quiet moments to stop and review whether you have communicated clearly and understood correctly the communication of others.

Key terms

Active listening: close listening, accompanied by an awareness of non-verbal communication of self and others

Routes of communication

In your work role you will use a number of routes to communicate information. Each time you need to decide on the most appropriate route. Sometimes you will use more than one route, such as a conversation followed up by a letter, or a committee meeting followed up with written minutes. Figure 1.5 outlines the positive and negative aspects of different communication routes.

Your assessment criteria:

2.2 Describe the factors to consider when promoting effective communication.

Figure 1.5 Positive and negative aspects of different communication routes

SPOKEN WORD	
Face to face conversation	
Positive aspects	*Negative aspects*
• Able to observe body language • Able to observe non-verbal responses of others • Able to question and clarify	• May take time to arrange a meeting • May not have privacy
Conversation over telephone	
Positive aspects	*Negative aspects*
• Quick method of communication • Immediate method of communication • Able to hear tone of voice	• Cannot observe body language responses of others • Person might not be in to receive call
WRITTEN WORD	
Letters and reports	
Positive aspects	*Negative aspects*
• Able to relay long/complex messages • Able to expand on thoughts without interruption • Able to present information in a formal way • Recipient has time to absorb information	• Takes time to compose letter • Need literacy skills • Letter could get lost in the post • Person may take a long time to respond, or not do so at all
Emails and texts	
Positive aspects	*Negative aspects*
• Fast, easy way to send messages • Able to send information in an abbreviated form • Able to send one message to many recipients • Able to edit and change message before sending	• Recipient could misinterpret abbreviated messages • Need the technology to use these methods • Have to wait for recipient's response

Case study

Ronan is a support worker for Ellen and Stevie, a married couple who both have special needs. They have recently responded to an unsolicited (junk) mail invitation to take out life insurance, something they don't need, because they have a trust fund, and that they can't afford on their budget. Ronan needs to explain things so they can understand and persuade them to cancel the arrangement, but in a way that does not undermine their confidence or infringe their independence.

1. What method or methods would you choose to communicate with Ellen and Stevie?
2. What are your reasons for these choices?
3. What factors must Ronan take into consideration during this communication?

Reflect

Think about the different routes you use to communicate. What is your preferred way of communicating? Why is this?

Touch can express concern and caring, providing comfort and reassurance

Using a range of communication methods and styles

Communication is a complex process made up of many different elements to do with verbal and non-verbal language. These are reflected in a range of communication styles and methods. Communication is also a two-way process that must take into consideration the reactions of others and respond appropriately. To be a skilled communicator and interpreter of communication you must pay close attention to your words and actions, as well as the words and actions of others.

Non-verbal communication

Non verbal communication is a form of communication that takes place almost **subconsciously**, that is, without being aware of thinking. It provides clues about the meaning of spoken language. You have already looked at some aspects related to non-verbal communication to do with proximity, orientation, posture and touch. The main aspects of non-verbal communication are illustrated in Figure 1.6 and described here.

Body language

Body language relates to the way your body reflects your thoughts and feelings. This can add emphasis to your words, but if you don't really mean what you are saying it can also reveal a truer and contradictory message beneath your words. For example, exclaiming, 'How fascinating' might sound as though you are interested, but body language of tapping fingers, poor eye contact and stifled yawns betrays that you are actually bored.

Gestures

Gestures are signs made with the hands and arms to illustrate or emphasise your words or to stand in place of words. People often gesticulate during conversations without really thinking about it. You may see someone gesticulating while talking on a phone, even though the person receiving the call cannot see their gestures. Some gestures are understood across many different countries of the world, such as thumbs up, meaning 'good news', but be careful because not all gestures are universal and instead of clarifying a message, could create confusion.

Key terms

Subconsciously: happening at a level without conscious thought or full awareness

Body language: communication expressed through gestures, poses and posture

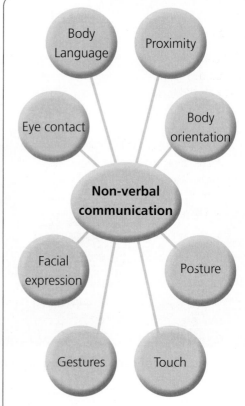

Figure 1.6 Non-verbal communication

Facial expression

Facial expression reveals a great deal about our feelings. Think of a grimace of pain, a wide grin of happiness, a worried frown. In fact, a blank facial expression makes it much harder to interpret what is being said.

Eye contact

Eye contact is very important and sometimes it is difficult to know if a person is telling the truth unless you can look into their eyes. Holding someone's gaze is a sign of intimacy, but to do so with a person you don't know well can feel uncomfortable, even threatening. During most conversations it is normal for your gaze to flit to and from another's face.

When working with service users who have communication difficulties it can help to exaggerate elements of non-verbal communication to provide more clues about your spoken message.

Verbal communication

Verbal communication is about the choice of words being spoken, but also the way the words are said.

Vocabulary

Choosing words that are appropriate to the service user's level of understanding is important. Perhaps English is not their first language, or they have communication difficulties associated with a physical condition. At the same time, you need to be aware of not being too simplistic and coming across as patronising.

Tone of voice

Tone of voice concerns the emotional message being conveyed alongside the spoken words. When these don't match, people can become aware of your emotions and will pick up whether you are irritated or anxious, for example.

Pitch of voice

Pitch of voice concerns how low or high your voice sounds. Speaking in a low voice can be calming and soothing, but too low and you can sound boring. In contrast, a high pitch can sound shrill and be unpleasant to listen to.

Reflect

Take some time to watch people in conversation with each other and notice their non-verbal communication. Be aware of body language, gestures, facial expression, eye contact, proximity, orientation, posture and touch.

Most communication takes place while undertaking other activities

Reflect

Make a point of listening to yourself and others when speaking. Notice the tone and pitch of voice and how this contributes to the message being communicated.

Responding appropriately

The following qualities will help you respond appropriately to the communication of others.

▶ **Awareness** of how your communication is being received. Look for non-verbal cues that indicate the recipient's interest and understanding and equally those that indicate misunderstanding or boredom.

▶ **Sensitivity** to tune in to your recipient's emotional responses to your words.

▶ **Flexibility** to change the way you say something in order to clarify your meaning and increase understanding.

Your assessment criteria:

2.4 Demonstrate how to respond to an individual's reactions when communicating.

By tuning into and mirroring the body language of service users you increase rapport and understanding

Communication techniques

Some communication techniques assist with the process of responding to the reactions of others.

Echoing

Echoing is a technique where you repeat back what a person has said in a way that both checks your understanding of their words and also affirms the underlying feeling being expressed. For example, if a distressed resident of a care home tells you she thinks someone has stolen items from her room, you might say, 'It must be upsetting for you to think someone has been interfering with your personal belongings.'

Mirroring

Mirroring is a communication technique used to improve **rapport** with another person. In many cases it happens naturally, where one person reflects the other person's physical positions and mannerisms, their tone of voice, word use and communication style.

Asking questions

If you want a person to express their ideas and feelings you are best to ask **open questions** which invite broader responses. 'How are you feeling today?' is an example, where a service user is free to respond in any way they choose. If you ask a **closed question** the answer is usually reduced to one word, for example, 'Are you feeling better today?' invites a 'yes' or 'no' response.

Key terms

Closed questions: questions that are worded in a way that invites a one word, yes or no answer

Open questions: questions that are worded in a way that invites a full response in answer

Rapport: a relationship of mutual understanding or trust and agreement between people

Reflect

Think about people you know who you would judge to be good communicators. What is it about the words they use and the way they say them that makes their communication successful? Have you noticed them using any particular communication techniques to good effect?

Practical Assessment Task   2.1 2.2 2.3 2.4

An important part of your role as a health or social care practitioner is to facilitate and promote effective communication with service users, their families and with your colleagues, all of whom will have different communication needs, wishes and preferences. To complete this assessment task you need to focus on a service user with whom you work and show that you are able to:

1. Establish the communication and language needs, wishes and preferences of the individual.

2. Describe factors that influence the effectiveness of communication with this person and demonstrate how you take these into consideration.

3. Show how you use a range of communication methods (verbal and non-verbal) and styles to meet the individual's communication needs, wishes and preferences.

4. Show how you respond to the individual's reactions appropriately when communicating with them.

Make sure you protect the confidentiality of the person you select for this task, by changing names. The evidence for this task must be assessed in a real work environment and must result from your practice.

Be able to overcome barriers to communication

How do people from different backgrounds use and interpret communication methods differently?

Communication is all about sharing with one another and yet each person communicates slightly differently according to their different background and experience.

The impact of differences

Diversity is something to be celebrated and enjoyed, but our differences can also lead to misunderstanding and different interpretations of the same communication. Have a look Figure 1.7 for some of the major causes of difference.

Cultural background

Cultural differences refer to a variety of different influences, such as family background, peer group, religion, and ethnicity. These all play a part in shaping the way a person views the world and responds to it. Cultural differences are revealed by particular attitudes, values and practices, all of which have a bearing on how a person communicates and understands the communication of others. For example, if an individual comes from a family where it is usual to make decisions through noisy and heated discussions, this person might find it difficult to accept an order without question.

Individual personality

Although individuals share personality traits in common with others, the unique make-up of these and the way they operate together is individual to that person. One individual might be quiet and reserved, another enthusiastic and bubbly and this will affect the way each communicates and responds to communication.

Your assessment criteria:

3.1 Explain how people from different backgrounds may use and/or interpret communication methods in different ways.

Key terms

Diversity: being varied or different

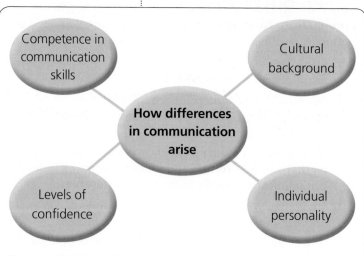

Figure 1.7 How differences in communication arise

- Competence in communication skills
- Cultural background
- How differences in communication arise
- Levels of confidence
- Individual personality

Levels of confidence

All communication requires a certain amount of confidence to speak up, make a statement, or share with others through spoken or written words. Sometimes a person has had their confidence undermined by a previous experience of communication, such as being misunderstood, or laughed at for mispronouncing a word, or perhaps an experience from childhood, such as failing their English exams. Confidence builds up over time but can be knocked down in seconds by a thoughtless or unkind response.

Competence in communication skills

Literacy skills refer to a person's competence in reading, writing and speaking in a particular language. The service users you work with may be at different levels of competence in literacy and need to be communicated with at a level they can cope with. Some adults struggle with literacy and may feel embarrassed by their difficulties. As well as literacy skills, some individuals will have better access to and be more competent using information and computer technology (ICT) than others. You should not assume that everyone you have dealings with at work has access to the internet and email, or mobile phones, or that they are competent in using such technology.

Reflect

Think about the different influences on your communication, in terms of cultural background, personality, confidence and competence. Can you work out what might have shaped the way you communicate and respond to the communication of others? How is this similar and different to the experiences of friends and colleagues?

Practical Assessment Task   3.1

Each individual communicates slightly differently according to their different background and experience and the service users you work with may have a diverse range of communication needs and preferences. To complete this assessment task you need to:

1. Identify three individuals whom you provide care for or work with (as colleagues) who use or interpret communication methods in different ways

2. Explain how the different backgrounds of the people you have chosen to focus on affect the way they use and/or interpret communication methods.

The evidence for this task must be assessed in a real work environment and must result from your practice. You should ensure that you protect the confidentiality of the people you refer to in any discussion or written work you produce.

Identifying and overcoming barriers to communication

Communication is a complex process and can be interrupted at any stage by a number of different barriers. These might be to do with forming a coherent message, or relaying it to another person. Problems may also be encountered with reliably receiving a message, or making sense of its content.

Where communication goes wrong

It is useful to look at different barriers to communication in relation to each stage of the communication process, as shown in Figure 1.8.

Figure 1.8 Communication process and barriers

Stage	Barrier	Example
Selection of information: to be relayed in a message	• Sender speaks different language • Sender cannot speak well • Poor or incomplete information selection	Mr Appleby has told the doctor in Accident and Emergency that his wife has a high fever, but forgets to let him know she has had two different types of antibiotics for a chest infection this month
Encode message: by deciding on method of transfer: via conversation or written means	• Sender chooses an inappropriate method • Sender cannot express message clearly, in speech or writing	Ralph texts his mother when she first gets a mobile phone, but she doesn't understand the abbreviated text language
Transfer message: speak face to face speak by phone write an e.mail/text write a letter	• Equipment may fail • May be interrupted • May be interfered with • May go astray	Leta was given a letter for her GP following a minor knee operation, but she forgot to deliver it
Receive message:	• Hearing difficulties • Visual difficulties • Distraction • Recipient may not recognise the message is aimed at them	Tobias saw the message from his manager saying, 'Please come to my office at 12', but thought it was meant for his colleague
Decode message:	• Wrong interpretation • Difficulties understanding • Lack of time	Viv was so frightened by her husband shouting at her for forgetting things that she couldn't take in what he was saying
Respond to message:	• Recipient may fail to respond • Response may be late • Response may be inappropriate	Alexi didn't understand that RSVP meant she must reply to the invitation to attend a conference, so her friend didn't book her a ticket

Finding ways around barriers to communication

Reflect

Can you recall a situation where you experienced a communication 'breakdown'. At what stage in the communication process did the break occur? How was it resolved?

As well as written and spoken words there are other routes to communicate information. Some of these can be used alongside spoken or written words to strengthen communication and some can be used in place of words:

▶ **Public information signs** – convey important information without any (or many) words using commonly understood symbols, such as on road and health and safety signs. These are especially vital for those who do not speak English and those who have difficulties with reading and writing.

▶ **Sign language** – British Sign Language (BSL) is a recognised language helping people who are deaf to communicate with others. It uses a sign for each letter of the alphabet and signs for different objects and places, as well as having signs that express ideas and concepts.

▶ **Language supports** – such as language boards where a person points to communicate need, or systems that illustrate and therefore emphasise spoken words (there is more about this on page 25)

  – **Picture Exchange Communication System** (PECS)

  – **Makaton**

▶ **Technology support** – uses computer programmes to provide voice simulators and other electronic communication aids.

Practical Assessment Task   3.2   3.3

Communication is not always straightforward and a number of barriers can be encountered when working in health and social care settings. Think about barriers that occur where you work that affect communication with service users, family members or with colleagues and other practitioners. To complete this assessment task you need to:

1. Identify three potential barriers to communication that arise in your work setting.

2. Explain how each barrier makes communication less effective.

3. Demonstrate ways to overcome each barrier to communication.

Your evidence for this task must be based on your practice in a real work environment and must be witnessed by or be in a format acceptable to your assessor.

What strategies clarify misunderstandings?

Communication is a complex process and health and social care is a complex area, so it is inevitable that misunderstandings will arise from time to time. When a misunderstanding happens it is important to have a range of methods to clarify the situation and improve communication.

Adapt your message: Sometimes the message needs to be said or written in a different way. Perhaps the tone needs to change, or the message's style. The language you have used might need to be simplified. Maybe a phone conversation has been unsatisfactory in some way, but a face to face meeting would help to establish better communication.

Change the environment: It might be necessary to make changes to the environment to enable better communication. For example, if you are conducting a meeting in an office where people are constantly coming in and out, or the phone keeps ringing, you will need to find a quieter place to speak.

Ask for feedback: In most situations it is acceptable to stop the flow of conversation with the person you are speaking with to check that you have understood correctly what is being spoken about. Equally, you can check that the person you are communicating with can hear you and understand you.

Allow time: Much communication happens while we are busy doing other things, but sometimes in order to make sure a message is received and understood you need to make time to have a proper conversation. By doing this you may find you actually save time.

Make an apology: Sometimes it is important to take responsibility for a misunderstanding and say you are sorry. A sincere apology can help to restore confidence and allow for the relationship to continue to build, on a firmer foundation.

Your assessment criteria:

> **3.4** Demonstrate strategies that can be used to clarify misunderstandings.

When using the phone you need to manage without the additional communication provided by body language

Reflect

Think about the last time you apologised about something. Was a breakdown in communication part of the problem? What was the effect of your apology? How did it make you feel?

Practical Assessment Task   3.4

An awareness of strategies to sort out communication misunderstandings is vital when you work with service users and their families. To complete this assessment task you need to focus on situations in which misunderstanding could potentially arise in your work setting, or which you have experienced or witnessed. These might involve a service user, their family members or a colleague. You need to:

1. Briefly describe two situations where a communication misunderstanding occurred (being careful to change names and maintain confidentiality if these actually occurred in your workplace).

2. Describe the strategies you used, or would use, to clarify the misunderstanding in each case.

3. Explain why you think each strategy would help.

Your evidence for this task must be based on your practice in a real work environment and must be in a format acceptable to your assessor.

How can you access support and services to enable effective communication?

There is a range of support available to enable effective communication with the service users you work with and members of their family. Importantly, individuals need to be informed about these services and be able to access them. For example:

▶ Support is available via local authorities and services, such as the NHS and adult social services departments. Help is also available from national charities, such as ICAN, for speech and language needs and the National Autistic Society for those with autism.

▶ The Citizens Advice Bureau (CAB) is another source for advice and assistance on advocacy, translation and interpretation.

▶ In addition there may be projects operating in local areas and these are likely to be advertised at a local library or community centre, or in a health centre.

Communication support tends to include these categories:

▶ speech and language services
▶ translation and interpreting services
▶ language service professionals (LSP)
▶ advocacy services.

Speech and language services

Speech and language therapy is concerned with the management of disorders of swallowing, speech, language and communication. Speech and language therapists (SLT) work closely with service users, their families, carers and other health and education professionals. They help those who have communication problems due to mild, moderate or severe learning difficulties, physical disabilities, such as cleft palate and spasticity, language impairment, hearing difficulties, speech impediments such as stammering, as well as autism and social interaction difficulties.

Service users are usually referred for speech and language therapy via health services. It is also possible to self-refer by contacting the local service directly.

As a care worker you might have to work closely with a SLT. This might mean supporting a service user to carry out exercises, or using language aids such as Makaton, which is a signing system, or the Picture Exchange Communication System (PECS) which is a visual system, both of which support language.

Your assessment criteria:

3.5 Explain how to access extra support or services to enable individuals to communicate effectively

Key terms

Autism: a developmental disorder which makes it difficult to make sense of the world and affects communication and social interaction

Makaton: a system that uses signs and symbols alongside speech to help people with learning and/or communication difficulties to communicate

Picture Exchange Communication System (PECS): a system used particularly with people with autism who have little or no ability to talk or use sign language, where a picture of an object is exchanged for an item which they want or need

Speech and language therapist (SLT): a practitioner who assesses and treats speech, language and communication problems in people of all ages

Translation and interpreting services

Translation services may be required for service users and their family who speak a language other than English. Information leaflets about services and benefits are now widely available in different languages.

Similarly, interpreters can be brought in to help translate conversation and discussions during meetings. Interpreters are trained not to give their own opinion, but to reflect whatever those present wish to convey.

If meetings are of a specialist nature and particular terms or jargon are likely to be used the interpreter will need notice of this to enable them to prepare.

Language Service Professionals (LSPs)

There are also translation and interpreter services for people with sensory impairment. Local authorities and services, such as the police and National Health Services are obliged to provide communication support for individuals:

▶ when visiting a doctor, optician or hospital

▶ if interviewed by the police

▶ when attending court or at a public meeting.

Support for those with sensory disability includes:

▶ British Sign Language (BSL) interpreters

▶ deafblind interpreters

▶ lip-speakers

▶ notetakers and speech-to-text reporters (palantypists).

Your assessment criteria:

3.5 Explain how to access extra support or services to enable individuals to communicate effectively.

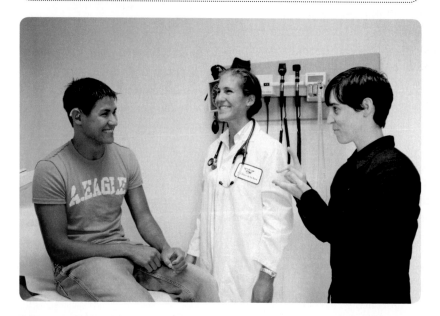

Advocacy services

An **advocate** is a supportive person who speaks in an official capacity on a person's behalf and in their best interests. Service users will be assigned an advocate in circumstances where there is no other person, such as a carer, who can speak up for them, for example, a service user from an asylum seeking family where no one speaks sufficient English to understand or be understood.

Reflect

Think about all the resources you know of locally and nationally.

▶ Do you know what support and advice is available in your care setting?

▶ What about local authority projects or national charities?

Key terms

Advocate: a supportive person who speaks in an official capacity on a person's behalf

Practical Assessment Task   3.5

Some people have communication difficulties that require extra support or services to enable them to communicate effectively. To complete this assessment task you need to explain how you would access extra support or services to enable individuals to communicate effectively where you became aware of barriers affecting communication with them.

Your evidence for this task must be based on your practice in a real work environment and must be in a format acceptable to your assessor.

Be able to apply principles and practices relating to confidentiality

Your assessment criteria:

4.1 Explain the meaning of the term confidentiality.

4.2 Demonstrate ways to maintain confidentiality in day to day communication.

What does confidentiality mean?

When you work in a health or social care setting you will regularly deal with information to do with the service users in your care and their families. Some of this is personal and private. **Confidentiality** refers to the need to handle personal and private information in ways that are appropriate, safe and professional and meet legal requirements. There are three main reasons why confidentiality is an important issue in a health and social care setting.

Trust

The relationships you build with service users and their families are central to your care role. If you share their personal information with others who have no need or right to know you risk breaking their trust in you. Individuals also need to know there are secure systems and procedures operating in the care setting to protect confidential information.

Safety

Some information must be kept confidential for safety reasons. For example, some service users are categorised as vulnerable adults, such as a person with special needs whose whereabouts might need to be protected from a relative who abused them in some way in the past.

The law

It is a legal requirement for organisations to manage and safeguard personal information correctly.

How do you maintain confidentiality?

A great deal of information will pass around at your place of work through conversations, hand-over reports, letters, written reports and emails. Some of it will be confidential and you need to know

Key terms

Confidentiality: the requirement to keep personal information private and only share it with those who need to know

Reflect

Think about the information you receive and give at work. Are you aware of the information that is confidential? Do you know how to handle this information?

how to manage this appropriately in a care setting. If you are unsure whether information is confidential, ask a senior member of staff.

Spoken information: Oral information can be transferred via face to face conversations, or over the phone. These might take place during meetings, or in less formal settings. If you need to discuss a confidential matter with a service user, family member, or with a colleague or visiting practitioner, make sure you find somewhere private where you will not be interrupted or overheard. In care settings it is not generally the policy to discuss confidential matters over the telephone, unless you can verify the person is who they claim to be. Never leave confidential messages on an answering machine. Do not at any time be tempted to gossip about confidential work matters.

Paper information: Personal records including notes, reports and letters concerning individual service and their families should be kept together in a file which is locked in a safe place. Remember a lockable filing cabinet is only safe if keys are not left lying around. Equally, rooms with keypads are not secure if the door has been propped open! Be aware of leaving documents around such as diaries, telephone messages and faxes if these contain confidential information. Many organisations have a policy that personal records must not be removed from the workplace, because these could be lost, damaged, seen by others, or the information could be taken and used wrongly.

Electronic information: These days a great deal of information is stored and transferred electronically, via computer. Computer files should be protected using passwords which are only shared with authorised individuals. Care must be taken to close private documents after use, to prevent individuals who are passing from catching sight of the screen. Be vigilant when transporting information between computers via memory pens or discs. Make sure the memory pen doesn't get lost and that the information doesn't remain on the hard drive of the computer it was played on.

Reflect

How is confidential information handled where you work? What are the security measures like? Are you careful with computer passwords?

Practical Assessment Task   4.1   4.2

When you work in health and social care settings you will need to communicate different types of information by a range of different methods, recognising in each case what is private and how to keep it confidential. In order to complete this task, use the example of a particular service user you work with to describe:

1. What keeping information 'confidential' means.
2. Which types of information concerning them and their family are 'confidential' (making sure you consider spoken information such as conversations, both in person and over the phone, both casual and more formal and written information in notes, records and assessments).
3. The ways in which you keep the information confidential.

Your evidence for this task must be based on your practice in a real work environment and must be in a format acceptable to your assessor.

Your assessment criteria:

4.3 Describe the potential tension between maintaining an individual's confidentiality and disclosing concerns.

Reflect

Think about the sorts of information you would not want others to know about you. How would you feel if this information was made public by others? Thinking in this way helps you to understand the importance of confidentiality at work.

When should information be kept confidential?

There will be a confidentiality policy where you work that includes procedures to guide the way confidential information is recorded, handled, stored and shared. As a care worker you have a responsibility to find out about these and work within the guidelines.

Privacy law

There is no specific privacy law in the UK, but issues related to privacy and confidential information are included in legislation.

▶ Privacy is highlighted as a right in the **United Nations Declaration of Human Rights (Article 8)**.

▶ **The Data Protection Act 1998** concerns the way personal information must be acquired, handled and stored.

▶ **The Freedom of Information Act 2000** protects the rights of individuals to have access to personal data that is held about them (see table).

The Information Commissioner's Office (ICO) is an independent authority set up to ensure organisations understand their responsibilities and the public their rights, about confidential information. Most care settings are required to register with the ICO.

Confidential information and the law

You will need to follow legal requirements for confidentiality set out in the health or social care setting where you work, as shown in Figure 1.9.

Investigate

Find out whether your employer keeps information relating to disclosure checks for employees. If so, for how long are they held?

Figure 1.9 Confidential information and the law

Legal requirements	Example
You may only obtain information that is relevant to your requirements.	Carly was told it breached privacy to record whether the adults with special needs in her support group were sexually active.
You may only use information for the purpose for which it was collected.	Aibileen cannot use medical records information from the dementia care ward for her research study unless she approaches the service users' next of kin for permission.
Do not disclose information to others unless there is a legitimate reason.	The care worker needs to know Julian is HIV positive because he helps with his personal care.
You must keep personal information up to date and do not keep records longer than necessary.	Gregor checked the care plans regularly and altered them as necessary to reflect changes and developments.
You must keep information in a safe place.	The lunch club purchased a lockable filing cabinet to keep service user's contact details.
You must keep to guidelines about transferring information out of the country.	When Alfie emigrated his carers spoke to his consultant for advice about transferring medical records.
Individuals have a right to know what information is held about them and in most cases may access this.	Elizbar's written request to read the medical records was acknowledged and he was sent a copy.
Inaccurate information must be corrected as soon as you realise there is an error.	Aba was upset to see 'father unknown' recorded in her notes because in fact he had died before she was born.

Your assessment criteria:

4.3 Describe the potential tension between maintaining an individual's confidentiality and disclosing concerns.

Disclosing confidential information

There are some situations when confidentiality needs to be breached to report information to a higher authority. The **disclosure** of private and personal information should only take place when:

▶ withholding the information is likely to threaten the safety and wellbeing of others

▶ a crime has been, or is likely to be committed.

How to disclose confidential information

It is your responsibility to check the policy and procedure at your place of work about disclosure of confidential information, in order to be clear about how to act and who to contact should the need arise.

Speak to a senior person within or outside of your work setting who is able to act on the information appropriately.

It is a mistake to think this is only a matter for senior care staff, because it is common for service users to prefer to confide in a junior member of staff who they feel they can relate to more closely.

Never promise confidentiality to an individual, but reassure the person you would only share the information if necessary and that you will inform them if you need to do so.

Whistle-blowing

Whistle-blowing is a term used to describe the disclosure of wrong-doing within an organisation to a higher authority, or the media. This might be about unsafe or illegal working practices or abuse within the system. The Public Interest Disclosure Act 1998 protects whistle-blowers but requires firm evidence, including evidence that it would not have been possible to use the internal system for complaints within the company.

Key terms

Disclosure: the breaching of a confidence in order to report information that may threaten the wellbeing of an individual

Whistle-blowing: a person who reveals wrongdoing within an organisation to the public, via the media, or to a higher authority

---

Reflect

You may hear colleagues talk about sharing confidential information on a 'need to know' basis only. What do you think is meant by this term? Does your place of work ask parent's permission to collect and store certain information about the service users in your care?

Case study

Dena, who has Down's syndrome is furious with her support worker Latif. She screams at him that he's ruined her life and she's reporting him to the police. Latif is shaken by this outburst and worries that he may have made a mistake by informing Dena's mother about a friendship she has made with someone she met in the shopping centre. Latif's concern is that Dena regularly lends this person money and the last time she persuaded her to go to the bank so she could loan her £20. He feels Dena's open and caring nature is being taken advantage of by this woman and that she is very vulnerable to being financially abused.

1. What is the dilemma that Latif finds himself in?
2. Do you think he was right to disclose this confidential information?
3. How would you have handled the situation?

Discuss

Talk with colleagues about occasions you have experienced or heard about where confidentiality has needed to be breached.

▶ What do you think are the most difficult aspects of breaching confidentiality?
▶ How would you manage these situations?

Practical Assessment Task   4.3

When you work in health and social care settings you will need to know about confidential information concerning service users. It is also likely there will be occasions when information must be disclosed to maintain a person's safety or wellbeing. To complete this assessment task you need to:

1. Identify a situation where tension between maintaining, or breaking confidentiality could potentially occur.
2. Complete the table by describing both the reasons why information relating to the situation should remain confidential and alternative reasons why this information should be disclosed.

Confidentiality situation	Reasons why information should remain confidential	Reasons for disclosing confidential information

Your evidence for this task must be based on your practice in a real work environment and must be in a format acceptable to your assessor.

Are you ready for assessment?

AC	What do you know now?	Assessment task	✓
1.1	Identify the different reasons why people communicate	Page 5	
1.2	Explain how communication affects relationships in the work setting	Page 9	

AC	What do you know now?	Assessment task	✓
2.1	Demonstrate how to establish the communication and language needs, wishes and preferences of individuals	Page 19	
2.2	Describe the factors to consider when promoting effective communication	Page 19	
2.3	Demonstrate a range of communication methods and styles to meet individual needs	Page 19	
2.4	Demonstrate how to respond to an individual's reactions when communicating	Page 19	
3.1	Explain how people from different backgrounds may use and/or interpret communication methods in different ways	Page 21	
3.2	Identify barriers to effective communication	Page 23	
3.3	Demonstrate ways to overcome barriers to communication	Page 23	
3.4	Demonstrate strategies that can be used to clarify misunderstandings	Page 24	
3.5	Explain how to access extra support or services to enable individuals to communicate effectively	Page 27	
4.1	Explain the meaning of the term confidentiality	Page 29	
4.2	Demonstrate ways to maintain confidentiality in day to day communication	Page 29	
4.3	Describe the potential tension between maintaining an individual's confidentiality and disclosing concerns	Page 33	

2 | Engage in personal development in health and social care settings (SHC 32)

Assessment of this unit

Personal development is fundamental to the role of a health and social care practitioner. The focus of this unit is on developing your own practice when working with service users and their families. You will look in detail at the duties and responsibilities of your work role and see how these relate to the laws and standards required of you in the work place. It will provide tools to help you reflect on your practice, evaluate your progress and create your own personal development plan. You will need to:

1. understand what is required for competence in your own work role.

2. be able to reflect on practice.

3. be able to evaluate your performance.

4. be able to agree a personal development plan.

5. be able to use learning opportunities and reflective practice to contribute to personal development.

The assessment of this unit is partly knowledge-based (things you need to know about), but mostly competence-based (things you need to do in the real work environment). To successfully complete this unit, you will need to produce evidence of both your knowledge and your competence. The charts below and opposite outline what you need to know and do to meet each of the assessment criteria for the unit.

Your tutor or assessor will help you to prepare for your assessment and the tasks suggested in the chapter that follows will help you to create the evidence that you need.

CHAPTER 2

AC   What you need to know

1.1   Describe the duties and responsibilities of own work role

1.2   Explain expectations about own work role as expressed in relevant standards

AC   What you need to do

2.1   Explain the importance of reflective practice in continuously improving the quality of service provided

2.2   Demonstrate the ability to reflect on practice

2.3   Describe how own values, belief systems and experiences may affect working practice

3.1   Evaluate own knowledge, performance and understanding against relevant standards

3.2   Demonstrate use of feedback to evaluate own performance and inform development

4.1   Identify sources of support for planning and reviewing own development

4.2   Demonstrate how to work with others to review and prioritise own learning needs, professional interests and development opportunities

4.3   Demonstrate how to work with others to agree own personal development plan

5.1   Evaluate how learning activities have affected practice

5.2   Demonstrate how reflective practice has led to improved ways of working

5.3   Show how to record progress in relation to personal development

---

This unit also links to some of the other mandatory units:

SHC 34   Principles for implementing duty of care in health and social care settings

HSC 025   The role of the health and social care worker

Some of your learning will be repeated in these units and will give you the chance to review your knowledge and understanding.

Understand what is required for competence in your own work role

Your assessment criteria:

1.1 Describe the duties and responsibilities of own work role.

What duties and responsibilities does your work role involve?

To be an effective health and social care practitioner and to successfully gain your diploma qualification you need to recognise the specific requirements of your own work role. You must understand:

▶ the duties and responsibilities of your role

▶ the knowledge and skills you need to carry out your role

▶ the appropriate attitude needed for the different aspects of your work.

Your job description

Everybody who is employed or working voluntarily in health and social care settings should have a **job description**. Your job description should be written for your particular work role and should clearly outline your work-related **duties** and **responsibilities**.

It is common during the recruitment process for employers to also give you a **person specification** that identifies the qualifications, experience, skills and qualities required to carry out the particular job you have applied for.

If you are a student on placement you will not have a job description, but your school or college and the placement organisation should jointly produce guidelines relating to your role.

Key terms

Duty: something a person is required to do

Job description: a written outline of the duties and responsibilities of a work role

Person specification: a written outline of the qualifications, experience and qualities needed to perform a particular work role

Responsibility: something a person is obliged to carry out

Investigate

What does your job description or work guidelines say about the duties and responsibilities associated with your work role? If there is anything you don't understand ask your manager, tutor or assessor.

Understanding job requirements

Job descriptions indicate what your employer expects for your work role:

▶ 'Experienced' and 'qualified' – mean previous experience or a certain level of expertise is required. Most job descriptions will specify whether a skill is required or just desired.

▶ 'Willing to be trained', or to 'undergo further study' – mean previous experience is not necessarily needed, but personal and professional development is expected.

▶ 'Assist with' and 'help out' – indicate that your role supports a more senior role.

▶ 'Organise' and 'operate' suggest you will be expected to take the initiative and perhaps lead others in carrying out a duty.

Understanding your duties and responsibilities

Job descriptions differ from job to job, but many ask for similar basic requirements. Most job descriptions include the following information:

▶ **Duties:** the roles and tasks you are expected to regularly carry out at work, doing so in ways that keep to the law, fulfil the professional standards expected and follow policy and procedure in your workplace.

▶ **Responsibilities:** the obligations you hold, particularly towards service users and their families, but also to the colleagues within your team, any visiting practitioners and your employer. These are likely to include working in ways that protect vulnerable adults and maintain the health and safety of yourself and others.

Your work role and qualities required

The duties and responsibilities associated with your work role will depend on the kind of setting you work in and the priorities and focus of the organisation that employs you. For example, if you work as a support worker in a day centre for older people, your practical duties and responsibilities are likely to be different to those of a person who works with adults as a healthcare assistant (HCA) in a hospital setting.

In carrying out your duties and responsibilities you will need to show the qualities set out in Figure 2.1.

Reflect

Think about your work role.

▶ What aspects of your duties and responsibilities do you carry out competently at the moment?

▶ Which areas of your practice could you improve on, perhaps through further training or by gaining more experience?

Figure 2.1 Qualities required to carry out duties and responsibilities

The knowledge and skills needed

Your knowledge will be demonstrated in the way you perform your duties and apply your learning and understanding to your role. Knowledge must be kept up to date, taking into account any changes to laws, policies and procedures, as well as new guidelines on practice. This means being aware of what is new in your area of work and putting yourself forward for learning opportunities and further training.

Your skills are demonstrated through the competence and confidence with which you carry out your work tasks. A range of **functional skills** will be necessary for this, for example, you will need a certain standard of reading, writing and speech in English in order to communicate with service users and staff members and receive and write reports. You may also need the ability to use a computer, as well as sufficient confidence with numbers, perhaps to carry out audits and manage basic statistics.

Appropriate attitude

An appropriate attitude refers to your manner and approach as you respond to a range of different people and situations at work. This includes having good **social skills** where you are able to relate with **empathy** to many different types of people in a health and social care setting. You also need to be flexible and adaptable to cope with sometimes challenging situations, while continuing to meet people's differing needs. Most health and social care workers work in a team where you must be able to co-operate and **collaborate** with other colleagues, as well as a range of different practitioners, in order to provide a comprehensive service to meet people's varied needs.

Your assessment criteria:

1.1 Describe the duties and responsibilities of own work role.

Key terms

Collaborate: work together with others to achieve a shared goal

Empathy: the ability to identify with another person and understand what they are feeling

Functional skills: (previously known as core or key skills) literacy, numeracy and ICT skills needed to enable you to carry out work tasks

Social skills: an ability to interact and communicate well with others

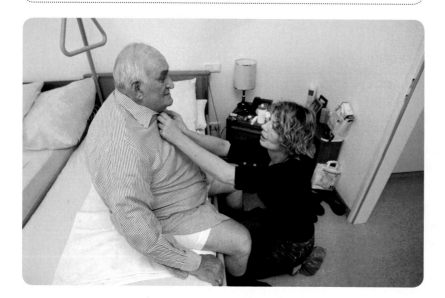

Starting a new job

When you begin a new job there will be a period of settling in when you find out what your role will involve. You should be given an **induction** which covers:

- an introduction to your colleagues and other visiting practitioners
- an introduction to the service users and their relatives who use the setting
- the layout of the work setting, including fire exits
- the daily routines
- any philosophy or particular principles that guide the work setting
- relevant **policies** and **procedures**.

The induction phase of a new job is a good opportunity to ask questions and clarify anything you don't understand. Don't expect to know everything all at once and give yourself time to get to know everyone gradually.

Contractual responsibilities

Your work contract, to which you will be asked to sign your agreement, sets out what is expected of you. This includes practical details such as your hours of work and shift patterns. It may also state the correct line of reporting, which means the responsible person to whom you pass on information, such as a senior worker or your manager. This person, in turn reports further up the hierarchy and so on, to the top of the organisation. Your contract will include any special duties that your work role demands and will state that you must keep up to date with policies and procedures and any changes made to these.

Key terms

Induction: a period of basic training

Policies: written documents that set out an organisation's approach towards a particular issue

Procedures: documents that set out in detail how a particular issue should be dealt with or how particular tasks should be carried out

Case study

Jagathi is 18 and has never worked in healthcare before, but she has helped to look after her disabled grandmother who lives with her family. She helps her to go the toilet, wash and dress and feeds her when she is too exhausted to do this herself. Her grandmother comments on how gentle Jagathi is and how her smile brings sunshine into the room. Jagathi answers an advert for a senior healthcare assistant in the local community hospital, because she is sure her personal experience means she will be able to manage a senior role. She receives an application form, along with a job description and person specification. It's a lot to read so she decides to complete the application form and only read the other information if she gets an interview.

1. From what you know of Jagathi, what qualities (knowledge, skills, attitude) does she show that would make her suitable for the duties and responsibilities of healthcare work?

2. Do you think Jagathi is suitable for the job she has applied for?

3. What do you think about Jagathi's decision not to read through the job description and person specification yet?

How do expectations for your work role correspond to relevant standards?

All health and social care services must operate according to a framework of standards. These include UK legislation, which incorporates European laws, as well as guidance and rules from **regulatory bodies**. This framework of standards is designed to protect the health and safety of service users and workers and to ensure the quality of services. Some care organisations have developed around a philosophy or ethos and there may be standards associated with this that workers are expected to uphold.

Some of the standards you are expected to meet within your role as a health and social care practitioner could include:

- ▶ Laws, for example health and safety law
- ▶ National Minimum Standards
- ▶ Codes of practice
- ▶ National Occupational Standards
- ▶ Policies and procedures in the work setting
- ▶ Underpinning philosophy or ethos of an organisation.

Your assessment criteria:

1.2 Explain expectations about own work role as expressed in relevant standards.

Key terms

Regulatory body: an organisation that sets standards and rules for care practitioners to follow

Investigate

Find out about a national regulatory body which regulates the area you work in. For example, the Care Quality Commission (CQC) regulates health and adult social care services and the General Social Care Council (GSCC) is the regulator of the social work profession and social work education in England.

Health and safety law

Have a look at Figure 2.2 to learn more about health and safety law and how these relate to your duties and responsibilities.

Figure 2.2 The Health and Safety at Work Act

Health and Safety at Work Act 1974

About the law:

- Covers all workplaces and personnel, not just those to do with health and social care
- Sets out employer and employee responsibilities:

Employers must:

- provide a safe and secure work environment
- provide health and safety equipment, such as personal protective equipment (PPE) and fire-fighting equipment
- provide information and training about health, safety and security
- develop policies and procedures to keep workers, service users and the public safe, such as fire and evacuation procedures
- carry out health and safety risk assessments
- report serious health, safety and security incidents to the authorities

Employees must:

- behave in ways that do not risk your or others' health, safety and security
- use health and safety equipment correctly at the appropriate times, keeping it in good order, reporting faults and need for new stock
- read health, safety and security information, attend training and act upon it
- be aware of policies and procedures and work in ways that follow the guidance given
- contribute to health and safety risk assessments
- report any health, safety and security hazards to the manager
- tackle directly any health, safety and security incidents that occur, but only when it is safe to do so

Reflect

Think about the specific ways in which the Health and Safety at Work Act impacts on your work role.

▶ Have you read and understood any health and safety information posters on the notice board or looked at the health and safety file at work recently?

▶ Do you know how to contribute to a health and safety risk assessment?

Regulatory body standards and your work role

The standards you are expected to uphold in your work setting will depend on the area of health and social care you work in. Standards also differ between England, Wales, Scotland and Northern Ireland. Professional standards often link to a system of registration, where you can only be a member of a professional body if you provide evidence to show you uphold the standards it sets. Check Figure 2.3 for some examples of standards, but find out from your manager those that relate directly to your role.

Your assessment criteria:

1.2 Explain expectations about own work role as expressed in relevant standards.

Figure 2.3 Regulatory body standards

Example of regulatory body standard	Information
National Minimum Standards – developed to fulfil the Care Standards Act 2000	Developed for employers and employees working in care homes for older people. It covers seven areas of care, where health and personal care and daily life and social activities are most relevant to the role of a care worker.
Essential standards of quality and safety – developed by the Care Quality Commission (CQC) to comply with the Health & Social Care Act 2008	Provides guidance for employers, employees and service users. The information is given in the form of desired outcomes with prompts to indicate what you should be doing at work to meet the standards.
National Occupational Standards (NOS)	Used to develop care qualifications such as this one, and courses that seek to improve practice in the health and social care sector. Employees and students are responsible for working to the NOS. Your employer should provide ongoing support and training opportunities and you have a duty to make the most of these.
Codes of practice for social care workers developed by the General Social Care Council (GSCC) England (NISCC – Northern Ireland; SSSC – Scotland; CCW – Wales)	Covers six areas of care for employers and employees where protecting rights and promoting interests, establishing trust and promoting independence are most relevant to the care worker role.

Case study

Lily has recently been promoted to senior care worker in The Priory, a residential care home for older people. Her manager has asked her to join a mixed group of staff and residents looking at standard twelve of the National Minimum Standards for Care which is concerned with daily life and social activities. The manager feels that the routines of the care home have become rather inflexible, where residents are expected to fit into their timetable for personal care, mealtimes and activities, rather than the other way round. She is concerned that the personal choice of individual residents is sometimes overlooked and asks Lily and the others in the group to come up with some ideas.

1. Why do you think this standard is important to the care of older people?

2. Can you think of ideas to introduce flexibility and choice around mealtimes at the home?

3. What ideas do you have about making routine care, to do with washing and dressing, more individual and personalised?

Policy and procedure and your work role

Your employer has a duty to develop policies and procedures that reflect laws and regulatory body standards and you have a duty to put these into practice in your work setting. Your employer should make you aware of the relevant standards expected of you and you should read these and keep updated about any changes. Most work settings keep a file of policies and procedures in the office available for staff members and service users and their relatives to look through. If you don't understand anything, ask your manager to explain further.

Underpinning philosophy

An underpinning philosophy or ethos may reflect the origins of a service, such as a charity, or a reputation that has been built up over many years of service. Some organisations will have a 'mission statement' that explains the aims and objectives of its underlying principles and this will provide a useful indication of the ways in which you will be expected to work. Before you apply to work for an organisation it is a good idea to find out about any underpinning philosophy so that you can understand the basis for its standards and the expectations for your role.

Regularly check notice boards for information on health and safety and other aspects of your work role

Knowledge Assessment Task   1.1   1.2

Duties and responsibilities and standards provide a framework within which you are able to practice safely and effectively. This task requires you to show how your duties and responsibilities at work link to standards and the ways in which your working practice reflects these. Make a table with three columns that:

1. Describes two duties and responsibilities expected of you in your work role.

2. Explains the standards linked to these duties and responsibilities, such as laws, codes of practice, policy and procedure, and so on.

3. Gives examples of some of the ways in which your working practice reflects these.

You should keep the written work that you produce for this activity as evidence towards your assessment.

How does reflective practice improve the quality of service provided?

Reflective practice is a process to help evaluate your work. It provides opportunities to learn from your experience and develop your working practice. It is both a tool to help you analyse specific interactions or incidents that have occurred at work, as well as a method of working in the moment that is **mindful** and **self-aware**.

The function of reflective practice

Reflective practice offers a range of opportunities to develop the way in which you work. Through the regular practice of reflecting on your work your powers of observation will improve, allowing you greater insights into those responses and interventions that bring the most positive results. By incorporating these insights into your working practice you will be able to improve your performance at work. If you work with others who are equally committed to the reflective practice process it can transform team working and thereby improve the overall quality of the service provided. Have a look at Figure 2.4 opposite, which shows the function of reflective practice.

Sharpening observation and insights

Working with people is unpredictable. This is because each person is a unique individual with different needs and preferences, which may change from day to day and even hour to hour. This means that no one approach (even to similar situations) can be guaranteed to work for every person all the time. You must be adaptable and responsive to each person and every unique situation that arises. Reflective practice is a method of working that sharpens observation and offers insights during potentially complex processes.

Key terms

Mindful: being in touch with and fully aware of the present moment, rather than operating in an automatic, routine manner

Reflective practice: a process for analysing personal work, in order to develop personal working practice and improve overall quality of service

Self-aware: taking careful note of your inner experience, especially your thoughts and feelings and recognising the way these might impact on others

Reflect

Native American folklore recommends that before you make a judgement about a person you should walk a mile in their moccasins.

▶ How would you express this in your own words?
▶ How does the Native American folklore relate to reflective practice?

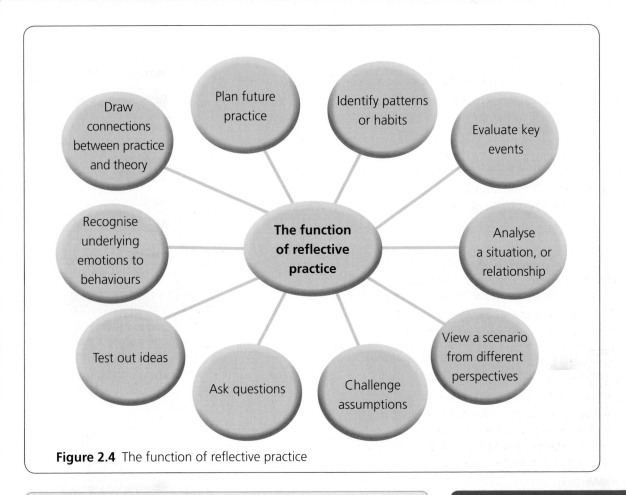

Figure 2.4 The function of reflective practice

Case study

Sarah works for a home-care service. She visits Hilda, who lives alone and has dementia, for a 15-minute appointment to give her lunch. This is enough time to heat and serve a pre-cooked meal, but not long enough to build up much of a relationship. Some days Hilda needs persuading to let Sarah in and can be easily distracted from sitting down to eat. On most days Sarah finds evidence of the previous meal in the bin or left untouched. She wants to talk to her manager about the need for a longer appointment, but is nervous because there is concern about streamlining services and saving money.

1 How might reflective practice help Sarah think about this situation?

2 What questions could Sarah consider during the reflective practice process, to do with the quality of service she provides for Hilda?

3 How might reflective practice help Sarah think about the needs of Hilda, which she has found to be more complex than simply providing a meal?

Investigate

Using library, internet or workplace sources find out about different models and tools for reflective practice. Have a look at what has been useful for others and think about the models and tools you would like to try.

How do you carry out reflective practice?

Reflective practice brings the most benefit when you take time to carry it out on a regular, preferably daily basis. You also need to make it a priority, rather than considering it an occasional luxury that you only manage if time allows. In the long term reflective practice is a process that will save you time and which helps you use the time you have productively. In order to use reflective practice effectively you must understand:

▶ Reflective practice methods

▶ The reflective practice process.

Reflective practice methods

Reflective practice is carried out in two main ways:

▶ Reflecting-in-action: takes place in the moment while an issue arises or an event takes place

▶ Reflecting-on-action: giving consideration afterwards to what worked well and how the situation could have been managed differently.

It is carried out using different methods:

▶ **Thinking:** bringing your self-awareness to a situation and considering it from all points of view

▶ **Writing:** through a reflective journal, setting down your experiences and observations on a day by day basis; using writing exercises to explore a specific event or occurrence; writing what happened from another person's point of view to bring fresh understanding

▶ **Discussion:** share experiences and explore possibilities with colleagues and other practitioners at work

▶ **Role play:** acting out a scenario so as to better understand what occurs between individuals - perhaps to do with emotions and relationships - brings insights.

Your assessment criteria:

2.2 Demonstrate the ability to reflect on your practice.

Reflect

▶ There may be a method for reflective practice that suits you best as an individual.

▶ Have you worked out the best way for you to reflect on your work?

▶ Is it through thinking, writing, discussion or role-play, or a combination of all of these?

Investigate

Find out about reflective journaling by getting yourself a notebook and having a go at it! There are no rules – just write! Make sure you use initials or code to protect the privacy of others.

The reflective practice process

Here is an explanation for each step of the reflective practice process as shown in Figure 2.5:

▶ **Time and place:** if you are reflecting-*in*-action, this takes place on the spot while you are interacting. You need to bring your awareness to the situation in a way that enables you to reflect while you continue to carry out whatever task or activity you are involved with. If you are reflecting-*on*-action you need to set aside time and find a quiet place where you won't be distracted or get interrupted. You might need to let those around you know so they make a point not to disturb you.

▶ **Self-awareness:** identify and, as far as possible, set aside your own defences and prejudices. These influence the way you see things and how you judge others. Try to apply a more objective view and see things from different perspectives.

▶ **Honesty:** remember that this process is all about seeing what is happening as clearly as possible. This is an exploratory process and there are usually no right or wrong answers.

▶ **Pose questions:** it is useful to ask yourself a number of searching questions:

   ▶ What did I do, say and feel during this scenario?

   ▶ What were the reasons behind my words and actions?

   ▶ How do I feel about the situation?

   ▶ Is there evidence to back up the way I am feeling?

   ▶ What was the response of each individual involved and the outcome for each?

   ▶ What was it that I wanted to achieve through my words and actions?

   ▶ What else could I have tried?

TIME and PLACE:
Set aside time to reflect

POSE QUESTIONS:
To help structure your thinking/writing/role-play

SELF-AWARENESS:
Set aside defences and prejudices – aim for objectivity

HONESTY:
Explore in a truthful way to provide clarity

Figure 2.5 The reflective practice process

Case study

Gahan works as a support worker at Ivy House, which provides supported living accommodation for adults with special needs. He has taken Ross, who has severe autism, out to a local cafe for breakfast. Although the cafe staff are very accommodating of the needs of Ivy House residents a new waiter serves Ross his breakfast and the beans spill over to touch the egg, a situation which upsets Ross. He immediately tips the plate over and starts making loud noises. The waiter looks really alarmed as Ross begins to rock and other customers have noticed the disturbance.

1. In what ways might reflecting-in-action help Gahan deal with this situation?

2. What questions could he ask himself to help this process?

3. How might reflecting-on-action help after the event?

What is the potential impact on working practice of personal values and experience?

Every individual, from early childhood, is influenced and shaped by their unique experience of life. This will include the values they have been brought up with, perhaps passed on by significant people, such as parents and teachers. It also includes beliefs, such as a religious faith or a political ideology, which guide the way you behave. Values, beliefs and experiences influence the way you look at life and make it difficult to maintain **objectivity**. This is not necessarily a bad situation, because who you are and how you think and behave makes up the unique person you are, but it is important to be aware of these influences and to recognise that other people's influences and experiences will be different from your own.

Influences to consider

There will have been many influences in your life – here are just a few to consider:

▶ **Family background:** the makeup of your immediate and extended family and their impact; whether you were an only child or there were many children; sibling rivalry; a mix of genders; the history of your family; whether there was harsh discipline or a permissive attitude, and so on.

▶ **Environment:** the type of home you grew up in and its location – within a town or rural setting, within a certain geographical area, or a different country.

▶ **Finances:** whether you were wealthy; reasonably well off; or struggled to have your basic needs met.

▶ **Education:** the ethos of your school; whether single or mixed sex; boarding or day school; inspirational teachers; whether you succeeded academically or not; whether you were bullied; whether you developed special interests.

▶ **Religious or spiritual belief system:** including whether you embraced or rejected this.

▶ **Moral influences:** values passed on to you as being of central importance to the way you live your life, such as not stealing or lying.

Your assessment criteria:

2.3 Describe how your own values, belief systems and experiences may affect working practice.

Key terms

Objectivity: the ability to view or describe something without being influenced by your own feelings and prejudices

Investigate

Ask colleagues who you know well if they would mind telling you why they came to work in a health or social setting. Try to work out whether there are any common factors that influenced their career choice, or whether people have come into care work for very different reasons.

Reflect

Think about the different influences on your life.

▶ Can you see the specific ways in which these may have an impact on the way you view life?

Practical Assessment Task   2.1 2.2 2.3

Reflection is an important part of practice when you work in health and social care. Use the stages set out below to demonstrate your use of reflective practice to improve your work performance and the quality of the service provided. Show how you maintain an awareness of the ways that values, belief systems and personal experience might be having an influence on this. Record your reflections using an appropriate method, such as a written or audio journal.

1. Select a scenario that has occurred recently in your workplace. This might be an occasion you were involved with, or something you witnessed happening.

2. Give a brief description of what happened, making sure you do not use real names so as to protect the confidentiality of the individuals involved.

3. Continuing with this example, complete the reflective practice process diagram (see page 49).

4. Make a note of any values, beliefs and personal experiences which might be influencing your reflective process findings.

5. Describe the insights you have gained from applying the reflective practice process to this scenario.

6. Explain the ways in which reflective practice continuously improves the quality of your individual work performance and the quality of the service provided.

Your evidence for this task must be based on your practice in a real work environment and must be witnessed by or be presented in a format that is acceptable to your assessor.

Be able to evaluate your own performance

How do you evaluate your performance and use feedback to develop working practice?

When you have identified and understood the expectations of your work role and become familiar with the process of reflecting on your working practice, the next step is to evaluate your progress. In a similar way to the reflection process, evaluation of your performance needs to be carried out in an ongoing way. As well as your own evaluation it is useful to consider the feedback of others, who will be able to view your performance from a different perspective.

Evaluation

Evaluation is the process of examining and questioning what you do, to assess it against an agreed standard. There may be a range of standards that are relevant to health and social care against which to evaluate your knowledge, understanding and performance at work. The requirements of your job description will be one standard, combined with the expectations of your manager and the satisfaction of service users and their relatives. Remember, there will probably be additional standards or codes of practice to adhere to if you work within a particular profession and this may link to yours or the organisation's registration. Also, an element of following a course of study, such as this one, is the requirement to evaluate whether you have reached the necessary standard for the qualification.

Knowledge, performance and understanding are broad terms which can be reflected in the particular skills and areas of expertise related to your role. To evaluate your performance you will need to ask yourself questions in each relevant area of your work, as shown in Figure 2.6.

Producing evidence of achievement

By creating a chart in which to record the answers to your evaluation questions and by gradually adding to this as your working practice develops, you can create your own personal evaluation tool. This provides a useful reference which, if you complete it regularly, will map your progress over time.

Have a look at the beginnings of an evaluation chart that a senior care worker in a care home for older people is using to evidence her achievement, in Figure 2.7 opposite.

Your assessment criteria:

3.1 Evaluate own knowledge, performance and understanding against standards.

3.2 Demonstrate use of feedback to evaluate own performance and inform development.

Key terms

Evaluation: a process of close examination and questioning to assess and judge performance, usually against an agreed standard

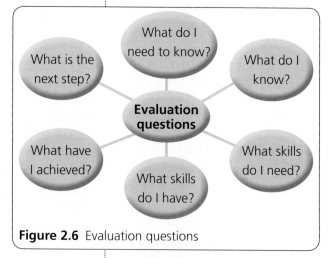

Figure 2.6 Evaluation questions

Investigate

Using the internet, look up The National Occupational Standards (NOS) for health and social care (www.skillsforcare.org.uk). Have a look around the website to see what they do and find out from the map provided what is going on in your region.

Relevant standards for evaluation:
Essential standards of quality and safety (Care Quality Commission (CQC))
Outcome 1: Respecting and involving people who use services

Knowledge; Performance; Understanding.	Evidence	Development

I have downloaded a copy of the Essential Standards and read through the outcomes to identify which are relevant to my level of practice. I focused on Outcome 1	• Have made notes on the outcome concerning ways to:
	  – Involve residents in making decisions to do with the way the home is run
	  – Assist residents to express their views
	  – Take resident views and experiences into account
	  – Regularly provide residents and their relatives with information about the home
	
	• Held an information evening for residents and relatives, which was also a social event, to find out ways they would like to be involved more.
	  – GS remarked that a regular newsletter which highlighted up-coming events and any new developments would be helpful
	  – G said, "Can we be in it too?"
	  – Mrs P pointed out not all the residents can read and wondered about a recorded version
	
	• I looked over the satisfaction questionnaires we send out to relatives every 6 months
	  – Need more space for comments
	  – How do we get responses from residents with communication difficulties?
		• Request a copy of 'High Elms' newsletter and ask to speak to their manager for ideas.
		
		• Get a group of interested staff, residents and relatives to meet to discuss format and content
		
		• Aim for trial newsletter to go out by next month
		
		• Need to create a simplified questionnaire to ask residents who have communication difficulties, to be completed through an interview with residents.

Figure 2.7 Example evaluation chart for a senior care worker in a care home, to show evidence of achievement

Evaluation areas to consider

You will need to think about your knowledge, performance and understanding at work in order to evidence your learning and be able to identify how to develop your practice. It is a good idea to evaluate knowledge, performance and understanding against specific duties and responsibility described in your job description and standards. Examples of evaluation areas are health and safety; risk assessment; safeguarding; first aid; activity planning; observation skills; showing leadership; managing others; communication skills; multi-agency working; record keeping and confidentiality issues.

Gaining feedback

Feedback is gained from formal and informal sources at work.

Formal sources are provided through a structured system:

– **Appraisal** every six months or year when performance is reviewed.

– **Supervision** sessions should occur regularly with a manager or senior colleague. Supervision can sometimes get squeezed out when work pressures are high, but actually these are the times when feedback can be most valuable, so remind your manager.

– **Study courses** where feedback comes from assessors/tutors.

– **Surveys and questionnaires** which are used to gather feedback about service users' and their relatives' levels of satisfaction. These can be completed by the respondent, or used to interview a service user, where the responses are noted. If you are making up a questionnaire try to ask **open questions** that encourage a fuller response, rather than a 'yes' or 'no' answer. Also leave space for comments. Remember that the information in questionnaires need to be analysed and fed back to service users, or the exercise will be pointless.

Informal sources are through everyday encounters and conversations:

– **Discussions** with colleagues or fellow learners.

– **Body language** where responses are picked up from 'reading' the non-verbal cues (gestures, facial expressions and so on) communicated by all you work with.

Responding positively to feedback

Hearing another person's evaluation of your knowledge, performance and understanding will help you recognise how others perceive your work. This can be affirming and encouraging when feedback is positive, but if the person has something critical to say it can feel uncomfortable. Try to keep an open mind and not be defensive, but concentrate on using the feedback to improve your performance. If you feel the person has overlooked or misinterpreted something, ask if you may speak with them about it at a convenient time.

Your assessment criteria:

3.1 Evaluate your own knowledge, performance and understanding against standards.

3.2 Demonstrate use of feedback to evaluate own performance and inform development.

Key terms

Feedback: written or spoken information about your performance from another person's perspective

Appraisal: an expert or official evaluation of your work and progress, undertaken every six months to a year

Supervision: The practice of regular meetings with a senior colleague or mentor to discuss professional development and set goals

Open questions: questions that are worded so they cannot be answered with a simple yes or no, but require a more developed answer

Body language: non-verbal communication involving gestures, posture and facial expressions that reveal a person's feelings

Case study

During a supervision session Amy points out to Tomas that he appears to be avoiding Roxanne, a patient on the psychiatric unit where they work. Amy suggests he uses reflective practice methods to consider what is going on before discussing it again.

Tomas replies, "Reflective practice is a bit soft. I can't see the point of doing it. Roxanne avoids *me* actually and anyway, you can't have a rapport with all the patients. It's best if the female staff look after Roxanne, because she has real temper outbursts which are bound to be something to do with hormones and they'll understand that better than I can."

Tomas respects Amy as a charge nurse, but he leaves the session feeling really annoyed.

1. What effect has the supervision session had on Tomas and why?

2. In what ways do you think Tomas' attitude is affected by his attitudes, ideas and beliefs?

3. What would you say to Tomas to persuade him of the benefits of listening to Amy's feedback?

Investigate

Ask your manager, tutor or assessor to show you examples of service user questionnaires. Have a look through to understand the sorts of questions being asked and the areas these cover. Can you see how responses to questionnaires can be used to inform practice?

Practical Assessment Task

3.1 **3.2**

It is important to be able to link your knowledge and learning, as well as the way you perform your duties, to the standards expected of you at work. This process is enabled by feedback from others, both formal and informal and together it contributes to your professional and personal development.

To complete this activity:

1. Identify two different sorts of standards expected of you at work, perhaps to do with the profession you work within, or your workplace policies and procedures.

2. Focus on a specific aspect of your work role that relates to these standards, such as providing personal care or communication skills.

3. Evaluate your progress in terms of knowledge, performance and understanding in relation to the standards and write it up to provide evidence for your evaluation.

4. Make a note to demonstrate how you have used feedback in this process.

5. Remember to respect confidentiality, for example, by using initials for any names you may need to mention in the evidence for your evaluation.

Your evidence for this task must be based on your practice in a real work environment and must be witnessed by or be presented in a format that is acceptable to your assessor.

Reflect

Think about the last time you received formal or informal feedback about your work?

How did it feel and do you think the person's observations and assessment were accurate? Was the feedback helpful and in what ways were you able to use it to develop your work practice?

What sources of support are available to plan and review your personal development at work?

A **personal development plan** is, above all, personal. There is no set format to follow, but it is helpful to find a structure that helps to give an overview of your work, shows the progress within your working practice and your aims for the future. You will find that the tools you have been developing through this diploma course, such as reflective practice and methods to evaluate your work will help you to plan and review your personal development. This is not something that happens overnight, but it is an ongoing process. Reviewing looks back at where you have come from and planning builds on this to meet future aims.

The reasons for support

Personal development reviewing and planning is greatly helped by using the resources and support of others.

As you review and plan your personal development you will be asking yourself such questions as:

▶ How am I doing?

▶ What am I looking for in my work?

▶ What do I need to do to reach the next level?

▶ What are my goals and ambitions?

▶ Am I making the right decisions to take me where I want to be?

To answer these questions you will need:

▶ The right information to make informed choices.

▶ Supportive people around who know the area you work in and who you can trust.

▶ Opportunities to experiment and test your abilities and limits.

▶ Opportunities to extend your knowledge and skills.

▶ Experts and specialists to guide you.

Sources and methods of support

There is a range of support available to you as you plan and review your personal development, as shown in Figures 2.8 and 2.9.

Key terms

Personal development plan: a structure to help you reflect upon and appraise your learning and work performance, record your findings and plan how to develop in stages towards future goals. It is also known as an individual development plan or a personal enterprise plan

Reflect

Take a moment to think about the support available to you:

▶ Note down the names of relevant individuals, or organisations.

▶ Include the sort of support each is likely to be able to offer.

▶ Consider whether there are any gaps and ways to fill these.

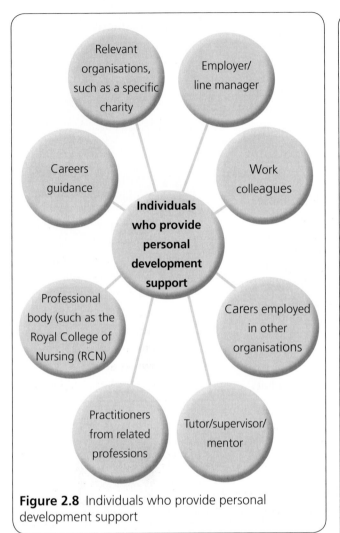

Figure 2.8 Individuals who provide personal development support

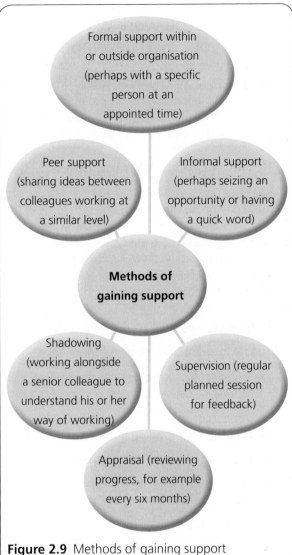

Figure 2.9 Methods of gaining support

Case study

Nina and Jake attend a college of further education. Nina hopes to get enough qualifications to apply for a social work degree course, but wonders whether some work experience in the holidays might be a good idea to make sure this really is the career for her. Jake is thinking about applying for a psychiatric nursing course in America or Australia. Nina comments that her brother is a psychiatric nurse. The college they attend run these courses but Nina and Jake haven't spoken to the students on the courses.

1. What formal sources of support would you suggest Jake and Nina turn to for advice?

2. What informal sources of support might be available to them?

3. How might a personal development plan help both Nina and Jake focus their attention on the future?

How can you work with others to review and agree your own development plan?

The process of creating your personal development plan comes out of reviewing your learning needs, professional interests and development opportunities. It is greatly aided by having one particular person to help work on it with you – perhaps a senior colleague or tutor.

Reviewing your learning needs

Learning needs will become clear through recognising first those areas where you are already competent, with established skills and the knowledge that informs these. You will then be able to recognise where there are gaps in skills or knowledge. Some skills will be specific to an area of work, such as using a hoist to transfer a service user from bed to chair and others will be transferable, such as being able to carry out a risk assessment. Try using a structure such as a table to list your skills and the corresponding knowledge in all areas related to your work.

You might want to think about these areas:

- Experience of working with service users (older people/ adults with special needs/ adults with mental health difficulties)

- Aspects of physical care (giving personal care, administering medication, providing nutrition and so on)

- Including all service users equally

- Planning and leading small and large group activities

- Communication with service users with different communication needs

- Observing and recording service user's progress

- Making sure service users are offered a healthy diet

- Keeping service users safe from harm

- Building positive relationships with service users

- Partnership with relatives

- Managing a budget

Skill areas

Each skill-area will relate to a knowledge base. For example:

▶ the skill of carrying out a risk assessment relates to knowledge about health and safety and safeguarding vulnerable adults

▶ the skill of changing a catheter bag relates to knowledge about infection control, maintaining healthy skin and making sure a service user is comfortable.

Carrying out this exercise will take quite a while, but it is useful to do so in a thorough manner over a period of time.

Professional interests and development opportunities

Professional interests and development opportunities will present as you become keen to discover more about a particular area and this may relate closely to the way you wish your career to develop.

There are a number of ways in which you can pursue professional interests:

▶ **Newspaper articles and professional journals** keep you up to date about what is current in your area of work

▶ **Books** provide an established foundation on a subject, but do be aware of when they were written as they can go out of date

▶ **Training sessions and courses** offer a focus on a particular area of your work

▶ **Self study materials** such as DVDs and CDs allow you to study in your own time and at your own pace

▶ **Conferences** provide an opportunity to hear the current thinking on a topic with the added stimulation of being able to meet and talk with fellow practitioners

▶ **Workshops** are usually practice based and allow you to try new ways of working. These are often run at a local level allowing colleagues to collaborate and share thoughts and ideas

▶ **Shadowing another practitioner**, such as a speech and language therapist or clinical psychologist to better understand their role and how it relates to your own.

Investigate

Using library, internet or workplace sources find out about an area of professional interest to you. This could be an area of care such as palliative care for the dying, or safeguarding vulnerable groups, or a skill such as communication techniques. You could put interesting articles related to areas of interest in a folder for reference purposes.

Your assessment criteria:

4.2 Demonstrate how to work with others to review and prioritise your own learning needs, professional interests and development opportunities.

4.3 Demonstrate how to work with others to agree your own personal development plan.

Prioritising your needs

You cannot do everything at once and will need to prioritise your learning needs, professional interests and development opportunities into a hierarchy. Priority might be determined by:

- ▶ relevance to your work
- ▶ availability of courses or materials or funding
- ▶ opportunities arising that you can take advantage of
- ▶ practicability in terms of whether you have the time to spare and can find money to fund it.

Using the input of others

People are one of the most valuable resources you are likely to come across, so it important that you use them well! These might include colleagues, other practitioners in different professions and school or college staff. Your relationships need to be based on honesty, where you are able to speak frankly about your strengths and about areas that require attention.

Use the time you have together well. Prepare for your sessions by planning what you need to achieve and note down particular areas you would like to discuss during your session.

Knowing yourself well will help you find people to support you who can give encouragement when you need it most and in ways that build on your strengths.

Reflect

Think about the ways you work best.

- ▶ Are you self-disciplined or do you need someone to keep you focused?
- ▶ Do you get on with things, or does your energy go into finding excuses about why tasks have not been done?

Practical Assessment Task

4.1 **4.2** **4.3**

Prioritising and planning your learning needs and reviewing your development are greatly helped by seeking support and collaborating with others. To complete this activity:

1. Make a list that identifies the sources of support available to you for planning and reviewing your own work.

2. Show the ways in which specific people provide help with the process of reviewing and prioritising your learning needs, professional interests and development opportunities.

3. Show the ways in which you can work with others to agree your own personal development plan.

The evidence that you produce for this assessment task must be based on your practice in a real work environment.

You need to demonstrate to your assessor and provide evidence on how you review and prioritise your own learning needs, professional interests and development opportunities, and work with others to agree your own personal development plan. You may want to make notes to help you to prepare for your assessment reflecting the:

▶ review of your learning needs, skills area and knowledge base
▶ development opportunities and ways in which you would like to pursue your professional interests
▶ way you have prioritised your needs
▶ way you have used the input of others.

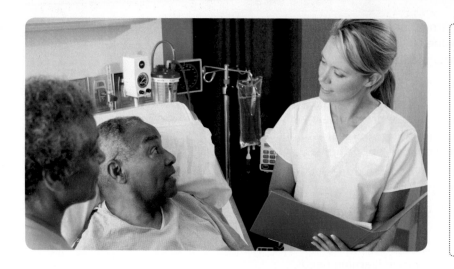

Your assessment criteria:

5.1 Evaluate how learning activities have affected practice.

5.2 Demonstrate how reflective practice has led to improved ways of working.

5.3 Show how to record progress in relation to personal development.

How can you evaluate how learning activities and reflective practice have affected your working practice?

Learning activities and reflective practice offer opportunities to:

▶ develop skills and expertise

▶ discover insights

▶ increase your understanding

▶ apply your learning to your practice

▶ model good working practice to others.

Recording your progress provides a comprehensive document that plots your journey, identifies how far you have come and plans the way ahead.

Evaluating learning activities

Learning activities refer to self-directed learning opportunities as well as attending study days and training courses and also include less formal opportunities such as observing colleagues. Taking part in study days and training courses are valuable activities, but these hold little meaning and do not contribute to your development unless you make connections between the theory and the practice of your work. Learning activities should stimulate your interest, broaden your knowledge, extend your skills and deepen your understanding.

Reflecting on learning activities

Reflective practice helps you draw together the different aspects of your learning experiences and apply them to your work. You might want to reflect on:

- knowledge and learning
- your relationships with the service users in your care and their relatives
- how well you work in a team
- your communication with other practitioners from different professions
- the interventions you make and activities you run.

Recording professional development progress

Record your professional development progress in order to:

1. **Gather the information together for easy reference** – keeping all the information in one place about personal study, training, attendance at conferences, as well as any certificates you have gained, makes it is easy to find and refer to.

2. **Provide a document of evidence** – which you can show to prospective employers to demonstrate how you have kept up to date in your practice, or as evidence to use for applying to colleges and university for courses of study.

3. **Demonstrate to you how far you have come** and remind you of the steps along the way.

It is advisable to keep your professional development records in a box or ring-binder file that can be added to. Keep this in a place you can easily access at home or at work.

Agreeing a personal development plan

When you agree your personal development plan it is helpful to set it out as an action plan with targets to aim for. A useful tool for setting out a personal development plan is to use the SMART method:

- **S**pecific – with clear and well defined targets
- **M**easurable – so you can see what you have achieved in a tangible way
- **A**chievable – it is manageable given your resources, ability and time
- **R**elevant – an identified goal which links to your area of practice
- **T**ime limited – with a realistic timeframe (and deadline!) for achievement

Case study

Ailise has worked for two years in a care home for older people. The aspect of her work she enjoys most is communicating with the residents. She is fascinated by the stories of their life, loves hearing about their families and their thoughts about life. That's the bit of her job she sees as fun, not real work. Ailise has heard about a reminiscence therapy study day, but she wonders if it might help her chances of promotion better if she did a more practical course in infection control or continence. Sometimes she thinks she'd like to train as a nurse, but other times decides she'll stay in residential care, but look for a job as an activities co-ordinator.

1. How might reflective practice help Ailise recognise and value the time she spends building relationships with the residents?

2. What learning activities would you suggest to Ailise to build on her strengths as a care worker?

3. How might advice from others and a system such as the SMART approach help Ailise work out her career priorities?

Your assessment criteria:

5.1 Evaluate how learning activities have affected practice.

5.2 Demonstrate how reflective practice has led to improved ways of working.

5.3 Show how to record progress in relation to personal development.

Practical Assessment Task   5.1 5.2 5.3

It is important to use learning opportunities and reflective practice to contribute to your personal development. To complete this task, create a personal development file and gather material to go in it:

1. Identify two learning activities you have undertaken and show the specific ways in which these have affected your working practice.

2. Show the specific ways in which reflective practice has led to improved ways of working.

3. Show how you have recorded your personal development in a way that shows the process of your progress (for example, by using the SMART approach on page 63).

The evidence that you produce for this assessment task must be based on your practice in a real work environment.

Are you ready for assessment?

AC	What do you know now?	Assessment task	✓
1.1	Describe the duties and responsibilities of your own work role.	Page 45	
1.2	Explain expectations about your own work role as expressed in relevant standards.	Page 45	

AC	What do you know now?	Assessment task	✓
2.1	Explain the importance of reflective practice in continuously improving the quality of service provided.	Page 51	
2.2	Demonstrate the ability to reflect on practice.	Page 51	
2.3	Describe how own values, belief systems and experiences may affect working practice.	Page 51	
3.1	Evaluate own knowledge, performance and understanding against relevant standards.	Page 55	
3.2	Demonstrate use of feedback to evaluate own performance and inform development.	Page 55	
4.1	Identify sources of support for planning and reviewing own development.	Page 61	
4.2	Demonstrate how to work with others to review and prioritise own learning needs, professional interests and development opportunities.	Page 61	
4.3	Demonstrate how to work with others to agree own personal development plan.	Page 61	
5.1	Evaluate how learning activities have affected practice.	Page 64	
5.2	Demonstrate how reflective practice has led to improved ways of working.	Page 64	
5.3	Show how to record progress in relation to personal development.	Page 64	

3 | Promote equality and inclusion in health and social care settings (SHC 33)

Assessment of this unit

This unit focuses on the importance of working with people in health and social care settings in ways that ensure each individual is treated equally and included fairly, in a manner that accepts and celebrates their differences. It looks at how individuals are sometimes treated unfairly and excluded and at ways to prevent this from happening.

You will develop your understanding of key words and ideas relating to equality and inclusion and will look at forms of discrimination that can occur in health and social care settings, as well as the relevant laws, standards and policies that tackle these. You will develop your knowledge about working in ways that are inclusive and anti-discriminatory, where you value diversity, respond to individuals equally, regardless of their difference and challenge discrimination. You will need to:

1. Understand the importance of diversity, equality and inclusion.

2. Be able to work in an inclusive way.

3. Be able to promote diversity, equality and inclusion.

The assessment of this unit is partly knowledge-based (things you need to know about) and partly competence-based (things you need to do in the real work environment). To successfully complete this unit, you will need to produce evidence of both your knowledge and your competence. The charts below and opposite outline what you need to know and do to meet each of the assessment criteria for the unit.

Your tutor or assessor will help you to prepare for your assessment and the tasks suggested in this chapter will help you to create the evidence that you need.

AC	What you need to know
1.1	Explain what is meant by diversity, equality and inclusion
1.2	Describe the potential effects of discrimination
1.3	Explain how inclusive practice promotes equality and supports diversity

AC	What you need to do
2.1	Explain how legislation and codes of practice relating to equality, diversity and discrimination apply to own work role
2.2	Show interaction with individuals that respects their beliefs, culture, values and preferences
3.1	Demonstrate actions that model inclusive practice
3.2	Demonstrate how to support others to promote equality and rights
3.3	Describe how to challenge discrimination in a way that promotes change

Assessment criteria 2.2, 3.1 and 3.2 must be assessed in the workplace or in conditions resembling the workplace.

This unit also links to some of the other mandatory units:

HSC 024	Principles of safeguarding and protection in health and social care
HSC 036	Promote person-centred approaches in health and social care
DEM 304	Enable rights and choices of individuals with dementia whilst minimising risks

Some of your learning will be repeated in these units and will give you the chance to review your knowledge and understanding.

What is meant by diversity, equality and inclusion?

Your assessment criteria:

1.1 Explain what is meant by diversity, equality and inclusion.

It is important to understand the meaning of the terms diversity, equality and inclusion in order to recognise how they fit together as a principle to guide the care you give to people and their families.

Diversity

Every person is unique and made up of different characteristics. As a practitioner you will work with colleagues, service users and other adults from a wide range of social, cultural, language and ethnic backgrounds. You will work with men, women, people with different types of ability and disability, individuals who speak different languages and who have different cultural traditions, as well as people who could be described as middle class, working class, as 'black', 'white' or of mixed heritage. You should value and treat each person fairly and equally.

The **diversity** in the United Kingdom population is vast; if you think about the local area where you live, you can probably identify a number of different sub-groups within the community. This means that the population consists of individuals with a huge range of different characteristics. These differences impact on people's needs. As a result, you have a responsibility to value difference as a way of meeting the needs of the service users you work with.

Equality

You will probably know from your own experience of service users, and perhaps from being a service user yourself, that people want to be treated equally and fairly. It does not mean you must treat everyone the same, because that fails to take people's different needs, wishes and preferences into account. **Equality** in health and social care settings is about supporting each person to live their life as they wish, giving them appropriate opportunities to make choices and decisions to the best of their ability about care, treatment and management. Your role as a practitioner will involve informing and supporting each individual so that they benefit from the type of care, services and facilities that are best suited to their particular needs. Valuing service users as individuals is a very important first step in promoting this kind of **equality of opportunity**.

Discuss

Share with colleagues or fellow learners your ideas about including all service users equally within your care setting. Is there more that can be done to appreciate and accept the diversity among your service users?

Investigate

Think about your care setting and the service users you work with. Make a note of examples of diversity within this group, perhaps to do with ethnicity, culture, age, gender and background. Do you think each service user is valued and treated equally to the next?

Inclusion

A health and social care service must promote **social inclusion** in order to offer equality of opportunity to those who use it. An inclusive health and social care service works hard at:

▶ identifying and removing barriers to access and participation

▶ enabling people to use the full range of services and facilities

▶ welcoming, valuing and supporting everyone who uses the care setting.

Inclusion does not happen by chance. The people who work in health and social care settings have to:

▶ be honest and reflective about how their workplace operates

▶ be critical in a constructive way, so that positive changes can be made

▶ work at identifying *actual* barriers to access and participation

▶ remain alert to *potential* barriers that may exclude some people

▶ act in practical ways to remove actual and potential barriers

▶ place the individuals who need care at the centre of planning and support-giving processes.

Key terms

Social inclusion: the process of ensuring that all members of society have access to available services and activities

Reflect

Think about your friends, family and colleagues and the ways in which you differ from and are similar to one another.

▶ Do you think your differences ever lead to inequalities and to individuals being excluded?

▶ Is there anything you can say or do to make individuals you know feel more included?

How might diversity lead to inequality and exclusion?

The ways in which individuals are different are too numerous to itemise. Look at Figure 3.1 below to examine those differences that most commonly lead to individuals and groups being treated unfairly and excluded. You have a responsibility to ensure each person is valued equally and included as a unique individual in your health and social care setting. This concept goes further than mere tolerance of difference – it embraces diversity and explores its potential.

Your assessment criteria:

1.1 Explain what is meant by diversity, equality and inclusion.

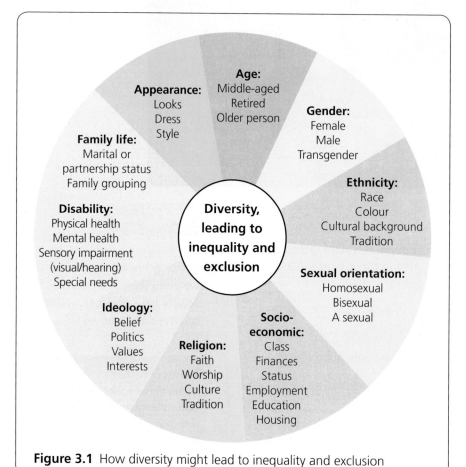

Figure 3.1 How diversity might lead to inequality and exclusion

Situations where inequality might occur

Here are some examples that show how differences can mark out an individual or group with potential for inequality and unfairness.

- ▶ A family living in poverty.
- ▶ A person with mental health problems trying to find work.
- ▶ A small community of Muslims in a predominantly Christian area.
- ▶ An older person who can no longer manage at home.
- ▶ A community of travellers needing to park their homes safely.

Investigate

Using the website **www.ageuk.org.uk** find out about ageism in UK society.

- ▶ Identify the different ways that ageism affects older people.
- ▶ Reflect on whether your own attitudes and behaviour towards older people reflects some prejudiced ideas.

Case study

Bill is seventy four and goes to see his GP. He has severe pain in one knee which has steadily increased and stops him going out as much, but he's also staying home because he is concerned his memory is getting worse. He's forgetful about where he's put things and worst of all he didn't remember his daughter's birthday.

Sometimes he finds it hard to follow conversations and his friend joked recently that he was 'losing his marbles' because he called him the wrong name. Bill's GP says it's just part of getting older and that everyone is more forgetful when they reach a certain age.

When asked about his knee, the GP advises him to take it easy and let others run around after him. Bill feels foolish and as if he has been making a fuss, so he goes home and continues to manage as best as he can without complaint.

1. In what ways does Bill's condition exclude him from living his life as normal?
2. What do you think about the GP's attitude to old age?
3. How might a different response have had a better outcome for Bill?

Knowledge Assessment Task

1.1

When you work in health and social care settings you will care for a diverse range of people each of whom must be valued and included equally as a unique individual. To complete this task read each statement below which illustrates an example of diversity. Note down whether the difference leads to inequality and exclusion and briefly justify your answer.

1. The way the care home got round Mr Ahmet's vegetarian needs was to provide the same vegetables as for the normal menu, but substituting meat with eggs and grated cheese on alternate days.
2. Staff members have got used to finishing the sentences of one of the regular attendees at the drop-in who has a severe stammer and takes a long time to express himself.
3. The interview panel appreciated that Kros discussed the mental health difficulties he experienced as a teenager and felt this might be an advantage in helping him empathise with the client group he would be working with.
4. The hospital fundraising committee decide to call their event a 'Spring', rather than an 'Easter' concert in recognition that the community includes many other faiths, cultures and traditions than Christianity.
5. Janek was asked to accompany a service user on a shopping trip to buy clothes, because as a gay man he was considered most likely to have an eye for fashion.

Keep a copy of your written work as evidence for your assessment.

Grafitti expressing extreme racism. It is your responsibility to challenge discrimination and promote equality and inclusion

Key terms

Direct discrimination: obvious and deliberate unfair treatment

Discrimination: unfair or less favourable treatment of a person or group of people in comparison to others

Indirect discrimination: unfair treatment that occurs inadvertently

What are the potential effects of discrimination?

Diversity is not welcomed or celebrated by everyone. Diversity and difference frightens some people, leading to a view of people as either 'them' or 'us'. This can result in unfair treatment or discrimination against those who are different from the majority.

What is discrimination?

Two forms of discrimination are recognised under UK law:

▶ Unfair discrimination that is obvious and deliberate which results in intentionally unfair treatment is known as **direct discrimination**. For example, if a care worker refuses to look after black residents, on grounds of their race and colour.

▶ Unfair discrimination that happens inadvertently or which is carried out in a secretive, hidden way is known as **indirect discrimination**. Normal procedures or rules can result in the exclusion of certain individuals or groups who are not able to comply with these. For example, if a club is held in a hall that has steps up to it, a person with physical disabilities may not be able to gain access. The club does not state, 'no wheelchair users allowed', which would be direct discrimination, but practical reasons prevent their attendance, which is indirect discrimination.

Investigate

Try to identify examples of indirect discrimination. These might be found in newspaper reports, or be examples from your own community.

▶ Do you think the service users you work with experience indirect discrimination?

▶ Is there anything you can do to change this indirect discrimination or minimise its impact?

How prejudice leads to discrimination

Prejudice is at the root of discrimination. A prejudice is an opinion, feeling or attitude, often of dislike concerning another individual or group of people. Prejudices are typically based on inaccurate information or unreasonable judgements. When a person acts on a prejudice, they become involved in discrimination. Acknowledging diversity, challenging prejudices and tackling all forms of discrimination are important elements of anti-discriminatory practice in health and social care work. Prejudice is revealed and expressed through the things people say and the way they behave towards individuals or groups who are different in some way. Prejudice:

▶ is often expressed through derogatory name-calling and by drawing attention to any physical differences, such as skin colour, facial and bodily features and behaviours

▶ thrives where there is uncertainty, anxiety and fear about an individual, or group who are different, or unfamiliar in some way

▶ asserts that people are less intelligent, less able or abnormal because of their differences

▶ claims a person is inferior – less valuable, less worthy of attention and less deserving – because of their differences

▶ states that a person is wrong and unnatural, rather than just different.

The expression of prejudice can range from petty insults to extreme violence towards individuals, or groups who are different in some way. It can be expressed through unfair or unkind treatment, or by isolating and excluding a person or group. You have a responsibility to recognise discrimination and prejudice at work and to encourage understanding, by providing an inclusive setting where each person is valued.

Key terms

Prejudice: an unreasonable or unfair dislike or preference towards a person or a group of people

It is your role to provide an inclusive setting where each person is valued

The negative effects of discrimination

Deliberate direct discrimination within health and social care services is relatively unusual and where discrimination does occur it usually happens inadvertently or due to an oversight. However, institutional discrimination is often so entrenched within the systems and routines of an organisation it is more difficult to recognise (see page 14 for more information). It is useful to be familiar with a number of terms that help you to identify and tackle prejudice and discrimination in health and social care settings.

Bias

Bias is a tendency to favour one side, or be influenced in a particular direction when making a judgement, rather than remaining impartial. An example is a biased care worker who tends to respond first to the needs of the male service users rather than the women.

Bigotry

Bigotry is the practise of remaining firmly persuaded by a prejudiced opinion and behaving with aggressive intolerance towards the object of that prejudice. An example of a bigot is someone who starts fights with Asian people, because he thinks this particular ethnic group are using free health services that are meant, by right, for white British people.

Labelling

Labelling means using terms that are often derogatory to identify a type of person or behaviour that then influences the way the person continues to be viewed and treated. An example is of an elderly male resident of a care home who once referred to a care worker as a 'pretty young thing' and is ever after labelled a dirty old man by the other staff members.

Stereotype

A **stereotype** is a generalisation that characterises a type of person or group of people in an oversimplified way, which fails to recognise individual differences. Stereotypes can be positive, such as that all people with glasses are intelligent, or negative, such as that all women are over-emotional. Some stereotypes include elements of truth that make them recognisable, but they never provide a fair or complete picture.

Stigma

Stigma is a trait that a person carries which marks them out by some as being less deserving, or causes others to avoid or reject them. For example, the stigma of old age sometimes means older people are not taken seriously.

Your assessment criteria:

1.2 Describe the potential effects of discrimination.

Key terms

Bias: tendency to a 'one-sided' perspective, favouring one side over the other

Bigotry: strong partiality to one's own group or belief, and intolerant of those who differ

Labelling: derogatory terms used to identify a type of person or behaviour

Stereotype: set and often ill-informed generalised ideas, for example, about the way people from certain backgrounds behave or feel

Stigma: a trait which causes a person to be disapproved of socially, and avoided or rejected

Reflect

Consider different groups of people who are commonly discriminated against and reflect on your own views.

► Do you hold any stereotypical or biased ideas?

► What can you do to challenge these?

How discrimination affects people

Discrimination has a negative impact on the targeted individual or group and often ripples out to also impact on their family and friends. It can spread more widely to affect organisations, communities and society as a whole. There is also a negative impact for those who inflict discrimination – the perpetrators – because they fail to experience the benefits of diversity, equality and inclusion and the consequent broadening of their horizons.

Look at Figure 3.2 below for the specific ways in which discrimination impacts negatively on individuals.

Reflect

Think about common stereotypes you are aware of to do with gender.

► In what ways do these limit the way people think about or act towards a man or a woman?

► Do you think your judgement is sometimes affected by stereotypes to do with gender, race or age?

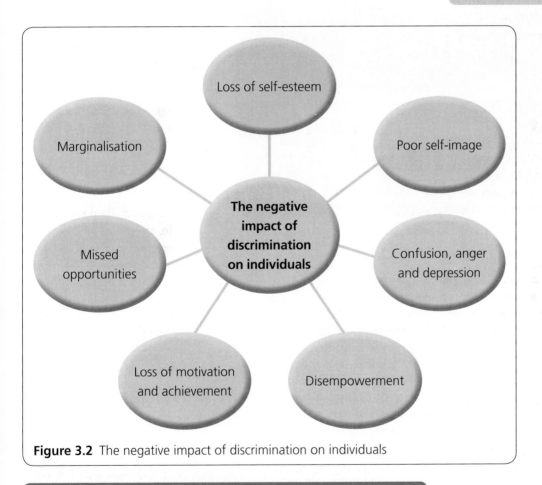

Figure 3.2 The negative impact of discrimination on individuals

Discuss

Talk together with colleagues or fellow learners about your experiences of discrimination.

► Have you, or has someone you know experienced discrimination?

► How did it make you (or the person you know) feel?

► What were the immediate and long-term effects?

Your assessment criteria:

1.2 Describe the potential effects of discrimination.

Key terms

Cycle of disadvantage: a person is discriminated against and the negative impact brings about a chain reaction of further disadvantages

The cycle of disadvantage

One negative effect of discrimination can impact on another, having a snowball effect. This is sometimes referred to as a 'cycle of disadvantage'. For example, a person with learning difficulties who suffers teasing or physical abuse increasingly avoids going out. The person stops attending a social club which leads to isolation, lack of friendship and a loss of many of the social skills the person had gained during their school years. The impact of discrimination can be so debilitating that ultimately a person's potential for good health, sound education, work opportunities and personal fulfilment is severely reduced.

Impact on family and friends

Those who are close to a person who is discriminated against can also be negatively affected, even though they are not directly discriminated against. For example, a person whose partner has disabilities might find certain holidays or recreational activities are not open to them, because of access difficulties for their partner or issues to do with providing for their partner's care needs. Not only is the person with the disability discriminated against in this case because they are unable to participate, but their partner and children who don't have disabilities miss out as well.

Case study

A project providing supportive housing for six adults who have special needs has been set up. Two live-in workers will ensure the house and garden are maintained, as well as assisting the residents to find and keep employment and learn skills such as cooking, cleaning, laundry and managing finances. A large house in a residential area has been purchased and planning permission sought for a change in usage, but neighbours have begun a campaign against the project. They claim that:

▶ there will be unacceptable levels of noise from shouting

▶ there will be unsocial behaviour, e.g. urinating in the garden

▶ residents will be a nuisance, ringing on doorbells and demanding assistance

▶ children and older members of the community will be placed in unacceptable danger

▶ the value of their property will decline because of the home's proximity.

1. List all the prejudices the neighbours have against people with special needs.

2. Describe how you would feel if you were a worried neighbour concerned for the wellbeing of your family.

3. Describe how you would feel if you were one of the prospective residents in the home.

Discuss

Talk with colleagues about the potential cycle of disadvantage that can occur with the service users you care for. What interventions could be made to reduce the chance of one disadvantage impacting on another?

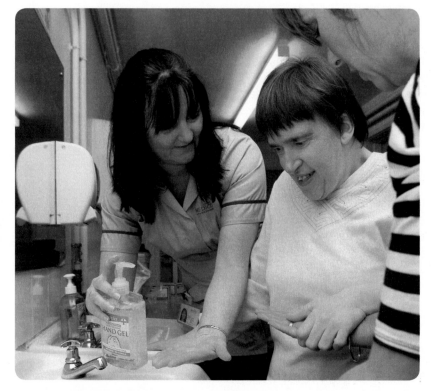

Sometimes a person requires only minimal assistance to take part in everyday activities

Discrimination within society

Discrimination can occur within certain sections of society where particular groups become associated with disadvantage and are less likely to prosper and advance. The word 'ghetto' is used to describe impoverished and neglected residential areas within cities that might be associated with a particular ethnic group, or socioeconomic class, and be characterised by higher levels of unemployment and crime. The term 'ghettoised' can also be used in a broader way to refer to any group which is disadvantaged and socially excluded.

Institutional discrimination

Institutional discrimination describes the unequal treatment of a particular group by an organisation, where discrimination has become so established it is almost written into its systems. Stephen Lawrence was a young black man who died after a racist attack in 1993 in London. A public enquiry found that institutionalised racism within the police force undermined the investigation of the crime, where there was a failure to provide an appropriate and professional service to the Lawrence family and other witnesses because of their colour, culture and ethnic origin. This was revealed in processes, attitudes and behaviour that showed unwitting prejudice, ignorance, thoughtlessness and racist stereotyping.

Institutionalised ageism

In health and social care services many people, including those working in this area claim that institutionalised ageism is common, where older people appear to not be given equal access to investigations and treatments that might improve their health and where the needs of those under the age of sixty five take precedence. Most examples of ageism are based on thoughtlessness and wrong assumptions, rather than being the product of positive prejudice, but this means many of those involved fail to recognise their behaviour as discriminatory.

Impact on the perpetrator of discrimination

There is also a negative impact on the person who inflicts discrimination on others, in that they fail to experience the stimulus of diversity and the benefits of variety. Their narrow view remains and unless challenged may become more deeply entrenched.

Your assessment criteria:

1.2 Describe the potential effects of discrimination.

Key terms

Institutional discrimination: unequal treatment of a group through practices or policies operating within an organisation

Knowledge Assessment Task   1.2

The potential effects of discrimination

Discrimination, whoever its target is, has the potential to negatively affect individuals and whole groups and can spread more widely to affect organisations, communities and society as a whole. To complete this assessment task you need to read the description below and suggest what the potential short and long term effects of discrimination might be.

1. Baghadur has recently married his English wife, who he met when she was on holiday in Turkey. He is finding it hard to adjust to his new life, more so now his relatives have returned home following the celebrations. He's managed to get a work in a care home and his wife reassures him his English is improving daily, but it's taking time for him to settle. The staff find the pronunciation of his name difficult and have decided to call him Bobby, which he hasn't got used to yet. A few of the residents claim they can't understand a word he says and one of the gentlemen refers to him as 'that darkie' which makes everyone laugh.

2. In the past Rex has had periods of time in psychiatric hospital for depression, but with the insights and support provided by regular psychotherapy sessions and the help of medication he is much more able to manage his condition. Rex applies for a new job and decides to be open about his mental health difficulties. The employer is concerned about Rex coping, saying his employees need to have strong personalities and be absolutely reliable. 'I couldn't have you throwing a wobbler and getting violent', he warns, 'and I've no time for whining and crying at the first sign of hard work!' Rex is shocked by his prospective employer's prejudices about mental illness and suddenly fears many people think this way.

Keep your notes as evidence for your assessment.

Reflect

Think about times you might have perpetrated prejudice and discrimination, perhaps in very minor ways through your words or actions. Can you understand why you acted in this way? Raise awareness so that others are not hurt or marginalised in your setting.

Being a wheelchair user need not affect a person's ability to carry out many duties and responsibilities required for a job

How does inclusive practice promote equality and diversity?

Viewing each service user you work with as an individual with unique qualities and particular needs is an important way to avoid prejudice and discrimination. Health and social care practitioners and organisations generally aim to be inclusive and welcoming to everybody who wishes to use their services.

What is inclusive practice?

Inclusive practice is based on a number of principles (truths that inform actions). The principles of inclusion are that each person is to:

▶ be valued as a unique individual

▶ feel confident about their self-identity

▶ have their individual needs recognised and met

▶ feel safe and have a sense of belonging

▶ be given the opportunity to communicate in the way they prefer

▶ be able to participate equally in activities

▶ have an equal chance to follow opportunities.

The positive outcome of inclusive behaviour

There are immediate benefits to inclusive behaviour for individual people, but there are also ongoing and wider-reaching benefits. The way in which gender, ethnicity, culture and social background are portrayed has an impact on communities and society as a whole. All people, whatever their background and ability should be able to believe that everyone can:

▶ take an active role in society

▶ achieve success in a variety of ways

▶ aspire to valued, responsible and influential positions in life.

Key terms

Inclusive practice: behaviour that ensures individuals are accepted and included equally

Discuss

Talk together with colleagues or fellow learners about:

▶ Your positive experiences of being included.

▶ Your negative experiences of being excluded.

▶ Think about ways to apply these insights to your working practice.

Reflect

Think about specific ways in which your life has been enriched by diversity within your friendship circles and with colleagues.

▶ Are there people in your life now, perhaps colleagues or acquaintances, who are different in some way and have different life experiences who you could get to know better?

Case study

Alister has a diagnosis of Asperger Syndrome. He attended mainstream primary and secondary schools, receiving input from a specialist autism service and his university was very supportive also. Alister has achieved a good degree and found work in the research laboratory of a pharmaceutical company. There were a few problems initially, mostly to do with his employer trying too hard to make him feel supported, which Alister found suffocating, and Alister interpreting regular supervision as a system to interfere with his work. After six months there is new understanding on both sides. Alister's manager has recognised his particular strengths and changed his role to suit these and Alister is pleased to be independently out in the world of work, bringing in a good income.

1. What are the positive outcomes of inclusion for Alister?
2. What are the positive outcomes of inclusion for Alister's manager and colleagues?
3. What might have happened if Alister's employer had not acted inclusively?

How can you promote equality and inclusion?

You can encourage others to embrace difference, rather than rejecting it, just because it isn't familiar, through:

▶ **Reducing fear and anxiety.** Fear of the unknown is often at the root of discriminatory behaviour and being supported to ignore or overcome this can help to provide positive outcomes which go on to reduce anxiety generally. It is hoped that individuals will find they had nothing to be afraid of and much to welcome by including people who are different in some way to themselves.

▶ **Broadening experience.** Inclusive behaviour opens up opportunities to share more widely with others from different backgrounds and experiences. When aspects of a different culture and traditions are made available it provides new interest and opens up new possibilities.

▶ **Increasing understanding.** Including those who come from a diverse range of backgrounds provides different perspectives on issues and allows new insights into an individual or group point of view. This develops understanding between different people.

▶ **Encouraging collaboration:** Sharing thoughts and ideas with a wide range of individuals encourages the generation of new ideas and brings fresh creativity.

Investigate

Ask your colleagues what they understand by the term 'inclusive practice.'

Make a note of the responses you receive and discuss these with your supervisor or manager.

Consider whether there is a potential need for further training and understanding in this area.

Knowledge Assessment Task

1.3

There are immediate and long-term benefits to inclusive behaviour where individuals are accepted and appreciated, whatever their differences, and the positive effects of diversity spread out to communities.

1. Think about your work setting or a health and social care setting with which you are familiar.
2. Produce a poster that identifies how inclusive behaviour in this work setting benefits service users, staff members and the wider community.
3. Include in the poster specific examples of inclusive practice which promotes equality and supports diversity.

How does legislation and codes of practice about diversity, equality and inclusion relate to your work role?

Diversity, equality and inclusion are such important issues they are protected by laws and promoted through codes of practice.

What is the legal framework for health and social care practice?

Health and social care practitioners have to work within a framework of **legislation**, **codes of practice**, **policies** and **procedures** that are designed to promote equality and inclusion and prevent discrimination.

The health and social care legal framework promotes diversity and protects the rights of individuals (service users, families and practitioners) in care settings. You need to be able to explain how legislation, codes of practice, policies and procedures relating to equality, diversity and discrimination impact on your role. You should also be able to explain the legal responsibilities that health and social care employers and employees have for promoting diversity and rights.

Figure 3.3 opposite outlines the main laws relevant to health and social care settings.

Your assessment criteria:

2.1 Explain how legislation and codes of practice relating to equality, diversity and discrimination apply to own work role.

Key terms

Code of practice: a document setting out standards for practice

Legislation: another term for written laws, such as Acts of Parliament

Policies: a plan of action and the principles that underlie this

Procedures: documents that specify ways of doing something or dealing with a specific issue or problem

Reflect

What differences do you think legislation about equality, diversity and inclusion have made within UK society?

Investigate

Using library, work-place or internet sources find out about the Equality Act 2010 and those elements of the law that have particular relevance for your work setting.

Figure 3.3 The main laws relevant to health and social care settings

UK Law	About the law	How it affects you
• European Convention on Human Rights 1953	A treaty to protect human rights and fundamental freedoms in Europe, based on the United Nations Convention on Human Rights 1948 that was drawn up after World War 11.	All citizens are protected under this convention and can appeal decisions and rulings through the European Court of Human Rights.
• The Human Rights Act 1998	Inspires and informs the basis of a lot of legislation and guidance to do with diversity, equality and inclusion.	You must work in ways that acknowledge and uphold the human rights of service users and their families, as well as colleagues and other practitioners you work with.
• Race Relations Amendment Act 2000	Enacted following the Stephen Lawrence case, where police work was affected by institutionalised racism.	If you work in the public sector, your service must be accessible and offer equal opportunities to all racial groups.
• Disability Discrimination Act 2005	Protects those with a substantial and on-going physical or mental impairment. Most of this Act is now covered by the Equality Act (below), except for the Disability Equality Duty.	If you work in the public sector, your service must promote equality of opportunity for disabled people.
• The Equality Act 2010	Brings together and simplifies previous legislation associated with difference (race, gender, disability, age, and so on). Aims to protect people and prevent discrimination in work, education, services, facilities, transport, access to goods.	You must make sure all service users and their family members are treated fairly and able to access and benefit from services and facilities. Also that colleagues and other practitioners are not discriminated against.

Your assessment criteria:

2.1 Explain how legislation and codes of practice relating to equality, diversity and discrimination apply to own work role.

Codes of practice

Codes of practice provide guidelines and rules for implementing the often complicated legislation that is relevant to health and social care. By working within these you will remain within the law. Codes of practice set out the standards expected within your profession and guide your working practice.

Some examples of codes of practice related to work in health and social care include:

▶ the codes of practice on equalities issues produced by the Equalities and Human Rights Commission

▶ the codes of practice for social care workers and employers of social care workers produced by the General Social Care Council (**www.gscc.org.uk**)

▶ the standards of proficiency for registered health professionals produced by the Health Professions Council (**www.hpc-uk.org**)

▶ the code of conduct for registered nurses and midwives produced by the Nursing and Midwifery Council (**www.nmc.org.uk**).

Government charters, such as the National Health Service (NHS) Patients Charter (1997) set out the standards that service users should expect, as well as the rights which must be upheld by law and these are reflected within codes of practice. Local authorities also produce charters relevant to the services they provide, such as Adult Social Services Charter Standards.

Your employer will use codes of practice, professional standards and service-user charters to produce policy and procedure documents. By working in accordance with these you will be keeping to the law and working in an inclusive way.

Discuss

Talk with colleagues or fellow learners about the ways you notice codes of practice being implemented in your work setting.

▶ How are service users informed about these?

▶ How are staff members informed about these?

Practical Assessment Task   **2.1**

As a health and social care practitioner you must work within a legal framework that promotes equality and inclusion and prevents discrimination, protecting the rights of service users, their families and other practitioners. To complete this activity you need to:

1. Identify specific aspects of the laws, codes of practice, policies and procedures about equality, diversity and discrimination that are relevant to your work role.

2. Produce a table that explains, by giving examples, how this links to your working practice with service users and their families.

Your evidence for this task must be based on your practice in a real work environment and must be presented in a format acceptable to your assessor.

How can you show respect in your interactions?

Interacting with service users and their families in ways that clearly demonstrate respect is a very important part of inclusive practice in health and social care settings. Everybody who uses your setting should be valued and respected for who they are, whatever their physical characteristics or their social or cultural background. People feel respected when you:

▶ treat them as an equal while recognising their individual needs, wishes and preferences

▶ acknowledge and recognise that their beliefs, culture and traditions are an important part of who they are

▶ use inclusive, non-discriminatory language that avoids stereotypes, labelling, prejudices, slang and **stigmatised** or derogatory terms

▶ are open-minded and prepared to discuss their needs, issues and concerns in a way that recognises the unique qualities of each person, as well as the characteristics they share with others

▶ show interest in their cultural and religious traditions and take part in an appropriate way in celebrating festivals and events that are significant for them and their community.

Case study

Bettina is key worker to Jock who is a resident in a care home for people with dementia. She has never been to Scotland and is interested to find out about the place Jock came from. She brings in a map and gets him to point out his hometown and describe the surrounding countryside of mountains and lochs. Jock has very poor short term memory, but still remembers stories from his childhood and even sings her some Scottish songs. Bettina can see how much it means to Jock to be reminded of his life before dementia and she asks him if he would like to make a memory book. His wife brings in photos and they cut out pictures from magazines and piece together his life story. When the book is finally finished Jock grips Bettina's arm and with tears in his eyes he says 'Lass, you've given me back my life'.

1. What impact has dementia had on Jock's sense of himself?

2. How does Bettina show her respect towards Jock?

3. In what ways might the memory book change Jock's impression of himself?

Your assessment criteria:

2.2 Show interaction with individuals that respects their beliefs, culture, values and preferences.

Key terms

Stigmatised: to characterise an aspect of an individual as being shameful, even disgraceful and therefore disapproved of by society

Investigate

Using the internet go to the website for the Alzheimer's Society (www.alzheimers.org.uk) and look for the section about sharing your experiences. Read the personal stories of those who have dementia and try to imagine what it might be like to experience this yourself.

Discuss

Talk to a colleague or fellow learners about how you imagine it feels to be stigmatised because of some difference. Think about a person with a disability, such as visual impairment, or a condition such as Asperger syndrome. Consider the difficulties of everyday living and the impact of negative attitudes and the prejudice of others.

Providing information in many languages is an example of inclusive practice

Practical Assessment Task

2.2

As a health and social care practitioner you must interact in an inclusive manner with service users and their families in ways that demonstrate respect for their beliefs, culture, values and preferences. To complete this task you need to:

1. Keep a reflective journal for one week at your work setting.

2. Record examples of instances where your approach, manner and behaviour shows respect towards the beliefs, culture, values and preferences of service users and their family members.

3. Where possible make sure a senior colleague, your workplace assessor or your manager witnesses these interactions and can confirm you demonstrated respect.

Your evidence for this task must be based on your practice in a real work environment and must be witnessed by or be in a format acceptable to your assessor.

Be able to promote diversity, equality and inclusion

How can you model inclusive practice in a care setting?

Your assessment criteria:

3.1 Demonstrate actions that model inclusive practice.

The basic principle of inclusion is to be receptive to and accepting of diversity, underpinned by the idea that all people are of equal value and therefore have equal entitlement to have their needs met and their individuality respected. In relation to health and social care settings, inclusion means equal access to appropriate care, which is given with respect for the individuality of each person.

Inclusive practice begins with the individual. It does not matter what your position is within the hierarchy of your care setting, because everyone has a crucial role to play in promoting diversity and equality by modelling inclusive behaviour.

Have a look at Figure 3.4 which sets out different ways to promote inclusion:

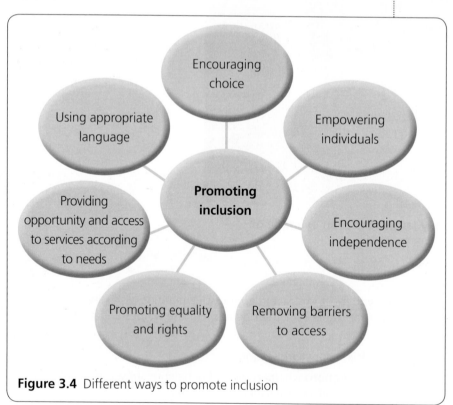

Figure 3.4 Different ways to promote inclusion

Reflective practice

Reflective practice is about being mindful and giving yourself time to think carefully about the ways in which you work. It requires you to re-play in your mind the various situations you have encountered during the day and the conversations you have been involved with at work. You need to apply self-awareness to this process, such that you can lay aside the influence of your own beliefs, justifications and prejudices and identify occasions where you missed an opportunity to behave more inclusively. Make sure you also notice and develop the positive aspects of your working practice.

Being a role model

The ways in which you work and respond to those around you will be seen and experienced by the service users you work with, their families, your colleagues and practitioners who visit your place of work. Others may view you as a practitioner with expertise and take their lead from you, including less experienced colleagues. This is your chance to be a positive role model for inclusive behaviour and make a difference where you work.

Promote opportunities for inclusion

In most cases individual practitioners and service users do not behave in discriminatory and exclusive ways, but as people get older they can tend to be a bit stuck in their ways and less open to new ideas and experiences. Emphasise the positive aspects of inclusion and the opportunities that diversity and equality offer in giving people new experiences that enrich life. Here are some ideas:

▶ Focus on some of the differences represented within the service user and staff group within your work setting and find ways to celebrate these. For example, asking about including the traditional food from different countries on the menu.

▶ Make sure the care you give is personal and individualised, for example, by supporting service users to make choices about the clothes they wear and the activities they take part in.

▶ Celebrate special days associated with a range of faiths, religions and traditions.

▶ Show an interest and find out about the individual life experiences of service users, asking family and friends to provide information where the service user cannot.

▶ Learn about various aids and support systems relevant to the needs of service users, such as signing for those with hearing impairment and those with special needs.

▶ Have a fundraiser at work for a charity relevant to the service users you work with.

Key terms

Reflective practice: being mindful and giving yourself time to think carefully about the ways in which you work

Reflect

How aware are you of the differences among the service users you work with?

Try noting down the range of differences and finding ways to acknowledge these in the way you work.

Discuss

Talk with a colleague or fellow learner about the ways in which you role model inclusive behaviour in your work setting, when carrying out your duties and responsibilities. Share together your ideas for finding new ways to extend this behaviour.

Investigate

Using library or internet sources find out about those who adhere to the social model of disability. For example, look for information about those in the deaf community who value sign language more highly than learning to communicate with spoken language, or those diagnosed with an autistic spectrum disorder who resent efforts to help them fit in to society, or people diagnosed with a mental disorder who argue that they are just different and not unwell.

The social model of disability

The social model of disability views disability in positive ways that do not focus on illness and inability. It attempts to get away from the medical model which aims to cure and fix individuals and even considers this stance has the potential to harm the self-esteem and social inclusion of individuals to the point of being prejudiced and discriminatory. The social model of disability defends the unique culture of those who experience the world differently because of their condition, giving them a different, but equally valuable viewpoint and set of abilities.

Your assessment criteria:

3.1 Demonstrate actions that model inclusive practice.

The social model of disability values the unique qualities of each individual

Model different approaches

As you will by now be aware, diversity, equality and inclusion are not about treating everybody in exactly the same way, in order to be fair. Service users must all be treated with equal concern and valued alike, but their differences mean they have individual needs. You will need to alter your approach and manner accordingly and it is necessary to consider differences such as:

▶ personality traits and characteristics: a service user who is shy might not want to be put at the centre of attention, for example

▶ confidence and competence: gentle encouragement over a long period of time will probably be the best way to introduce changes

▶ preferences (likes and dislikes): you cannot insist service users try new experiences and some will be more suitable for particular service users than others

▶ cultural background and influences: some ethnic and religious beliefs mean there are traditions that need to be respected, especially if the service user wishes to observe them.

Case study

Kate works with Akara, who has profound learning difficulties and some limb spasticity following a birth trauma. She is from Cambodia and was adopted and brought to live in Wales when she was twelve and is now in supported living accommodation following the deaths of her adoptive parents. Kate is aware that Akara's adoptive parents took her on trips back to Cambodia because she found photo albums in the bottom of her wardrobe when she was tidying up. However, there is very little else that reflects her ethnicity and background. One of the other residents calls her 'the jap', which makes the others laugh. Akara also laughs and because she seems happy with it the staff don't intervene, but Kate feels uncomfortable and wonders whether Akara just joins in as a defence against feeling hurt. Kate would like to find some way of acknowledging Akara's roots and celebrating her background.

1. What is Kate's behaviour modelling when she doesn't join in with the laughter?

2. Why is it important that Kate follows up her intention to acknowledge Akara's roots?

3. Can you suggest ways she might achieve this?

How can you support others to promote equality and rights?

As well as working in ways that promote equality and rights for the service users you work with, you are also in a position to support their families and your colleagues to do the same. There are a number of ways in which you can do this, as Figure 3.5 shows.

Highlight areas of concern

If you work according to the principle that each individual has the right to be treated fairly regardless of their differences, you will become more alert to any potential discrimination taking place. This might come from service users or members of their family, or from less aware colleagues. Recognising and identifying discrimination is the first step to tackling it. In order to manage this it is advisable to first seek advice from individuals whose judgement you trust. In most health and social care settings there will be a staff meeting where you can discuss concerns.

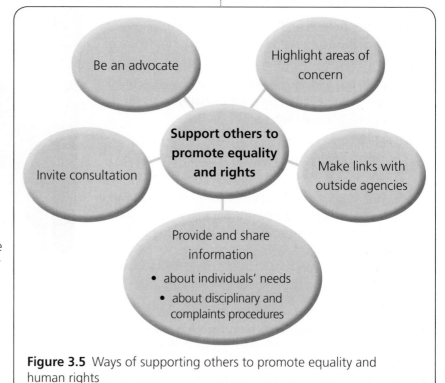

Figure 3.5 Ways of supporting others to promote equality and human rights

Provide and share information

Information is available about a range of issues to do with equality, discrimination and inclusion relevant to health and social care settings. You can make sure this literature has a high profile especially with those you have identified as needing this information. Make sure you know the policies to do with equality and rights at your workplace and talk about these with the adults you come into contact with at work. Policies should be displayed prominently for all to see and read, so if this is not the case do bring it to the attention of your manager. You could also suggest holding an information-giving session about equality and rights that explains how your place of work is ensuring these are implemented.

Service users and their families need to have access to information about how to make a complaint and who to contact. In addition, staff need to know there are disciplinary procedures in place in the event of experiencing discrimination.

Reflect

Think about whether there are aspects of your work that invite unfairness and infringe rights?

▶ What needs to change?

▶ What part could you play in supporting others to improve this situation?

Make links with outside agencies

There are a number of outside agencies that are particularly concerned with equality and rights. The Equality and Human Rights Commission (**www.equalityhumanrights.com**) is a good source for general information and provides links to other groups concerned with a particular aspect of rights and equality, such as disability or race relations.

Invite consultation and feedback

If service users you work with are part of a minority group, suggest to your manager that they be invited to share their experiences and contribute to a consultation on equality and rights. Check with these individuals that their needs are being met satisfactorily and explain to other staff why you are doing so. By making a point of including those who may feel on the fringes you prevent them from being overlooked and their needs ignored.

Be an advocate

Keep your awareness raised to the possibility of discrimination where you work. **Advocacy** is the process of standing up for those who are overlooked or put down because of their differences. You can be an advocate where you work by supporting individuals who are vulnerable to discrimination because of their differences. Speak up in your support of all voices being heard equally and every person being treated fairly.

Investigate

Using the internet, look up the work of the Equality and Human Rights Commission (**www.equalityhumanrights.com**). Search the website for information that particularly relates to your area of work and work role.

Discuss

Talk with colleagues about different ways of consulting with service users to make sure their opinions and wishes are included centrally in the management of their care.

Key terms

Advocacy: the act of interceding on behalf of another person, looking out for their rights and providing active support

Case study

Malik works for Care Matters, a company that provides support and care for people in their own homes.

His role involves assessing and managing the needs of service users, providing appropriate care to help them to continue to live as independently as possible.

He has been asked by his manager to join a team who are developing a questionnaire to gather the opinions of service users and their families about the quality and individuality of the service.

1. How do initiatives such as this reflect the principle of inclusion?
2. What questions could Malik suggest that would ask how diversity is acknowledged in the way service is delivered?
3. What ideas do you have for making sure as many service users and their family members respond to the questionnaire and provide the widest possible feedback for the Care Matters company?

How can you challenge discrimination and promote positive change?

Your assessment criteria:

3.3 Describe how to challenge discrimination in a way that promotes change.

Occasions may arise when you witness or are made aware of discrimination taking place. It is not acceptable to ignore or make excuses for this. You must act, but it is more productive to intervene in ways that lead to positive change in those you challenge, rather than negative resentment and misunderstanding. Have a look at Figure 3.6 about ways to challenge discrimination.

Figure 3.6 Ways to challenge discrimination

Understand why discrimination occurs

It is useful to understand something of the psychology behind discriminatory behaviour. The diagram in Figure 3.7 gives some examples of why discrimination occurs.

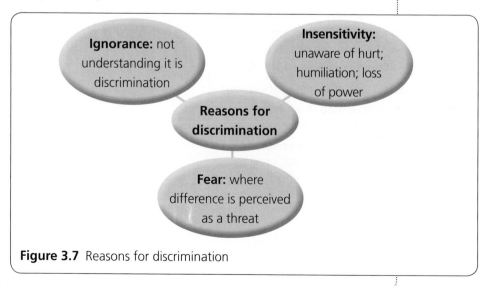

Figure 3.7 Reasons for discrimination

Positive methods of challenging discrimination

When challenging discrimination, your approach should take into consideration whether the perpetrator is a service user, one of their relatives, or a member of staff. It is always advisable to talk over the best approach for challenging discrimination with someone whose opinions you respect, such as your tutor or manager. There are a number of positive methods to challenge discrimination:

▶ **Direct confrontation:** an immediate response that gives a clear message of non-tolerance. At times this approach is appropriate where a person needs to be told in a straightforward manner why discriminatory behaviour is unacceptable and won't be tolerated. For example it is not acceptable to name-call or leave a person out because of some actual or perceived difference. However, it is important to maintain a calm manner and offer information that guides behaviour, rather than making the perpetrator feel uncomfortable or upset. Be aware that the perpetrator may be unwittingly repeating prejudiced ideas learnt from a young age at home.

▶ **Initiate discussion:** in some circumstances direct confrontation leads to angry arguments which could cause the perpetrator to act defensively and perhaps become even more entrenched in their discriminatory behaviour. Respectfully sharing your thoughts with the perpetrator is more likely to help the person engage with and explore the issues and hopefully reach a new understanding.

▶ **Support those who are discriminated against:** if you say nothing in the face of discrimination this could be interpreted as being in agreement with it. It is never acceptable to condone (go along with) discrimination. Without being confrontational it is possible to act assertively and refuse to get involved in discriminatory behaviour. Standing beside those who have been on the receiving end of discrimination is a supportive action in itself, but it also gives a message to others that you will always challenge discrimination.

▶ **Reporting discrimination:** ultimately it is illegal to act in ways that discriminate against individuals and groups and the law provides one of the major methods to positively challenge discrimination. Most organisations will have a reporting system and complaints procedure which can be used to record the incidence of discrimination and ensure the situation is followed up.

Discuss

Talk with a colleague or fellow learner about occasions when you have witnessed a person name-calling or acting in a discriminatory manner.

▶ Did you challenge the person, ignore it, or did you go along with it?

▶ What was your motivation for acting in this way?

Case study

Georgina is a new volunteer at a lunch club for older people. She is a cheerful person who is outgoing and quite loud.

You notice that her manner is sometimes a bit intrusive, for example she playfully pinches the waistline of Ted, who has been a member of the club since his wife died and who has only recently started to show an appetite. After she teased that he was, 'putting on the beef,' Ted took a noticeably smaller portion.

She laughs with staff that her friends think she works with 'mentalists' and she's had to tell them, 'it's just old folk – like helping out your granny'.

Things come to a head when Georgina is asked to go and buy a pint of milk, because they have run low and as she is going out of the door she calls back across the room, 'Should I just go to the paki shop on the corner, or the supermarket?'

1. Identify what is difficult about Georgina's manner.
2. How might this upset other people?
3. What approach would you use to deal with Georgina's case?

Your assessment criteria:

3.3 Describe how to challenge discrimination in a way that promotes change.

Using positive discrimination to promote change

Positive discrimination and **affirmative action** are terms to describe the favouring of groups who are discriminated against, in order to even the power balance. This is a direct method of challenging discrimination, but it is controversial.

Through positive discrimination, groups who are disadvantaged are promoted in some way to compensate for the inequalities they experience. An example is when organisations who are obliged to have a certain percentage of people with disabilities represented among their employees favour candidates with disabilities, in order to meet their quota. Another example concerns the debate regularly held in parliament as to whether women, who are grossly unrepresented in the House of Commons should have a quota of protected positions, where men are not permitted to compete for the same seat.

Those in favour of positive discrimination state that discrimination has created such deep-rooted disadvantage within society that it cannot be equalised without affirmative action. Those who are against positive discrimination state that it is patronising and dilutes the innate strength and power of these groups when they are shown partial treatment.

Key terms

Affirmative action: action that favours those who are discriminated against

Positive discrimination: discrimination in favour of those who are disadvantaged

Reflect

- What do you think about positive discrimination?
- Are you aware of it being practised at your place of work?

Investigate

Using library, internet and workplace resources find out about positive discrimination and affirmative action and the ways these are practised. Consider whether any of these approaches could be applied in the health and social care setting where you work.

Practical Assessment Task

3.1 **3.2** **3.3**

When you work in health and social care settings you must model inclusive practice, showing how you support both service users and staff members to promote equality and rights, and whenever it arises you must challenge discrimination in a way that promotes positive change. Imagine that you are about to take part in a performance and development review with the manager of your health and social care setting. The review will focus on your ability to promote equality, diversity and inclusion:

1. In preparation for the review you have been asked to work with a group of service users in a way that demonstrates your ability to use inclusive practice and to support others to promote equality and rights. Ideally you should organise, support or assist with activities that can be witnessed by your manager or assessor.

2. Following the activity you should reflect on your performance and write some brief notes on:
   - how your actions modelled or demonstrated inclusive practice
   - how you supported others to promote equality and rights during the activity.

Keep your written work as evidence towards your assessment. Your assessor may want to observe and question you about your performance. The evidence for this activity should be assessed in the workplace.

Are you ready for assessment?

AC	What do you know now?	Assessment task	✓
1.1	Explain what is meant by diversity, equality and inclusion	Page 71	
1.2	Describe the potential effects of discrimination	Page 79	
1.3	Explain how inclusive practice promotes equality and supports diversity	Page 81	

AC	What can you do now?	Assessment task	✓
2.1	Explain how legislation and codes of practice relating to equality, diversity and discrimination apply to own work role	Page 85	
2.2	Show interaction with individuals that respects their beliefs, culture, values and preferences	Page 87	
3.1	Demonstrate actions that model inclusive practice	Page 97	
3.2	Demonstrate how to support others to promote equality and rights	Page 97	
3.3	Describe how to challenge discrimination in a way that promotes change	Page 97	

4 | Principles for implementing duty of care in health and social care settings (SHC 34)

Assessment of this unit

The focus of this unit is on what is meant by the term 'duty of care' and how this obligation relates to your work role with individuals in health and social care settings. It addresses the potential tension between maintaining a duty of care and upholding an individual's rights and it sets out appropriate ways to deal with potential conflicts or complaints that might arise as a consequence.
You will need to:

1. Understand how duty of care contributes to safe practice.
2. Know how to address conflicts or dilemmas that may arise between an individual's rights and the duty of care.
3. Know how to respond to complaints.

To complete this unit successfully you will need to produce evidence of your knowledge as shown in the 'What you need to know' chart opposite. Your tutor or assessor will help you to prepare for your assessment and the tasks suggested in this chapter will help you to create the evidence you need.

CHAPTER 4

AC What you need to know

1.1	Explain what it means to have a duty of care in your own work role
1.2	Explain how duty of care contributes to the safeguarding or protection of individuals
2.1	Describe potential conflicts or dilemmas that may arise between the duty of care and an individual's rights
2.2	Describe how to manage risks associated with conflicts or dilemmas between an individual's rights and duty of care
2.3	Explain where to get additional support and advice about conflicts and dilemmas
3.1	Describe how to respond to complaints
3.2	Explain the main points of agreed procedures for handling complaints

This unit is designed to develop your working practice, which is relevant to every chapter of this book, but has particular links to other mandatory units:

HSC 024	Principles of safeguarding and protection in health and social care
HSC 025	The role of the health and social care worker
HSC 037	Promote and implement health and safety in health and social care

Some of your learning will be repeated in these units and will give you the chance to review your knowledge and understanding.

Understand how duty of care contributes to safe practice

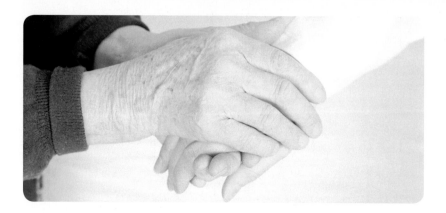

Your assessment criteria:

1.1 Explain what it means to have a duty of care in your own work role.

Key terms

Duty of care: the legal obligation to act toward others with careful attention and reasonable caution to protect their wellbeing and prevent harm occurring

Safe practice: working in ways that uphold laws and standards, prevent harm and protect and promote the safety and wellbeing of others

What does having a 'duty of care' mean?

'A **duty of care**' is a legal term. It refers to the obligation of all adults to be aware of the wellbeing of others and take reasonable steps to ensure no-one comes to harm, as a result of any action or inaction. According to UK law, a duty of care applies to all people you come into contact with, but it is of particular significance where children, young people and adults that require safeguarding are concerned, because they are unable to meet their own needs or may be unaware of potential dangers.

Your work role

As a care practitioner, you have a duty of care towards the people you provide care or support for in your work role. This means that you are expected to:

▶ put the needs and interests of those you provide care for at the centre of your thinking and practice

▶ ensure that what you choose to do – or choose not to do – does no harm to those you provide care for.

Care practitioners are accountable to their employer and to the law for providing care and support that is safe and which promotes the health and wellbeing of the individuals they work with. Your duty of care towards those you work with (individuals, their families and your colleagues), affects the way that you:

▶ exercise authority

▶ manage risk, and work safely

▶ safeguard the interests of individuals

▶ monitor your own behaviour and conduct

▶ maintain confidentiality

▶ store personal information appropriately

- ▶ report concerns and allegations
- ▶ make professional judgements
- ▶ maintain professional boundaries
- ▶ avoid favouritism
- ▶ maintain high standards of conduct outside the professional role.

As a result, when you work with adults who need care or support, having a duty of care brings specific responsibilities to:

- ▶ uphold their rights
- ▶ promote their interests
- ▶ ensure safe practice working within your own level of competence
- ▶ protect their health, safety and wellbeing.

Figure 4.1 The people to whom you owe a duty of care

Figure 4.1 shows those people to whom you owe a duty of care.

The consequences of failing in a duty of care

Care practitioners often only consider their duty of care after an incident has occurred and view the consequences with the benefit of hindsight. Even when no harm has occurred it is possible to be dismissed from your job or be removed from a professional register if you have failed in your duty of care. It is better by far to understand now what a duty of care requires of you in your work role.

Reflect

Can you think of occasions at home or at work when you need to be aware of having a duty of care towards others? Think about situations of potential negligence where something you do, or fail to do could result in harm to another person.

Knowledge Assessment Task | **1.1**

You should be clear that you have a duty of care towards others as part of your own work role. In this assessment activity you are required to show the specific ways in which you demonstrate a duty of care to the individuals for whom you are responsible during the course of a normal working day. Your response to this task will be submitted as evidence of your competence, and should be discussed with your manager, assessor or tutor before completion. You should:

- ▶ make a copy of your job description
- ▶ identify those aspects of your job description that particularly relate to holding a duty of care (you could underline or highlight them)
- ▶ give two examples for each of the three headings below that show the ways in which you fulfil your duty of care. You should have six examples in total.
  - ▶ upholding individuals' rights
  - ▶ promoting individuals' interests
  - ▶ protecting individuals from harm.

Keep a copy of the written work that you produce for this activity as evidence towards your assessment.

In what ways does a duty of care safeguard adults receiving care or support?

At the point in their life where an individual needs care or support, they are potentially vulnerable to exploitation, abuse and neglect.

Users of health and social care services depend to varying degrees on care practitioners, relatives and even neighbours acting as informal carers to fulfil their basic needs for nutrition, warmth and shelter, as well as psychological and emotional needs to be loved and nurtured.

Some people who use care services may not always be aware of risks and dangers, or the potential consequences of their actions.

Safeguarding is the term for the vigilant and nurturing care that people require in such circumstances and is an important element of a duty of care.

The safeguarding aspects of a duty of care

The main safeguarding aspects of a duty of care when working with adults in health and social care settings are reflected in the actions set out in Figure 4.2.

Reflect

Think over your most recent day's work. What activities took place, who was involved and in what different ways did you demonstrate your duty of care?

Key terms

Safeguarding: the process of looking after individuals in ways that protect them from illness, injury and abuse, promote their interests, and value and uphold their rights

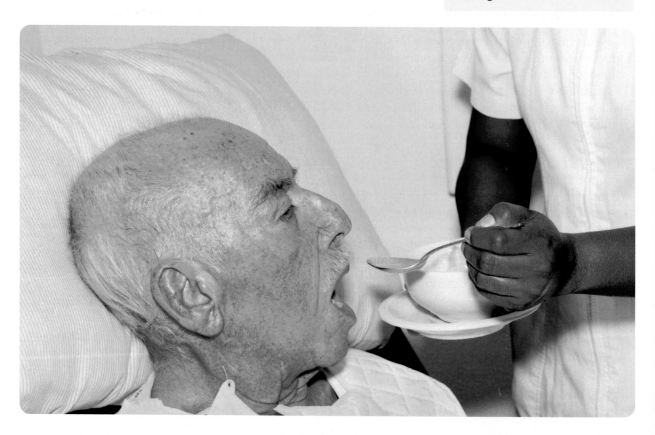

Figure 4.2 The main safeguarding aspects of a duty of care when working with individuals in health and social care settings.

Principle of safeguarding	Duty of care action
Recognise and meet physical, emotional and psychological needs.	1. Know what is required for health and wellbeing. 2. Observe and record physical, behavioural and psychological indicators that show a person is well. 3. Liaise with parents and practitioners. 4. Show empathy, support and caring.
Anticipate danger and manage risks.	5. Carry out risk assessments. 6. Take precautions to avoid hazards and prevent illness, accidents and injury.
Intervene and support in the event of illness or injury.	7. Intervene with appropriate first aid. 8. Seek appropriate treatment or support. 9. Liaise with practitioners and parents. 10. Report to appropriate authority.
Be alert to the potential of exploitation, abuse and neglect.	11. Knowledge and observation of the signs of abuse and neglect. 12. Follow safeguarding procedures. 13. Report to appropriate authority.
Provide guidance and supervision of recreation and activity.	14. Set clear expectations and appropriate boundaries. 15. Use strategies to manage challenging behaviour. 16. Support creativity and exploration.
Uphold and value rights.	17. Knowledge about the rights of the individual. 18. Treat as unique individuals with equality and fairness. 19. Protect from discrimination. 20. Communicate with others in support of their best interests.

Knowledge Assessment Task — **1.2**

Safeguarding is an important part of your duty of care towards the individuals you provide care or support for. In this activity you need to explain how duty of care contributes to the safeguarding or protection of the individuals you work with. You should:

▶ obtain the consent of your manager and two individuals with whom you work to describe their needs for safeguarding

▶ explain how care practitioners in your work setting apply their duty of care in practice to safeguard the needs and interests of each individual.

Keep a copy of the written work that you produce for this activity as evidence towards your assessment.

Your assessment criteria:

2.1 Describe potential conflicts or dilemmas that may arise between the duty of care and an individual's rights.

Duty of care dilemmas

When you work with adults in health and social care settings, situations will sometimes arise where a duty of care appears to clash with the principle of respecting an individual's (or their family's) rights. You need to be aware this might happen, be able to recognise the **rights** and **responsibilities** involved, and know how to deal with the dilemma that results from this. A dilemma arises when there are two or more alternative courses of action, none of which will provide a solution to suit everyone involved.

The potential tension between rights and responsibilities

Although you have a duty of care to the individuals you work with, the person and then their next of kin retains overall decision-making responsibility for issues relating to their care. That is why it is necessary for health and social care practitioners to obtain permission from an individual's next of kin to provide care or interventions when a person is unable to consent to these themselves.

The two main areas where conflict between duty of care and rights and responsibilities is most likely to arise are:

▶ taking risks

▶ maintaining confidentiality.

Key terms

Responsibilities: what a person is legally or morally expected or required to do

Rights: an individual's legal or moral entitlements

Taking risks

You have a duty to keep the individuals in your care safe, but this needs to be balanced with their right to live life as they choose. Some activities that individuals take part in involve physical risk, which may be increased if the person is frail. Stopping them from joining in might prevent an accident, but it also restricts their freedom and may damage their confidence or sense of self. Being risk avoidant is not necessarily the answer.

Managing risk and carer concern

Conflict also arises if the person's family or partner fear for their safety and insist on restricting the individual's freedom to take part in activities that involve some risk. In this situation your duty of care requires you to promote the individual's interests by enabling them to participate in activities that conflict with their relative's wish for caution while helping the relative recognise why this is important.

There is more about risk assessment and management in Chapter 8 on health and safety (pages 216–221).

Maintaining confidentiality

It is an individual's right for personal information about them to be kept private.

Confidences disclosed by individuals

Both individuals and members of their family are likely to confide in care practitioners from time to time. Sharing information in this way is a sign of trust, but on occasions it may be necessary for care practitioners to share this information with colleagues or higher authorities in order to carry out their duty of care to keep the person safe. For example, a person may disclose an incident of abuse, but beg a care practitioner not to tell anyone. The care practitioner would be failing in their duty of care if they did not pass this information on and the person remained at risk of further abuse.

Confidences from care practitioners

There may also be occasions where upholding confidentiality by not passing on information places other people at risk. For example, a care practitioner who tells his colleague he still feels intoxicated after a heavy drinking session the night before, but is sure he's fine to drive the work place minibus to take residents on an outing is breaching his duty of care. It would be negligent for the person he confided in to keep the information quiet when the residents are at risk of being involved in an accident.

There is more about confidentiality in Chapter 8 on health and safety (page 206).

Reflect

Can you think of occasions when you have been concerned enough about the safety of an individual in your care that you have restricted their access to or participation in activities?

▶ What were your concerns?
▶ Do you think you were justified in your actions?

Your assessment criteria:

2.2 Describe how to manage risks associated with conflicts or dilemmas between an individual's rights and the duty of care.

2.3 Explain where to get additional support and advice about conflicts and dilemmas.

How do you manage risks and find support and advice when responsibilities conflict with rights?

Managing risks when responsibilities conflict with rights requires your thoughtful attention and careful judgement. On occasions it will not be possible to reconcile fully the two different positions between maintaining a duty of care and upholding individuals' rights. There will seldom be one right answer to the dilemma and a difficult decision may need to be made to give one a higher priority over the other. This is why it is important to seek support and advice as part of the process of managing risks.

Support for balancing duty of care and rights

The way you go about managing risks that arise when a duty of care conflicts with rights is probably as important as the decision you finally make. There are a number of steps you can take to help you make your decisions, as shown in Figure 4.3.

Promote partnership with parents

By working closely together in **partnership with individuals and their relatives**, a trusting relationship will build between you. Take time to recognise and understand what is important to them about the care or support they need and expect. At the same time explain your role and how at times it may be necessary to come to a compromise in order to resolve dilemmas. It is usually helpful and appropriate to include individuals in discussions, to help them understand decisions.

Key terms

Partnership with individuals/relatives: working together with an individual and/or their relatives to understand their priorities and point of view and explain your responsibilities towards the person

Figure 4.3 Support for balancing duty of care and rights

Refer to standards, policies and procedures

You might find it useful to look at standards, such as the National Occupational Standards for care, or the policies and procedures used in your work setting, to check whether your decision fulfils the guidance given. In particular, have a look at policies such as the confidentiality policy, safeguarding policy and health and safety policy that set out the principles you should follow.

Carry out risk assessments

The process of carrying out a formal risk assessment helps to identify the risks in a clear way and points to steps that can be taken to minimise risk to an acceptable level. It also provides evidence of the reasoning behind your decision, which may be useful if this is later questioned.

Liaise with others

You can speak to a senior colleague, or approach a practitioner with specialist information. It can also be useful to discuss difficult situations with others who may bring a fresh angle to the dilemma or have past experience to draw on. However, make sure you do not breach confidentiality during discussions.

Seek advice

Advice can be sought by phoning or via a website from a number of different sources:

▶ professional bodies, such as the Care Quality Commission

▶ service providers, such as the police or Adult Social Services

▶ advisory service, such as the Citizens Advice Bureau

▶ charity, such as MIND, SCOPE or Age Concern

▶ supportive organisation, such as a union, who are particularly qualified to provide legal information.

Reflect

▶ What sources of advice and support are available to you in your work role?

▶ Who might you speak to if you are faced with a dilemma between your duty of care, an individual's rights or a parent's responsibility?

Knowledge Assessment Task 2.1 2.2 2.3

Care practitioners need to be able to identify and respond to situations where there are potential conflicts or dilemmas between the duty of care they have and an individual's rights. With reference to your own knowledge and practice:

▶ Describe the potential conflicts or dilemmas that may arise between the care practitioner's duty of care and an individual's rights

▶ Describe how to manage risks associated with conflicts or dilemmas between an individual's rights and the duty of care

▶ Explain where you would obtain additional support and advice about each conflict and dilemma.

How should you respond to complaints using proper procedures?

It is inevitable that from time to time complaints will arise about the quality of a care service. Commonly these will concern the tension between maintaining a duty of care and upholding the rights of an individual. Perhaps a person's partner believes that the individual has not been looked after with sufficient care, or that a right due to him or her has been overlooked. How the complaint is handled is very important for finding a satisfactory resolution, as well as learning from the experience.

Dealing with complaints

Sometimes a complaint can be handled with a quick conversation in passing that clears up a misunderstanding or gives information that had been overlooked. At other times it is a more serious situation. You will need to judge what is required and ask for the support of a colleague if you feel out of your depth.

Dealing with complaints can feel uncomfortable and it is easy to react in a defensive manner when a person complains to you. Figure 4.4 highlights some suggestions for handling a complaint in a professional way.

De-escalate emotion

Privacy

Respect

Handling a complaint

Confidentiality

Listening

Acknowledgement

Figure 4.4 Handling a complaint

Privacy

It is best to find a place to talk where the complaint can be discussed in private, away from the work area and the presence of other individuals and visitors to the setting. During your conversation avoid answering the phone or dealing with any other interruption.

De-escalate emotion

If the person is angry and upset you can help them calm down and settle if you speak calmly and quietly in response. Suggest that they sit comfortably and offer refreshment to help the person relax and let go of intense emotions.

Respect

Respect is shown by the way you respond to the person. Be aware of your **body language**, such as facial expression, tone of voice, proximity and gestures. For example: allow some space between you and the person, do not cross your arms in front of your body in a defensive manner and have frequent eye contact, but without staring.

Listening

The most important response is to listen carefully, giving your full attention and clarifying the person's words when necessary to make sure you understand their point correctly.

Acknowledgment

Emphasise the person's right to complain and show them you are taking their complaint seriously. If you try to ignore a complaint it is unlikely to go away and could escalate to a more serious level.

Confidentiality

The person making the complaint should be reassured that the matter will be dealt with in confidence and only shared with those who need to know about it.

Reflect

▶ Has anyone ever complained to you or about you, or your work?
▶ How did it make you feel?
▶ How did you respond?

Key terms

Body language: the non-verbal messages communicated through facial expression, tone of voice, proximity and gestures

Case study

Mrs Orrock is 89, unmarried and proud that she has lived independently until being transferred to a care home for a period of respite, following a fall. 'I don't wish to be babied', she states to a carer when she arrives at High Elms. 'I didn't have a husband to mend fuses and paint and decorate – I learnt to do everything myself.' Concerned that the cause of the fall has not yet been established, the carer tries to persuade Mrs Orrock to take the lift, but she prefers the stairs and becomes angry and upset, threatening to lodge a complaint if anyone objects.

1. How do you understand the situation from Mrs Orrock's point of view?
2. How would you describe the conflict between the carer's duty of care and the rights of the individual?
3. What suggestions do you have for handling the situation to avoid an official complaint being made?

Your assessment criteria:

3.1 Describe how to respond to complaints.

3.2 Explain the main points of agreed procedures for handling complaints.

Key terms

Complaints procedure: an official process to deal with a complaint, where specific steps are taken to ensure it is thoroughly investigated with fairness shown to all parties

Reflect

▶ Have you read the complaints procedure in operation at your place of work?

▶ Do you know who you should go to for support and advice if a complaint is made about you or your work?

Complaints procedures

Complaints at work should always be dealt with according to a **complaints procedure** that is set down in a complaints policy. This ensures the rights of individuals and their families are supported in a proper way, while also protecting the practitioner. For example, while it is right that you should listen to a complaint, you are not expected to tolerate aggression or verbal abuse.

The complaints process

The policy must be available for everyone to see at any time and should include information about who to take their complaint to if they are not satisfied with the way it is being handled.

Complaints procedures should set out each stage of the process, including a timescale, so the complainant knows what to expect:

1. A verbal response within a certain timeframe.

2. A meeting arranged at a mutually agreed time and place.

3. A written response following the meeting.

4. If this does not resolve the matter, the complaint to be put in writing to a higher authority.

Knowledge Assessment Task   **3.1** **3.2**

Complaints must always be handled according to agreed procedures. To complete this task you need to produce a leaflet for use by staff in your workplace that:

1. Describes how you should respond if a service user or their relative makes a complaint to you.

2. Includes the key points of procedures for dealing with complaints in your workplace.

Keep a copy of the written work that you produce for this task as evidence towards your assessment.

Are you ready for assessment?

AC	What do you know now?	Assessment task	✓
1.1	Explain what it means to have a duty of care in your own work role	Page 103	
1.2	Explain how duty of care contributes to the safeguarding or protection of individuals	Page 105	
2.1	Describe potential conflicts or dilemmas that may arise between the duty of care and an individual's rights.	Page 109	
2.2	Describe how to manage risks associated with conflicts or dilemmas between an individual's rights and the duty of care	Page 109	
2.3	Explain where to get additional support and advice about conflicts and dilemmas	Page 109	
3.1	Describe how to respond to complaints	Page 112	
3.2	Explain the main points of agreed procedures for handling complaints	Page 112	

5 | Principles of safeguarding and protection in health and social care (HSC 024)

Assessment of this unit

This unit is relevant to people working in a wide range of health and social care settings. It introduces the importance of safeguarding individuals from abuse, identifies the different types of abuse that can occur as well as the signs and symptoms that might indicate a person is experiencing abuse. The unit also considers when individuals might be particularly vulnerable to abuse and what you can do if abuse is suspected or alleged. You will need to:

► know how to recognise signs of abuse

► know how to respond to suspected or alleged abuse

► understand the national and local context of safeguarding and protection from abuse

► understand ways to reduce the likelihood of abuse

► know how to recognise and report unsafe practices.

The assessment of this unit is entirely knowledge-based. To successfully complete this unit, you will need to produce evidence of your knowledge as shown in the table opposite. Your tutor or assessor will help you to prepare for your assessment, and the tasks suggested in this unit will help you to create the evidence that you need.

AC	What you need to know
1.1	Define the following types of abuse: • physical abuse • institutional abuse • sexual abuse • self-neglect • emotional/psychological abuse • neglect by others. • financial abuse
1.2	Identify the signs and/or symptoms associated with each type of abuse
1.3	Define factors that may contribute to an individual being more vulnerable to abuse
2.1	Explain the actions to take if there are suspicions that an individual is being abused
2.2	Explain the actions to take if an individual alleges that they are being abused
2.3	Identify ways to ensure that evidence of abuse is preserved
3.1	Identify national policies and local systems that relate to safeguarding and protection from abuse
3.2	Explain the roles of different agencies in safeguarding and protecting individuals from abuse
3.3	Identify reports into serious failures to protect individuals from abuse
3.4	Identify sources of information and advice about own role in safeguarding and protecting individuals from abuse
4.1	Explain how the likelihood of abuse may be reduced by: • working with person-centred values • encouraging active participation • promoting choice and rights.
4.2	Explain the importance of an accessible complaints procedure for reducing the likelihood of abuse
5.1	Describe unsafe practice that may affect the well being of individuals
5.2	Explain the actions to take if unsafe practices have been identified
5.3	Describe the action to take if suspected abuse or unsafe practices have been reported but nothing has been done in response

This unit also links to some of the other units:

SHC 33	Promote equality and inclusion in health and social care settings
SHC 34	Principles for implementing duty of care in health and social care settings
IC 01	The principles of infection prevention and control

Some of your learning will be repeated in these units and will give you the chance to review your knowledge and understanding.

Key terms

Vulnerable: more prone to risk and harm

Adult at risk: any person aged 18 years and over who is or may be in need of community care services

Consent: giving informed permission for something to happen

Capacity: the mental or physical ability to cope with or to do something

Coerced: being forced to do something against your will

Omission: where something is either deliberately or accidently left out or not done

Commission: the deliberate act of doing something while knowing the implications and consequences

What is 'abuse'?

Abuse can occur when individuals are deprived of their rights to:

▶ privacy

▶ independence

▶ choose for themselves

▶ a decent quality of life

▶ protection and security.

Abuse is a significant and serious problem within society; anyone is potentially at risk of harm or abuse. However, most of us are able to take steps to protect ourselves. Most of us are not **vulnerable** to abuse. However, individuals accessing health and social care services have a greater level of vulnerability, and this places them at a greater risk of harm or abuse. This greater level of vulnerability is often associated with that individual's need for support. A key responsibility of every health and social care practitioner therefore is to safeguard and protect **adults at risk**.

In 2000 the Department of Health published *No secrets*, which provided guidance for organisations to enable them to develop and implement multi-agency procedures to protect adults at risk from abuse. In *No secrets* abuse is defined as: 'a violation of an individual's human and civil rights by any other person or persons'.

It goes on to add that abuse may:

▶ be a single act or repeated acts

▶ be physical, verbal or psychological

▶ be an act of neglect

▶ be a failure to act

▶ occur when a vulnerable person is persuaded to do something to which they cannot **consent** or have not consented

▶ occur in any relationship

▶ result in significant harm to or exploitation of the person subjected to abuse

▶ occur in situations in which the individual is unable to protect themselves or prevent abuse happening to them.

People can experience abuse in a number of different ways. It is more usual that a person will experience more than one type of abuse at the same time. For example, physical abuse or violence is generally accompanied by verbal threats and intimidation, so the person is both physically and emotionally abused.

Key terms

Norm: the standard pattern of behaviour accepted as normal

Investigate

What do you know about the different types of consent. Do you know what guidance there is regarding consent in your work setting? Find out how consent is established with the individuals you support in your work setting and what happens when an individual is unable to consent to care or treatment.

Figure 5.1 Types and examples of abuse

Type of abuse	Definition and examples of abuse
Physical	The deliberate use of physical force that results in bodily injury, pain or impairment. This includes the inappropriate application of techniques or treatments, involuntary isolation or confinement, misuse of medication.
Sexual	Direct or indirect involvement in sexual activity without valid **consent**. Consent to a particular activity may not be given because: the individual doesn't wish to consent; lacks **capacity** and is unable to consent; or feels **coerced** into an activity because the other person is in a position of trust, power or authority.
Emotional/ psychological	Any action by another that damages an individual's mental wellbeing. The use of threats, humiliation, bullying, swearing and other verbal conduct, or any other form of mental cruelty that results in mental or physical distress. It includes the denial of basic human and civil rights, such as choice, self-expression, privacy and dignity.
Financial	This is the theft or misuse of an individual's money or personal possessions to the advantage of another person.
Institutional	This is the mistreatment or abuse of an individual by a regime or people within an institution. It occurs when the routines, systems and **norms** of an institution override the needs of the people that they are there to support.
Self-neglect	This is where an individual fails to adequately care for themselves and meet their own basic needs for food, warmth, rest, medical care, personal care. This may be intentional or unintentional, due to physical or mental health issues.
Neglect by others	This is the deliberate or unintentional failure to meet an individual's basic needs for personal care, food, warmth, rest, medical care, social stimulation, cultural or religious needs. This can be either acts of **omission** (not doing something) or acts of **commission** (doing something on purpose).

What are the signs and symptoms of abuse?

There are a number of ways you can recognise that an individual may have been abused, though the signs and symptoms are not always obvious. Knowing the individual and how they normally behave is an important part of being able to protect them, as changes in behaviour can be subtle and easily overlooked.

Physical abuse

Physical abuse is possibly the easiest to recognise as it is often more visible. However, it can also be missed, especially if explanations are accepted without questioning and careful monitoring. Some forms of physical abuse – such as denying an individual's needs or the misuse of medication – can be difficult to recognise. Any explanation that is inconsistent with an observed physical injury should raise concerns and prompt reporting and further investigation.

Your assessment criteria:

1.2 Identify the signs and/or symptoms associated with each type of abuse

Signs and symptoms of **physical abuse**

▸ multiple or minor bruising of different areas with inconsistent explanations

▸ burns and scalds

▸ odd-shaped bruising/burns – such as the outline or shape of a weapon or cigarette end

▸ marks on the skin consistent with being slapped, scratched, bitten or pinched

▸ splits on the side of the lips consistent with the mouth being forced open

▸ broken bones

▸ evidence of old injuries, e.g. untreated broken bones

▸ black eyes and bruising around the mouth and ears

▸ smell of urine and faeces

▸ indicators of malnutrition or general signs of neglect

▸ misuse of medication, such as withholding pain relief or giving additional doses of sedatives

▸ bruising to wrists indicating forced restraint

▸ unexplained bruising to normally protected areas of the body – abdomen, fingertip marks on underarms or inside of the thigh

▸ unexplained falls

▸ guarding reactions by the individual when approached by anyone

▸ a reluctance to undress in front of others.

Sexual abuse

Sexual abuse can take many forms and can include contact or non-contact.

Sexual abuse through contact may be vaginal or anal rape; touching or forcing an individual to touch another in a sexual manner without consent.

Sexual abuse through non-contact can include: forcing an individual to watch pornographic or adult entertainment without fully understanding what this involves; subjecting an individual to indecent exposure, sexual innuendoes, harassment or inappropriate photography; and not giving choice regarding the gender of the carer giving personal care.

Sexual abuse is closely associated with power, and is generally accompanied by both physical and psychological abuse.

Signs and symptoms of **sexual abuse**

- ▶ anxiety and fear of physical contact
- ▶ injury, bleeding, irritation or infection of the genital area
- ▶ sexually transmitted disease
- ▶ bruising, bites, scratches on the breast or inner thigh
- ▶ inappropriate conversations of a sexual nature
- ▶ unexplained crying and distress

- ▶ withdrawal from social contact
- ▶ acute confusion
- ▶ depression
- ▶ nightmares
- ▶ torn clothes
- ▶ self-harm
- ▶ self-neglect.

Emotional/psychological abuse

Psychological abuse is often difficult to recognise as it is generally hidden, and happens over time. It may involve the removal or denial of the individual's right to make decisions and result in the restriction of their choices. The deliberate withholding of care, affection, companionship and love, as well as verbal threats, are often used by the abuser to intimidate and force the individual to do what the abuser wants.

Signs and symptoms of **emotional and psychological abuse**

- ▶ changes in appetite
- ▶ changes in sleep pattern, e.g. nightmares or insomnia
- ▶ attention-seeking behaviour
- ▶ self-isolation – especially when the individual was previously outgoing and sociable to others
- ▶ unusual weight gain or loss
- ▶ sadness or uncontrollable crying
- ▶ being passive, with no spontaneous smiles or laughter
- ▶ self-abuse or self-harm, e.g. misuse of alcohol, nicotine or illegal drugs; refusing food or medication

- ▶ withdrawal and disinterest
- ▶ depression
- ▶ avoidance of contact with others
- ▶ unexplained fearfulness or anxiety, especially about being alone or with particular people
- ▶ increased tension or irritability
- ▶ low self-esteem
- ▶ lack of self-confidence.

Financial abuse

Financial abuse can take many forms.

Your assessment criteria:

1.2 Identify the signs and/or symptoms associated with each type of abuse

Signs and symptoms of **financial abuse**

- sudden, unexplained inability to pay bills
- unpaid bills resulting in utilities being discontinued
- a reluctance to spend any money (even when finances should not be a problem)
- no food in the house
- sudden, unexplained withdrawals of money from the individual's accounts
- missing money, chequebook, bank card, credit card or possessions
- being under pressure to make or change the terms of a will
- other people showing an unusual interest in the individual's assets.

Institutional abuse

In situations of institutional abuse, the policies and the way people work add to the risk of abuse rather than safeguard against it. For example, organisations that impose fixed care routines and which put pressure on practitioners and service users to just accept how things are done without question, are likely to be places where abusive practices occur.

Signs and symptoms of **institutional abuse**

- rigid routines
- lack of choice offered
- activities arranged solely for the convenience of staff and the organisation
- cultural or religious needs not being met
- difficulty in relatives/friends accessing individuals – e.g. inflexible visiting times
- restriction of access to food and drink
- restriction of access to toilet, bathing facilities or a comfortable place to rest during the day
- inappropriate use of restraint
- misuse of medication, e.g. overuse of sedation to benefit staff not the individual
- lack of privacy, dignity or respect
- restriction of access to medical or social care
- inflexible mealtimes and bedtimes
- inadequate guidance, policies and procedures for staff
- inadequate access for individuals to complaints procedures
- inappropriate, inadequate and poor standards of care
- repeated examples of poor professional standards and behaviour.

Self-neglect

Self-neglect can be accidental as well as deliberate. An individual who is confused or has memory problems may neglect themselves unintentionally. Deliberate self-neglect can also be a way of expressing mental health problems or it may be a symptom of abuse, especially sexual abuse.

Reflect

How involved in making decisions about the support they receive are the people for whom you provide care? Do you think that the service you work in is flexible and responsive in meeting individuals' preferences about mealtimes, bedtimes and food choices, for example?

Signs and symptoms of **self-neglect**

▶ neglecting personal hygiene
▶ not seeking medical or social care
▶ not taking prescribed medication
▶ not eating
▶ overeating
▶ self-harm, e.g. misuse of alcohol, or illegal drugs, cutting themselves
▶ not taking exercise
▶ unsanitary living conditions that are a risk to health, e.g. presence of vermin.

Neglect by others

Neglect can be passive or active. An individual may experience neglect in a variety of ways: as a lack of attention; as abandonment; or as confinement by their family and by society. Whether neglect is intentional or unintentional, by acts of omission or commission, the result is the deterioration of the individual's wellbeing.

Signs and symptoms of **neglect by others**

▶ denial of access to health or social care
▶ denial of individual rights and choices
▶ the withholding of appropriate and adequate care to meet needs
▶ the withholding of medication
▶ isolation of the individual by denying others access
▶ failure to meet the individual's physical, emotional, social, cultural, intellectual and spiritual needs

▶ prevention of others from meeting the individual's needs
▶ failure to provide adequate and appropriate food, drink, warmth, shelter and safety
▶ failure in the 'duty of care'
▶ exposure of the individual to unacceptable risks and dangers.

Your assessment criteria:

1.3 Define factors that may contribute to an individual being more vulnerable to abuse

Factors that contribute to abuse

There are a number of factors that contribute to an individual being more vulnerable to abuse. They may depend on physical, emotional, psychological or social support. If this support is either withdrawn or manipulated by an abuser, this will leave the individual more vulnerable to abuse as they become more isolated. Factors that may contribute to increased vulnerability to abuse include those related to the individual and those related to the situation or care-giver (see Figure 5.2).

Figure 5.2 Examples of factors contributing to abuse

Factors related to the individual	Factors related to the situation or care-giver
• Isolation • Physical illness creating dependency • Mental health issues, e.g. dementia • Communication problems, e.g. speech or hearing impairments or a learning disability • Behavioural changes resulting from condition, e.g. following a stroke or head injury • Where violence is viewed as the norm within the environment or relationships • Past history of accusations	• Prejudice, resentment and hostility towards the individual • High levels of care-giver stress • Lack of support for care-giver • Care-giver is drug or alcohol dependent • Care-giver has physical or mental health issues • Care-giver has previously been abused themselves • Powerlessness and isolation of the care-giver • Lack of understanding about the individual's medical condition • Lack of leadership and clear roles, responsibilities, policies and procedures • Lack of training and competence in giving care • Lack of or poor monitoring of care provision • Staff shortages • Lack of continuity of care, e.g. over-reliance on agency/temporary staff

Environmental factors that contribute to abuse can lead to institutional abuse, especially those relating to inadequate management. These are likely to result in failures in the duty of care, as incompetence and poor practice becomes the norm within a given organisation. When this occurs, it constitutes an abuse of the fundamental rights of the individual. You have a **moral** and legal duty of care to raise your concerns using the appropriate mechanisms.

Case study

Mrs Porter is a 73 year-old woman who lives alone in a large house. Her husband of 50 years died two years ago and since that time her health and memory have deteriorated. She has no other family. Mrs Porter receives two visits a day to provide personal care and support at mealtimes. You haven't visited Mrs Porter for two weeks and you are covering as the usual carer has had an accident. You are alarmed and shocked when you see Mrs Porter. She has lost a considerable amount of weight, her hair is matted, and her clothes are dirty. She is frail and appears very frightened. When you move towards her, she puts her arms up in front of her face as if to shield herself. You manage to reassure her and calm her. When you ask if she would prefer a wash or a shower, she tells you the usual carer doesn't normally bother. When you undress her in the bathroom, you are shocked to find her body is covered in bruises. You are particularly concerned about the bruising on the inside of her thighs. When you enquire about the bruising, Mrs Porter starts crying: 'I don't like him! I don't like him! He hurts me'. She then tells you that 'he' is the male carer who comes in at lunchtime visits. You also discover that there's no food in the fridge, and little in the cupboards. You know that shopping is part of Mrs Porter's care package.

1. What signs and symptoms lead you to suspect Mrs Porter is being abused?
2. What types of abuse may be taking place?
3. What factors have made Mrs Porter vulnerable to abuse?

Knowledge Assessment Task

1.1 1.2 1.3

Part of your role and responsibility as a health or social care practitioner is to safeguard individuals from harm and abuse. To do this effectively you will need to be able to recognise the different signs and symptoms of abuse. You will also need to understand the factors that increase an individual's vulnerability to abuse. Complete the questions below to demonstrate your knowledge and understanding of this area of responsibility.

1. Define the different types of abuse.
2. Identify the signs and symptoms associated with each type of abuse.
3. Describe the different factors that may make individuals more vulnerable to abuse.

Keep the written work that you produce as evidence towards your assessment.

How to respond to suspected or alleged abuse

What to do if you suspect abuse

Your organisation will have an agreed policy and procedure for what to do in the event of suspected, actual or alleged abuse. You will need to follow the procedures as described by the organisation in charge of your workplace or placement.

If you suspect abuse YOU MUST:

▶ always raise an **alert** and report your suspicions

▶ follow the agreed procedures

▶ not be persuaded by others that it is 'unimportant' or 'minor', and not worth reporting

▶ seek advice and support from a trustworthy and more senior or experienced member of staff

▶ maintain confidentiality within your role and the procedures

▶ keep the individual safe

▶ remember that you have a duty of care and moral responsibility to act.

In cases where abuse occurs, it is often by linking together seemingly minor incidents that the pattern of abuse is uncovered. If these incidents go unreported, the pattern cannot be established, leading to systematic and repeated abuse becoming accepted practice.

So, if in doubt, always report. Reporting a manager, colleague, or someone who is a member of the individual's personal network, such as a family member or carer, is a highly sensitive and difficult task. It is important therefore to be sure of your facts, and to discuss these with either a more senior member of the team and/or Adult Social Care services before making a decision. However, you must raise the alert. Not doing so constitutes a form of abuse.

If you suspect abuse DO NOT:

▶ ignore it or hide it for fear of the consequences to you if you have unintentionally been involved in the abuse

▶ **collude** with colleagues or others and fail to report your suspicions

▶ make the situation worse by covering up for others

▶ confront the person you think is responsible for the abuse

▶ leave the individual in an unsafe situation or without appropriate support

▶ destroy anything that might be used as evidence.

Your assessment criteria:

1.1 Explain the actions to take if there are suspicions that an individual is being abused.

Key terms

Alert: make another person aware of a possible danger or difficulty

Collude: cooperate with somebody in order to do something illegal or undesirable, or to keep it secret

Adult at risk: the individual adult who may have been subject to, or at risk of, abuse

Investigate

Do you know where the safeguarding adults at risk policies and procedures can be found in your work setting? Find out where they are, and what they say, so that you understand what actions to take if you suspect an individual is being abused.

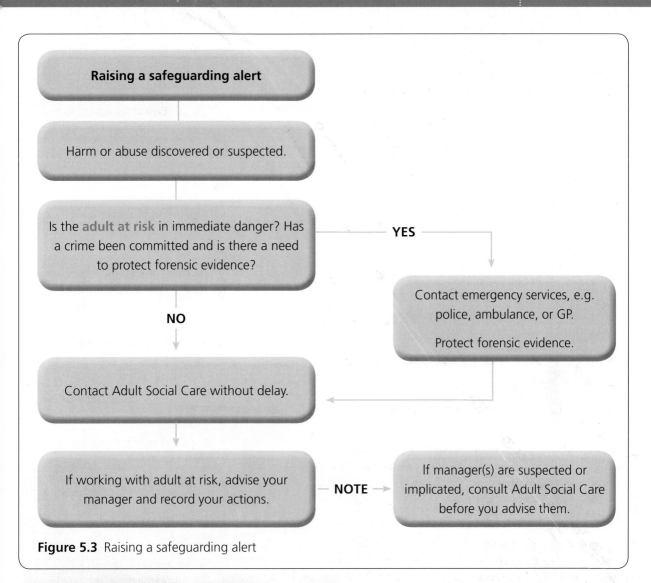

Figure 5.3 Raising a safeguarding alert

Incidents of suspected or actual abuse must always be documented and reported

Reflect

Think about the following in a situation where you witness an individual being abused by another worker and you fail to report it.

1. How do you think the individual might feel towards you, knowing you witnessed the incident and did nothing?
2. How do you think the abuser might feel towards you?
3. What is likely to happen to the individual being abused?
4. How you would feel about not reporting the incident?

What to do if an individual alleges abuse

If an individual makes an allegation of abuse remember what can and cannot be done. They are described in the previous section. In addition, ensure that you DO:

▶ follow agreed procedures

▶ take the individual's allegations seriously

▶ take them somewhere safe and private

▶ remain calm and try not to look shocked or angry

▶ listen without interrupting or prompting

▶ respect the individual's wishes

▶ offer reassurance and tell them they have done the right thing

▶ remember they are likely to feel shocked, frightened, distressed, blameworthy, ashamed or embarrassed

▶ be honest about your responsibility to act and the limits of this

▶ offer them the opportunity to talk to someone more senior (if appropriate)

▶ tell the individual what you are going to do to deal with the situation

▶ record what they tell you accurately and completely.

Ensure that you DO NOT:

▶ make assumptions or judge the individual

▶ put them in any further danger

▶ ask them any leading questions

▶ pressure them to talk or give you details they're not comfortable to give

▶ promise the individual a level of confidentiality beyond your role and responsibility

▶ discuss the information with anyone outside the individuals who need to be informed.

How to preserve evidence of abuse

In the event of an allegation of abuse, your first duty of care will be to the alleged victim. However, you must also take steps to preserve any evidence vital to a case where a criminal offence may have taken place.

Key terms

Leading question: a question which strongly suggests the answer the person asking the question wants to hear

DO NOT:

- ▶ move or remove anything
- ▶ touch anything unless you have to make the area, thing or person safe
- ▶ clean or tidy up
- ▶ allow access to anyone not involved in investigating.

DO:

- ▶ record any visible signs of abuse, such as bruising, or physical injuries, torn clothing, signs of distress
- ▶ if you have to touch something, keep it to a minimum and try not to destroy fingerprints
- ▶ keep anything of interest dry and safe, especially anything that may have been used to injure the individual
- ▶ preserve clothing, footwear, bedding and other such items, and handle them as little as possible
- ▶ preserve anything used to keep the individual warm
- ▶ record in writing
- ▶ record any injuries
- ▶ preserve and record the state of the individual and the alleged abuser's clothing (if appropriate)
- ▶ record the condition and attitudes of the people involved.

If items need to be preserved, then this can be done by placing:

- ▶ most items in a clean brown paper bag or in a clean unsealed envelope
- ▶ liquids in clean glassware.

Reflect

An individual you support returns from a visit to the shops tearful and distressed. Their coat is torn and dirty. They are holding their arm as if it hurts and will not let you look at it. When you ask them what has happened they just mumble that they have 'lost' their bag and shopping. You suspect something more has happened. What would you do in this situation?

Who would you involve?

How would you preserve any evidence?

Knowledge Assessment Task   2.1   2.2   2.3

Having a good working knowledge and understanding of the reporting processes is part of a health and social care practitioner's responsibilities. Knowing what to do, what not to do and whom to report to are all important aspects of safeguarding individuals from abuse. Completing the following questions will help you to demonstrate your knowledge and understanding of this area of practice:

1. What would you do if you suspect abuse?
2. What would you do if someone tells you they have been abused?
3. How would you preserve any evidence of abuse to ensure it is not contaminated?

Keep the written work that you produce as evidence towards your assessment.

National and local policies and systems for safeguarding

Two key national policy documents that relate to safeguarding adults at risk are:

▶ *No secrets – guidance on developing and implementing multi-agency policies and procedures to protect vulnerable adults from abuse* (2000)

▶ *Safeguarding adults – a national framework of standards for good practice and outcomes in adult protection work* (2005)

Together, these two documents provide best practice guidance on establishing local multi-agency policies and procedures, and clearly outline multi-agency roles and responsibilities. They also reinforce the need for rigorous, transparent recruitment practices. As a result of the recommendations made, prior to being employed in health and social care all prospective employees and volunteers are required to undergo a Criminal Records Bureau (CRB) check. This check is repeated every three years. In addition, all health and social care employees and volunteers are required by law to be registered with the Independent Safeguarding Authority (ISA).

Your assessment criteria:

3.1 Identify national policies and local systems that relate to safeguarding and protection from abuse

Investigate

Do you know where the Safeguarding Adults at Risk policy and procedures can be found in your work setting? Does your workplace have a copy of *No secrets*? Find out if and when individuals using your service are given a leaflet/information about Safeguarding Adults at Risk procedures. If they are not given any information, find out why this is the case?

Figure 5.4 National legislation with regards to safeguarding

Legislation or national policy	Summary of key points
Legal powers to intervene	There are a range of laws that enable abusers to be prosecuted. These include: • Offences Against the Person Act 1861 – relates to physical abuse • Sexual Offences Act 2003 – relates to sexual abuse • Protection from Harassment Act 1997 – relates to psychological abuse • Section 47, National Assistance Act 1948 – relates to neglect.
Human Rights Act 1998	All individuals have the right to live their lives free from violence and abuse. Rights include: • Article 2: 'The right to life' • Article 3: 'Freedom from torture (including humiliating and degrading treatment)' • Article 8: 'Right to family life'.
Mental Capacity Act 2005	Provides the statutory framework to empower and protect adults at risk who are unable to make their own decisions. The five key principles are: • a presumption of capacity • the right for individuals to be supported to make their own decisions • individuals must retain the right to make what might be seen as eccentric or unwise decisions • anything done must be the in the individual's best interests • least restrictive intervention. The Act includes guidance regarding care and treatment and restraint and particularly relates to financial abuse.
Safeguarding Vulnerable Groups Act 2006	Resulted from the Bichard Inquiry in 2002 into the Soham murders. Recommendations led to creation of the Independent Safeguarding Authority (ISA) which is responsible for: • the Vetting and Barring Scheme (VBS) • maintaining children and adults barring lists.
Health & Social Care (HSC) Act 2008; HSC Act (Regulated Activities) Regulations 2010; CQC Regulations 2009	Established the Care Quality Commission (CQC) to regulate the quality and safety of health and adult social care services. Replaces National Minimum Standards. Introduced essential standards of quality and safety, which are 28 regulations and associated outcomes.

In February 2011 the UK government decided that the Criminal Records Bureau and the Independent Safeguarding Authority would merge to form a single streamlined authority to provide a barring and criminal recording checking service.

What roles do different agencies play in safeguarding?

Part of the duty of care remit requires a working knowledge of safeguarding procedures. Understanding how to use national and local safeguarding procedures is a crucial aspect of health and social care work. This responsibility includes volunteers as well as employees.

Figure 5.5 Agencies involved in safeguarding

Agency	Key responsibilities
Local authority adult social care services	These agencies: • receive safeguarding alerts • ensure action is taken to keep individual safe – may require immediate intervention/assessment/provision of additional care services • liaise with all individuals/agencies involved • provide information and advice • coordinate investigations • arrange, chair and record meetings and case conferences • remove the alleged abuser, if required • are represented at police interviews.
All agencies, including police, NHS, GPs, medical services, councils, emergency services, independent, voluntary, private providers, Trading Standards, CQC	These agencies: • implement and work to the agreed safeguarding adults policies and procedures • cooperate and collaborate with other agencies to ensure the safety of adults at risk • ensure all staff can recognise signs and symptoms of abuse • ensure all staff receive regular awareness training of safeguarding policies, reporting and recording procedures • provide information and advice to people who access services to ensure they understand how they can protect themselves and others • ensure all employees and others required by law are CRB checked and registered with the ISA prior to employment • inform the ISA of anyone who is unsuitable to work with adults at risk.

In addition to the above, the following have additional roles and responsibilities:

Police	The police: • investigate allegations of abuse if a crime is suspected • gather evidence • pursue criminal proceedings if appropriate • protect people in vulnerable situations.
Medical Services e.g. GP, NHS Acute Trusts	These agencies: • provide immediate treatment if required • undertake evidential investigations or medical examinations, if required and following consent.

What reports are available regarding serious failures in safeguarding adults at risk?

As a health and social care worker, it is important that you learn from the findings and recommendations of inquiries into failures in practice. You must also be able to relate these findings and recommendations to your organisation's policies and care practice.

In the past five years there have been a number of inquiries into failures in safeguarding. The following are just three of the resultant reports:

1. *Six lives – the provision of public services to people with learning disabilities* (2009): a report by Ann Abraham, Health Service Ombudsman, and Jerry White, Local Government Ombudsman. This inquiry was launched in response to complaints by Mencap on behalf of the families of six people with learning disabilities who died whilst in NHS or local authority care between 2003 and 2005. Details were initially highlighted in the Mencap report *Death by Indifference* (2007). As a result an urgent review of health and social care for people with learning disabilities was recommended.

2. *The Francis Inquiry Report* (2010): a report on the level of care provided by Mid Staffordshire NHS Foundation Trust (see page 98 in SHC 24 for more about this report).

3. *Care and Compassion?* (2011): a report by Ann Abraham, Health Service Ombudsman, on 10 investigations into NHS care of older people. The investigations highlighted the gaps between the actual experiences of older people and their families, and the principles and values of the NHS. The report identified that:

   ▶ fundamental needs were consistently neglected

   ▶ staff attitudes were dismissive

   ▶ staff had a total disregard for the older person's rights, dignity and privacy

   ▶ poor communication, planning, coordination and thoughtlessness left people in excessive pain and discomfort

   ▶ inflexible attitudes led to families being excluded at mealtimes, resulting in patients unable to feed themselves becoming malnourished and dehydrated.

Reflect

Read one of the inquiry reports mentioned in this last section. Think about the following:

1. How were the individuals involved in the failures abused?

2. What types of abuse did they experience?

3. Who else do you think was abused?

4. Could similar failures and abuses as those identified in the report happen in your work setting?

Where can you go to seek information and advice?

Advice and guidance on safeguarding procedures are available in your organisation's safeguarding policy and procedures document. Your employer will also provide training and updates on safeguarding and protecting adults at risk. Policies and procedures documents, training and updates will contain information about:

▶ types of abuse

▶ signs and symptoms

▶ how to respond to suspected, actual or alleged abuse

▶ what to do and who to go to if you suspect someone more senior than yourself

▶ how to report and record suspected, actual or alleged abuse

▶ a list of contact numbers and names.

Supervision meetings are a good opportunity for you to seek advice and guidance about your role. These should occur regularly. Your manager or a senior member of the team will provide you with advice and support at any time.

Your assessment criteria:

3.4 Identify sources of information and advice about own role in safeguarding and protecting individuals from abuse

4.1 Explain how the likelihood of abuse may be reduced by:
- working with person-centred values
- encouraging active participation
- promoting choice and rights

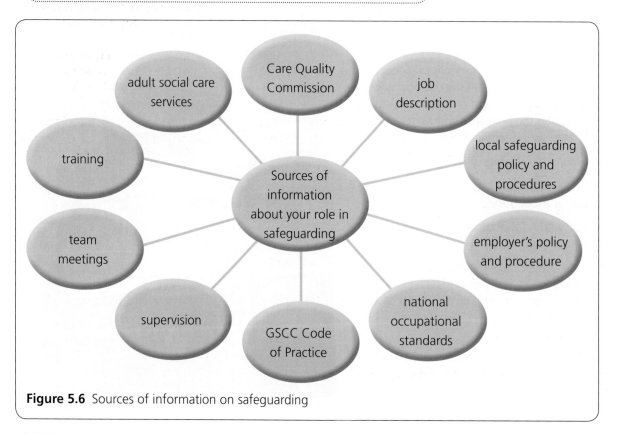

Figure 5.6 Sources of information on safeguarding

Person-centred approaches

Person-centred approaches have been successfully used in the support of adults with learning disabilities and individuals with dementia. Person-centred approaches place the individual at the centre of all activities. This kind of approach reduces the likelihood of abuse occurring by means of the following core values:

▶ **individuality** – planning support around the unique needs of the individual

▶ **rights** – never doing things that may ignore or go against the individual's rights

▶ **choice** – making sure choices are appropriate to the individual and in their best interests

▶ **privacy** – making sure the individual is free from unwanted intrusion by others

▶ **independence** – giving the individual time and opportunity to self-manage

▶ **dignity** – supporting the individual to maintain emotional control and sense of self-worth in difficult and sensitive situations

▶ **respect** – always treating the individual in a way that demonstrates their sense of self-worth and their importance to others

▶ **partnership** – working with others with a focus on achieving outcomes that are always in the best interests of the individual.

Investigate

Find out which policies and procedures underpin person-centred approaches in your work setting. Find out what advice and training is available to existing and new employees about person-centred approaches.

Reflect

Think about the individuals you support. Consider how you support them to ensure you work in a person-centred way.

1. How do you demonstrate that you see them as a unique individual?

2. What do you do to ensure you really understand their point of view, wishes and expectations?

3. How do you ensure they are involved in decisions about their support and care?

Knowledge Assessment Task | 3.1 | 3.2 | 3.3 | 3.4

Safeguarding individuals from abuse is the responsibility of everyone involved in providing support. Understanding the roles and responsibilities of other agencies and how to clarify your role is an important way of learning from failures in practice that lead to abuse. Complete the following questions to demonstrate your knowledge and understanding about joint working, clarifying your role and what can be learnt from inquiry reports to improve safeguarding procedures:

1. What are the national policies and local procedures that relate to safeguarding and protecting adults at risk?

2. Outline the roles of different agencies in safeguarding and protecting adults at risk?

3. Identify at least two inquiry reports regarding serious failures in care practice that led to abuse taking place.

4. Where would you obtain information and advice about your role in safeguarding and protecting adults at risk?

Keep the written work that you produce as evidence towards your assessment.

How can working with active participation reduce the likelihood of abuse?

An impersonal support regime, which allows infringement of individual rights, generates the conditions in which abuse can occur. The individual is depersonalised, disempowered and ceases to be an active, social agent in their own right. Active participation is a way of working that recognises an individual's right to participate in the activities and relationships of everyday life. The individual is given as much independence as possible. Crucially, the individual is viewed as an *active* participant or partner, and not as the *passive* recipient of health and social support. The main result of an active participatory approach is the **empowerment** of the individual concerned. The individual is empowered to make choices about how their personal support is delivered. This way the individual's needs are met, and care regimes that are simply convenient to the provider are ended.

The increased access to, and use of, self-directed budgets, where individuals manage their own care package, is one example of how active participation has changed the way health and social care services are delivered. Being in control of how care and support is provided enables individuals to enter into more equal partnerships with providers. This further reduces the potential for an individual's rights to be disregarded.

In 2009 the government carried out a consultation process to review the effectiveness of *No secrets*. Of the 12,000 people involved, 3,000 were members of the public, and many were people to whom the guidance applied. The following recommendations with regards to procedure are a good example of active participation on a national scale. The process recommended that care organisations ensure:

▶ that the abused individual is empowered and listened to

▶ that the individual is fully involved in safeguarding decisions

▶ that the individual who lacks capacity to independently participate in the decision-making process is represented and able to participate as fully as possible.

Your assessment criteria:

4.1 Explain how the likelihood of abuse may be reduced by:
- working with person-centred values
- encouraging active participation
- promoting choice and rights

Key terms

Empowerment: gaining more control over your life by being given greater self-confidence and self-esteem

Reflect

Think about the individuals you support.

1. How do the assessment and care planning processes used take account of the individual's life story?

2. How is understanding of their life experiences used to create a person-centred approach to supporting their needs?

3. How do you think taking a person-centred approach enables you to safeguard them from harm and/or abuse?

Investigate

Investigate all the different ways in which individuals being supported within your workplace are empowered. Find out how individuals are:

▶ supported to make their views and opinions known

▶ involved in the processes of assessment, care planning and reviewing care

▶ given easily understandable and accessible information about their rights and responsibilities.

Establishing positive, empowering relationships minimises the possibility of abuse happening in care settings

Case study

You work in a residential care home for individuals with dementia. The residents have moderate levels of dementia and many are still physically active. Most require frequent prompting when undertaking daily living activities. Most of the residents are in their 90s and very few have relatives who visit frequently.

1. What factors make the residents of the home vulnerable to abuse?

2. How can you apply person-centred values to working with the residents to reduce the likelihood of abuse?

3. How can you encourage the residents to actively participate in their support to reduce the likelihood of abuse?

How can promoting choice and rights reduce the likelihood of abuse?

In organisations where it is common practice to work in ways that actively promote individual choices and rights, the potential for abuse is reduced. This is because the way support is provided will be organised in such a way as to ensure the individual is actively involved in everything that happens. It encourages a culture of care based on listening to the individual, and making decisions based on the individual's expressed wants. Carers, family members and friends share the same beliefs and values; and understand the benefits of choice and the necessity of rights. Such a practice actively promotes the individual's rights, including the right to choose, on a daily basis. It is a transparent practice, and as such it is much more difficult to abuse. Finally, in the event that abuse does occur, the chances that it is discovered – and discovered early – are high.

How to actively promote individual choices and rights:

- ► Spend time getting to know the individual.
- ► Understand their needs and abilities.
- ► Understand how their situation/condition affects their day-to-day life and activities.
- ► Understand their likes and dislikes.
- ► Understand what is important to them and what their priorities are.
- ► Understand their values and beliefs.
- ► Understand how their past experiences impact on their view of life/their current situation.
- ► Respect their uniqueness.
- ► Understand the duty of care.

How can an accessible complaints procedure reduce the likelihood of abuse?

An organisation that is actively involved in reducing the likelihood of abuse occurring will be one that accepts complaints as a form of feedback. In this way, the organisation will be able to constantly review and improve its procedures for the detection of abuse. It is essential therefore that care organisations develop complaint procedures that are easily accessed – available, easy to understand and easy to use – and that remove the fear of **retribution**.

Your assessment criteria:

4.1 Explain how the likelihood of abuse may be reduced by:
- working with person-centred values
- encouraging active participation
- promoting choice and rights

4.2 Explain the importance of an accessible complaints procedure for reducing the likelihood of abuse

Key terms

Retribution: something done to injure a person in any way as punishment for something that person may have done

Making the complaints procedure accessible to all encourages openness. Providing individuals vulnerable to abuse with a user-friendly complaints procedure further diminishes the likelihood of abuse taking place. Accessible complaints procedures should:

▶ be written in plain English and made available in different formats – i.e. in pictures, other languages, on tape or in Braille

▶ be available as copies to anyone using the service

▶ include an explanation as to how to use the procedures

▶ include a way of checking that the user has understood the procedure

▶ be displayed in the public areas of the service

▶ be provided by staff trained to respond positively to a complaint

▶ encourage individuals to complain if they are dissatisfied with their support

▶ involve the use of a key worker system to ensure individuals are listened to and given the opportunity to complain informally

▶ confidentially inform individuals using the service when complaints have been dealt with

▶ confidentially inform individuals as to the outcome of individual complaints.

Information must be accessible, easy to understand and available in a variety of formats

Knowledge Assessment Task   4.1   4.2

As a health and social care practitioner the way that you support individuals will have a direct impact on how safe or vulnerable they are to abuse. Complete the questions below using examples to demonstrate how current approaches can improve safeguarding and reduce an individual's vulnerability.

1. Use examples to explain how the following reduce the likelihood of abuse:
   ▶ working with person-centred values
   ▶ encouraging active participation
   ▶ promoting choice and rights
2. How is making sure the complaints procedure is accessible an important way to reduce the likelihood of abuse?

Keep the written work that you produce as evidence towards your assessment.

What are unsafe practices?

Any practice that puts the service user or care worker at risk could be considered as unsafe. An **unsafe practice** can take place due to: poorly observed procedures; insufficient resources; operational difficulties.

Poor working practices include:

▶ not wearing personal protective equipment

▶ not following correct procedures

▶ not undertaking risk assessments

▶ ignoring strategies to manage risk

▶ lack of monitoring, supervision and guidance.

Insufficient resources may include:

▶ not having the appropriate equipment to undertake a task

▶ not having enough equipment or materials to undertake a task safely

▶ one person doing a task that should be done by two people

▶ not allocating enough time to safely carry out activities and tasks.

Operational difficulties may include:

▶ not having enough staff to adequately meet individuals needs

▶ lack of appropriate staff training

▶ lack of policies, procedures and guidance for staff

▶ lack of regular and appropriate staff supervision

▶ lack of leadership and management.

What action should you take if you identify unsafe practices?

When practices are unsafe it suggests that they are being carried out without due care and attention to the potential danger and harm that may result. You have a duty of care to make your employer aware of any unsafe practices, and to take action to protect yourself and others (see page 86).

An organisation's written procedures will outline the action to be taken in the event of unsafe practice. These procedures will differ from organisation to organisation, but all procedures concerning unsafe practice will share the same core elements:

Your assessment criteria:

5.1 Describe unsafe practices that may affect the wellbeing of individuals.

5.2 Explain the actions to take if unsafe practices have been identified.

Key terms

Unsafe practice: a level of care that puts individuals at risk

Reflect

Think about the individuals you support. Consider how you support them to ensure you work in a person-centred way.

1. How do you demonstrate that you see them as a unique individual?

2. What do you do to ensure you really understand their point of view, wishes and expectations?

3. How do you ensure they are involved in decisions about their support and care?

1. If possible and safe to do so, make the situation safe, e.g. identify an unsafe area with a hazard sign.

2. Report the situation without delay to the person in charge:

   ▶ verbally – to the senior person on duty

   ▶ in writing – in the daily record, and complete an incident form/maintenance form.

3. Ensure others are aware of the potential danger. If appropriate, remove and label broken equipment.

4. Follow up to check if the situation has been remedied. Keep your own records.

Safety is everyone's responsibility. In some situations unsafe working practices may have become normalised over time. In these situations, care workers who refuse to carry out a procedure they may deem unsafe can be made to feel incompetent or negligent. Should this occur, check the procedure against the organisation's written procedures. If you are correct, and it is unsafe, seek advice from a senior colleague, and if necessary register a complaint. Remember to act. Doing nothing supports the unsafe practice.

Investigate

Think about your work setting. Find out what the correct procedures are. How would you use the procedures to help report and record the following:

▶ unsafe working practices?

▶ unsafe equipment?

▶ suspected/actual abuse?

Find out the procedure for making a complaint, and what further steps to take if no action results from the initial complaint.

Case study

You have been working as a domiciliary care worker for nine months in a rural area. When you first started you had a two-week induction which included both the mandatory training and shadowing a more experienced worker for a week. You work in the evenings and one day at the weekend. During your five-hour shift you normally undertake eight 30-minute visits. However, for the past month your manager has allocated you ten visits in the same time. You have explained to your manager several times that this is not possible to do as your calls are all at least 10 minutes apart and each individual you visit has a 30-minute allocation to carry out the agreed care plan. Your manager has told you to ignore the care plan and just to do what you can. When you question your manager as to what should be recorded now that you don't have enough time to complete the care plan, your manager tells you to write that everything was done as stated on the care plan. You tell them you don't agree. You say that are unhappy about the situation. They indicate to you if you don't do as asked, your hours could be reduced.

1. What is unsafe about this situation?

2. What are the potential consequences of these unsafe practices for the individuals you visit?

3. What action can you take to resolve the situation?

4. Who is being abused in this situation?

What action should you take if there has been no response to reported suspected abuse or unsafe practices?

Your assessment criteria:

5.3 Describe the action to take if suspected abuse or unsafe practices have been reported but nothing has been done in response

When you raise a concern and report either suspected abuse or unsafe practices always ensure you put this in writing, and that you keep a copy for your own records. This will protect you and the people you are trying to protect, and allow you to produce written detailed evidence when your alert or complaint is investigated.

Most procedures operate agreed timescales that stipulate when a complaint, concern or incident should be dealt with. These timescales will entail a number of time-related step-by-step procedures, one of which guarantees the time it will take to respond to an alert. However, depending on the severity of a case, or the danger posed by an incident, timescales may be overridden by senior care managers and other associated external services, such as the police. Make sure you know and understand which procedures apply.

In the event that you have been asked to carry out a task you deem unsafe, and have followed in-house procedures with regards to complaints and alerts, and the times within which the incident should have been responded to have passed, then you will need to follow your organisation's procedures for grievances. An employee or volunteer grievance procedure should provide details of persons and organisations to contact. These may include a more senior person within the organisation; an external body, such as the Adult Social Care Services; the Care Quality Commission (CQC). Depending on the nature of the grievance, you may also want to notify your trade union, which will provide information, advice and help (see also page 94).

Knowledge Assessment Task   5.1   5.2   5.3

As a health and social care practitioner you have a responsibility to recognise and take appropriate action when you become aware of unsafe practices that place you, individuals you support or other people at risk of harm or abuse. Complete the following questions to demonstrate your knowledge and understanding in relation to unsafe practices:

1. Use examples to describe unsafe practices that may affect the wellbeing of individuals.

2. Explain what you would do if you identified unsafe practices.

3. Describe what you would do if suspected abuse or unsafe practices had been reported but no action had been taken to respond to or resolve the situation.

Keep the written work that you produce as evidence towards your assessment.

Are you ready for assessment?

AC	What you know now	Assessment task	✓
1.1	Define different types of abuse	Page 123	
1.2	Identify the signs and/or symptoms associated with each type of abuse	Page 123	
1.3	Describe the factors that may contribute to an individual being more vulnerable to abuse	Page 123	
2.1	Explain the actions to take if there are suspicions that an individual is being abused	Page 127	
2.2	Explain the actions to take if an individual alleges that they are being abused	Page 127	
2.3	Identify ways to ensure that evidence of abuse is preserved	Page 127	
3.1	Identify national policies and local systems that relate to safeguarding and protection from abuse	Page 133	
3.2	Explain the roles of different agencies in safeguarding and protecting individuals from abuse	Page 133	
3.3	Identify reports into serious failures to protect individuals from abuse	Page 133	
3.4	Identify sources of information and advice about own role in safeguarding and protecting individuals from abuse	Page 133	
4.1	Explain how the likelihood of abuse can be reduced by working with person-centred values, encouraging active participation and promoting choice and rights	Page 137	
4.2	Explain the importance of an accessible complaints procedure for reducing the likelihood of abuse	Page 137	
5.1	Describe unsafe practice that may affect the wellbeing of individuals	Page 140	
5.2	Explain the actions to take if unsafe practices have been identified	Page 140	
5.3	Describe the actions to take if suspected abuse or unsafe practices have been reported but nothing has been done in response	Page 140	

6 | The role of the health and social care worker (HSC 025)

Assessment of this unit

This unit will introduce you to the knowledge and skills needed to understand working relationships in care settings, the importance of working in ways that are agreed with your employer, and the role that partnership working now plays in the health and social care sector. You will need to:

▶ understand working relationships in health and social care

▶ be able to work in ways that are agreed with the employer

▶ be able to work in partnership with others.

The assessment of this unit is partly knowledge-based (things you need to know about) and partly competence-based (things you need to do in the real work environment). To successfully complete this unit, you will need to produce evidence of both your knowledge and your competence. The tables on the page opposite outline what you need to know and do to meet each of the assessment criteria for the unit.

Your tutor or assessor will help you to prepare for your assessment and the tasks suggested in the unit will help you to create the evidence that you need.

CHAPTER 6

AC   What you need to know

| 1.1 | Explain how a working relationship is different from a personal relationship |
| 1.2 | Describe different working relationships in health and social care settings |

AC   What you need to do

2.1	Describe why it is important to adhere to the agreed scope of the job role
2.2	Access full and up-to-date details of agreed ways of working
2.3	Implement agreed ways of working
3.1	Explain why it is important to work in partnership with others
3.2	Demonstrate ways of working that can help improve partnership working
3.3	Identify skills and approaches needed for resolving conflicts
3.4	Demonstrate how and when to access support and advice about: • partnership working • resolving conflicts

Assessment criteria 2.1–2.3, and 3.1–3.4 must be assessed in a real work environment.

This unit also links to some of the other units:

SHC 32	Engage in personal development in health and social care settings
SHC 34	Principles for implementing duty of care in health and social care settings
HSC 038	Promote good practice in handling information in health and social care settings

Some of your learning will be repeated in these units and will give you the chance to review your knowledge and understanding.

Relationships with service users and colleagues are a key part of care practice

Reflect

Can you think of examples of different types of relationship in your own life? Which relationships are most important to you, and most influential in your life?

Different types of relationship

We all experience a number of different types of relationship throughout our lives. These include:

▶ family relationships (with partners, parents and siblings, for example)

▶ friendships

▶ intimate personal and sexual relationships

▶ working relationships.

These different relationships can have both a positive and a negative impact on our personal development and wellbeing. They each perform a different function and meet our needs in different ways. The nature and significance of the relationships we have depend on the life stage that we are in; the relationships change as we grow older.

Family relationships

Whatever type of family structure a person lives in (see Figure 6.1), their relationship with their parent(s) or main carers, and with their siblings, will play a big part in their personal

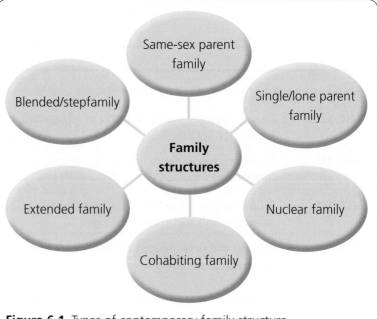

Figure 6.1 Types of contemporary family structure

development and wellbeing. An infant generally forms their first relationship with one or both of their parents. Close physical contact, the provision of food, and regular, reassuring care and communication between the child and their parents will create an **attachment relationship**. The child who feels loved, with complete trust in their parents' affection and support, develops a sense of emotional security and self-confidence.

A child's parents continue to play an important role in their development as they get older. Parents become role models, socialising the child, providing care and support, and helping them to learn how they should behave towards others. During this stage of life parents have a strong influence on their child's self-concept and self-esteem.

When a person moves into adolescence their relationship with their parents tends to change. In particular, there is less of a focus on **socialisation** and providing physical support, and more of a focus on emotional support. Despite the growing desire for independence, and the strains and tensions that this can bring to family relationships, adolescents need to feel that their parents love and support them. Adolescents who have a trusting, supportive and affectionate relationship with their parents will tend to have better self-esteem and be better equipped for the transition to adulthood than adolescents who lack this relationship.

A person's family relationships may change significantly during adulthood. The majority of people leave home and begin new relationships with people outside of their birth family, perhaps getting married or living with a partner and starting a family of their own. As a result, adults tend to alter the relationship they have with their parents. Whilst still being their parent's child, an adult is now independent, able to manage their own life and perhaps also committed to relationships in their new family. Despite this, parents can still play an important part in an adult's emotional life and may be consulted about important decisions or issues that the person faces.

Parental relationships are based on attachment

Discuss

What impact do you think a person's early relationships have on them later in life? Share thoughts and ideas on this with a work colleague or a classmate. Do you think that a person's early, childhood relationships provide a 'blueprint' for the relationships they develop later in life?

Reflect

Have your family relationships changed over time? Think about how they have changed and the impact that this has had on you.

Intimate, personal and sexual relationships

People generally first start to become interested in more personal relationships in their early teens. Adolescents tend to fall in and out of love quite frequently as they experience 'crushes' (infatuations) during puberty. This can be emotionally painful but most teenagers use these experiences to learn more about the emotional aspects of relationships and to extend their understanding of their own needs and preferences. For many teenagers their first intimate relationship is an intense emotional experience rather than a sexual one. Intimate personal relationships tend to be short-lived during early adolescence but become longer and more emotionally and physically involved in later adolescence. Sexual relationships can be long- or short-term but tend to be seen as significant because of the level of physical intimacy and emotional closeness they involve. People usually establish longer-term intimate, personal and sexual relationships when they are emotionally mature and have a stronger sense of personal identity.

Friendships

Friends are people whom we generally see as likeable, dependable and with whom we can communicate easily. People form friendships for a variety of reasons, including: shared attitudes, values and interests; emotional support and companionship. Friendships tend to boost a person's self-esteem and self-confidence and help people to develop social skills. Friendships make an important contribution to an individual's emotional and social development and the formation of their self-concept.

Friendships play an important role in a person's social and emotional development. An individual will first learn how to behave and relate to others through family relationships during infancy. As they move into early childhood, the person will begin meeting other children and increase their range of friendships. Friendships can be especially important during adolescence, when young people are trying to forge an identity separate from their parents, and also in adulthood when friendships form the basis of our social lives outside of the family. Friendships in later adulthood can be a vital source of companionship and connection to a person's past. Throughout life, an individual's personality, social skills and emotional development are all shaped by their friendships. Friendships play a role in helping people to feel they belong, are wanted and liked by others, and that there are people to whom they can turn for support.

Working relationships

Working relationships are different to other forms of relationship because the relationship serves a particular, non-personal purpose to do with achieving tasks or coordinating roles in an organisation. Most working relationships are formed between individuals who are not of equal status, and have clear boundaries. A person's job description, and the line management arrangements that exist in the work setting, often define these boundaries. As a result, one person usually has more power or authority in the relationship than the other. Relationships between students and teachers, between employers and employees, and between colleagues, are examples of working relationships. Effective working relationships tend to be based on good communication, trust and respect between the people involved. Figure 6.3 identifies some other qualities of good working relationships.

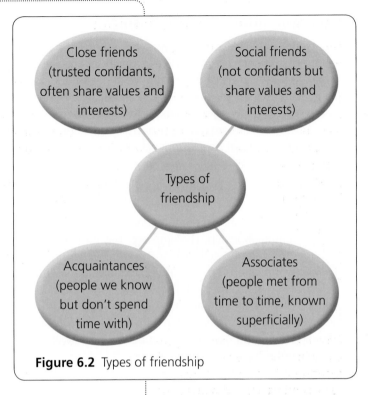

Figure 6.2 Types of friendship

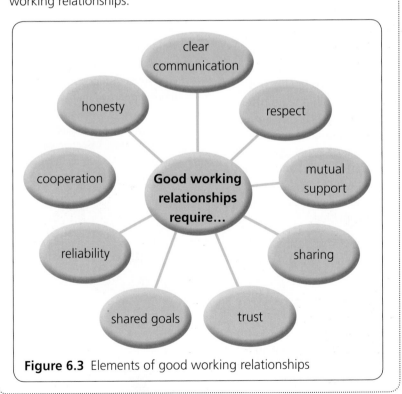

Figure 6.3 Elements of good working relationships

Reflect

What qualities or skills do you have, and what strategies do you use, which contribute to the effectiveness of your working relationships?

Employer/employee relationships

The relationship that you have with your employer has a very important influence on your role as a health or social care worker. There are a vast range of different roles in health and social care. Many, such as adult social worker, paramedic and occupational therapist, involve giving care directly to service users. Some other roles, such as care manager or residential home manager, have a significant but usually indirect impact on the care that people receive.

The employer-employee relationship is an example of a **formal relationship**. That is, it is based on a set of rules and expectations about how people should relate to each other because of their employment relationship. The employer has the most power and authority to direct the activities of the employee in these situations. Employment relationships can affect an individual's self-image, their social skills and their intellectual development, depending on the type of work they do and the development opportunities they are given. A person's relationship with their employer may also influence their attitudes, values and behaviour as well as their self-concept.

Relationships with colleagues

Care practitioners need to form effective working relationships with colleagues as they tend to work in teams or in collaborative partnerships, such as multi-agency arrangements, when providing care and support. Trust, mutual support and cooperation are important features of team working. However, each health and social care team is different and relationships within a team often change or need to be adapted each time someone joins or leaves the team. Within your work setting, some of your colleagues will also be your peers. That is, they will be people of equal status and similar background to you. Being supported, liked and valued by your work colleagues will have a positive effect on your self-confidence and self-esteem as well as your effectiveness as a team member. Key points for effective team work include:

▶ understanding communication processes within your workplace (and in your team in particular) and knowing how you can contribute to effective communication

▶ recognising and valuing the contributions of others

▶ valuing and accommodating individual differences

▶ carrying out your own role effectively so that you make an appropriate and expected contribution to the team.

Key terms

Formal relationship: relationship based on agreed, formal terms, such as that between colleagues in a workplace

Reflect

Think about the different people you work with. Why are some of your relationships stronger and more supportive than others? Are there any colleagues with whom you would like to have a better or more effective working relationship? What could you do to improve this?

There will be numerous occasions when you have to communicate effectively in order to provide high quality care to service users or information to others regarding an individual's care. In addition, you and your colleagues are likely to meet and communicate as a team in:

- ▶ planning and review meetings
- ▶ staff support meetings
- ▶ staff development meetings
- ▶ training and education sessions
- ▶ handover or report meetings.

You can use these occasions to develop your knowledge and understanding of care and team working issues, share best practice or discuss different approaches, and resolve any disputes or concerns about practice in your care setting.

Reflect

Which of these meetings take place in your work setting? Do you attend and make a contribution to team discussions? Think about how you might be able to improve or increase your involvement in the different kinds of team meetings that take place in your work setting.

Supportive relationships

It is important that relationships between colleagues are supportive. You can promote this by recognising when individuals are:

▶ feeling stressed by personal or professional matters

▶ performing their work effectively

▶ over-stretched, struggling to cope with their workload and needing help.

Effective health and social care teams tend to involve colleagues who are supportive of each other. Sharing information, showing new or less experienced colleagues how to do things, and being available when a colleague needs practical or emotional support, all contribute to this supportive environment. Supportive relationships tend to be mutual so the support that you provide for others should be reciprocated (returned) to help make your work life a little easier and less stressful.

Relationships with service users

The relationship that a health or social care practitioner has with the individuals for whom they provide care or support plays a crucial part in their professional work. Care relationships are different to the other types of relationship that the care practitioner may have. One of the unusual and defining features of a care relationship is that it can involve a higher level of non-sexual physical contact and an emotional closeness with the person than is present in other relationships. As a result, care relationships depend heavily on the development and maintenance of trust and mutual respect between care practitioners and service users.

Providing personal and physical care, and listening and responding to the often very personal problems and difficulties that a service user has, puts the care practitioner in a powerful and privileged position in the care relationship. It is vital that care practitioners do not abuse or misuse the power or privileged position that the care relationship gives them. Because the relationship with the service user is the cornerstone of all the work that they do as a care provider, it must be based on trust. Good care relationships must also promote and support service users' rights to make their own decisions and to have their safety and security protected during care interventions and when they are most vulnerable and unable to care for themselves.

Reflect

Who are the supportive people in your work setting? Why do you find these people more supportive than others? Think about what it is that makes these people more supportive than others.

Case study

Geraldine is 32 years old and a single parent. Since the age of 25 she has suffered from multiple sclerosis. Her condition has left her without the ability to walk, has impaired her eyesight and has reduced her energy to care for herself and her two children, Eddie (10) and Sara (13).

Geraldine's children provide all the home care their mother needs when she has an episode of illness and is unable to care for them or herself. These periods of ill health are becoming longer as Geraldine's condition progresses. During the week Eddie and Sara take it in turns to cook, wash the dishes, clean the house, wash and dress their mum, make her comfortable and make sure that she has her medication. They also go to school most days. At weekends Eddie and Sara take their mum out to see friends of the family, push her around the local park so that she gets fresh air, wash their clothes at the launderette and do the shopping at the supermarket.

Claudette Gidens, the district nurse who comes to see Geraldine, has got to know Eddie and Sara very well. They try to do the things she says and ring her when they feel worried about their mum. Geraldine wants to stay at home with her children as long as she can. She feels loved and cared for by her children but now feels they are under too much pressure to keep meeting her needs. Eddie and Sara say it's tiring but they don't want their mum to go away to hospital or a home.

1. How might Eddie and Sara's relatiosnhip with their mum be changed by her periods of illness?

2. List some of the positive and negative feelings and responses that carer like Eddie and Sara may experience when caring for a close relative at home.

3. How might Claudette's relationship with Geraldine be different to the relationship that Eddie and Sara have with their mum?

Knowledge Assessment Task

1.1 **1.2**

Imagine that you are applying for a new job in your health or social care organisation. Your employer has asked all applicants to complete an application form detailing their qualifications, skills and experience. As a final way of selecting the most suitable candidates for interview, your employer has included a written task. You are required to:

▶ describe examples of different working relationships in health and social care settings

▶ explain how a working relationship is different from a personal relationship.

Write an account of 300–500 words that demonstrates your understanding of working relationships in health and social care. You should also be prepared to answer any questions that your assessor may ask you about the work you produce. Keep a copy of your work as evidence towards your assessment.

Working in ways agreed with your employer

Your assessment criteria:

2.1 Describe why it is important to adhere to the agreed scope of the job role

2.2 Access full and up-to-date details of ways of working

2.3 Implement agreed ways of working

Adhering to the scope of the job role

Everybody who works in your work setting has been employed to work within a particular role. If you are a student on placement in a care setting you should also have a clear role, even if you are **supernumerary**. Service users and your colleagues will expect you to work within the boundaries of your particular role, and these boundaries should be clear from your job description. The job description should refer to the:

▶ responsibilities of your job

▶ supervision and line management arrangements for your job

▶ setting where you will work

▶ management or supervisory responsibilities attached to your work role, if appropriate.

Health and social care organisations usually produce a job

Key terms

Supernumerary: a member of staff, usually a student or trainee, who is not counted in the number of people required to staff a care setting

description outlining the expectations and tasks associated with each job. This is typically produced when a job vacancy occurs and is given to all applicants for the post, so that people are very clear about what is expected of them from the beginning of their employment. A job description may include a clear, detailed and structured set of duties and responsibilities associated with a work role. Alternatively, it may consist of a much looser set of tasks and responsibilities that are described in a general way. If this is the case, it is important to clarify with your employer any aspects of the job description that seem vague, confusing or unclear.

Your employer will expect you to fulfil all aspects of your work role because they have identified a need for somebody to carry out the range of tasks or activities associated with it. That is, your job has been designed and created as part of a broader **workforce planning** process within your care organisation. Your role covers work tasks and duties that need doing. Each of your colleagues will also have a job description associated with their work role, and will also be expected to complete particular work tasks and duties. You therefore need to do your job at the prescribed level and in the expected way to fit in with others. If you ensure that you always meet your own responsibilities and your colleagues do the same, service users should receive appropriate care and support. Taking over other people's responsibilities or doing random tasks not expected of you can disrupt workload management and the daily allocation of tasks. However, your manager or supervisor may occasionally request that you undertake work not normally associated with your work role. Where you agree to do this you should always ensure that you work within the boundaries of your own level of competence, qualifications and experience.

Reflect

Can you remember what your job description says? When was the last time that you looked at this document? Think about whether your job description actually describes the role and responsibilities that you undertake in the work setting.

Key terms

Workforce planning: the planning carried out by employers to determine the size of their workforce, the different work roles, and the management structure

Case study

Alice Bell is 79 years old and lives alone. She has some memory impairment and forgets what time of day it is, whether she has eaten, and the names of all but her closest relatives and Betty Edwards, her community nurse. Betty visits Alice every other day. She knows that this is a little bit too often but she says that Alice likes (and needs) to see a friendly face. Betty is supposed to monitor Alice's physical and mental health and change the dressing on a leg ulcer that Alice has recently developed. Betty says that she is doing these things but she has also started to take shopping for Alice and washes and styles her hair once a week. Alice doesn't complain about this but has now become very dependent on Betty's help.

1. Do you think that Betty is adhering to the scope of her job role?
2. Which activities described in the case study are likely to be outside of her job description?
3. Explain why Betty's approach to providing care for Alice may be seen as problematic and inappropriate.

Agreed ways of working

The policies and procedures designed and written by your employer set out how you should provide care and support for others and how you should deal with specific issues in your work setting. These should include policies and procedures relating to:

▶ health and safety

▶ equal opportunities

▶ confidentiality

▶ data protection

▶ supervision

▶ waste management

▶ moving and handling

▶ managing medication

▶ security and safeguarding.

The workplace policies produced by your employer identify the general approach that the organisation takes towards an issue. For example, the moving and handling policy may outline a 'no manual lifting' approach to moving and supporting service users. The procedures that accompany the policy would then outline the detailed way of putting the 'no manual lifting' approach into practice, such as through the use of lifting aids and equipment. You should know about and understand all of the procedures that affect your work role. For example, there should be detailed procedures explaining how to:

▶ respond to a fire incident

▶ deal with the receipt of medication

▶ deal with an accident or a death in the work setting

▶ assess and manage risks.

The policies and procedures written by your employer should incorporate all of the legal requirements affecting care work and should reflect the safest and most effective ways of carrying out particular tasks. It is essential that you understand and follow these policies and procedures to ensure that you are working in ways agreed by your employer.

It is important, and your responsibility, to make sure that you know about agreed ways of working in your work setting

Reflect

Do you know where to find copies of these policies and procedures in your work setting? When was the last time that you consulted or read through one of these documents? Could you explain how the different policies and procedures used in your work setting impact on your particular work role?

Case study

Daniel McClaren is a residential support worker in a care home for older people. he works shifts on a rota system which means that he works two weekends per month, three months of nights and day shifts in between. Daniel is very keen to progress in his career and hopes to become a residential home manager one day. However, at his recent appraisal, Daniel's line manager drew attention to reports that she had received about Daniel's work practices. Despite having residents' best interests at heart, Daniel has a habit of taking short cuts 'to get the job done' as he explained to his line manager. This has recently involved lifting an individual into the bath on his own and not checking the water temperature before doing so. Daniel has also been reminded on several occasions that he should not take residents out for walks on his own.

1. In what ways is Daniel failing to follow the agreed ways of working in his care setting?

2. How could Daniel clarify what the agreed ways of working are?

3. Explain why it is important that Daniel does know about and actually follows the agreed ways of working for his care setting.

Practical Assessment Task   2.1 2.2 2.3

The duties and responsibilities of your health or social care work role should be set out in your job description. In signing a contract of employment you have stated that you will work in ways agreed with your employer, which are described in the policies and procedures that apply in your work setting.

For this assessment task you need to:

▶ describe why it is important to adhere to the agreed scope of your job role

▶ show that you can access full and up-to-date details of agreed ways of working

▶ implement agreed ways of working in your care setting.

You may want to make notes to help you to prepare for your assessment. The evidence that you produce for this assessment task must be based on your practice in a real work environment.

Working in partnership with others

Your assessment criteria:

3.1 Explain why it is important to work in partnership with others

3.2 Demonstrate ways of working that can help improve partnership working

3.3 Identify skills and approaches needed for resolving conflicts

3.4 Demonstrate how and when to access support and advice about:
- partnership working
- resolving conflicts

How would you describe your role as a care practitioner to someone you have just met? What would you say? Would you describe your role as *working with* people or *doing things for* people? In the past, there was a general expectation that care practitioners would do things *for* people. Now the emphasis has changed and you are expected to work in partnership with the people you care for or support. There are, in fact, many different types of partnership in the health and social care field. These include partnerships with:

- ▶ colleagues
- ▶ practitioners from other agencies
- ▶ people receiving care or support
- ▶ the partners and families of the people you are caring for.

Partnerships with individuals

Part of your role as a care practitioner involves providing people with enough care and support to enable them to get on with their daily life. The relationship that you develop with an individual, and the approach that you take to providing support for them, should be based on the idea of partnership. Partnership is all about working together in a relatively equal and collaborative way. Within the care partnerships that you develop you should enable and support individuals to make as many decisions as possible and to do as much as they can for themselves. An individual's problems may well be made worse by a care practitioner who provides too much care and support even though this may be given with the best of intentions.

Reflect

What different kinds of partnerships are you involved in within your work role? Think about the range of other people with whom you work.

Discuss

In a small group, discuss examples of how you work in partnership with the individuals for whom you provide care or support. Does this actually happen in your care setting or does pressure to 'get the work done' lead to a lack of collaboration and partnership working with service users?

Care practitioners are sometimes tempted to do too much for individuals because they are trying to compensate for skills and abilities that people have lost or because they do not like to see people struggle, take risks and sometimes fail in their efforts to be self-caring. However, encouraging and supporting individuals to be involved in their own care and to take as much control as possible is a crucial way of helping them to maintain their skills and their self-esteem.

Team work and partnerships

Effective partnerships are based on teamwork. Health and social care practitioners increasingly work in integrated **multi-agency** and **multi-disciplinary** teams, bringing different skills and specialisms together to provide the range of services and high quality care that service users often require. They provide a way of pooling resources and expertise and are an efficient means of reducing duplication or overlap of service provision.

Multi-agency teams working in partnership with each other and with the individual need to have a clear understanding of and approach towards issues such as:

▶ communication

▶ information sharing and confidentiality

▶ decision-making procedures

▶ each practitioner's role and responsibilities

▶ ways of resolving conflicts

▶ agreeing objectives.

It is important that people working in partnership situations all have a clear, common understanding of the problems or needs of the individual and of the shared goal they are all seeking to achieve.

Key terms

Multi-agency: collaboration between practitioners employed by different agencies or organisations

Multi-disciplinary: arrangements that involve practitioners from different care professions working together in the same team

Partnership working requires cooperation, collaboration and a willingness to compromise

Investigate

Is your care setting a multi-disciplinary or multi-agency environment? Find out about the roles and specialist skills or responsibilities of other people who practise within your work environment.

Investigate

What role do the care or support plans written for individuals in your work setting play in coordinating the work of different care practitioners?

Improving partnership working

Good communication is essential for building trust and establishing efficient working arrangements. Trust and goodwill are needed to make partnerships work, as are respect and appreciation of others' involvement. As a care practitioner you should:

▶ value equally the different skills, contributions and approaches of others

▶ acknowledge the efforts and contributions of other people.

Clear decision-making that follows agreed processes and procedures enables practitioners working in partnership teams to feel more confident about the process of working together. It is important to ensure that you do not exclude any practitioners or team members from taking part in the decision-making process, as they may well then feel rejected, demotivated and less committed to a shared, team-based approach to providing care.

Resolving issues and difficulties

Partnership and team-based working can produce conflicts between individual practitioners or between practitioners from different agencies. This can result from the fact that practitioners with different professional training and backgrounds may approach situations differently or have different priorities. A community-based health care support worker may, for example, want to focus on completing particular tasks each day. A community nurse or social worker may have a longer-term view and may wish to work in a way that promotes active participation and independence.

To avoid potential problems, there need to be ways of resolving problematic relationships and conflict within teams and partnerships. Cordial, professional working relationships must be established even if people are not as cooperative or compatible on a personal level. Professional, not personal, standards apply to these situations. It is essential that you communicate and relate to others effectively and courteously, even when you have a different perspective on what ought to happen or on how a procedure should be carried out.

Accessing support and advice

You may need advice and support about partnership working in relation to:

▶ sharing information

▶ issues of confidentiality

▶ clarification of roles and responsibilities, including professional boundaries

▶ understanding agreed ways of working.

Reflect

Have you ever become involved in a conflict or disagreement over a practice-related issue in your work setting? How did you resolve this? Did you seek out or make use of any support or advice services?

Reflect

How do people resolve sensitive issues or personal difficulties in your work setting? What would you do if you became involved in a dispute or had cause to complain about a colleague or a practitioner from another agency?

Advice and support on issues such as these can be obtained from several different sources – firstly, from your manager or supervisor. You also need to know about and understand your organisation's policies and procedures relating to partnership working. These should provide detailed information and guidance on a range of issues. Seeking advice from senior colleagues and your manager will also be helpful.

Your manager and senior colleagues will see asking for help and support as a sign that you have a conscientious, professional approach, not as a sign of weakness or incompetence. Other sources of advice and support include mentoring organisations, independent advisory organisations, trade unions and the occupational health service provided by your employer. Whenever you are considering whether you need to seek support or advice, you should always prioritise the needs of people for whom you provide care and support. Asking for help when you need it is usually in everyone's best interests.

Practical Assessment Task   3.1 3.2 3.3 3.4

Health and social care practitioners are increasingly likely to be working in partnership with others. This assessment task requires you to engage in some form of partnership working activity and to:

▶ explain why it is important to work in partnership with others
▶ demonstrate ways of working that can improve partnership working
▶ identify skills and approaches needed for resolving conflicts
▶ demonstrate how and when to access support and advice about:
   ▶ partnership working
   ▶ resolving conflict.

The evidence that you produce for this assessment task must be based on your practice in a real work environment. Your assessor may wish to observe you in practice and may ask you questions relating to the way you work in partnership with others.

Are you ready for assessment?

AC	What do you know now?	Assessment task	✓
1.1	How a working relationship is different from a personal relationship	Page 151	
1.2	How to describe different working relationships in health and social care settings	Page 151	

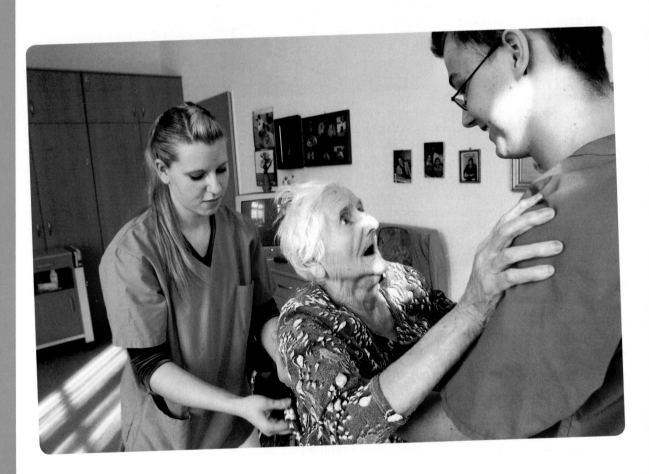

AC	What can you do now?	Assessment task	✓
2.1	Describe why it is important to adhere to the agreed scope of the job role	Page 155	
2.2	Access full and up-to-date details of agreed ways of working	Page 155	
2.3	Implement agreed ways of working	Page 155	
3.1	Explain why it is important to work in partnership with others	Page 159	
3.2	Demonstrate ways of working that can help improve partnership working	Page 159	
3.3	Identify skills and approaches needed for resolving conflicts	Page 159	
3.4	Demonstrate how and when to access support and advice about: • partnership working • resolving conflicts	Page 159	

7 | Promote person-centred approaches in health and social care (HSC 036)

AC What you need to know

1.1	Explain how and why person-centred values must influence all aspects of health and social care work
1.2	Evaluate the use of care plans in applying person-centred values
7.1	Compare different uses of risk assessment in health and social care
7.2	Explain how risk-taking and risk assessment relate to rights and responsibilities
7.3	Explain why risk assessments need to be regularly revised

CHAPTER 7

AC What you need to do

2.1	Work with an individual and others to find out the individual's history, preferences, wishes and needs
2.2	Demonstrate ways to put person-centred values into practice in a complex or sensitive situation
2.3	Adapt actions and approaches in response to an individual's changing needs or preferences
3.1	Analyse factors that influence the capacity of an individual to express consent
3.2	Establish consent for an activity or action
3.3	Explain what steps to take if consent cannot be readily established
4.1	Describe different ways of applying active participation to meet individual needs
4.2	Work with an individual and others to agree how active participation will be implemented
4.3	Demonstrate how active participation can address the holistic needs of an individual
4.4	Demonstrate ways to promote the understanding and use of active participation
5.1	Support an individual to make informed choices
5.2	Use own role and authority to support the individual's right to make choices
5.3	Manage risk in a way that maintains the individual's right to make choices
5.4	Describe how to support an individual to question or challenge decisions concerning them that are made by others
6.1	Explain the links between identity, self-image and self-esteem
6.2	Analyse factors that contribute to the wellbeing of individuals
6.3	Support an individual in a way that promotes their sense of identity, self-image and self-esteem
6.4	Demonstrate ways to contribute to an environment that promotes wellbeing

Assessment criteria 2.1–2.3, 3.2, 4.2–4.4, 5.1–5.3 and 6.4 must be assessed in a real work environment

This unit links to some of the other units:

SHC 31	Promote communication in health and social care settings
SHC 33	Promote equality and inclusion in health and social care settings
SHC 34	Principles for implementing duty of care in health and social care settings
DEM 312	Understand and enable interaction and communication with individuals who have dementia
HSC 3020	Facilitate person-centred assessment, planning, implementation and review

Some of your learning will be repeated in these units and will give you the chance to review your knowledge and understanding.

Understand the application of person-centred approaches in health and social care

What are person-centred values?

The main principle underlying any person-centred approach to care or support is that the individual plays a central role. That means they are involved in every aspect of their care or support; for example, needs assessment, care or support planning. When an organisation's activities are based on a person-centred approach, policies and procedures are designed and developed *with* individuals *for* individuals.

Person-centred approaches are underpinned by **values**. These are the principles which guide how individuals are treated as shown in Figure 7.1.

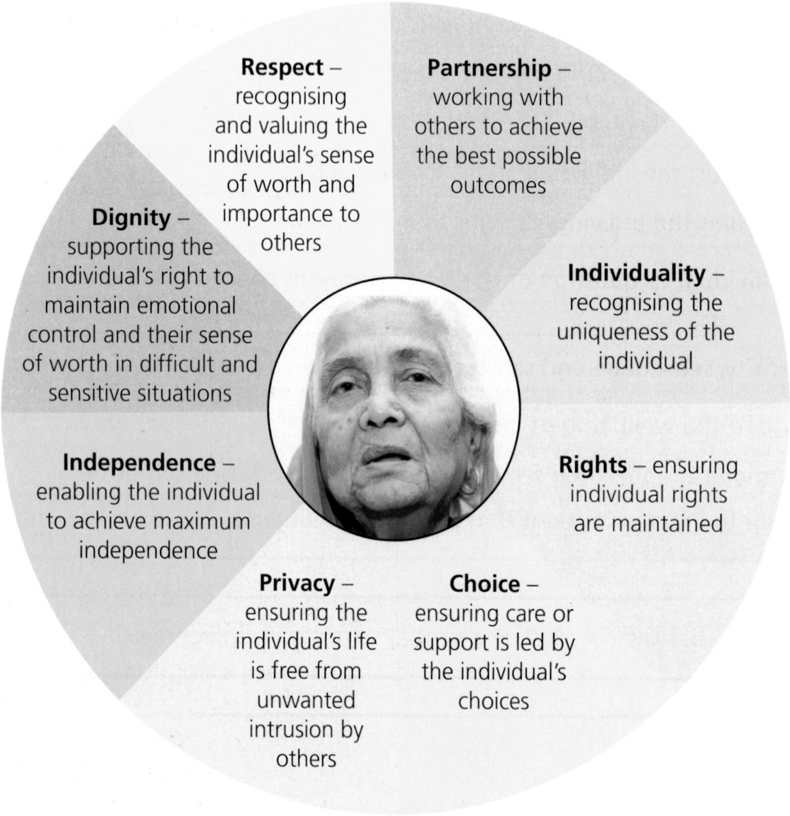

Your assessment criteria:

1.1 Explain how and why person-centred values must influence all aspects of health and social care work.

Key terms

Inclusion: being a part of something, involved

Medical model of disability: in this model disabled people are defined by their illness, condition and medical diagnosis. It promotes the view that disabled people are dependent and need to be cured or cared for. Their lives are controlled by 'professional experts', not the individual. This impacts on access to education, welfare, employment and all aspects of social activity

Social model of disability: considers that it is the wider factors within society – e.g. systems and negative attitudes – that directly or indirectly determine who is and is not disabled within society

Values: the accepted principles or standards of a person or a group; a person's judgement of what is important in life

Figure 7.1 Person-centred values

How can person-centred values influence all care?

Person-centred values and approaches demonstrate the practical outcome of the **social model of disability** and **inclusion**. For this reason they must influence all aspects of health and social care provision.

Models of disability

For many decades the **medical model of disability** was the dominant influence on attitudes in society towards disability. As a result, the focus in health and social care services was on the 'disability' and what the individual was *unable* to do as a result. The disabled person was viewed as 'being the problem' needing professional 'experts' to determine what was best for them. This resulted in things being 'done to them', creating a **disempowering** 'learned helplessness'.

The social model of disability views the attitudes and structures of society as 'the problem'. The way society is structured is instrumental in 'disabling' people and creating 'helplessness' rather than being an inevitable consequence of disability.

The social model of disability has had a significant influence on attitudes to disability. People with disabilities are no longer hidden away and separated from society. Equal rights have led to improved access to education, employment and all aspects of life. These changes have resulted in higher expectations and an improved quality of life and outcomes for disabled people. Changes in attitude have also challenged health and social care providers to work in a different way which puts the individual more in control. The social model of disability and **social inclusion** are now the foundations of health and social care provision.

Person-centred approaches are about sharing **power**. The emphasis is on 'doing things with' the individual and that means including the individual in decision-making. Person-centred approaches focus on:

▶ who the person is

▶ who the important people are in their lives

▶ what they can do together to achieve a better life for the person – in the present and in the future.

Empowering individuals

If people with disabilities are to be **empowered** and seen as equal partners, then person-centred values have to be embedded into every aspect of provision. Inclusion and involvement needs to be meaningful: individuals may require independent support to express their views or to fully understand the implications of decisions. Care workers need to understand the individual in depth: their preferred means of communication as well as their perspective on their life.

The focus in a person-centred approach is on finding ways to enable the individual to achieve their potential. To achieve this it is important to listen to individuals, to ensure they are involved in developing solutions to meet their needs as well as their ideas for their future. If a solution is agreed, it is more likely to succeed.

Key terms

Disempower: to remove or reduce the power an individual has to control decisions

Empowerment: gaining control over life, leading to increased self-confidence or self-esteem; being aware and using personal and external resources to become more involved in decision-making and overcoming obstacles including discrimination and oppression

Power: the ability, strength or capacity to do something; having authority, control or influence over others

Social inclusion: ensuring that those in society who might otherwise be prevented (marginalised) through circumstances, receive opportunities which enable them to make decisions and participate in society and improve their wellbeing

Investigate

Find out how person-centred values influence your workplace policies and procedures.

1. Which policies and procedures include specific reference to person-centred values?

2. How are individuals who use your service involved in developing policies and procedures?

3. How are individuals involved in recruiting new employees?

165

Evaluating care plans

A **care plan** defines the 'path' between where an individual is currently is and where they want to be – i.e. how they want their needs to be met and their life to change. Often, care plans contain only basic information on:

▶ assessed needs and circumstances

▶ options to meet needs

▶ the individual's views

▶ their current level of support

▶ desired outcomes (what they want)

▶ required outcomes (what they need to keep them healthy and safe)

▶ planned support

▶ timescales for implementing and reviewing.

Your assessment criteria:

1.2 Evaluate the use of care plans in applying person-centred values.

Key terms

Care plan: a document which details an individual's needs and wishes, how these will be met and who is involved in meeting those needs

Person-centred care plans

All too often too care plans reflect a service approach to care or support with 'needs' identified in terms of what can be provided rather than what the individual really needs. The care plan presents a key opportunity for developing a person-centred approach. This can be achieved by involving the individual at every step to ensure it reflects their individuality.

A person-centred care plan will include the individual's:

▶ views about their needs and circumstances

▶ priorities, and the needs they consider to be most important

▶ strengths

▶ interests, likes and dislikes

▶ ideas about how they want their life to be

▶ ideas about how to have their needs met (balancing desired and required outcomes)

▶ support network – people who are important to and contribute to their life.

Reflect

Think about the care planning process used in your workplace. Look at a variety of care plans and compare them in terms of how they demonstrate person-centred values.

1. How are person-centred values demonstrated within each care plan?

2. If there is no evidence of person-centred values within the care plan, how could this change?

3. What recommendations could you suggest to include person-centred values?

Evaluation criteria for care plans

When **evaluating** anything it is important to start with a set of criteria against which you will make a judgement.

Figure 7.2 opposite provides some suggestions of questions to ask when evaluating the effectiveness of care plans. You may find there is more evidence in some areas than in others: areas with more evidence can be considered as demonstrating a person-centred approach; areas with little or no evidence can be viewed as requiring development and improvement. Your evaluation will enable you to make recommendations.

Your assessment criteria:

1.2 Evaluate the use of care plans in applying person-centred values.

Key terms

Evaluate: to consider or examine something in order to make a judgement about its value, quality, importance, relevance or usefulness

Knowledge Assessment Task · 1.1 · 1.2

Person-centred values are central to effective health and social care practice. As a practitioner you will need to show that you have the knowledge and understanding to support individuals using these values and that evidence for this can be found in your work.

1. Explain how and why person-centred values must influence all aspects of health and social care work.
2. Using at least two examples of care plans for your workplace evaluate their use in applying person-centred values.

Keep your notes as evidence towards your assessment.

Figure 7.2 Evaluating care plans using a person-centred approach

Person-centred value	Does the care plan:
Individuality	• reflect the individual? • show how the plan of care is designed to maintain this on a day-to-day basis? • include the individual's views, wishes and preferences? • include the individual's own words?
Rights	• show how the individual's rights have been maintained – for example, were their communication needs met so they could express their views? • show how the individual was included in decision-making? • include their explicit agreement and/or consent to decisions made? • show how the care plan is designed to maintain this on a day-to-day basis?
Choice	• show how the individual expressed their personal choices? • include all the options discussed with the individual and their responses to each one? • show that the choices suggested reflected the individual's needs, wishes and preferences, not just a 'service solution'? • show how the plan is designed to maintain this on a day-to-day basis?
Privacy	• show how the individual was protected from unwanted intrusion by others during the process – i.e. did they have a say in who participated in the care planning process? • show how the plan is designed to maintain this on a day-to-day basis?
Independence	• show that the focus of the plan is to enable the individual to achieve maximum independence? • show that risk assessments are designed to 'enable' and not 'disable'? • show how the plan is designed to maintain this on a day-to-day basis?
Dignity	• show how the individual was supported to maintain emotional control and their sense of worth during the care planning process as well as in difficult and sensitive situations? • show how the plan is designed to maintain this on a day-to-day basis?
Respect	• show how each aspect of the individual's care and support will recognise and value their sense of worth and importance to others? • show how the plan is designed to maintain this on a day-to-day basis?
Partnership	• show how all those involved in the individual's care and support will work together to achieve the best possible outcomes? • show what measures and processes are in place to monitor and review agreed support provided by each person/agency involved? • show how concerns will be addressed before there is a detrimental impact on the individual? • show how the plan is designed to maintain this on a day-to-day basis?

Find out what matters to an individual

Working in a person-centred way means placing the individual at the centre of all your thinking and activities. To do this effectively you first need to really understand the individual. This means finding out about them, their life story and their personal history. This will involve spending time with them as well as the other people who are important to them within their social network. This could include family and friends as well as other professionals who support them.

Life history

Too often the emphasis is placed on their current situation. However, past experiences are a strong influence and so it is important to understand these too if care or support is to be appropriate and beneficial.

Individuals who require care or support are often described only by the labels that accompany them – for example, a medical diagnosis or current need. However, their present circumstance is only a part of who they are, not the whole picture. Finding out about an individual's life, their experiences, culture and values will help you to understand what is important to them, their likes and dislikes. It may also provide important information to help you understand how past experiences have influenced their current behaviour. This can be done by:

▶ talking and listening to the individual to gain insights into who they are and what makes them unique

▶ asking the people who are significant to them, in particular their family and friends

▶ listening to other people's recollections of the individual

▶ looking at photographs, mementos etc.

▶ observing behaviour – especially if the individual has limited verbal communication

▶ finding out about their interests and past experiences to help plan meaningful activities

▶ collating a life story book to help others get to know them

▶ offering choices and observing and testing out responses – especially if they have communication difficulties

▶ reading case notes and information from others.

It is useful to remember that preferences, wishes and needs change. Never assume that because an individual liked something a month ago they still do. So, if in doubt, ask, watch and listen.

Your assessment criteria:

2.1 Work with an individual and others to find out the individual's history, preferences, needs and wishes.

Case study

Lydia is an 86 year-old woman originally from the Caribbean. She has dementia, and finds communication difficult, but is physically fit.

When Lydia first arrived at the residential care home she found it difficult to adapt. She spent a lot of time in her room, often refused meals and refused to join in with any activities. Her mood was low and she was restless and unsettled.

Her key worker Josie was concerned about Lydia and discussed the situation with her supervisor. Josie felt that she needed to understand more about Lydia if she was to support her. It was therefore agreed that Josie would spend at least an hour of each shift just with Lydia, to try and encourage her to settle and improve her mood and activity levels.

Josie has spent time with Lydia's family to find out more about her past life, her interests and life experiences as well as what is important to Lydia. Josie has asked Lydia's family to work with her to collate a life story book that could be used to engage Lydia in reminiscence and also help other staff to understand Lydia and interact with her.

Josie has also spent time with Lydia encouraging her to talk about her life and interests. She has also arranged for Lydia's daughter to talk to the cook about organising a Caribbean-themed meal. Josie and the cook have involved Lydia in preparing the meal and have discovered that she has retained more skills than had first been assessed.

Lydia's family have brought in some Caribbean music and Josie has used this to evoke Lydia's memories. As Lydia has always enjoyed music and used to dance and sing they have been able to use this to encourage her to become more active.

As a result of what Josie has learnt, the next person-centred care plan meeting with Lydia and her family has enabled them to develop a more personalised support plan which reflects Lydia's past, her present abilities and future wishes. Lydia's wellbeing has improved and she has become more active and her days more meaningful.

1. How did working with Lydia and her family help Josie to work in a person-centred way?

2. How did Josie's work with Lydia demonstrate person-centred values?

3. What else could Josie do to further develop a person-centred approach to Lydia's support?

Working in complex and sensitive situations

Working in health and social care means that you are often supporting individuals to deal with issues and situations which are distressing, traumatic or very personal. The key to a helping role is to build a relationship with individuals whom you support. As you will be supporting individuals at times in their life that they may find very difficult to cope with, you need to establish trust and respect. At these times they will need you to work sensitively with them and to be clear about your role, responsibilities, professional boundaries and confidentiality.

Situations that may be considered complex or sensitive could include:

▶ distressing events such as bereavement, family or relationship breakup, illness, dying

▶ traumatic situations such as sudden death, accident or abuse

▶ threatening or frightening situations, such as abuse, assault, family dispute or violence

▶ personal crises, such as ill health or relationship problems

▶ situations where there are complex communication or **cognitive** needs; for example, where the individual has multiple profound disabilities.

Applying person-centred values to practice

Applying person-centred values to your day-to-day work may require you to make some changes in your practice. In order to support individuals in ways that promote their rights, choices, preferences, wishes and dignity you will need always to listen, learn and act upon what you learn.

You will need to:

▶ think about your role in the individual's life

▶ think about how you can bring about action or change for that individual

▶ think about and analyse what life is like for the person now: what is working for them; what is not working for them; what needs to change so that it does work for them.

When the situation is complex or sensitive this will require you to be even more alert, not only to verbal but also non-verbal communication. Individuals in these situations are often experiencing a range of emotions which they may communicate through behaviour more than in speech. Communication can be more difficult due to a heightened emotional state. You may need to repeat information several times before it is understood and acted upon. Figure 7.3 outlines factors in applying person-centred values in complex or sensitive situations.

Your assessment criteria:

2.2 Demonstrate ways to put person-centred values into practice in a complex or sensitive situation.

Key terms

Cognitive: relating to thought processes – thinking, reasoning or perception

Investigate

Find out what your organisational policy says about supporting individuals when they are distressed. Think about how you can determine your professional boundaries when dealing with complex or sensitive situations. Who would you talk to if you are unsure? What do you think are the potential problems that can arise if sensitive situations are not dealt with in a professional manner?

Respect – Gary's views are listened to about how to resolve difficult issues

Partnership – Gary is involved in every decision affecting his daily life

Dignity – when he becomes distressed Gary is supported to move to a private space

Individuality – use Gary's preferred means of communication

Independence – Gary decides whom he wants to support him and how he is supported

Rights – Gary decides how much and with whom information is shared

Privacy – all discussions about Gary take place in private and are confidential

Choice – Gary decides what he wants to do about each situation

Figure 7.3 Applying person-centred values in complex or sensitive situations

Practical Assessment Task   2.1 2.2

As a health and social care practitioner you will need to produce evidence based on your practice at work which demonstrates that the support you provide is underpinned by person-centred values. Identify one individual you support – for example, someone for whom you act as key worker.

Write a case study which demonstrates how you have found out about and used their history, preferences, wishes and needs to apply person-centred values to your work with that person. Include how what you do:

▶ recognises their **individuality**
▶ promotes their **rights**
▶ ensures that you support them to make their own **choices**
▶ respects and maintain their **privacy**
▶ supports them to achieve as much **independence** as possible
▶ respects and maintains their **dignity**
▶ **respects** and values them for themselves
▶ works in **partnership** with them and others to achieve their goals and wishes.

Keep your notes as evidence towards your assessment.

Adapting to changing needs and preferences

When an individual's needs are assessed this is a statement of the situation at that point in time. However, needs and circumstances will change. For some individuals change may occur frequently, while for others change may be more gradual or occur suddenly without warning.

Examples of changes that may occur are:

▶ poor/limited mobility in the morning for an individual with arthritis

▶ frequent fluctuations in cognitive ability for an individual with dementia

▶ frequent mood swings due to mental illness affecting behaviour and capacity

▶ changes due to pain or discomfort

▶ sudden change due to illness or an accident – for example, an acute infection, a fall or medical emergency

▶ gradual change due to deteriorating health – for example, failing eyesight or hearing.

Change of any kind will impact on an individual's ability to function, and you will need to be able to adapt your approach to accommodate those changes. For example, if when you went to move an individual you found they were in pain, you should deal with this first and wait until the pain relief had taken effect before supporting them to move.

An individual's preferences may also change frequently as a result of their mood, situation, interests, new information or experiences. It is therefore important to never assume that just because they liked something yesterday they will like it today. Always make a habit of asking and check their preferences before acting.

Your assessment criteria:

2.3 Adapt actions and approaches in response to an individual's changing needs or preferences.

Reflection

Think about the people you support and their care and support needs.

▶ In what circumstances might their needs change?

▶ Who would be involved in assessing any changes in needs?

▶ How are any changes to their needs and preferences recorded and shared with others in your team?

Case study

David is 58 years old and has chronic obstructive pulmonary disease (COPD) as a result of smoking for 30 years.

He lives at home with his wife, who is his main carer. He took early retirement a year ago due to his deteriorating health and mobility. He had worked as a teacher prior to this. His condition has deteriorated over the past six months and he now has oxygen at home. He has 'good days' and 'bad days'.

On his good days he is able to manage his personal care himself and likes to be as active as his condition allows him. However, on his bad days he finds it difficult to breathe, which limits his ability to manage any activity without considerable help. He is prone to chest infections and has some heart failure.

His condition is deteriorating overall and his recent care plan meeting discussed palliative care arrangements.

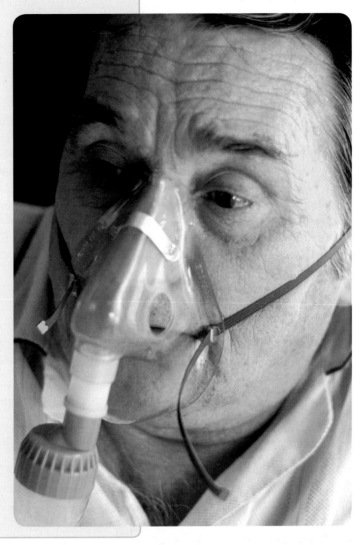

1. How could David's person-centred support plan reflect his fluctuating needs?
2. How could you adapt your support to accommodate David's needs on a 'good day'?
3. How could you adapt your support to accommodate David's needs on a 'bad day'?

Practical Assessment Task   2.3

Individuals' needs and circumstances change for a variety of reasons. Health and social care practitioners need to be able to respond to individuals' changing needs and preferences. This task requires you to produce evidence of your ability to adapt your actions and approaches in response to an individual's changing needs or preferences. Your assessor may wish to observe how you do this in practice and may also ask you questions about this aspect of your practice.

What influences the capacity to express consent?

Our mental **capacity** – that is, the ability to think and reason – develops as we grow, given the right opportunities and conditions. These abilities enable us to understand complex and abstract ideas or concepts without requiring direct evidence. They enable us to weigh up the arguments for and against a course of action and then reach a decision. For example, we can think about situations and assess what the risks might be. We can imagine a situation and use our judgement to consider the potential benefits and harms of actions which involve risk. Our ability to think and reason is a significant factor in being able to **consent**.

Other factors include:

▶ understanding the situation and any risks and benefits

▶ being free to express thoughts and to ask questions

▶ personal values and beliefs

▶ being given time to understand any and all implications

▶ education level – i.e. poor educational attainment may have resulted in a lack of opportunity to develop higher thinking skills

▶ communication skills – i.e. being able to make others understand and/or access to advocacy

▶ the quality and quantity of information available to inform the decision

▶ being treated with respect by those requiring a decision

▶ having privacy and dignity respected

▶ being free from coercion and fear of retribution.

Your assessment criteria:

3.1 Analyse factors that influence the capacity of an individual to express consent.

Key terms

Capacity: the mental or physical ability for something or to do something

Consent: means giving informed permission for something to happen. Giving consent implies that the person knows and understands the implications of their decision

What is capacity and consent?

When an individual gives consent, this means they agree to an action or decision that affects them, having been made aware of the full implications of the issue in question. The process of establishing consent will vary according to an individual's assessed capacity – i.e. their ability to give their consent.

Having capacity means being able to undertake the four stages of decision-making. This means the individual is able to:

▶ understand the information they are being given that is relevant to the decision

▶ retain that information long enough to make a decision

▶ analyse (use and weigh up) that information

▶ communicate their decision to others (verbally, using sign language, or pictures).

There are different types of consent that apply within health and social care work. These are:

▶ **informed consent** – the individual has capacity, has access to all relevant information, and is fully aware of the implications of the decision. There is a formal agreement, usually in writing.

▶ **implied consent** – the actions of the individual give the impression that they are consenting. There is no formal agreement. An example is an individual attending their GP. The implication is they are consenting to the GP making a diagnosis and offering treatment.

▶ **continued consent** – informed consent is ongoing during a period of treatment, care or support.

▶ **consent by proxy** – if the individual is unable to provide informed consent there may be times when decisions are made in their best interests by an appropriate person – e.g. a family member, next of kin.

Practitioners have a legal and moral obligation to establish consent prior to any intervention, not only those that are viewed as invasive. Consent is frequently sought through a verbal exchange – for example, asking an individual if they are ready to be moved or have a bath.

Establishing consent also shows respect for the individual's dignity and is likely to establish their trust and cooperation, so that the individual is more likely to work with you to achieve the intended action. Doing something to an individual without their consent is an infringement of their rights and if it involves physical contact may be viewed as assault.

Investigate

Find out how an individual's capacity to give consent is established in your workplace. What policies and procedures are in place to ensure an individual is free from coercion when being asked to give consent? For which particular activities is written consent obtained in your workplace? Where is an individual's **consent** recorded and any evidence of this kept?

How to establish consent

Part of your role and responsibility is to make sure you support individuals to make informed decisions. To establish consent to undertake an action affecting an individual you must ensure that you:

▶ understand their individual needs and circumstances in relation to capacity and decision-making

▶ have all the relevant information available regarding the decision, including all the available options

▶ understand and can clearly explain the different options and any potential or actual risks.

If an individual lacks the capacity to make informed decisions alone then you will need to establish who else needs to be involved. This information is usually found in their care plan or a communication chart, having been previously established to cover a range of circumstances.

Your assessment criteria:

3.2 Establish consent for an activity or action.

Gaining consent is the first step when gathering personal information from individuals

Reflect

Think about the following situations and decide what type of consent may apply:

1. attending an appointment with your GP
2. participating in research by completing a face-to-face survey in the supermarket
3. receiving medical treatment following a consultation with a specialist
4. an adult with learning difficulties being given contraception by their GP.

Implementing consent

To establish consent to an action or activity:

▸ explain what the action is using language familiar to the individual

▸ describe what it involves

▸ explain the benefits to the individual

▸ explain any potential or actual risks involved in carrying out the action

▸ explain any potential or actual risks involved in not carrying it out

▸ listen and observe the individual's response

▸ encourage them to ask questions

▸ give them time to process the information

▸ confirm consent again immediately prior to commencing the action.

In day-to-day activities consent is very often verbal and informal – e.g. consent to taking part in daily living activities. If the action is more invasive – for example, a treatment, medical procedure or legal process – consent is generally formal and therefore recorded in writing on a consent form.

Reflect

Think about the day-to-day work you undertake with the individual you support.

1. How do you find out about their capacity to consent?
2. How do you establish their consent to actions and activities?
3. What do you do if they do not consent?

Practical Assessment Task 3.1 3.2

Consent is an important aspect of maintaining an individual's rights. As a health and social care practitioner you need to provide evidence of your competence in establishing consent in a variety of different circumstances. Using examples from your work with two different individuals:

▸ Analyse factors that influence the capacity of each individual to express consent

▸ Establish consent for an activity or action with each individual.

You should write a reflective account summarising the above points as evidence for your assessment. Your assessor may wish to observe how you establish consent with individuals and may wish to ask you questions about this area of your practice.

What steps to take if consent cannot be readily established

Your assessment criteria:

3.3 Explain what steps to take if consent cannot be readily established.

Gaining consent from the individual

It is useful to remember that if the individual is tired, in pain or discomfort, hungry, thirsty or anxious they may not be able to concentrate sufficiently, or they may find the information overwhelming. The individual's response in these circumstances may not be a reflection of their true feelings.

If the individual has dementia, for example, their ability to make decisions may fluctuate due to their disease. In this case strategies may be required that do not assume the individual's *inability* to make a decision or provide consent, but seek to respond to a changing situation: for example, there may be a best time of the day to gain consent or the individual may need to be asked several times, and be given time to process the information.

Finding out about the individual's past history may also help. For example, the individual may associate giving consent with negative consequences, or they may not previously have been given the opportunity to make decisions for themselves and so find it overwhelming or fear the consequences.

Gaining consent from a responsible person

In some circumstances individuals are assessed as being unable to give consent. This can be as a result of congenital or childhood problems – for example, a learning disability, injuries (e.g. a head injury), illness or disease (e.g. dementia). An individual may temporarily or permanently lack capacity, and in either case it may be difficult to establish consent.

The Mental Capacity Act (MCA) 2005 outlines the circumstances in which another person can make a decision or take action on behalf of the individual who lacks capacity. The action or decision must relate to the care or treatment of the individual concerned. The principles of the MCA then require that:

▶ the responsible person reasonably believes that the individual lacks the capacity to make a decision in the circumstances and at that time

▶ the action or decision is in the individual's best interests

▶ the action or decision is the least restrictive alternative.

In these circumstances details regarding what has been consented to will be formally recorded in the individual's care plan or another document within their records.

In many circumstances in which consent cannot readily be established, it is useful to ask a family member about the individual's preferences and wishes.

Case study

Jon is a 48 year-old man with learning disabilities and early signs of dementia. He lives with his younger brother and his brother's wife, who are his main carers. His disability means that his ability to make decisions fluctuates during the day. He becomes particularly anxious when he is given too much verbal information at once. He finds it difficult to concentrate unless the person talking to him is facing him. Jon likes to be spoken to using a soft tone of voice. He likes to be called 'Jon' not Jonathan, as he associates this with his grandmother who brought him up. His grandmother was very strict and his brother says Jon was frightened of her.

Jon is a morning person and this is the best time to plan his day with him. He has a pin board in his room and his brother uses pictures to remind Jon of the things he is doing that day. Jon has a support worker who visits three times a week to support Jon to attend his voluntary job at the local garden centre and two evenings a week when Jon goes swimming or to a local activity club.

1. What strategies could you use to establish Jon's consent to actions or activities?
2. What would you do if it was difficult to establish Jon's consent?
3. How can a person-centred approach help when supporting Jon?

Investigate

Find out what policies and procedures are in place relating to establishing consent in your workplace.

▶ Research how the Mental Capacity Act 2005 has been integrated into your organisations' policies and procedures.

▶ Find out when an Independent Mental Capacity Advocate (IMCA) might be used and the process for doing this.

Practical Assessment Task   3.3

Establishing an individual's consent to your carrying out activities or actions relating to their care needs can sometimes be difficult and even impossible in a care setting. However, there are ways of dealing with such situations. In this task you are required to reflect on your own practice and to explain what steps you would take, or have taken, when faced by a situation where consent cannot be readily established.

The evidence that you produce for this assessment should be based on your care practice in the work place. Your assessor may also wish to observe and ask questions about this aspect of your practice.

What is active participation?

Active participation is a way of working that recognises an individual's right to participate in the activities and relationships of everyday life as independently as possible. The difference in this approach is that the individual is viewed as an active participant or partner rather than as a passive receiver of support.

How can active participation be applied to meet individual needs?

Active participation focuses on the individual, their wishes and abilities, and uses these to design ways of working that maximise their independence, as shown in Figure 7.4 opposite. Finding out an individual's history, likes, dislikes, abilities and wishes is an important starting point in encouraging active participation.

Taking a person-centred approach to care or support means looking for ways to fulfil and meet the individual's needs and wishes, This is quite different from trying to make them 'fit' in to available services whether they are right for them or not.

Being made to 'fit' into something that isn't shaped for you means you are unlikely to enjoy it and want to make it work. To show your unhappiness you are likely to fight against it, object if you are able to, be unhappy and un-cooperative. The chances of failure are high. You are likely to feel unimportant or a burden and this will make the situation worse.

Matching something to create a best fit or tailoring it to fit specifically is more likely to result in a positive outcome for all involved.

Reflect

Think of an individual that you or someone else has supported to actively participate in everyday life and reflect on the following:

1. How does this demonstrate active participation?

2. How has active participation changed the way professionals support this person?

3. How could you encourage individuals you support to actively participate?

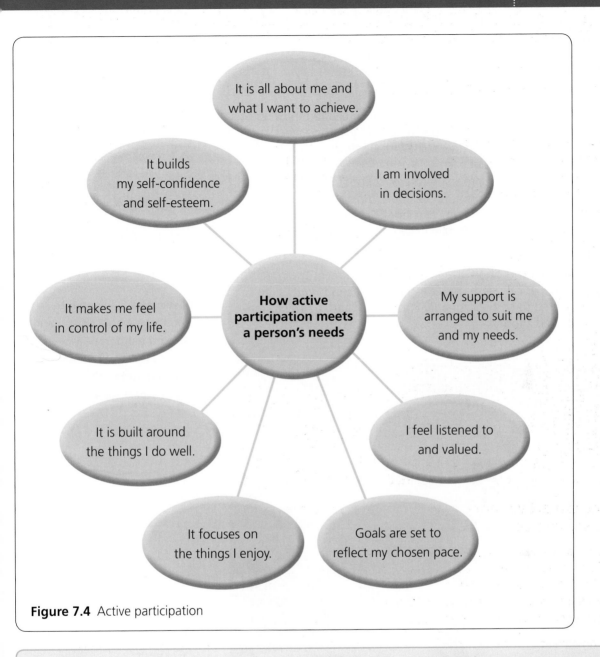

Figure 7.4 Active participation

Case study

Jamal is 28 years old with a history of clinical depression. He has attempted suicide on three occasions which resulted in hospital admissions each time. Doctors believe that Jamal's alcohol and substance misuse since his early teens have been contributing factors in his condition. His periods of depression are characterised by feelings of hopelessness, self loathing, apathy and agitation. During these times he finds it difficult to be motivated and concentrate. As a result of the changeable nature of his illness he has been unable to maintain education or employment opportunities. All of which further reduce his motivation and self esteem. His interests include music and creative arts such as painting and textile work.

1. How could you apply the principles of active participation to support Jamal?
2. What activities could you encourage Jamal to become more involved with to build his confidence?

How can active participation address holistic needs?

The idea behind active participation and person-centred thinking is that the whole person is considered and not just the aspect concerning a disability or vulnerability. A **holistic** approach means taking into account each area of the individual's life and considering these when providing care or support. It means looking at the implications of, for example, a physical disability and thinking about how this impacts on their emotional state, their ability to work or participate in leisure opportunities and their relationships with others.

Care and support is often arranged primarily to meet the individual's physical needs; other aspects of the individual's life are considered to be of secondary importance and, at worst, may be overlooked altogether.

Your assessment criteria:

4.1 Describe different ways of applying active participation to meet individual needs.

4.3 Demonstrate how active participation can address the holistic needs of an individual.

Key terms

Holistic: means taking into account the whole person and how all the different aspects of their life impact on their wellbeing, rather than looking at each aspect separately

Case study

Heather is a 45 year-old woman who is paralysed from the neck down following a car accident five years ago.

She lives with her husband, Rob, and two children: Clare, six years, and Ellie, eight years. The house has been adapted to accommodate her needs, including her electric wheelchair. Rob is her main carer; he works full-time about a 30 minute drive away from home.

For the first three years following her accident Heather was isolated at home and received a standard package of care with morning and evening visits to support personal care. Rob was unable to work and this placed considerable strain on the family relationships as well as their finances. The family became quite isolated as there was little opportunity to do things as a family. Heather also became very depressed and felt she was a burden on her family.

Two years ago Julia became Heather's social worker and encouraged Heather to actively participate in her support arrangements. They started to explore self-directed support and now Heather manages her own care and support through her individual budget. They have employed Sophie as a personal assistant and she supports Heather each weekday while Rob is at work.

Heather has returned to work part-time as a journalist, which she is able to carry on doing from home. Having an individual budget has enabled Rob to return to full-time work as now Sophie takes the children to and from school as well as caring for Heather's physical needs during the week.

Active participation has enabled Heather to express her need for mental stimulation and to continue working. Heather feels more in control of her life and has become more active.

1. Which of Heather's needs were unmet before she became an active participant in her support?

2. How has Heather's care and support changed as a result of her active participation?

3. Which of her needs would be unlikely to be met if she were not actively participating in decision-making and arranging her support?

Self-directed support: a system of funding that enables the individual to have control over how their care or support is provided. All benefits due can be amalgamated into one fund and used according to the wishes and preferences of the individual. It is also known as an individual budget, a personal budget, a direct payment or a personal health budget

Active participation in practice

Active participation can be applied in many ways. For some it might involve managing their own care through self-directed support or an individual budget. Putting active participation into practice means being able to recognise and reduce the potential barriers to implementation. It also means ensuring that everyone involved is committed to working with the individual to achieve the best possible outcomes.

Implementing active participation

Active participation is more likely to enable individuals to achieve their potential and improve their life experience. However, it can require a significant shift in thinking. Encouraging active participation challenges:

▶ the individual – to believe they can be active rather than passive

▶ family/friends – to view the individual as an equal

▶ health and social care workers – to work with the individual as an equal partner in care or support

▶ health and social care organisations – to provide flexible, personalised care or support

▶ society – to view people with disabilities as 'givers', i.e. able to contribute, and not 'takers', i.e. dependent.

Changing attitudes is the key to reducing the barriers to active participation. Improving society's attitudes to and expectations of people with disabilities is an important part of that. The **social model of disability** has already created a shift in thinking. Information, education and training will help to move that further. Involving the individual and all those people who are significant to them is also crucial to success. For active participation to be implemented, organisations need to:

▶ review their policies, procedures and ways of working

▶ ensure they involve the individual in all processes that have a direct impact on them

▶ provide support to enable individuals to express their views

▶ consider renegotiating funding to facilitate active participation

▶ support individuals to understand active participation

▶ provide staff training to support understanding and commitment

▶ monitor and review processes to ensure consistency

▶ learn from successes and failures.

Your assessment criteria:

4.2 Work with an individual and others to agree how active participation will be implemented.

4.4 Demonstrate ways to promote understanding and use of active participation.

Investigate

Find out how people with disabilities are viewed in society today. Look at how people with disabilities are represented in the media: on television, in films, in newspapers and magazines.

Find out about how people with disabilities are viewed in your local area – for example, how welcome are they in shops, restaurants, cinema, theatres and sports facilities? How do you think these influence the opportunities individuals have for active participation?

Promoting active participation

To promote and encourage the implementation of active participation you will need to:

► take time to ensure those involved understand the individual's personality, history, health, cognitive status and social abilities

► view the individual as capable of being an active partner

► keep the individual's goals central to planning

► focus on what the individual can do and have higher expectations of their ability to achieve

► work in partnership with the individual and the other important people in their life

► break goals down into small, achievable steps

► celebrate every small achievement as significant to the individual

► set longer timescales for reaching goals

► monitor and review frequently and avoid using non-disabled criteria for measuring success

► get into the habit of a 'review, adjust, review, adjust' approach

► don't be afraid to make changes and move in a different direction if it's not working

► be creative and flexible in your thinking

► be committed, patient, and tenacious

► be realistic about timescales and cost

► engage other people in making the individual's goals a reality

► think about risk assessment as a means by which to make things possible

► integrate active participation into care or support so that it becomes the norm

► consider resistance (barriers) as opportunities for creative solutions to change attitudes.

Practical Assessment Task   4.1   4.2   4.3   4.4

This task requires you to demonstrate how you use active participation approaches in your care practice. With reference to your own practice, you need to:

► Describe different ways of applying active participation to meet an individual's needs
► Work with the individual and others to agree how active participation will be implemented
► Demonstrate how active participation can address the holistic needs of the individual
► Demonstrate ways to promote the understanding and use of active participation.

The evidence that you produce for this assessment should be based on your care practice in the work place. Your assessor may also wish to observe and ask questions about this aspect of your practice.

Support the individual's right to make choices

Making informed choices

Having the opportunity to make choices is something most of us take for granted. However, for many of the people you support, being presented with choices may be a confusing or new experience for them.

Being able to make a choice assumes an understanding of the options available and the potential consequences of those options. There is always the danger that care workers make assumptions about individuals' ability to understand; in the past such individuals may have had little opportunity to be involved in making choices. However, everyone has a right to make their own choices about their life and this is an essential care principle.

Your assessment criteria:

5.1 Support an individual to make informed choices.

It is important to understand your choices fully in order to make an informed decision

Understanding options

Making an informed choice means knowing what will be gained as well as potentially lost with each option. It is important, when supporting an individual to make a choice, to:

▶ understand the individual's needs and abilities

▶ provide relevant information in the way the individual prefers (e.g. words, pictures, signs, another language); in quantities that the individual can deal with; at a time which suits the individual

▶ explain how each choice may benefit/suit the individual

▶ explain what they may lose by making each choice

▶ use an even tone of voice without emphasising the choice you prefer

▶ ensure there is no bias and that you are objective in the way you present each choice

▶ give the individual time to consider

▶ check they understand each choice

▶ repeat if this is what they prefer or is what works for them.

Reflect

Think about your workplace and the individuals you support. Reflect on how choices are presented to them. Think about the different types of choices they are offered each day. Identify at least two individuals you support and answer the following questions:

1. Do you know how each individual likes to be presented with choices?

2. How much choice do they exercise in their day-to-day activities?

3. How are they supported to make informed choices?

Using your role and authority to support individuals' choices

Within your role you will have a responsibility not only to promote an individual's rights and choices but to support them to make choices.

To the individuals you work with, and their families or friends as well as other professionals, your role signifies that you have knowledge, understanding and skills as well as experience. Your role therefore brings with it a certain amount of authority and power to make things happen. There are, potentially, three types of power that can be exercised within your role.

These are:

▶ **legitimate power** – which results from your role

▶ **expert power** – which results from your knowledge and skills

▶ **referent power** – which results from your personality, worthiness and right to respect from others.

When used appropriately this authority and power will enable you to influence the reactions of others and compel them to listen to what you have to say. As a result you will be able to advocate for individuals you support and ensure their views and opinions are heard.

Supporting an individual to challenge decisions

There may be times when an individual is unhappy about decisions that have been made about them or for them. This may be when:

▶ others believe the individual is not capable of making complex decisions

▶ others do not agree with the individual's decision

▶ others use 'duty of care' and risk assessment to override individual choice

▶ others believe it is their right to make the decision on the individual's behalf – for example, a parent, carer

▶ others believe their decision is in the individual's best interests

▶ the individual's decision does not suit other people – i.e. they feel it creates more work for them

▶ it is the norm for others to make decisions without really involving the individual

▶ others have coerced the individual into making a decision that suits them and not the individual.

In situations where an individual's right to make their own choices and decisions has been infringed, they have a right to question or challenge these decisions.

Your assessment criteria:

5.2 Use own role and authority to support the individual's right to make choices.

5.4 Describe how to support an individual to question or challenge decisions concerning them that are made by others.

Ways of supporting a challenge

In situations where an individual wishes to question or challenge decisions concerning them that have been made by others, there are a number of ways that they can be supported. These include:

▶ helping the individual decide what they want to do, how they want to raise their concerns, and who they wish to involve

▶ supporting the individual to identify and think through their reasons for questioning or challenging the decision

▶ identifying how the individual's views were not considered

▶ identifying others who can support the individual's view

▶ arranging an informal meeting to raise the concerns

▶ using the complaints procedure if informal processes don't work

▶ involving an independent **advocate** if this is the best option.

Key terms

Advocate: a person responsible for expressing the views, wishes and feelings of an individual, and who will speak on their behalf if they are not able to do so

Investigate

Find out what your workplace policy and procedure is for individuals to question or challenge decisions made by others concerning them. Find out who is involved in this process. Find out if there are any independent advocacy services available in your area. Are there any specialist advocacy services? How can you contact them?

Case study

Florence is a 93 year-old woman with mobility problems due to arthritis. She also has poor circulation and deteriorating eyesight due to type 2 diabetes, and a heart condition. Over the past month she has had three falls, the last of these causing her to break her arm. Her family believe it is no longer safe for her to remain living in her own home and are very keen for her to move into residential care. Florence doesn't want to do this as it would mean losing her dog and cat and her independence. Florence feels her family are pressurising her to move because they are keen to sell her large house and profit from it. Florence feels she manages well with the support from the domiciliary care agency, with two visits a day to support her personal care needs. She has domestic support and meals delivered which she heats in her microwave. Following a visit from the rehabilitation officer for the visually impaired, Florence now has a number of aids and adaptations in place to help her manage the issues resulting from her failing eyesight. Her GP has reviewed her medication following her falls and changed some of her medication. This seems to have improved her steadiness and mobility. However, her GP has told Florence that he agrees with her family that perhaps it is time to consider residential care. Florence is very unhappy about this as it is not what she wants. Her family have already found a home for her to move into.

1. As a care worker how could you support Florence's choices?

2. What evidence could you use to support Florence's point of view and wishes?

3. Who else may be able to support Florence to challenge decisions being made about her?

Practical Assessment Task   5.1   5.2   5.4

Write a case study which provides evidence of your competence in using your role and authority to support individuals to make informed choices and to question or challenge choices made on their behalf by others. Keep your notes as evidence towards your assessment.

Managing risk to maintain the right to make choices

Risk assessments

Risk assessments are often viewed in a negative way, as a means to justify stopping an individual from doing something. Viewed in a positive way, however, they are about assessing risk to support choices and enabling an individual to do something.

Person-centred risk assessments:

▶ explore the risks to an individual in an area of their life

▶ help to manage the risk and enable the individual to carry out a task or activity

▶ positively enable safe independence for individuals to carry out tasks and activities

▶ looks at the possible risks and hazards for the individual

▶ minimise possible risks and hazards using guidelines and measures to enhance the skills and abilities of the individual.

The following people need to be involved:

▶ the individual

▶ other people within their circle of support

▶ anyone involved in the task or activity.

Attitudes to risk

Everyone has had past experiences of risk and this tends to influence our attitude towards it. Some people are risk takers and thrive on the challenge this presents. Other people are more conservative and like to 'play it safe' by weighing up every aspect of an action or activity before committing themselves to it.

If past experience has taught us that there is a great deal to be gained by taking a risk then we are more likely to view risk as something to welcome. If, however, taking a risk has resulted in negative experiences and memories then it is likely to be viewed as something to be wary of and avoided if at all possible.

Your assessment criteria:

5.3 Manage risk in a way that maintains the individual's right to make choices.

Investigate

Find out what the risk assessment policies and procedures are in your workplace. Find out how workers in your workplace are trained to carry out risk assessments. Look at a selection of completed risk assessments and evaluate them using the following criteria:

▶ How person-centred are they?

▶ Who was involved in the risk assessment?

▶ Was risk assessed to enable the individual to do something or to justify them not doing something?

▶ How often are risk assessments monitored and reviewed?

Making informed choices

Once a risk assessment has been undertaken it is essential that the identified risks are discussed and understood by all those involved. It is important to ensure that the individual is able to make an informed choice. Excluding the individual or anyone involved is likely to increase the risk as they have no investment in managing the risk to avoid harm or danger.

It is therefore essential that you remember that when involving the individual in the management of risk they will need:

▶ accessible information about the potential risks – i.e. information that is communicated in a way that meets their needs and preferences

▶ time and appropriate support to understand the implications of any potential risk

▶ the opportunity to ask questions, clarify and challenge the risk assessment

▶ a clearly reasoned argument for any decisions made

▶ the opportunity to suggest acceptable control measures

▶ the opportunity to take an informed risk.

If the individual wishes to challenge the risk assessment outcome they will also need:

▶ access to an independent advocate, if appropriate and requested

▶ the opportunity to have a second opinion, i.e. a repeated risk assessment.

In most cases, if the individual is involved in any risk assessment and the discussion regarding appropriate safeguards and control measures, these can generally be agreed. Often, once the risk is analysed and evaluated, this increased awareness reduces the risk and this, along with safeguards, enables activities to proceed.

In some cases, however, the best way to manage risk is to take things in incremental steps as this reduces the overall risk whilst maintaining an individual's choice.

On occasions, maintaining an individual's right to choose may not be possible: if the risk is considered to be too great – i.e. it may result in significant harm, injury, death or is illegal, or in some other way is in conflict with the 'duty of care'. At these times the individual's right to be protected from harm overrides their choice. In this case, you will need to undertake negotiations with all involved to determine if safer and acceptable alternatives can be found.

Reflect

Think about your own attitude towards risk and taking risks in your person life. Think about your attitude towards risk within your job role.

1. What has influenced your attitude towards risk?
2. How does that affect the way you assess risk in your personal life?
3. How does that affect the way you assess risk as part of your job role?

Practical Assessment Task
5.3

Write a reflective account of a real work example of how you managed risk in a way that maintained the individual's right to make choices. Keep your notes as evidence towards your assessment.

How are identity, self-image and self-esteem linked?

Our identity is more than our name and our picture in a passport. Identity is what makes us stand out in a crowd as an individual.

Self-image is how we view ourselves – our worth and value is more often bound up with our attractiveness to others and our intelligence. **Self-esteem** is about having confidence in who we are and our worth and value to others and to society.

Identity, self-image and self-esteem are therefore all closely linked, with one dependent on the other. If an individual has little sense of who they are as an individual then they are likely to struggle with a sense of low worth and value and this creates a negative self-image and low self-esteem Figure 7.5 shows aspects of identity.

Many people who grew up in large institutions struggle with their sense of identity, as all the time they lived there they were never treated as an individual – only as part of a group. They were never treated as if they had unique value or worth and so had low self-esteem and a poor self-image. This meant they found it difficult to express themselves or to exercise choice, even over simple everyday matters.

Our identity, self-image and self-esteem are influenced by the following factors:

- ▶ inherited characteristics
- ▶ family, upbringing, shared history – including how we were treated, or mistreated, as children
- ▶ primary care givers
- ▶ friends
- ▶ educational and life experiences
- ▶ culture, religion, nationality
- ▶ the media and images and representations of 'beauty', 'perfection' and what is 'ideal' (e.g. 'size 0' models)
- ▶ feedback we get from other people about who we are, our value and worth as individuals.

Many people who were abused as children grow up with a very poor self-image and low self-esteem; generally, any abuse involves an element of emotional abuse as the individual is repeatedly told they are worthless and a bad person, and that is why they are being abused. This poor self-image and low self-esteem makes it difficult for the individual to have a realistic idea of their own identity and this can lead to behaviours that are in many ways self-destructive. This can reinforce the negative views they already have about themselves.

Your assessment criteria:

6.1 Explain the links between identity, self-image and self-esteem.

6.2 Analyse the factors that contribute to the wellbeing of individuals.

Key terms

Self-esteem: having confidence in who we are and our sense of our value as a unique individual

Self-image: how we see ourselves, our opinion of our own worth, attractiveness, intelligence and so on.

Figure 7.5 Aspects of identity

(Personality · Our essential characteristics · Distinctive features · What makes us unique · Individuality · 'Identity – Who I am')

Which factors contribute to wellbeing?

Wellbeing is often described as a state of feeling that you are doing well and feeling good. These feelings create a 'wellness cycle' in which the individual does well because they are feeling good, and so on. Factors that influence wellbeing include the following:

▶ **practical aspects of life**

  ▶ education and skills

  ▶ employment

  ▶ income

  ▶ physical and mental health

  ▶ access to services and amenities

  ▶ quality of the living environment

▶ **personal and social relationships**

  ▶ intimate relationships, involving love and care

  ▶ support networks

  ▶ relationships with wider society

▶ **values and attitudes**

  ▶ ideas about self and personality

  ▶ hopes, fears and aspirations

  ▶ moral and/or spiritual codes of behaviour

  ▶ sense of purpose and meaning to life

  ▶ levels of satisfaction and dissatisfaction with life

  ▶ levels of trust and confidence in life and relationships.

Understanding who we are, our value and worth to ourselves, to people we respect and care about, and to society as a whole, are important aspects of our sense of wellbeing. The way that other people and the systems within society treat an individual will reinforce either their sense of worth and value or their sense of worthlessness. For example, discrimination and abuse damage self-esteem because they make the individual feel they are worth less than others. In the past, people with disabilities were excluded from education and employment. The result was a reduced ability to participate in society and a feeling of having less importance and worth because of that disadvantage.

The recognition, acceptance and promotion of the cultural and spiritual aspects of an individual are also important. For some, these will be central to their identity and every aspect of their life. For others, they may play a lesser role. It is important to find out what each means to the individual and not make assumptions.

Reflect

Think about yourself. How would you describe yourself to someone you didn't know? What do you consider to be your unique characteristics? What do you think your family or friends consider to be your unique characteristics? Are the similar or different from your view?

Attitudes that promote identity and wellbeing

If an individual feels worthless – i.e. has low self-esteem or a poor self-image – this will affect how they interact with others. A lack of self-worth and self-esteem will lower motivation and reduce the individual's ability to develop their potential and improve their sense of self and wellbeing: it is a vicious cycle. However, that vicious cycle can become a virtuous cycle if the attitudes and behaviour of the people around the individual are positive and nurturing, as shown in Figure 7.6.

Your assessment criteria:

6.3 Support an individual in a ways that promotes a sense of identity and self-esteem.

6.4 Demonstrate how to contribute to an environment that promotes wellbeing.

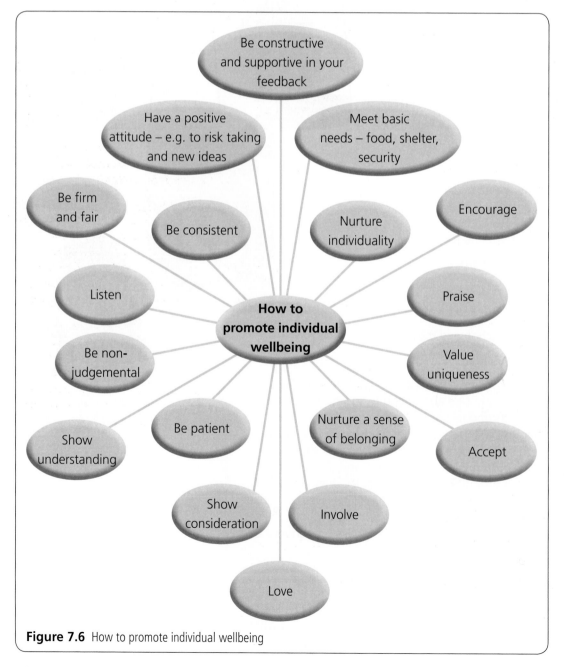

Figure 7.6 How to promote individual wellbeing

Creating an environment that promotes wellbeing

An individual's wellbeing will be promoted if they are surrounded by people with positive 'can do' attitudes. However, the physical living environment and the systems that operate within this are also important to promoting wellbeing.

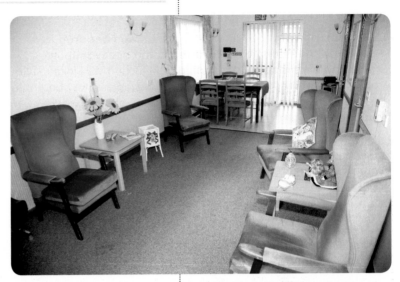

The physical environment can contribute to wellbeing by being:

▶ accessible

▶ welcoming

▶ well maintained

▶ comfortable

▶ light and airy

▶ appealing to the senses – e.g. colours, smells, textures, low noise levels

▶ designed to accommodate individuality

▶ temperature controlled

▶ safe and secure

▶ well equipped to meet individual needs

▶ equipped with areas that provide privacy and quiet as well as space for large groups.

Systems and structures within an environment can contribute to wellbeing by using:

▶ person-centred approaches to care or support

▶ risk assessments which focus on enabling activities

▶ creative and flexible approaches to meeting needs and enabling individuals

▶ user feedback and involvement to make decisions about how and what services are provided

▶ good evidence-based practice to develop services

▶ staff supervision and training to develop positive attitudes to care or support

▶ monitoring and review processes to make changes and improvements.

How can you improve an environment to promote individual wellbeing?

Investigate

Look around your workplace. Identify how the environment promotes individual's wellbeing. Find out what else could be done to improve the environment and promote wellbeing.

Now look at the systems and structures (i.e. how things are done) within your workplace. How do you think these promote individuals' wellbeing? How could they be improved?

Case study

Rachel is 25 years old and her background is one of poverty, abuse and domestic violence. She spent her early life in an out of children's homes and has a long history of drug and alcohol misuse.

As a result of a particularly violent assault and her drug use Rachel has some cognitive impairment and needs support managing her money and planning daily activities. Since leaving rehabilitation she has made good progress and is now beginning to feel more positive about her future. Rachel's key worker, Caro, has been working with her to build her self-esteem, confidence and resilience.

Rachel has expressed a wish to use her experience in a positive way to help others. Caro has been encouraging Rachel to look at youth work and has been supporting her to volunteer at a local youth centre.

As a result of her progress there they contacted a charitable foundation who have agreed to support Rachel to gain experience and qualifications in youth work.

1. How do you think Rachel's background may have affected her sense of identity, self-image and wellbeing?
2. How do you think Rachel's sense of identity and self-image may now have changed?
3. What factors may have influenced a change in her self-image and self-esteem?
4. How have the attitudes and behaviours of other people in Rachel's life made
   a) a negative impact?
   b) a positive impact?

Your assessment criteria:

6.3 Support an individual in a ways that promotes a sense of identity and self-esteem.

6.4 Demonstrate how to contribute to an environment that promotes wellbeing.

Reflect

Think about yourself.

▶ What do you consider to be the essential ingredients of your identity?

▶ What factors have been significant in forming your identity and sense of self?

▶ How do you think your self-image compares with how others see you?

Practical Assessment Task   6.1   6.2   6.3   6.4

Identity, self-image and self-esteem are closely linked and have a strong influence on an individual's wellbeing. As a health and social care practitioner you will need to show evidence of your knowledge, understanding and competence in promoting an individual's wellbeing. With reference to your own care practice, you need to demonstrate the ability to:

▶ Explain the links between identity, image and self-esteem

▶ Analyse factors that contribute to the wellbeing of individuals

▶ Support an individual in a way that promotes their sense of identity, self-image and self-esteem

▶ Demonstrate ways to contribute to an environment that promotes wellbeing.

The evidence that you produce for this assessment should be based on your care practice in the work place. Your assessor may also wish to observe and ask questions about this aspect of your practice.

Understand the role of risk assessment in enabling a person-centred approach

Risk assessment in health and social care

Risk is a part of everyday life which enables individuals to develop their skills, self-confidence and self-esteem. As we develop our self-confidence we also learn to manage risk by weighing up the options to help us reach a decision. Our experiences will influence our attitude to risk and what we consider to be acceptable and not acceptable.

In health and social care, risk assessment involves a judgement made by a practitioner about an individual. It represents a balance between the individual's and others' rights and responsibilities, and the duty of care.

Risk assessment and limitations

Many health and social care organisations are risk averse, fearing litigation and public scorn if things go wrong. As a consequence, risk assessment is cautious and defensive in nature, meaning that risk is avoided as far as possible.

In many organisations this approach is reinforced by a 'blame culture' in which, if risks are taken, there is no shared responsibility within the organisation's management so that practitioners bear sole responsibility for any adverse consequences. This results in risk assessments being a tool to stop an individual doing something or to provide the proof that a decision is unsafe. They were almost exclusively carried out by practitioners with little or no involvement of the individual or others who may be affected.

For the individual this reduces their opportunities for developing and achieving their potential, limits their life experience and increases their dependence on others.

As so few 'risks' are taken there is little or no opportunity for the organisation, practitioners or individuals to gain confidence in managing risk. This lack of experience and confidence further compounds the aversion to risk.

Risk assessment and enabling potential

More recent person-centred approaches are about enabling the individual to achieve their potential through exercising choices and developing independence. If this is to be achieved then risk must be a part of the care or support provided. Sharing responsibility for assessing and managing risk is an essential part of this approach and one which is changing attitudes towards risk.

In a person-centred approach an element of risk is inevitable, as individuals have their own:

▶ views and opinions

▶ attitude to risk

▶ likes, dislikes and choices

▶ wishes and aspirations.

If individuals are to be fully involved in decision-making regarding their care or support, they are likely to want to try new things to realise their potential and achieve their wishes and aspirations. They must be supported to do this even if it involves an element of risk. Part of any planning process will involve risk assessment, which should aim to avoid overstating risk whilst maintaining the safety of the individual.

Investigate

Find out about risk assessment in your workplace. What do the policies and procedures tell you about attitudes towards risk? Who is involved in assessing risk? How are workers and others trained to undertake risk assessments? How do the risk assessments used in your workplace promote individuals' rights and responsibilities? How could they be improved?

Rights and responsibilities in risk-taking and risk assessment

Often the emphasis when considering risk-taking and risk assessment is on maintaining individual rights. However, it is important to recognise that the exercise of individual rights must be accompanied by the individual taking responsibility for the outcomes of their decisions.

Workers must therefore ensure that individuals have the capacity to fully understand the potential consequences of taking a risk so that their choice is an informed one.

Taking a consistent approach

As attitudes to risk vary it is important that organisations establish a consistent approach to risk-taking and risk assessment. It is important that:

▶ everyone involved receives appropriate training in undertaking risk assessments

▶ everyone involved uses risk assessment tools fairly and consistently

▶ individuals are fully involved in risk assessment, as is their right

▶ risk assessments are reviewed by a more senior practitioner to ensure they are:

  ▶ carried out according to policies and procedures

  ▶ objective

  ▶ consistent in their recommendations

▶ there is an accessible mechanism for challenging the outcome of risk assessments

▶ individuals are given support, as necessary, to make informed decisions regarding risk-taking.

Individual choice and disclaimers

Sometimes an individual may decide to take a risk against recommendations. If they have the capacity to make that informed decision then an organisation may ask them to sign a disclaimer, so that the individual takes full responsibility for that decision and releases the organisation of their duty of care in that circumstance.

Your assessment criteria:

7.1 Compare different uses of risk assessment in health and social care.

7.2 Explain how risk taking and risk assessment relate to rights and responsibilities.

7.3 Explain why risk assessments need to be regularly reviewed.

Reviewing risk assessments

It is essential that risk assessments are reviewed regularly and as an individual's needs and abilities change. A risk assessment may initially have been carried out to enable an individual to undertake activities which will develop their skills and confidence. As their skills and confidence grow the risk assessment will need to be reviewed. Failure to do this will undo all the progress that has been made as well as infringing the individual's rights.

Alternatively, a risk assessment may have been carried out when individuals' abilities were greater; as their health deteriorates there may be an expectation that they can do more than is safe for them to do. This could result in harm and a failure in the duty of care.

Case study

Steve is 28 years old and has a learning disability. He lives at home with his parents. He works two days a week at a local factory and attends a day centre on the other three days. At his last review and care plan meeting Steve expressed a wish to live independently; this is supported by his parents who are getting older and are concerned about Steve's future. Jack is Steve's support worker and they have been working on a number of areas to develop Steve's independent living skills. Currently Steve has a taxi to take him to and from work and the day centre. Jack has been working with Steve to develop his road awareness and skill at managing travel on buses. Steve has now told his parents that he wants to use the bus on his own. His parents have stopped him as they say the risk is too great and that he will get lost. Steve is very unhappy about this and asks Jack to help him sort it out.

1. What are Steve's rights and responsibilities in this situation?

2. What can Jack do to support Steve?

Knowledge Assessment Task   7.1   7.2   7.3

Your manager has asked you to write a fact sheet for individuals and their families to explain how risk assessment is used in a person-centred approach. He has asked that you use real work examples in your explanation and that you include the following:

▶ a comparison between the different uses of risk assessment in health and social care

▶ an explanation of how risk-taking and risk assessment relate to rights and responsibilities

▶ an explanation of why risk assessments need to be regularly revised.

Keep your notes as evidence towards your assessment.

Reflect

Think about your own attitudes toward risk.

▶ Are you a caution person or a risk taker?

▶ What factors have influenced your attitude towards risk?

▶ Has your attitude towards risk changed as you become older?

▶ How does your attitude to risk impact on your daily life and choices?

Are you ready for assessment?

AC	What do you know now?	Assessment task	✓
1.1	How and why person-centred values must influence all aspects of health and social care work	Page 168	
1.2	How to evaluate the use of care plans in applying person-centred values	Page 168	
7.1	How to compare the different uses of risk assessment in health and social care	Page 203	
7.2	How risk taking and risk assessment relate to rights and responsibilities	Page 203	
7.3	Why risk assessments need to be revised regularly	Page 203	

AC	What can you do now?	Assessment task	✓
2.1	Work with an individual and others to find out an individual's history, preferences, needs and wishes	Page 173	
2.2	Demonstrate ways to put person-centred values into practice in complex or sensitive situations	Page 173	
2.3	Adapt your actions and approaches in response to an individual's changing needs and preferences	Page 175	
3.1	How to analyse the factors that influence the capacity of an individual to express consent	Page 179	
3.2	Establish consent for an activity or action	Page 179	
3.3	How to explain what steps to take if consent cannot be readily established	Page 181	
4.1	How to describe the different ways of applying active participation to meet individual needs	Page 187	
4.2	Work with an individual and others to agree how active participation can be implemented	Page 187	

AC	What can you do now?	Assessment task	✓
4.3	Demonstrate how active participation can address the holistic needs of an individual	Page 187	
4.4	Demonstrate ways to promote the understanding and use of active support	Page 187	
5.1	Support an individual to make informed choices	Page 191	
5.2	Use your own role and authority to support the individual's right to make choices	Page 191	
5.3	Demonstrate how to manage risk in a way that maintains the individual's right to make choices	Page 193	
5.4	How to support an individual to question or challenge decisions concerning them that are made by others	Page 191	
6.1	How to explain the link between identity, self-image and self-esteem	Page 199	
6.2	How to analyse the factors that contribute to the wellbeing of individuals	Page 199	
6.3	Support an individual in a way that promotes a sense of identity and self-esteem	Page 199	
6.4	Demonstreate how to contribute to an environment that promotes wellbeing	Page 199	

8 | Promote and implement health and safety in health and social care (HSC 037)

Assessment of this unit

This unit introduces you to the knowledge and skills that health and social care practitioners need to work safely and to manage the security of themselves and others in care settings. In this wide-ranging unit, you will learn about health and safety legislation, risk assessment, ways of responding to accidents and incidents and demonstrate your moving and handling ability, use of security measures and infection control procedures. You will need to:

1. Understand your own responsibilities, and the responsibilities of others, relating to health and safety.

2. Be able to carry out own responsibilities for health and safety.

3. Understand procedures for responding to accidents and sudden illness.

4. Be able to reduce the spread of infection.

5. Be able to move and handle equipment and other objects safely.

6. Be able to handle hazardous substances and materials.

7. Be able to promote fire safety in the work setting.

8. Be able to implement security measures in the work setting.

9. Know how to manage stress.

The assessment of this unit is partly knowledge-based (things you need to know about) and partly competence-based (things you need to do in the real work environment). To complete this unit successfully, you will need to produce evidence of both your knowledge and your competence. The tables opposite outline what you need to know and do to meet each of the assessment criteria for the unit. Your tutor or assessor will help you to prepare for your assessment and the tasks suggested in the chapter will help you to create the evidence that you need.

AC	What you need to know
1.1	Identify legislation relating to general health and safety in a health or social care work setting
1.2	Explain the main points of health and safety policies and procedures agreed with the employer
1.3	Analyse the main health and safety responsibilities of: • self • the employer or manager • others in the work setting
1.4	Identify specific tasks relating to health and safety that should not be carried out without special training
3.1	Describe different types of accidents and sudden illness that may occur in own work setting
3.2	Explain procedures to be followed if an accident or sudden illness should occur
9.1	Describe common signs and indicators of stress
9.2	Describe signs that indicate own stress
9.3	Analyse factors that tend to trigger own stress
9.4	Compare strategies for managing stress

CHAPTER 8

AC What you need to know

2.1	Use policies and procedures or other agreed ways of working that relate to health and safety
2.2	Support others to understand and follow safe practices
2.3	Monitor and report potential health and safety risks
2.4	Use risk assessment in relation to health and safety
2.5	Demonstrate ways to minimise potential risks and hazards
2.6	Access additional support or information relating to health and safety
4.1	Explain own role in supporting others to follow practices that reduce the spread of infection
4.2	Demonstrate the recommended method for hand washing
4.3	Demonstrate ways to ensure that own health and hygiene do not pose a risk to an individual or to others at work
5.1	Explain the main points of legislation that relates to moving and handling
5.2	Explain principles for safe moving and handling
5.3	Move and handle equipment and other objects safely
6.1	Describe types of hazardous substances that may be found in the work setting
6.2	Demonstrate safe practices for: • storing hazardous substances • using hazardous substances • disposing of hazardous substances and materials
7.1	Describe practices that prevent fires from: • starting • spreading
7.2	Demonstrate measures that prevent fires from starting
7.3	Explain emergency procedures to be followed in the event of a fire in the work setting
7.4	Ensure that clear evacuation routes are maintained at all times
8.1	Demonstrate the use of agreed procedures for checking the identity of anyone requesting access to: • premises • information
8.2	Demonstrate use of measures to protect own security and the security of others in the work setting
8.3	Explain the importance of ensuring that others are aware of own whereabouts

Assessment criteria 2.1 – 2.6, 4.1 – 4.3, 5.1 – 5.3, 6.1, 6.2, 7.1 – 7.4, and 8.1 – 8.3 must be assessed in a real work environment.

This unit is designed to develop your working practice, which is relevant to every chapter of this book, but has particular links to other mandatory units:

SHC 34	Principles for implementing duty of care in health and social care settings
IC 01	The principles of infection prevention and control
DEM 304	Enable rights and choices of individuals with dementia whilst minimising risks

Some of your learning will be repeated in these units and will give you the chance to review your knowledge and understanding.

Understand health and safety legislation in care settings

The health and safety responsibilities of employers and employees in health and social care settings result from the wide range of **legislation** that governs health and safety in all workplaces, and other laws which are specific to care settings. Legislation is necessary to ensure that safe working practices are followed when caring for people, and to protect the health and safety of both service users and care workers.

The Health and Safety Commission and Executive

The **Health and Safety Executive** is the body that monitors standards and enforces health and safety law in the workplace in England, Wales and Scotland. The Health and Safety Executive Northern Ireland has this responsibility in Northern Ireland. The Health and Safety Executive was created by the Health and Safety at Work Act 1974. One of its key tasks is to investigate all accidents in the workplace. The website of the Health and Safety Executive (**www.hse.gov.uk**) states that: 'Our mission is to prevent death, injury and ill-health in Great Britain's workplaces'. The Health and Safety Executive can:

▶ enter premises to conduct investigations or carry out spot checks on health and safety

▶ conduct investigations into accidents and safety **compliance**

▶ take samples and photographs to assess health and safety risks

▶ ask questions about health and safety procedures and risk control

▶ give advice on how to minimise risk

▶ issue instructions that must, by law, be carried out

▶ issue improvement and **prohibition** notices.

The Health and Safety Executive is most likely to visit care settings where there is evidence that health and safety is poor, there are hazardous substances that should be properly stored and controlled or a specific incident (accident, death or illness, for example) has occurred.

The purpose of Health and Safety Executive visits and investigations is to check that standards of workplace health, safety and welfare are satisfactory and to give advice on how risks to people being injured or becoming ill in the workplace can be minimised.

Your assessment criteria:

1.1 Identify legislation relating to general health and safety in a health or social care work setting.

1.2 Explain the main points of the health and safety policies and procedures agreed with the employer.

Key terms

Compliance: doing what others want

Health and Safety Executive: the government agency responsible for monitoring and enforcing health and safety laws in the workplace

Legislation: written laws, usually Acts of Parliament

Prohibition: prevention; stopping something from happening

The Health and Safety at Work Act 1974

The Health and Safety at Work Act 1974 is the main piece of health and safety law in the UK. It affects both employers and employees. Under this **statute**, care practitioners share responsibility for health and safety in care settings with the care organisation that employs them. The care organisation is responsible for providing:

▶ a safe and secure work environment

▶ safe equipment

▶ information and training about health, safety and security.

In short, care organisations must provide a work environment that meets expected health and safety standards. They must make it possible for health and social care practitioners to work safely. Health and social care practitioners in turn have a responsibility to:

▶ work safely within the care setting

▶ monitor their work environment for health and safety problems that may develop

▶ report and respond appropriately to any health and safety risks.

To meet their legal responsibilities the organisations must:

▶ carry out health and safety risk assessments

▶ develop health and safety **procedures**, such as fire evacuation procedures

▶ provide health and safety equipment, such as fire extinguishers, fire blankets and first aid boxes

▶ ensure that health and social care settings have appropriate safety systems, such as smoke alarms, fire exits and security fixtures (electronic pads on doors and window guards, for example)

▶ train their employees to follow health and safety **policies** and procedures, and to use health and safety equipment and safety features appropriately

▶ provide a range of health and safety information and warning signs to alert people to safety features such as fire exits and first aid equipment, and to warn them about prohibited areas and activities (no smoking, for example).

Health and safety regulations

The Health and Safety at Work Act 1974 enforces minimum standards of workplace health and safety and establishes a framework for safe working. In practice, a range of regulations that apply to care settings also extend and supplement this Act as outlined in Figure 8.1.

Figure 8.1 Health and safety regulations

Regulations	Effects on practice
Management of Health and Safety at Work Regulations 1999	This places a responsibility on employers to train staff in relation to health and safety legislation, fire prevention, and moving and handling issues. Employers must also carry out risk assessments, remove or reduce any health and safety hazards that are identified, and write safe working procedures based on their risk assessments.
The Manual Handling Operations Regulations 1992 (amended 2002)	These regulations cover all manual handling activities, such as lifting, lowering, pushing, pulling or carrying objects or people. A large proportion of workplace injuries are due to poor manual handling skills. Employers have a duty to assess the risks surrounding any activity that involves manual handling. They must put in place measures to reduce or avoid the risk. Employees must follow manual handling procedures and cooperate on all manual handling issues.
Health and Safety (First Aid) Regulations 1981	These cover requirements for the provision of first aid in the workplace.
Reporting of Injuries, Diseases and Dangerous Occurrences Regulations (RIDDOR) 1995	These regulations require employers to notify the Health and Safety Executive, or other relevant authorities, of a range of occupational injuries, diseases and dangerous events.
Control of Substances Hazardous to Health Regulations (COSHH) 2002	These regulations require employers to assess the risks from hazardous substances and take appropriate precautions to ensure that hazardous substances are correctly stored and used.

Your assessment criteria:

1.1 Identify legislation relating to general health and safety in a health or social care work setting.

1.2 Explain the main points of the health and safety policies and procedures agreed with the employer.

Key terms

Regulations: legal rules that are created using the authority of a statute

Care Quality Commission: the independent organisation that inspects and regulates all health and social care services in England

Discuss

How do these health and safety laws affect the way people practice in your work or placement setting? Talk to your fellow workers and colleagues; discuss the different ways in which legislation affects the way care is provided in your workplace.

Investigate

Go to the website of the Care Quality Commission (**www.cqc. org.uk**) and find a report on a health or social care organisation near to where you live. Alternatively look at a report on the organisation you work for. What does the report say about standards of health and safety in the organisation?

Health and safety policies and procedures

A health or social care organisation's policies and procedures should always incorporate the key points of health and safety law. This means that a care practitioner will be able to put health and safety laws into practice simply by following their employer's policies and procedures. Health and social care organisations need to develop a range of policies to ensure all aspects of the legal framework of care are covered. These will include policies on:

▶ health and safety

▶ dealing with, and reporting of, accidents, injuries and emergency situations, e.g. specific action to take, reporting procedures, and completing relevant documentation

▶ dealing with first aid situations, e.g. understanding specific hygiene procedures, dealing with blood and other body fluids, administering basic first aid (if trained to do so), reporting procedures and completing relevant documentation

▶ moving and handling procedures

▶ use of equipment, e.g. use of mechanical or electrical equipment, such as mechanical hoists

▶ healthcare procedures, e.g. administering personal care, procedures for individuals with specialised needs

▶ food safety procedures, e.g. food handling and preparation, and understanding of food hygiene regulations

▶ infection control policies, and dealing with hazardous substances, e.g. situations requiring strict infection control, use of protective clothing such as gowns, masks and gloves, procedures for disposing of clinical waste

▶ policies relating to security and personal safety, e.g. policies for personal security, and policies for **safeguarding** vulnerable individuals.

Using policies and procedures in practice

The way health and safety-related policies and procedures are used should be monitored to check that employees are actually using them appropriately in practice. Employees are under a contractual obligation to implement their employers' policies and procedures and may face disciplinary action and possible dismissal for not doing so. You should know, and be able to explain, what is said in the health and safety related policies and procedures used in your work setting, and how they affect your work role.

Health and safety responsibilities

Health and safety law makes every health and social care practitioner responsible for working in ways that protect their own and other people's health, safety and security.

Your responsibilities

A key aspect of your responsibility is recognising the limits to your own competence and ensuring that you always work within these limits. This is part of taking responsibility for your own health and safety.

Another aspect is that you must understand and apply relevant legislation and agreed ways of working in your workplace setting. You must undertake, and update, all of the health and safety training relevant to your work role and cooperate fully with others on health and safety issues. Where personal protective clothing or specialist equipment is provided to carry out care-related tasks, you should ensure that you know how to use this properly. Also, of course, you must make sure that you use any such equipment that is provided.

Responsibilities of employers

Your employer also has responsibilities to support health and safety in the workplace. Employers have a responsibility to:

▶ provide information, e.g. about risks to health and safety that might result from working practices, changes that may harm or affect health and safety, what is done to protect health and safety, how to get first aid treatment, and what to do in an emergency

▶ provide training so that employees can do their job safely

▶ provide protection, e.g. special clothing, gloves or masks

▶ provide employees with health checks, e.g. vision testing.

Responsibilities of others

There are others who also have a responsibility for health and safety. This includes team members, other colleagues, families and carers. These people have a responsibility to be aware of health and safety issues in relation to observation, practice, reporting and recording procedures.

You need to understand the advantages and disadvantages of others taking responsibility for health and safety issues. For instance, an advantage is that it widens the number of people who have health and safety responsibilities that could help potential problems to be identified and dealt with. A disadvantage might be that it is harder to manage health and safety when a number of different people are involved.

212

Specific tasks that need health and safety training

You should ensure that you receive specific training and health and safety guidance if your work role involves any of the following:

- ▶ using specialist equipment
- ▶ providing first aid and administering medication
- ▶ carrying out health care procedures (such as bandaging, changing catheters)
- ▶ preparing or handling food.

You must always let a senior member of staff know when you do not have the knowledge, skills or experience for a particular task.

Key terms

RIDDOR: Reporting of Injuries, Diseases and Dangerous Occurrences Regulations (RIDDOR) 1995

COSHH: the independent organisation that inspects and regulates all health and social care services in England (COSHH) 2002

Case study

Johanna has recently started work as a care assistant at the Spring Meadow care centre. As a new employee she received a pack of information including leaflets about the health and safety legislation that applies to care settings such as the Spring Meadow care centre. Johanna found the information complicated and hard to understand. Tony, the centre manager, has told Johanna that he will be asking her to explain:

1. what her health and safety responsibilities are, as an employee
2. what health and safety responsibilities she thinks the Spring Meadow care centre has, as her employer
3. how RIDDOR and COSHH might apply to the care setting.

How would you respond to each of these questions if you were in Johanna's position?

Knowledge Assessment Task   1.1   1.2   1.3   1.4

Health and social care practitioners need to understand their own responsibilities, and the responsibilities of others, relating to health and safety in their work setting. Summarise your understanding of health and safety by carrying out the following tasks:

1. Identify examples of legislation relating to general health and safety in your work setting.
2. Describe the main points of the health and safety policies and procedures that are used in your work setting.
3. Outline the health and safety responsibilities that apply to yourself, your employer and others in the work setting.
4. Identify tasks relating to health and safety that should not be carried out without special training.

Keep the work you produce for this activity as evidence towards your assessment.

Using health and safety policies and procedures

All employees in health and social care settings have a responsibility for health and safety. This includes working safely yourself, as well as making sure that others are also working safely around you. It also involves making sure that the environment is safe and free from hazards.

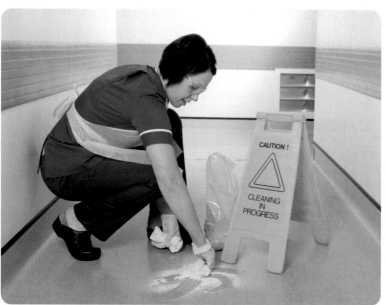

Your own working practice

One important aspect of safe working is having an understanding of how specific policies and procedures or agreed ways of working apply to your own practice. This means applying your knowledge of your workplace's policies and procedures to the way you carry out your own job. You are putting the policies and procedures into practice.

Your own health and safety responsibilities

Another aspect of working safely is to understand your own responsibilities in relation to different aspects of health and safety in the workplace. There are a variety of work situations where you will need to be aware of your responsibilities for health and safety. Examples of these situations include dealing with accidents, injuries and emergency situations; specific working conditions and the working environment; procedures relating to personal care, to security and to personal safety. In all of these situations you will need to know how to work safely and in line with the policies and procedures of your workplace.

Your assessment criteria:

2.1 Use policies and procedures or other agreed ways of working that relate to health and safety.

2.2 Support others to understand and follow safe practices.

Reflect

Working in health and social care puts you in a position of responsibility for the health and safety of clients and colleagues. Think about your own workplace and your role within it. How do health and safety concerns affect how you carry our your work?

Observing the environment for health and safety

You also have a responsibility to keep an eye out for health and safety risks around you as you carry out your work. This means that you need to observe the environment and assess whether a particular situation presents a risk to health and safety. Alongside this responsibility is the need to be aware of the procedures for reporting and recording any risks or hazards that you discover.

Good communication and keeping up to date

Good communication is important in maintaining a safe working environment. You need to share information about safe practices and procedures with your colleagues and fellow workers. It is also important to keep up to date with the latest recommendations and policies on safe working. You should attend any relevant training that is available to help you, and keep records of training and staff development sessions that you have attended.

Supporting others to understand and follow safe practices

As well as being aware of your own work practices, you need to be aware of the practices of others around you in the work environment. Even though you may be working safely you may notice that yourself, or other people, are being put at risk if your colleagues are not following safe working practices. You need to support others to understand and follow safe working practices, perhaps by bringing it to the attention of colleagues and offering advice where appropriate.

Discuss

Part of your responsibility for health and safety is to look out for ways that others may not be working safely. Discuss with your fellow workers how you could mention problems to colleagues without offending or upsetting them

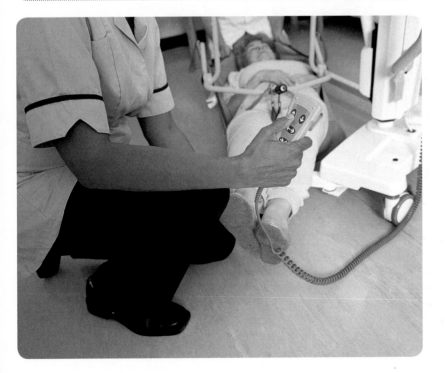

Monitoring and reporting on potential health and safety risks

Your assessment criteria:

2.3 Monitor and report potential health and safety risks.

It is part of your responsibility as a worker in health and social care to be aware at all times of situations where risks may be present. For instance, when you need to use equipment and machinery you should check that it is safe to be used and assess it for risks. You must report any problems you find to an appropriate responsible person in the organisation, and make sure that you never use unsafe or faulty equipment.

Keeping up to date with policies and procedures

It is also important to keep an eye on the policies, procedures and agreed ways of working that are used in your workplace. These should not be regarded as permanent. Policies and procedures need to be regularly reviewed and updated, with improvements implemented when they are found to be necessary.

Reporting issues and changes

Reporting any issues that you become aware of is an important aspect of your responsibility for health and safety as an employee. You must report any risks you identify immediately. Delay could lead to someone being harmed or injured. You should also report any changes that you notice, such as changes to working conditions or to the work environment. Such changes could have an impact upon the effectiveness of current safe working practices.

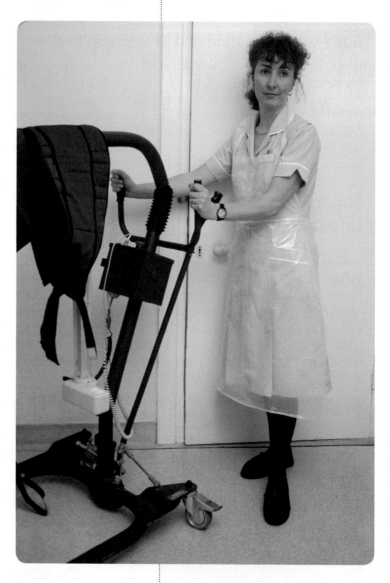

Using reporting procedures and records

It is important that you know how to go about reporting any health and safety problems that you have discovered. Make sure that you have found out the lines of communication you should follow when reporting any risks. What are the verbal reporting procedures in your workplace? Who do you speak to when you come across a situation that you think could potentially lead to a health and safety risk?

As well as verbal reporting it is important that written records are kept. Health and social care organisations generally have accident and incident books or forms that must be completed as part of the reporting procedure. You should know where these can be found and what kinds of information they require you to provide. Your employer has a legal obligation to report certain types of accident or incident to the Health and Safety Executive or the local authority environmental health department.

Written records need to be clear and accurate. They should include details of dates and times when risks are reported, and a simple description of the risks identified and the action taken. Recording systems may be paper based, or electronic using IT facilities.

Reporting of Injuries, Diseases and Dangerous Occurrences Regulations (RIDDOR) (1995, amended 2008)

These regulations require your employer to report all deaths, accidents, dangerous incidents or outbreaks of infectious diseases to the Health and Safety Executive's Incident Contact Centre. The Centre will then pass this information to the local authority or the Health and Safety Executive for an investigation to be carried out. This may result in further risk assessments being carried out or the existing risk assessments and procedures being modified.

Investigate

Your workplace should have procedures in place for recording and reporting accidents and incidents that have occurred. There may be an accident or incident book, or there may be forms for this purpose. Find out about the procedures in your workplace for reporting and recording accidents and incidents. Why do you think it is important for you to follow these procedures?

How do you use risk assessment for health and safety?

By law, health and social care organisations are required to carry out formal risk assessments of their workplaces and outside areas that employees or service users may use. **Risk assessment** aims to identify potential **risks** to the health, safety and security of service users, health and social care practitioners and anybody else who uses the care setting. The aim is to minimise risk by identifying **hazards** and putting measures in place to protect people from harm.

You have an important role to play in contributing to and using risk assessments appropriately. You will need to understand and use risk assessments in order to:

▶ protect yourself and others from danger or harm in the work setting

▶ ensure you are working within the law

▶ identify what could cause harm

▶ take precautions to prevent harm

▶ minimise accidents, injuries and ill health

▶ reduce the risk of individuals being injured at work.

Your assessment criteria:

2.4 Use risk assessment in relation to health and safety.

Key terms

Hazard: anything that can cause harm

Risk: the chance of harm being done by a hazard

Risk assessment: the process of evaluating the likelihood of a hazard actually causing harm

The risk assessment processes

Risk assessment recognises that health and social care provision, equipment and the care setting itself can all be hazardous. However, steps can be taken to remove or minimise the level of risk to people. All of the activities that take place within your workplace must be risk-assessed. Similarly, all of the equipment and facilities have to be checked for hazards. The ultimate aim of a risk assessment is to ensure that people can use care settings without coming to any harm. The Health and Safety Executive has identified five stages of a risk assessment process. These stages and their purpose are identified in Figure 8.2.

The risk assessment process is a continuous one. Hazard identification and risk reduction are an ongoing process because circumstances, people's behaviour and care practices change on a regular basis in health and social care settings.

Figure 8.2 The five stages of risk assessment

Stage	Key questions	Purpose
1. Identify the hazards, and differentiate between a hazard and a risk	What are the hazards? What risks could they lead to?	• to identify all hazards that could cause a risk
2. Deciding who might be harmed and how	Who is at risk?	• to decide who the risk applies to and what harm it could result in
3. Evaluating the risk and deciding on precautions to minimise it	What level of danger does the risk present? Who needs to do what to minimise it?	• to evaluate how dangerous the risk is, and identify risk control measures and responsibilities for reducing or removing the risk
4. Recording findings and implementing them	Are the risk control measures being implemented?	• to implement the risk control measures
5. Review of the risk assessment and updating of risk control measures if necessary	Is the risk controlled? Can the risk be reduced still further?	• to evaluate the effectiveness of current risk control strategies • to identify new risks or changes to risk levels • to consider new strategies for controlling risk

How can you minimise potential risks and hazards?

The Management of Health and Safety at Work Regulations (1999) place a legal duty on employers to carry out risk assessments in order to minimise risk and ensure a safe and healthy workplace. The risk assessments that are produced should identify clearly:

▶ the potential hazards and risks to the health and safety of employees and others in the workplace

▶ any preventive and protective measures that are needed to minimise risk and improve health and safety.

Carrying out risk assessments

Many larger organisations employ people as health and safety officers to carry out their risk assessments and manage health and safety issues generally. In smaller organisations this might be the responsibility of one or more of the managers, or of a senior practitioner. Risk assessments must be:

▶ communicated to all health or social care practitioners and users of the setting

▶ implemented through the way practitioners work

▶ monitored and reviewed on a regular basis

▶ linked to health and safety policies and to staff training.

Your assessment criteria:

2.5 Demonstrate ways to minimise potential risks and hazards

2.6 Access additional support or information relating to health and safety

Reflect

Have you seen any of the written risk assessments that are used in your work setting? Do you know who carried out or produced these risk assessments? How might you contribute to the risk assessment process in your work setting?

Accessing additional health and safety support and information

Information about health and safety should be provided in the health and safety policies and procedures relating to your workplace. You should be able to obtain additional information relating to specific health and safety issues from:

▶ the manager of your workplace

▶ your supervisor or mentor

▶ the health and safety representative for your workplace

▶ your tutor or assessor

▶ specialist websites such as the Health and Safety Executive (**www.hse.gov.uk**).

Health and safety training

Health and safety issues are a priority in all health and social care settings. You should receive basic health and safety training when you first begin your work role. You should also have opportunities to learn more and to update your knowledge and skills on a regular basis through workplace or external training opportunities.

Practical Assessment Task | **2.1** | **2.2** | **2.3** | **2.4** | **2.5** | **2.6**

Professional care practitioners prioritise health and safety issues and risk assessment processes in order to safeguard themselves and service users whilst providing effective care. In this task you will produce a short report that explains:

1. why it is important to assess health and safety hazards posed by the work setting or by particular activities

2. how and when to report potential health and safety risks that have been identified

3. how to access additional support or information relating to health and safety.

You should keep a copy of the report that you produce for this task as evidence for your assessment.

Types of accidents and sudden illness

Health and social care practitioners need to know how to react when an accident or sudden illness occurs in the care setting. Accidents can happen unexpectedly in all health and social care settings and adults can suddenly become unwell for a variety of reasons. In either of these situations, a person may need medical help. Part of your work role is to monitor individuals in the setting for signs of illness or injury, and to respond appropriately by getting help when necessary. The types of accidents and illnesses that you need to be prepared for are described in Figure 8.3.

Your assessment criteria:

3.1 Describe different types of accidents and sudden illness that may occur in own work setting.

Figure 8.3 Causes and possible effects of different types of accident

Type of accident	Causes and possible effects
Slips and trips	Wet floors, loose carpets or rugs, ill fitting shoes or slippers. The effects can include fractures (hips, collar bones, arms, ankles) sprains and bruising.
Falls	Tripping over objects, standing suddenly and experiencing a drop in blood pressure, loss of strength or stamina. The effects can include fractures, sprains and head injuries.
Needle stick injuries	Failing to dispose of a used needle safely – don't try to re-sheath it! This can lead to the transfer of infection from one person to another.
Burns and scalds	Excessively hot baths, hot water bottles or wash basins of water, spilled hot drinks, pans that fall or are pulled from a stove, sitting too close to a heat source (e.g. open fire or very hot radiator). Severe skin damage can result.
Injuries from operating machinery or specialised equipment	Lack of guards on equipment, poorly maintained or malfunctioning equipment or incorrect use/technique may result in injury. The nature of the injury will depend on the type of equipment but could include electrocution, fracture or lacerations.
Electrocution	Poorly wired electrical equipment, contact between electrical equipment and water and overloaded sockets can lead to electrocution. The effects include burns, altered heart rate/heart attack and death.
Accidental poisoning	This can result from ingestion of chemicals or other toxic fluids or overdose of medication, for example. Retching and vomiting, loss of consciousness and organ failure leading to death can result.
Sudden illness	For example: heart attack, diabetic coma or epileptic convulsion. These occurrences are the result of underlying medical conditions that an individual may have.

Identifying signs and symptoms of sudden illness

The **signs** of sudden illness are those things that you can see, such as a visible change in a person's normal appearance and behaviour – becoming pale in colour or not having the energy to respond in their usual way. People often know when they are unwell and will tell you about **symptoms** that they feel, such as feeling sick or having a headache. Figure 8.4 outlines the signs and symptoms of sudden illness. Observing and talking to people in the care setting should enable you to identify when they are unwell or have an injury.

Figure 8.4 Signs and symptoms of sudden illness

Type of sudden illness	Signs and symptoms
Heart attack	Chest pain: the chest can feel like it is being pressed or squeezed by a heavy object, and the pain can radiate from the chest to the jaw, neck, arms and back; shortness of breath; overwhelming feeling of anxiety
Diabetic coma	Increased thirst, the need to urinate frequently and tiredness; can be followed by a sleep-like state in which the person slips into a coma. They will be unresponsive and must be treated in hospital quickly.
Epileptic convulsion (seizure)	A tonic-clonic seizure has two stages: • stiffness in the person's body • twitching of the person's arms and legs. The person loses consciousness and some people will wet themselves. The seizure normally lasts between one and three minutes but they can last longer.

Key terms

Signs: visible indications that someone is unwell that are seen in their appearance or behaviour

Symptoms: physical changes indicating that a person is unwell. This could include something the person reports, such as nausea or a headache, or something measured, such as increased body temperature

Reflect

Can you think of any recent situations in which you noticed a person exhibiting the signs or symptoms of illness or injury? What was it you noticed and what were the causes of these signs or symptoms?

Procedures when accident or sudden illness occurs

Your assessment criteria:

3.2 Explain procedures to be followed if an accident or sudden illness should occur.

All health and social care settings have to be prepared for emergency situations and must have appropriate procedures in place so that staff can respond and people can be kept safe. You should know about and understand these and should take part in any accident or emergency response training that is provided by your employer.

It is important to follow the correct procedure as soon as you realise that an accident or incident has occurred or that a person has suddenly become unwell. In general this will require you to:

▶ remain calm

▶ raise the alarm or call for help

▶ assess the situation and prioritise the safety of yourself and others

▶ clear the area of people, furniture and, wherever possible, equipment

▶ assess the individuals affected by the accident, incident or by sudden illness for injuries and other symptoms of ill health

▶ administer first aid; but only if you are trained to do so

▶ stay with the person until help arrives

▶ reassure and observe the person or people involved, noting any changes in their condition

▶ provide a clear verbal report of what happened and the state of any casualties to medical staff or others who arrive to provide assistance

▶ be able to complete a full written report and any relevant documentation, such as an accident report or incident report.

Recording an emergency incident

Make sure that you understand the policies, procedures and agreed ways of working in the event of an accident or sudden illness in your work setting. You should know where the accident and incident forms are kept in your work setting. You will need to complete one of these if you are involved in or witness any kind of accident or incident. This must happen even if there are no injuries to the people involved.

Investigate

What do the emergency procedures in your work setting say about the following:

- raising the alarm
- getting help and assistance from the emergency services
- evacuating the building
- the assembly point outside of the building
- protecting and reassuring people during emergency incidents?

Knowledge Assessment Task   3.1   3.2

Accidents and sudden illness are unexpected occurrences in a care setting. Despite this care organisations, and the practitioners they employ, must be prepared for the unexpected. In this task you are going to produce a handout for trainees who are about to begin a placement in the care setting where you work, or where you are on placement. Your handout should:

1. describe different types of accidents and sudden illness that may occur in your own work setting

2. explain the procedures that people working in the setting need to follow if an accident or sudden illness should occur.

Keep a copy of the work you produce for this task as evidence for your assessment.

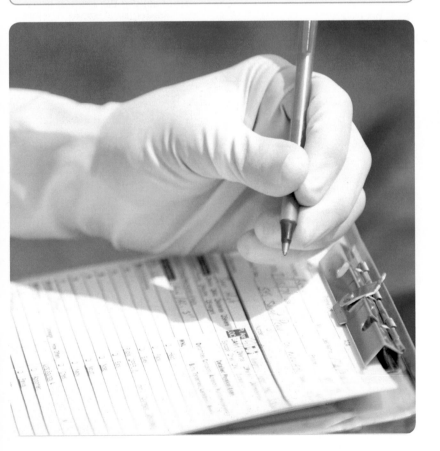

Be able to reduce the spread of infection

Supporting others to reduce the spread of infection

Infection control procedures aim to prevent bacteria and viruses from being passed from one person to another, causing illness. The **bacteria** and **viruses** that cause infections are present in everyday life. In most cases people gradually build up **immunity** to common infections and only suffer minor illnesses in the process. However, the weaker, sometimes impaired immune systems of people who are sick, frail or disabled can make them more vulnerable to both new and existing strains of infection that lead to significant health problems.

Following infection control procedures

Health and social care practitioners should always follow basic infection control procedures and follow practices that reduce the spread of infection. To do this it is important to understand how infection can be spread through airborne means, by direct contact and by indirect contact.

Measures can be taken to minimise the risk of infection taking place. These include:

▶ washing hands correctly as often as is necessary

▶ following hygienic procedures when dealing with food

▶ disposing of waste correctly.

Your assessment criteria:

4.1 Explain own role in supporting others to follow practices that reduce the spread of infection.

Key terms

Bacteria: single-cell organisms that can carry disease but which can also be helpful to human beings

Immunity: resistance to disease

Virus: a disease-carrying microorganism that infects other cells in the human body

Providing information and training

It is important that everyone working in health and care settings is aware of the procedures and practices that are followed to help reduce the spread of infection. Health and care environments often use posters and notices to communicate infection control procedures to members of staff and users of the service.

Staff training and updating of skills and knowledge is an important way to help reduce the spread of infection. Workers need to be aware of the risks of spreading infection, and about procedures that can help to minimise the risks. People working in health and care professions can help to reduce the spread of infections by encouraging and supporting each other. This could be by ensuring that others are familiar with policies, procedures and agreed ways of working that reduce the spread of infection.

Investigate

Go to the Health Protection Agency website (www.hpa.org. uk) and find the information and guidance on infection prevention and control in hospitals and care homes. Consider how this guidance can be used in your own work setting.

Using the recommended method for hand washing

Regular, effective hand hygiene is the single most important infection control measure you can undertake in a health or social care setting. Washing your hands thoroughly with a decontamination agent and drying them properly denies bacteria and viruses the conditions in which they can exist and develop. You should always wash and dry your hands before and after:

▶ helping a person to use the toilet or commode

▶ changing a person's incontinence pad, dressing or soiled clothes (remember to wear gloves)

▶ using the toilet yourself

▶ preparing or providing food for people, including yourself

▶ taking part in messy creative or outside activities.

Following the eight-step procedure

The Department of Health recommends an eight-step procedure for hand washing. The eight steps are:

1. Wet hands and apply soap. Rub palms together until soap is foamy

2. Rub each palm over the back of the other hand

3. Rub between your fingers on each hand

4. Rub backs of fingers (interlocked)

5. Rub around each of your thumbs

6. Rub both palms with fingertips

7. Rinse hands under clear running water

8. Dry hands with a clean towel.

Aspects of good practice

There are other aspects of good practice that should be followed when washing hands. Use liquid soap dispensers rather than bars of soap as this lowers the risk of picking up infection from others. Do not use detergents that are not intended for hands, such as those used to wash dishes. These detergents may dissolve natural oils in the skin. Do use air dryers to ensure that hands are completely dry. Also remember to wash your hands after covering your mouth when sneezing or coughing, particularly before carrying out procedures on clients or preparing food.

You should encourage and demonstrate good hand hygiene to the people for whom you provide care, assistance and support so that they develop effective hand washing habits too.

Reflect

When do you wash your hands at work? Think of the types of activities and tasks you do and reflect on the infection risks that these might involve. Are you protecting yourself and others appropriately through regular and thorough hand washing?

Ensuring your own health and hygiene

As a health and social care worker you need to be aware of how your own personal health and hygiene practices play a part in reducing the spread of infections. There are a number of practices that you should follow to help with this aim, for example:

▶ always wash your hands after using the toilet, or before preparing food

▶ cover your mouth when sneezing or coughing, and always use disposable tissues

▶ cover any cuts or abrasions that you have with appropriately coloured sticking plasters; for instance a blue plaster is used in a food preparation environment.

Your assessment criteria:

4.3 Demonstrate ways to ensure that own health and hygiene do not pose a risk to an individual or to others at work.

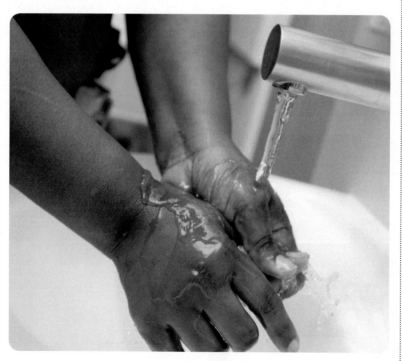

Avoiding the spread of infection

If you have been affected by an illness or infection it is important that you stay away from work. Being brave and struggling into work when you are ill may appear to be a positive and supportive act, but in fact it is a reckless one, and could lead to the spread of infection amongst colleagues and clients. Alongside this it is important to seek treatment promptly for any illness or infection that you contract. This will help you to return to work more quickly without introducing the danger of spreading infections to others in the workplace.

Case study

Karen is a health care assistant at her local health centre. The centre manager, Brian, has asked Karen to improve the information that the centre provides for new employees and trainees on placement. He is particularly keen to improve information about infection control in the Centre. Make notes, describing for Karen:

▶ the infection control procedures in your work setting
▶ the personal protective clothing that is used to avoid the spread of infection.

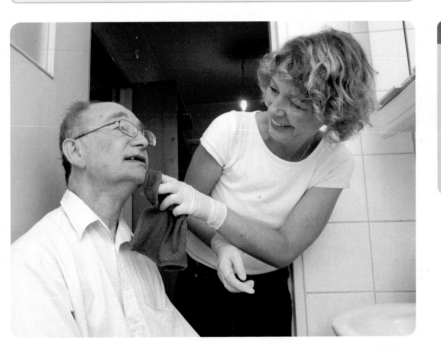

Investigate

Protective clothing such as masks and gloves are sometimes needed to protect health and care workers from infection. What types of protective clothing are available for you to use in your workplace? Do you know how to obtain protective items when you need to use them?

Practical Assessment Task   4.1   4.2   4.3

Your competence as a health or social care worker depends on your ability to demonstrate safe practice. For this task you need to show your assessor that you are able to demonstrate:

▶ the recommended method for hand washing
▶ ways to ensure that your own health and hygiene do not pose a risk to others at work.

You will need to demonstrate these skills in a practical, work-based situation. One way of doing this would be to apply these basic infection control procedures when providing personal care for a service user. You may be able to identify another situation where you can demonstrate these skills but should agree on the suitability of this with your assessor.

Moving and handling legislation

Your assessment criteria:

5.1 Explain the main points of legislation that relates to moving and handling.

Moving and handling people, equipment and other objects is a major cause of injury at work in the United Kingdom. According to the Health and Safety Executive more than a third of all over-three-day injuries reported each year to HSE and local authorities are caused by manual handling. Health and social care practitioners are particularly at risk of back injuries unless they understand and use safe moving and handling techniques. The importance of using correct moving and handling procedures is reflected in the fact that this area of care practice is regulated by a number of laws.

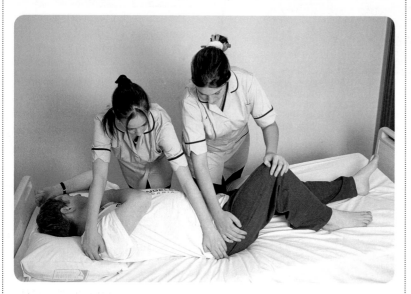

Manual Handling Operations Regulations

The moving and handling of people, equipment and objects is regulated by the Manual Handling Operations Regulations 1992 (as amended in 2002). This law requires employers to avoid all manual handling activities where there is a risk of injury 'so far as is reasonably practicable'. This might involve modifying the plan for a task or using specialist lifting equipment to carry it out. However, there are situations in health and social care settings where manual handling cannot be avoided. A suitable and sufficient risk assessment must be carried out and all reasonable steps taken to minimise risks to those involved in these situations.

Health and Safety at Work Act

Section 2 of the Health and Safety at Work Act 1974 requires employers to provide their employees with health and safety information and training. This should, where necessary, include more specific information and training on manual handling injury risks and prevention.

Provision and Use of Work Equipment Regulations

There are also other regulations that relate to manual handling. The Provision and Use of Work Equipment Regulations (PUWER) (1998) make employers responsible for ensuring that workplace equipment is:

▶ suitable for its intended use and for the conditions in which it is used

▶ safe for use, and maintained and inspected where necessary

▶ used only by those with adequate knowledge, training and experience to use it safely

▶ fitted with suitable safety measures (e.g. safety guards, brakes, protective devices, instructions and warning labels).

Where the use of equipment involves a risk to users it must be inspected by qualified people on a regular basis.

Lifting Operations and Lifting Equipment Regulations

Another set of regulations that affect manual handling are the Lifting Operations and Lifting Equipment Regulations (LOLER) (1998). Under these regulations employers must ensure that equipment used in the work setting is:

▶ strong and stable enough for its particular use and marked with any safe working loads if used for lifting

▶ positioned and installed to minimise risks

▶ used safely by competent people

▶ regularly checked by qualified inspectors.

All lifting equipment for handling objects must have an annual inspection. Lifting equipment for handling or moving people must be inspected every six months.

Reflect

Health and social care professionals often use a range of equipment as part of their work. What equipment do you use in your job, and what type of task is it intended to help with? How did you learn about how to use the equipment safely? If you are using equipment designed to aid in lifting people or objects it is particularly important that you have been trained to use it competently.

Principles of safe moving and handling

It is now rare to lift a person or object manually in a health or social care setting. Poor moving and handling techniques have been the most common cause of injury and sickness absence in health and social care workplaces. It is vital that you undertake training for this type of work before you take part in the moving and handling of individuals.

Where this does happen, a risk assessment must be carried out and risk control measures followed. This may involve using a team of people to carry out a lift or using specialist equipment. The safety of the person being moved or lifted as well as those carrying out the move is the key concern.

Responsibility for ensuring that moving and handling activity is carried out safely is shared between employers and employees.

The employer's responsibility

It is the employer's responsibility to:

▶ provide an induction and training course in current manual handling practice, with compulsory yearly updates

▶ produce and implement a manual handling policy

▶ provide equipment that meets both the specific and collective needs of the individuals concerned

▶ employ a competent person to monitor manual handling practice or seek advice from an expert, such as a back care adviser

▶ minimise risks in the workplace environment by providing adequately trained staff, clear guidelines and support and an appropriate uniform or clothing policy

▶ ensure that members of staff are fit to carry out work and that there are sufficient reporting mechanisms in place if injuries do occur

▶ investigate any injuries and aim to prevent any reoccurrence through risk assessment and clear policies and procedures.

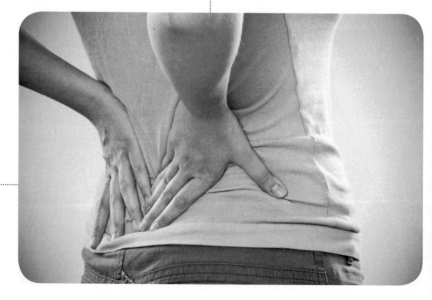

The employee's responsibility

It is the employee's responsibility to:

▶ be accountable for their own actions and to seek advice if unsure of safe practice

▶ undertake manual handling training and update practice at least once yearly

▶ report any manual handling concerns regarding individuals, equipment or staff to a manager or supervisor

▶ use moving and handling equipment appropriately and responsibly

▶ request and receive assistance regarding individuals with special needs or requirements

▶ carry out a personal risk assessment to consider safety of self, individual and equipment.

Moving and handling policies

Your care organisation should have an organisational policy on moving and handling. It is important – and your responsibility – to find out what this says, and to follow the practices and procedures that it sets out. The moving and handling policy should incorporate all of the latest moving and handling regulations and laws. You will not be covered by your employer's insurance policies, and may not have any legal redress, if you fail to follow the moving and handling policy and subsequently get a back injury due to unsafe practice.

Investigate

Employers have a responsibility to produce and implement a manual handling policy. Find out about the moving and handling policy in your workplace. Why is it important that you find out what the policy says, and that you follow it?

MANUAL HANDLING

Getting to grips with
MANUAL HANDLING
A short guide

HSE

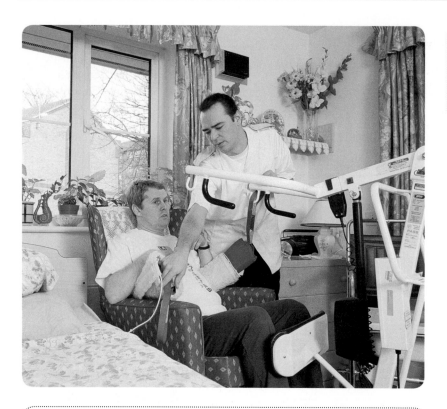

Using moving and handling equipment safely

The majority of health and social care settings have a policy of no manual lifting. This ensures that individuals are assisted to move with the aid of equipment or support aids. However, it is known that when there are staff shortages and equipment is lacking or defective, many care practitioners will continue to lift or manually handle individuals. In doing so, they are putting themselves at risk of sustaining back, arm and neck injuries and may also be endangering the safety of the individuals they are caring for.

Risk assessment will determine what constitutes safe handling practice in any situation. The starting point for risk assessment should be that lifting an adult's weight is likely to be unacceptably hazardous to an individual practitioner. The Department of Health also advises that certain moves, such as the shoulder or 'Australian' lift, are now considered to be unacceptable from a risk control point of view.

Detailed advice on safe moving and handling practice in your workplace should be sought from a specialist practitioner or adviser with responsibility for this area of work. You should also consult the safe moving and handling policy and any in-house training guidance that your employer provides on these matters. Remember that no one working in a hospital, nursing home or community setting should need to manually lift patients any more. Non-weight-bearing individuals should only be moved using appropriate equipment and safe techniques.

Good practice in manual handling

Follow these guidelines on good practice when you are faced with any task that involves manual handling:

▶ Before attempting any moving or handling, explain to the individual what you need to do and obtain their assistance where appropriate.

▶ Prepare the area first so that it is free from clutter and objects on the floor.

▶ Confirm that the equipment to be used has been checked and is safe to use. If this is not the case, do not use it.

▶ The correct sling or hoist should be used to suit the weight and size of the individual.

▶ Sufficient time and space must be allowed when carrying out the manoeuvre so that the individual does not feel rushed.

▶ The individual's dignity must be maintained throughout and they should not be unduly exposed or made to feel vulnerable.

▶ The hoist should be placed in a suitable position near to the person's bed, chair or bath, for example. At least two people should support the individual during the procedure: one person to operate the device and one to support the individual so that no injuries occur.

▶ If the individual is being transferred to another area it is advisable to transport them in a wheelchair first and then to use the hoist in the transfer area, such as a bathroom.

▶ The individual should never be left alone whilst in the hoist. To avoid this, before you begin take all of the necessary equipment, toiletries, clothing and belongings to the area where care will be provided.

▶ Provide the minimum level of manual handling required in the situation: encourage the person to do as much for themselves as they can.

Practical Assessment Task · 5.1 · 5.2 · 5.3

The safety of yourself and others should be your main priority when moving and handling equipment and other objects in your work setting. In this task you need to show that you are able to:

1. explain legislation that relates to moving and handling

2. explain the principles for moving and handling equipment and other objects safely

3. move and handle equipment and other objects safely.

The evidence that you produce for this task must be based on your practice in a real work environment. Your assessor may want to observe you moving and handling equipment or other objects and may wish to ask you questions about this and the legislation and principles involved in this area of practice.

Hazardous substances in the care setting

The various kinds of clinical and everyday waste that are produced in health and social care settings present an infection hazard unless they are dealt with correctly. The Control of Substances Hazardous to Health (COSHH) Regulations (2002) apply to any potentially hazardous substance. This includes substances that are corrosive, e.g. acid; irritant e.g. cleaning fluids; toxic e.g. medicines; highly flammable e.g. solvents; dangerous to the environment e.g. chemicals and clinical waste; germs that cause diseases e.g. legionnaires' disease; materials that are harmful e.g. used needles; potentially infectious materials e.g. used dressings; body fluids e.g. blood, faeces or vomit.

Records of hazardous substances

The regulations require every work setting to have a COSHH file that lists all of the hazardous substances used in the work setting. The file should identify:

▶ where hazardous substances are kept

▶ how they are labelled

▶ their effects

▶ the length of time a person can safely be exposed to each substance

▶ what to do in an emergency involving each hazardous substance.

You have a responsibility to know what the COSHH file says and to work in ways that minimise risk.

Employer responsibilities

Health and social care employers are required to:

▶ find out what the health hazards are with regard to each substance used

▶ decide how to prevent harm to health via risk assessment

▶ provide control measures to reduce harm to health

▶ make sure that all control measures are used

▶ keep all control measures in good working order

▶ provide information, instruction and training for employees and others

▶ provide monitoring and health surveillance in appropriate cases

▶ plan for emergencies.

Safe practices for hazardous substances

Health and social care workers should identify tasks or aspects of practice that expose them to hazardous substances. You should know how each substance may cause harm and what you can do to reduce the risk to you and others. Always try to prevent exposure at source by choosing an alternative or by minimising the contact you have with the substance to maximise your own safety.

Storing hazardous substances

You need to follow your workplace policies and procedures for storing hazardous substances. Drugs and medicines should be stored safely and out of the reach of people who should not have access to them. Materials must be stored in containers recommended by the manufacturer and must be clearly labelled. Containers must be securely sealed to prevent leakage. Substances that are incompatible, that is those which could pose a risk if mixed together, must be stored separately.

Using hazardous substances

When using hazardous substances it is important that you follow agreed ways of working and your workplace's policies and procedures. It is vital that you avoid exposure to hazardous substances, such as by inhalation, by contact with the skin or eyes, by swallowing or through skin puncture. You also need to know how and when to use protective clothing where necessary, such as latex gloves, masks and aprons. The COSHH Regulations (2002) outline a number of principles of good practice and require employers to:

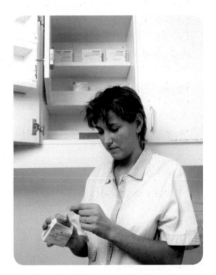

Drugs and medicines should be labelled and stored safely

▶ design and operate processes and activities to minimise emission, release and spread of substances hazardous to health

▶ take into account all relevant routes of exposure – inhalation, skin absorption and ingestion – when developing control measures

▶ control exposure by measures that are proportionate to the health risk

▶ choose the most effective and reliable control options that minimise the escape and spread of substances hazardous to health

▶ provide (in combination with other control measures) suitable personal protective equipment (PPE), where adequate control of exposure cannot be achieved by other means

▶ check and review regularly for their continuing effectiveness all elements of control measures

▶ inform and train all employees on the hazards and risks from the substances they work with and the use of control measures developed to minimise the risks

▶ ensure that the introduction of control measures does not increase the overall risk to health and safety.

Disposing of hazardous substances

There should be a detailed waste disposal policy and a clear set of procedures relating to waste disposal in your workplace. You need to know about these policies and procedures and must follow them carefully. If you are unsure about what to do with a certain type of waste, always ask your supervisor or a senior colleague for assistance. The waste disposal policy and procedures should identify how to dispose of different types of waste (see Figure 8.5) and contain information on how the waste should be stored and removed.

Your assessment criteria:

6.1 Describe types of hazardous substances and materials that may be found in the work setting.

6.2 Demonstrate safe practices for:
- storing hazardous substances
- using hazardous substances
- disposing of hazardous substances and materials.

Figure 8.5 Methods of disposal of different types of waste

Type of waste	Method of disposal
Linen and clothing	Soiled sheets, towels and clothing should be kept and washed separately from non-soiled linen. They should be washed as soon as possible after soiling.
Sharps	Needles, blades, glass and other sharps should be disposed of in a special sharps bin. Broken glass or pottery should be carefully wrapped and disposed of in the domestic waste bin or according to the local procedure.
Body products	Blood, urine, faeces, vomit and sputum should be cleaned up using the spillage procedure and flushed down the toilet or a sink, as appropriate. All spillage areas should be disinfected following the local policy and procedures.
Clinical waste	Dressings, plasters, bandages, gloves, aprons, nappies and pads should be put in the clinical waste bags in foot-operated bins. This should be stored in a designated area and removed by a specialist waste contractor.
Recyclable waste	Place recyclable materials in the appropriate recycling bin or, for clinical equipment that will be sterilised and reused, in the special packages/bags provided.
Leftover food	Put it in the kitchen bin or food bin as soon as a meal is finished.
Household waste	Dispose in the domestic rubbish bin using the waste disposal system provided by the local authority.

Investigate

Many people working in health and social care roles make routine use of products and substances that could be hazardous if misused, or incorrectly stored. What hazardous substances do you use in your work? Are you familiar with the procedures for storage, use and disposal of the hazardous substances that you encounter at your workplace?

Case study

Kim has recently started a new job as a care support worker at Pinesprings, a residential care home for frail, older people. Kim has been working alongside Charlotte, the manager of the Pinesprings care home. Charlotte was called away to deal with a phone call in the office. Whilst Kim was on her own she realised that Alan, a quiet 80 year-old resident, had wet his trousers and needed cleaning and changing. Kim wasn't sure what to do in this situation as she was new to the care home. Kim waited until Charlotte returned and then pointed out that Alan seemed upset about something.

1. Identify reasons why Kim should have got help sooner in this situation.

2. Describe the potential hazards that need to be dealt with in order to provide appropriate and safe care for Alan.

3. What should Kim have done to maximise health and safety and minimise the risk of infection in the situation described?

Practical Assessment Task   6.1   6.2

Your competence as a health or social care practitioner depends on your ability to demonstrate safe practice. For this assessment task you need to demonstrate that you are able to use safe practices to:

▶ store hazardous substances

▶ use hazardous substances

▶ dispose of hazardous substances and materials.

You will need to identify an appropriate opportunity to demonstrate these skills in a practical, work-based situation. One way of doing this would be to use safe practices when your work routine calls for you to deal with hazardous substances. Alternatively, you may be able to identify another type of situation where you can demonstrate these skills but should agree on the suitability of this with your assessor.

Preventing a fire from starting and spreading

Fire emergencies are frightening and can be very dangerous. Fire can be particularly dangerous in a health and social care environment because clients' needs often make it hard for them to escape or remove themselves from danger. The best way to deal with fire is to prevent a fire from starting, and if one has started to prevent it from spreading.

Minimising the risk of fire

Fires are caused when the right conditions occur together. That is when there is a source of ignition, fuel to catch fire and burn and oxygen to allow **combustion** to take place. When all three of these conditions are met a fire will start. This is known as the fire triangle, as shown in Figure 8.6.

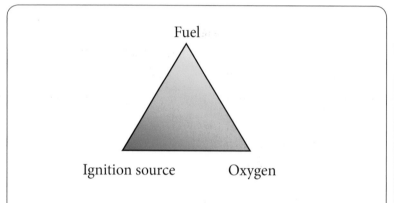

Fuel

Ignition source   Oxygen

Figure 8.6 The fire triangle

There is a source of oxygen in the air around us, and almost all environments have a range of flammable material in them. It is important, therefore, to prevent fires from starting by being aware of the sources of ignition that may be present and controlling or removing them. This could include lit cigarettes, naked flames, hot surfaces or faulty electrical equipment. Risk of fire starting can be minimised by actions such as regular checks on electrical equipment. Electrical equipment should be tested regularly; this is known as a Portable Appliance Test (**PAT test**).

Staff training

Staff training is also important so that everyone is aware of the risks, and what to look out for. Staff vigilance is one of the best ways to prevent fire starting and spreading.

Key terms

Combustion, combustible: able to be burned or set alight

PAT test: safety check made on electrical equipment. Stands for Portable Appliance Testing

Your responsibilities

There are several things that you, as a member of staff in a health and care environment, can do to help prevent the starting and the spread of fire. Figure 8.7 outlines some of these.

Figure 8.7 Actions you can take to prevent the start and spread of a fire

Areas of risk	Action
Take care with electrical appliances and equipment	• Do not overload power sockets • Check for worn or faulty wiring • Unplug appliances when not in use • Keep electrical equipment away from water • Never put anything metal into a microwave oven
Take care with heating devices	• Use only approved covers on heaters and radiators • Ensure that heaters are switched off or fully guarded at night
Take care with naked flames	• Do not use candles • Store matches and lighters safely • Enforcing strict procedures for designated smoking areas • Ensuring that cigarettes are fully extinguished

Good practice

Your workplace should carry out a risk assessment to check where there may be potentially dangerous situations that could lead to fire starting and spreading and minimise these by safe practices in the workplace. One aspect of this is the storage and disposal of flammable materials such as waste materials, paper wood, furnishings or flammable liquids. Another important practice is to keep fire doors shut; they are specifically designed to prevent a fire from spreading and are of no use if kept open! Also it is important to check smoke detectors regularly.

Practical Assessment Task 7.1 7.2

You need to demonstrate your competence in taking measures that prevent fires from starting. You will need to identify an appropriate opportunity to demonstrate these skills in a practical, work-based situation. One way of doing this would be to carry out a brief risk assessment on fire safety in an area that you are familiar with in your own work environment. A brief report on your findings could help to show that you are aware of the measures that need to be taken to prevent fires from starting and spreading. Alternatively, you may be able to identify another type of situation where you can demonstrate these skills but should agree on the suitability of this with your assessor.

Emergency procedures in the event of a fire

In the rare event that a fire does start in your care setting, you should understand what can be done to prevent it from spreading and also what your role is in any evacuation procedure. There should be a detailed fire and evacuation policy for your work setting. You must be familiar with this. You also need to know about any equipment that is to be used in the event of fire. This could include the use of appropriate fire extinguishers, fire blankets or other safety equipment. You need to know how to operate the fire alarm, and the procedures for alerting other personnel.

Actions to take

A care practitioner's role during a fire incident is to keep themselves and others safe. If you are the person who notices a fire (or smoke), you should first raise the alarm by activating a fire alarm, phoning 999 yourself or instructing someone else to do this. Other actions to take include:

▶ alerting other personnel in your work setting

▶ closing doors and windows to prevent draughts from fanning the flames and allowing the fire to spread

▶ tackling the fire if it is very small and manageable and you have the correct equipment

▶ ensuring that all service users are moved away from the area and are supervised by care practitioners

▶ reassuring people by staying calm and providing information about what is happening and what they need to do

▶ evacuating the building and going to the agreed **assembly point** with the people you are taking care of.

Your assessment criteria:

7.3 Explain emergency procedures to be followed in the event of a fire in the work setting

7.4 Ensure that clear evacuation routes are maintained at all times

Key terms

Assembly point: an agreed place everyone must go to when they are evacuated away from potential danger in an emergency

Case study

Merion is in the first week of his new job as a care assistant at the Pinebridge Centre, a residential care home for disabled older people. He has noticed that there are fire doors and extinguishers at different locations in the building, and that there are notices showing evacuation routes. He is concerned though that he has not been given details of procedures in case of a fire, and he has received no training from senior staff at the centre on what to do in a fire emergency. If you were in Merion's position:

1. What type of information about emergency fire procedures would you want to know about?

2. What training would you want to receive?

3. What improvements would you suggest the Pinebridge Centre management need to make to support staff in dealing with fire emergencies?

Maintain clear evacuation routes

You need to be familiar with the evacuation procedures of your workplace. Evacuation must use designated routes. Lifts are not to be used in the event of a fire, and you should close all doors to slow the spread of the fire. Very young children and individuals with mobility or other difficulties require special evacuation procedures and sometimes equipment, such as the use of an evacuation chair.

Be prepared

A successful fire evacuation depends on there being a clear set of fire procedures; good understanding of what to do developed through regular fire drills; and, very importantly, clear evacuation routes within the building. All corridors, fire exits, stairways and the usual entrance and exit doors to your workplace should be kept free of obstructions at all times. If you notice that any of the fire evacuation routes are blocked, you should inform the person in charge of your work setting at that point and have the items obstructing the evacuation route removed.

Follow procedure

The person in charge of an evacuation during a fire incident needs to keep a register of all people in the building to check that everyone is present at the assembly point. No one should return to the building unless authorised by the person in charge and/or the emergency services personnel. You should also remain at the assembly point until you are directed to go somewhere else or are allowed back into the building.

Practical Assessment Task · 7.3 · 7.4

Health and social care practitioners should attend a fire safety session to update their knowledge about fire prevention each year. For this assessment task, produce a handout for a fire safety briefing. In your handout:

1. describe practices that prevent fires from starting and spreading in your workplace

2. outline emergency procedures to be followed in the event of a fire

3. explain the importance of maintaining clear evacuation routes in your workplace at all times.

Keep any written work that you produce for this activity as evidence towards your assessment.

Investigate

Have you taken part in a fire drill at your workplace in the past three months? Can you remember where the assembly point outside of the building was?

Security procedures for access to premises or information

It is important to consider the security of the setting where you work as this affects the safety of the service users, visitors and care practitioners who use it. Security incidents can occur as a result of:

▶ intruders or unauthorised people entering the building

▶ service users leaving the building unexpectedly through unlocked doors or windows

▶ care practitioners giving confidential information to people who are not authorised to have access to it.

Procedures for entering the workplace

You should understand and implement agreed ways of working in your workplace when anyone requests access. The person's identity needs to be checked, and your workplace may require them to show an official ID. There is likely to be a signing in procedure, and a visitor badge system. Your workplace may also use biometric security systems, such as fingerprint scanners.

Procedures for protecting information

Information also needs to be held securely. Information stored electronically must be protected with secure passwords. Other records also need to be held securely. You need to be familiar with the systems used in your workplace to keep information confidential, and to use them at all times. On occasions you may need to deal with electronic requests for information. Make sure that you are familiar with the policies and procedures of your workplace for dealing with such requests, and always follow these procedures.

Your assessment criteria:

8.1 Demonstrate use of agreed procedures for checking the identity of anyone requesting access to:
- premises
- information.

8.2 Demonstrate the use of measures to protect own security and the security of others in the work setting.

Using measures to protect your own and others' security

You should never lend your identity badge to anyone else nor reveal the keypad code to non-staff members. If you are asked to check ground-floor windows and doors, you should do this thoroughly to ensure that they are safe and secure. You should always report any concerns that you have about visitors and about any apparent attempts to break into the building or inappropriately enter your workplace. The personal safety of people in the workplace is always a high priority in a care setting so if you have any serious suspicions or become aware of an intruder it is advisable to seek help quickly and to call onsite security staff and/or the police. Care organisations generally discourage staff from approaching or directly restraining intruders in order to minimise the risk of violence occurring.

Minimising security risks

Care settings can minimise the risk of security incidents by:

▶ having a single entry and exit point that is controlled by staff

▶ using a security system, such as a keypad or locked door, to control entry and exit to the setting

▶ ensuring that identity badges are worn by staff and visitors and that only authorised visitors accompanied by a member of staff are allowed entry

▶ training staff members to approach and politely challenge visitors who are not wearing appropriate visitor badges or who appear in the setting (including the outside areas) unexpectedly.

▶ ensuring that service users only leave the setting with the knowledge of a senior member of staff.

Ensuring that others know your whereabouts

There may be occasions where you have to leave the work setting to carry out a work-related task somewhere else, to escort visitors or service users to another part of the building or to visit a person in their own home. In all of these cases, your supervisor or the person in charge of the workplace should know where you are going, who you are with or will be seeing and what time you are expected to return. If you do have to visit a service user at home, your organisation should have a lone-working policy and must train you in ways of managing your own safety when working alone.

Your assessment criteria:

8.3 Explain the importance of ensuring that others are aware of own whereabouts

Investigate

Find out about the procedures in your workplace that are intended to ensure that others are aware of your whereabouts when you are at work. Why do you think it is important to be aware of these procedures?

Case study

Alice is a health care support worker at the Broadelm Health Centre. A patient of the Centre, John Francis, has forgotten to take his medication with him following a clinic visit. Alice knows John's address and, as she has no other duties that afternoon, she decides to drop in on John and deliver his medication to him. Alice tells her friend Natasha, a fellow health care support worker, that she is popping out for a minute. Natasha is worried that Alice is not behaving safely, and is not following the correct procedures. If you were Natasha:

1. Why would you think that Alice may not be working in a safe way?

2. What procedures would you expect Alice to follow before she left the Centre to visit a patient?

3. What would you say to Alice before she left the Centre?

Practical Assessment Task   8.1   8.2   8.3

Protecting the security of yourself and others is a key part of your role as a care practitioner. Health and social care organisations must always have security-related policies and procedures that safeguard members of staff and other people who use the care setting. In this activity you are required to produce evidence that shows you are able to:

1. use agreed ways of working for checking the identify of anyone requesting access to your work setting or to information relating to service users or care practice

2. implement measures to protect your own security and the security of others in the work setting

3. explain the importance of ensuring that others are aware of your whereabouts when you are working.

Your evidence for this task must be based on your practice and experience in a real work environment. Keep any written work that you produce for this activity as evidence towards your assessment. Your assessor may also want to observe or ask you questions about the way you implement security measures in the work setting.

Common signs and indicators of stress

'Stress' is the feeling of emotional tension, worry or pressure that a person feels when they face a demanding or challenging situation. It has both psychological and physical symptoms.

A person who is experiencing high levels of stress may display this through their behaviour: perhaps by being irritable, argumentative and quick to lose their temper or by smoking or drinking more heavily to cope with the anxiety that stress causes. Prolonged or extreme stress can lead to health problems. It can trigger mental health problems such as depression and anxiety-based illnesses. Stress is also associated with high blood pressure and heart disease, and leads some people to misuse drugs and alcohol as a way of coping with their symptoms.

What signs indicate your own stress?

You may experience some of the common signs and symptoms of stress outlined in Figure 8.8.

Figure 8.8 Signs and symptoms of stress

Signs and symptoms of stress		
Physical	• aches and pains • nausea • dizziness	• chest pain • rapid heartbeat
Emotional	• moodiness • irritability or short temper • agitation • inability to relax	• feeling overwhelmed • a sense of loneliness or isolation • depression or general unhappiness
Cognitive (or intellectual)	• memory problems • inability to concentrate	• poor judgement • constant worrying
Behavioural	• eating more, or less • sleeping too much or too little • neglecting responsibilities	• using alcohol, tobacco or drugs to relax • nervous habits, such as nail biting

Your assessment criteria:

9.1 Describe common signs and indicators of stress.

9.2 Describe signs that indicate own stress.

9.3 Analyse factors that tend to trigger own stress.

Reflect

Identify three occasions when you've felt very stressed. What were your symptoms? What caused your stress? Make a note of these points or discuss them with a colleague in your class. Remember that health and social care practitioners have diverse social and cultural backgrounds as well as differing lifestyles and personal circumstances. Your main sources of stress, or the work-related factors that trigger off your feelings of stress, may be different to those of your colleagues as a result.

Analyse factors that trigger your own stress

There are a number of things that can cause a person to become stressed.

Work factors

Factors at work can cause stress. This could include changes in routine that seem to make things harder or confusing. It could be due to having to deal with difficult situations. In some workplaces there may be pressure to meet targets, or expectations of managers about performance, which could lead to stress for the workers. Personal relationships at work can also be a source of stress. These could be between you and other work colleagues, or with clients. Demands of work can also lead to stress. These could be about working unsocial hours, or taking on special projects, that bring extra challenges and could lead to stress.

Personal factors

Personal factors can be another way that people become stressed. These could be financial problems, or relationship or family issues. Other personal factors include major life changes, such as moving home, the loss of a loved one, or the onset of illness or injury.

Understanding how stress affects you

You need to understand how these factors can trigger stress in yourself, and other individuals. These factors can operate singly, or in combination, to create stress.

Reflect

What are the three main stress triggers in your work life? If you could remove or at least control one of these sources of stress, which one would you choose?

Case study

Sue is a 37 year-old hairdresser. She wants to retire as a rich, happy woman when she is 50. Sue runs her own hairdressing business, working between 60 and 80 hours every week. She is feeling under a lot of pressure at the moment.

Sue has complained to her husband that she has had a headache for a week, feels faint at times and is having trouble sleeping. Sue will not go and see her GP as she says she is too busy.

Her husband is trying to persuade her to take a holiday but Sue is reluctant to do so because of the amount of work she has to do.

1. What symptoms of stress does Sue have?
2. What might be causing Sue's current stress problems?
3. Explain what might happen to Sue's health and wellbeing if she continues to experience high stress levels.

Comparing strategies for managing stress

Your assessment criteria:

9.4 Compare strategies for managing stress.

Awareness of the symptoms, causes and triggers of your stress is the first step to managing it. There are a variety of ways of managing stress as shown in Figure 8.9, though to be effective any strategy must respond appropriately to the underlying causes. For example, if your stress is triggered by working excessively long hours or by the emotionally draining nature of your work, an appropriate response would be to take time off and ensure a work–life balance.

Figure 8.9 Ways of managing stress

Confiding in others

Being able to confide in somebody and talk through an issue and your feelings about it with them can be a very helpful way of managing stress. A common strategy is to talk to a partner or close friend informally to express feelings and receive some support. Similarly, you should use the advice, guidance and support services provided by your employer to seek help for and manage work-related stress.

Using a variety of strategies

▶ Relaxation techniques can be effective in reducing stress. These include methods such as yoga, massage, aromatherapy or listening to music.

▶ Physical activity is another strategy that can help to relieve stress. This could be through joining a gym, or simply going for a run. A number of scientific studies have shown that regular physical activity improves a person's mental health.

▶ Social strategies can also help with stress. This could be meeting up with friends and family, or volunteering for work in the local community.

▶ Logical strategies could be another method. Doing things like making lists, or prioritising tasks, can help life seem less confusing and more under your own control.

▶ Creative strategies, like music, painting or other artistic pursuits can help relieve stress. These activities can promote feelings of being a creative person and take your mind off the immediate causes of the stress you may be feeling.

▶ Some people may find that stress leads them towards religious or other beliefs. This may have a positive effect in a few cases, but it may lead to attitude and lifestyle changes that have negative effects on relationships and mental health.

Emotional wellbeing and resilience

In any coping strategy that aims to relieve stress it is important that the individual understands the importance of emotional wellbeing and resilience. Health and social care work brings practitioners into regular contact with the needs of other people. In fact it is a basic element of such work. This means that emotional resilience is a key skill that practitioners need to develop so that they remain mentally healthy, and cheerful, despite the situations they sometimes need to deal with. It is important to recognise the things that bring about stress, and know when it is a good idea to take 'time out' to allow yourself space to regain your emotional energy. Thinking positively and being assertive (saying 'no' to extra work!) are all good ways of reducing stress levels.

Knowledge Assessment Task | **9.1** | **9.2** | **9.3** | **9.4**

Health and social care practitioners spend the majority of their time caring for and supporting others. This focus on the needs and wellbeing of other people can sometimes lead to practitioners failing to look after themselves! Produce a personal health and wellbeing plan as follows:

1. Describe common signs and indicators of stress.

2. Analyse factors that tend to trigger your own stress.

3. Describe ways in which you manage your own stress, or could do so if you became stressed in the future, and compare the different strategies that you could use.

Your written work for this task should relate to your health or social care role. Keep a copy of the work you produce as evidence for your assessment.

Are you ready for assessment?

AC	What do you know now?	Assessment task	✓
1.1	Identify legislation relating to general health and safety in a health or social care work setting	Page 213	
1.2	Explain the main points of the health and safety policies and procedures agreed with the employer	Page 213	
1.3	Outline the main health and safety responsibilities of: • self • the employer or manager • others in the work setting	Page 213	
1.4	Identify specific tasks in the work setting that should not be carried out without special training	Page 213	
3.1	Describe different types of accidents and sudden illness that may occur in own work setting	Page 225	
3.2	Explain procedures to be followed if an accident or sudden illness should occur	Page 225	
9.1	Describe common signs and indicators of stress	Page 253	
9.2	Describe signs that indicate own stress	Page 253	
9.3	Analyse factors that tend to trigger own stress	Page 253	
9.4	Compare strategies for managing stress	Page 253	

AC	What do you know now?	Assessment task	✓
2.1	Use policies and procedures or other agreed ways of working that relate to health and safety	Page 221	
2.2	Support others to understand and follow safe practices	Page 221	
2.3	Monitor and report potential health and safety risks	Page 221	
2.4	Use risk-assessment in relation to health and safety	Page 221	
2.5	Demonstrate ways to minimise potential risks and hazards	Page 221	
2.6	Access additional support or information relating to health and safety	Page 221	
4.1	Explain own role in supporting others to follow practices that reduce the spread of infection	Page 231	
4.2	Demonstrate the recommended method for hand washing	Page 231	
4.3	Demonstrate ways to ensure that own health and hygiene do not pose a risk to an individual or to others at work	Page 231	

AC	What do you know now?	Assessment task	✓
5.1	Explain the main points of legislation that relates to moving and handling	Page 237	
5.2	Explain principles for safe moving and handling	Page 237	
5.3	Move and handle equipment and other objects safely	Page 237	
6.1	Describe types of hazardous substances that may be found in the work setting	Page 241	
6.2	Demonstrate safe practices for: • storing hazardous substances • using hazardous substances • disposing of hazardous substances and materials	Page 241	
7.1	Describe practices that prevent fires from: • starting • spreading	Page 243	
7.2	Demonstrate measures that prevent fires from starting	Page 243	
7.3	Explain emergency procedures to be followed in the event of a fire in the work setting	Page 245	
7.4	Ensure that clear evacuation routes are maintained at all times	Page 245	
8.1	Demonstrate the use of agreed procedures for checking the identity of anyone requesting access to: • premises • information	Page 249	
8.2	Demonstrate use of measures to protect own security and the security of others in the work setting	Page 249	
8.3	Explain the importance of ensuring that others are aware of own whereabouts	Page 249	

9 | Promote good practice in handling information in health and social care settings (HSC 038

Assessment of this unit

This unit covers the knowledge and skills needed to implement and promote good practice in recording, sharing, storing and accessing information.

You will need to show that you can:

1. Understand requirements for handling information in health and social care settings.

2. Be able to implement good practice in handling information.

3. Be able to support others to handle information.

You will be assessed on your knowledge of the legislation and codes of practice which relate to the recording, storing and sharing of information in health and social care. You will need to show that you understand what the main points of these laws and codes of practice are as they apply to your work in the health and social care field.

The assessment of this unit is partly knowledge-based (things you need to know about) and partly competence-based (things you need to do in the real work environment). To complete this unit successfully you will need to produce evidence of both your knowledge and your competence. The charts opposite outline what you need to know and do to meet each of the assessment criteria for the unit. Your tutor or assessor will help you to prepare for your assessment and the tasks suggested in this chapter will help you to create the evidence that you need.

AC What you need to know

1.1 Identify legislation and codes of practice that relate to handling information in health and social care

1.2 Summarise the main points of legal requirements and codes of practice for handling information in health and social care

AC What you need to do

2.1 Describe features of manual and electronic information storage systems that help ensure security

2.2 Demonstrate practices that ensure security when storing and accessing information

2.3 Maintain records that are up-to-date, complete, accurate and legible

3.1 Support others to understand the need for secure handling of information

3.2 Support others to understand and contribute to records

This unit also links to the following units:

HSC 3020 Facilitate person-centred assessment, planning, implementation and review

SHC 31 Promote communication in health and social care settings

HSC 025 The role of the health and social care worker

Some of your learning will be repeated in these units and will give you the chance to review your knowledge and understanding.

Your assessment criteria:

1.1 Identify the legislation and codes of practice that relate to handling information in health and social care.

1.2 Summarise the main points of legal requirements and codes of practice for handling information in health and social care.

Key terms

Legislation: laws, in this case governing the use of information

Media: different ways of recording or conveying information, for example print or video

Governance: procedures and checks to ensure that the correct rules are followed

Legislation and codes of practice that relate to handling information

The main **legislation** affecting the recording, storage and sharing of information is outlined in Figures 9.1 and 9.2 on the following pages. The law concerns all kinds of information, not just written documents: it can include documents and emails on computers, CDs and memory sticks, as well as information that is shared verbally (spoken), for example on the telephone.

Figure 9.1 Legislation affecting information recording, storage and handling

The legislation	What it covers
Data Protection Act 1998	This Act covers the holding, obtaining, recording, using and disclosing of information held in all forms of electronic and paper media, including images. As well as patient or service user information, it covers things such as personnel records. Although it applies to living individuals, it would be good practice to take the same care with information about those recently deceased.
Freedom of Information Act 2000	Under this law most public authorities are obliged to provide information about their policies and services to people requesting that information through the agreed channels.
Health and Social Care Act 2008	This Act created a national Information Governance Board, which will determine the policies and procedures around information handling which your organisation has to follow.
Human Rights Act 1998	This Act sets out 16 rights that all people are considered to have while in the UK, starting with the right to life. If any of these rights are breached an individual has the right to look to a legal solution.
Equality Act 2010	This brings all types of discrimination under one law, including those covered by the Disability Discrimination Act (2005) and the Race Relations Act (2000). The Equality Act started to come into effect in October 2010, though some of its provisions did not come into effect until April 2011 and some further connected legislation is planned.
Various laws and case law relating to the protection of vulnerable adults	Adults who are deemed to be vulnerable may be protected, or their abusers prosecuted, under various laws, depending on the offence. This could potentially include inadequate entries in, or fraudulent use of, care records if this led to worse health or social care of an individual.

Codes of practice

In addition to actual laws there are codes of practice, which health or social care workers must follow in the same way that they follow legal requirements. There are specific codes of practice around various topics in health and social care, many of which will be based on the requirements of the law. Your employer and/or professional organisation (e.g. the Nursing and Midwifery Council (NMC) for nurses) will have codes of practice around information handling, which you should know where to find and become familiar with.

Investigate

Look up some information on paper or online about how your organisation is trying to comply with the new Equality Act. Can you find two things that could apply to the way you handle people's confidential information?

Legal requirements and codes of practice for handling information

Figure 9.2 Legislation and codes of practice affecting information handling

Legislation	What are the main points?
Data Protection Act 1998	This Act includes the principles that as well as being kept **secure**, information should be accurate, be adequate for its purpose, observe a person's rights and be kept no longer than is necessary. It must be used for limited purposes, in a fair and legal manner, and not be transferred to or shared with others without proper safeguards. The Act also gives people certain rights to see or have copies of their health or social care records.
Freedom of Information Act 2000	This Act only covers the activities of the organisation, and not personal information. You should know whom to ask in case someone approaches you with a request for certain kinds of information, for example the costs of a certain service.
Health and Social Care Act 2008	The information governance parts of this Act aim to ensure policies and practices which make information handling **confidential** and secure. It is intended to assure patients and service users that the information they provide is used and shared in a safe, secure and ethical way. It also means that health and social care staff have a single source of guidance and support they can trust: the National Information Governance Board.

continued...

Your assessment criteria:

1.1 Identify legislation and codes of practice that relate to handling information in health and social care.

1.2 Summarise the main points of legal requirements and codes of practice for handling information in health and social care.

Key terms

Secure: information that is not just physically safe (e.g. in a locked cabinet), but also protected from people who do not need to know about it

Confidential: this means that information is only shared with those who have a good reason and the authority or permission to know it

Legislation	What are the main points?
Human Rights Act 1998	The main rights which might be referred to in connection with health and social care are the rights to respect for private and family life, and freedom from degrading treatment. For example, even if a person is in care, or can no longer give their own consent for information about them to be shared, they have a legal right to have their privacy respected.
Equality Act 2010	This requires employers and carers to take all reasonable steps to treat all people the same – those with disabilities (of any kind) the same as people without disabilities, for example. Even if individuals do not have the capacity to understand issues themselves, they should not receive worse treatment than others. For example, staff should not talk about someone's care to others who are not appropriate, even if the service user involved does not understand what is being said. Another aspect of equality is that people with sight, hearing or learning difficulties have the right to information in an appropriate format about various choices they might want to make.
Case law around duty of confidentiality	The 'duty of confidentiality' is not laid out in a named Act as it has developed as a result of individual legal cases. This means that very clear decisions about how to apply confidentiality are not always possible, but general guidelines such as the Caldicott principles (below) should always be followed. For example, information is considered to be confidential where the information is sensitive (e.g. medical information) and also if it is given in circumstances where the giver could reasonably expect it to remain confidential.

Discuss

Have you heard or read about cases in the news where an individual or an organisation has been accused of handling information badly or illegally?

▶ What was alleged to have happened?

▶ Why did these actions allegedly break the law and/or codes of practice, or which laws/codes do you think may have been broken?

Codes of practice: the Caldicott principles

The most important general principles concerning information handling are the Caldicott principles. These were formulated for health care settings but are used also in the social care sector. They apply to the release of information that identifies individuals either by name or in some other way. There will be one or more senior people in your organisation who can give advice on this, but the principles apply broadly to all the work you are likely to do. For example, if you need to share information on someone with a doctor or social worker these principles will affect what you do and how you do it. They would also apply to sharing information within an organisation – for example, staff who work in the same care home but do not usually undertake direct care of residents.

The Caldicott principles state that:

▶ you must be able to justify the purpose of every proposed use or transfer of information

▶ you should not use or share personal information unless it is absolutely necessary

▶ you should use the minimum amount of personal information necessary to do a particular task

▶ access to personal information should be on a strict need-to-know basis

▶ everyone with access to personal information must be aware of their responsibilities

▶ everyone must understand and comply with the law.

Your assessment criteria:

1.1 Identify legislation and codes of practice that relate to handling information in health and social care.

1.2 Summarise the main points of legal requirements and codes of practice for handling information in health and social care.

Personal information should be held securely, with access on a strict need-to-know basis

The main points around information handling should be covered as soon as possible in the induction process

Case study

Jean is a senior carer who is helping Sunil, a new care worker, through the induction process at work. She wants to give him a brief introduction to his legal and ethical responsibilities as regards handling people's information. She particularly wants to show him how he is required to behave differently at work from how he might behave outside the workplace.

1. Which parts of the law might she mention to emphasise that Sunil has legal responsibilities around security and confidentiality of information?

2. Suggest three points she might make to show how information sharing at work is affected by a code of practice that would not affect sharing information about people socially outside the workplace.

Knowledge Assessment Task　　1.1　1.2

1. Identify the main laws that apply to information handling in health and social care. What is the main additional code of practice which deals with personally identifiable information?

2. What are the main points of the law as it applies to handling information in health and social care? What six principles need to be followed if identifiable information about an individual is used?

Be able to implement good practice in handling information

Your assessment criteria:

2.1 Describe features of manual and electronic information storage systems that help ensure security.

Ensuring security in storage systems

There are many different ways of recording, storing and sharing information, and this information may be stored on paper, or electronically on computer files or disks. However information is recorded or stored, you must ensure that it is done securely. If information about people is not stored – and disposed of – securely, it could get lost, stolen or damaged. Information about one individual could also get mixed up with someone else's, which could harm the care of both of them.

Information of any kind concerning patients or service users is usually deemed to be confidential, which means it should not be handled by or shared with people who have no right to it: to ensure this, it is essential to have good security measures in place.

Confidentiality

Confidentiality does not mean keeping things secret. It means making sure that only those people who really need to know it, as part of their work role, have access to information about an individual. Information is shared with these appropriate people, in appropriate ways, in the course of normal work. Information should not normally be used or disclosed in a form that might identify an individual without their consent; however, explicit consent does not normally need to be given if the information is being used for appropriate health and social care purposes only.

Discuss

With one or two other staff from your workplace, think about a patient or service-user well known to all of you. Making sure your discussion is in private and is respectful of that person, consider the information you hold on that person.

▶ With whom is that information shared, and for what purposes?

▶ How is the person made aware of information being recorded or shared about them, for example by or with medical staff?

▶ Has that person ever asked for information to be withheld from someone?

▶ Have there been, or could there be, any occasions where confidential information on that person needed to be given to an outside body such as police or social services?

Good practice

It is good practice to make the individual aware, as far as possible and as part of everyday treatment, that you are using or sharing their information – for example, noting medical details in their file or using personal details in a hospital referral letter. Individuals do have the right to ask for certain information to be withheld from others, in which case staff need to discuss respectfully with them what the negative effects on their care might be. If the individual is happy to accept this, that decision needs to be documented in their file.

(For further reading see, for example, 'Confidentiality: code of practice for health and social care in Wales', the main points of which apply across the UK. The document is available online.)

There are sometimes situations, outside of everyday health and social care settings, where other people need to be told information in order to protect someone or prevent a crime. Normal rules on confidentiality can be broken in the following circumstances:

▶ to protect a person at risk of harm

▶ to protect a person's health

▶ if the person appears to be about to commit a crime

▶ to protect the health or safety of others

▶ to help an investigation into suspected abuse

▶ if a court or tribunal orders certain information to be disclosed.

Reflect

Who has records or information about you? Think of an example, concerning your health, or income, or a family matter. Why would you want to keep this information private? What could happen if the information recorded was not correct or up-to-date? What could happen, and how would you feel, if this information was given to someone who didn't need to know it?

All the people you care for have the same rights as you to have their information recorded correctly, stored safely and only shared with those people who really need to know – usually with the person's consent.

Investigate

How many ways is information about individuals recorded in your workplace? See if your workplace uses any or all of the examples below.

▶ handwritten daily records
▶ care plans
▶ computer files
▶ hospital/GP letters
▶ medical charts and test results
▶ professional reports
▶ records of phone calls
▶ family/personal correspondence.

For how long does information of different kinds have to be kept in your workplace? How is information disposed of securely (by shredding, for example) and who is allowed to do it?

Features of manual information storage systems that ensure security

Physical security of information

The following guidelines apply to all care settings:

▶ Confidential records should normally be kept in a cupboard or cabinet which can be locked. It should be kept locked even if it is in a room which is normally itself kept locked.

▶ The cupboard or cabinet should be sited in a discreet place away from public areas of the workplace.

▶ Keys to the cupboard or cabinet, and access to the records, should be restricted to named staff (and any students, junior staff and visiting workers, as long as they are under staff supervision).

▶ Members of the public, including family and friends of staff or service users, should not be allowed unsupervised access to any area where records are stored.

▶ Open files, letters, notes, telephone messages etc. should not be left anywhere unattended where they could be seen by inappropriate people, or could be in danger of being lost.

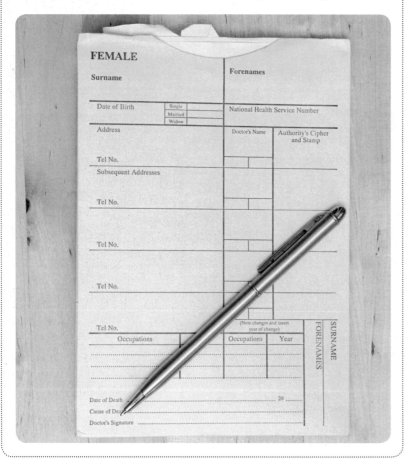

Your assessment criteria:

2.1 Describe features of manual and electronic information storage systems that help ensure security.

Discuss

In your experience, what are the most difficult aspects of trying to record, store or share information in a secure and confidential manner?

▶ Do you know of any instances where difficulties have led to less than perfect practice becoming the norm?

▶ Were there any consequences of this, or what might they have been?

▶ How have you motivated yourself and other staff to keep up good practice in this area?

Security of information in records

The following guidelines apply to all care settings:

▶ Each individual's name on their records should be clearly marked, easy to read and obviously different from all the others.

▶ Handwriting must be **legible** so mistakes are not made. Using handwritten records also encourages staff to read and enter in written records rather than just passing messages verbally or via other non-secure ways. It also makes clear who has written what, and – provided each entry is dated – when.

▶ Written information should be correctly spelled as far as possible, to avoid any confusion between similarly named people, places or procedures.

▶ Avoid the use of abbreviations (for example, 'ENT' for Ear, Nose and Throat Department) unless you are sure everyone seeing the record would understand the abbreviation, or unless there is a page in the records to note common abbreviations and their meanings.

▶ Staff should only write what is most important, so that relevant information is easy to find; security includes information being in the right place and available to those who might need to know it, as well as protected from those who don't.

▶ Regular staff and visiting professionals should sign and date everything they write. It may be important to know who has, or has not, been made aware of certain information about an individual.

▶ Make sure there is a tidy and secure place for different kinds of paper, such as test results or messages on bits of paper. There should be agreed ways of working in your workplace about what to do with this kind of information; generally, it is good practice to record things in a permanent form in an appropriate place, and as soon as possible. The original information may then need to be disposed of securely. There may be different sections of care records for different types of information. It may also be necessary to make a note in one part of the record about where to find information kept in another part.

▶ Don't erase or white-out mistakes; score through, initial or sign and then rewrite, according to your workplace policy.

▶ Only record factual information, not opinions or hearsay. This respects the human rights and privacy of individuals and ensures that records are accurate, which is particularly important if those records need to be shared with others.

Key terms

Legible: clear and easy to read

Care workers need to follow the agreed ways of working with information storage and systems in the workplace

Storing and recording information

▶ If you receive information verbally, decide whether any information needs to be recorded – if unsure then err on the side of caution. Make sure you know and record who is telling you any information and why, along with any contact details in case anyone needs to get back to them.

▶ Files should ideally not be taken out of their storage place (an office, for example) so try to write notes in this place. It is not ideal to write up notes in a lounge area, for example, while attempting to keep an eye on residents at the same time. If notes need to be taken to a meeting, check what the procedure is in your workplace – for example, take only the minimum pages necessary or take photocopies (these also need to be treated securely). Make sure a note is put in the file or cabinet as to what has been taken.

▶ Write up notes as soon as possible after the event – you may not remember all the details later on. This could be very important if the notes were ever used in court. Again, any temporary notes or messages must be disposed of securely.

▶ Do not write temporary notes with no indication as to which individual the notes concern, as the information could easily get entered into the wrong file: using initials only is one way to guard against this.

▶ Check what the procedures are in your workplace for disposing of sensitive or confidential material which is no longer needed: there may be shredding facilities, for example, but there may be safeguards in place against shredding material which may later be needed. Never assume that older material is unwanted – it may need to be **archived** in case the material needs to be referred to at a later date.

Your assessment criteria:

2.1 Describe features of manual and electronic information storage systems that help ensure security.

Key terms

Archive: to store old notes or other material safely in a special place, where they can be accessed later if needed; the place where this material is kept

It is good practice to write up notes and records in a safe environment where files are kept securely

To avoid mess and issues of security, records should not be taken out until needed and stored securely immediately after use

Case study

Your manager has sent round a cutting from a health and social care magazine, reporting on an inspection visit of another workplace. At this place, several instances of bad practice in information handling were found. These included the following:

► case notes left in an unlocked cabinet all day and night
► case records in illegible handwriting
► files of people with the same surname recorded but no first name
► scraps of paper lying around with client details on them
► staff discussing clients in the staff dining room area.

1. Why did the inspection team regard these practices as being unacceptable?
2. What should the staff have been doing instead?

Features of electronic information storage systems that ensure security

The following guidelines apply to all care settings:

▶ You may have to use **encrypted** files/emails to access or share information, or use passwords to get in to the work computer: never give anyone else your password(s). Many systems will prompt you to change your password(s) regularly; ideally, do not write these down, but at least make sure that they are recorded somewhere which is itself secure – e.g. a diary kept in a locked drawer.

▶ Always save any work you are doing on an individual's record, care plan etc., as you go along, so you do not lose anything vital. Only work on one individual's records at a time.

▶ If you are able to in your workplace, make sure essential records are backed up in case of computer or internet failure – for example, by putting records on disk. However, these need to be kept as secure as paper records, and also need to be updated as frequently as any other records so that the most up-to-date information is always available in any format.

▶ Normally you should not use people's names in emails or other 'public' communications; but if absolutely necessary, use initials only, or sometimes the first name (but this is not always an adequate safeguard against confusion). If someone sends you an insecure email, reply with a new email and use only the minimum personal information.

Your assessment criteria:

2.1 Describe features of manual and electronic information storage systems that help ensure security.

Key terms

Encrypted: refers to computer files or emails made secure by requiring passwords to open, send or receive them

Good practice

▶ Always log out if you have to leave a computer, even for a short time.

▶ Good practice which applies to paper records also applies to electronic ones: careful spelling; little or no use of abbreviations; entries as brief and relevant as possible; factual reporting only; signing and dating of entries written as soon as possible after the event.

▶ You may need to check if there are rules in your workplace about deleting files or parts of files: if in any doubt, don't delete.

▶ Staff should be well trained in using the computer at work for various tasks before they are left alone to use confidential records. All staff should know who to ask on a shift if, for example, they think they have deleted or transferred information which they should not have done.

▶ It is preferable not to use laptop computers, or to put information onto memory sticks, as both are easy to leave in insecure places. If these are permitted in your workplace there may be restrictions on what kind of data you can put on them: for example, standard diet sheets might be allowable but not someone's individual dietary records. If you need and are allowed to use them for completing confidential records or reports, you must make sure that the laptop or memory stick is not the only place where the information is stored, in case of the data getting physically or electronically lost. The laptop or memory stick should always be kept in a securely locked place if outside the normal workplace.

Reflect

Do you use a computer for everyday or occasional use at work?

▶ Consider whether you are following all the guidelines you have been given about accessing the computer and recording or finding information on it.

▶ If you don't currently use a computer, are you aware how other staff follow certain procedures to ensure good practice in information handling?

Practical Assessment Task   2.1

1. Describe the manual information storage systems which are used in your workplace, and explain what procedures are used to ensure that information is kept physically secure and used confidentially.

2. Describe the electronic information storage systems which are used in your workplace, and explain what procedures are used to ensure that information is kept physically secure and used confidentially.

Ensuring security when storing and accessing information

The organisation you work for has a duty to protect individuals' health, wellbeing and personal information. They should have procedures to ensure that all staff are aware of their responsibilities regarding personal information at all times – including not just regular staff but any contractors or volunteers who might be in the workplace.

In your workplace, there should be protocols and guidance about accessing, recording, storing and sharing information. As well as understanding these and the reasons for them, you need to show that you are following this guidance in your everyday work, in the areas of:

▶ physical security of information, both paper and electronic

▶ security of data contained in both paper and electronic records

▶ security of information shared verbally (spoken).

Sharing information verbally

In addition to manual and electronic means of recording, storing and sharing information, information is often received or shared over the phone or during conversations. You will need to show that you are aware of the particular problems that may arise in these situations. In particular:

▶ conversations about confidential matters should never take place in a public area

▶ even in an office setting, staff should be careful about whether anyone else in the office at the time needs to hear any of the conversation. The minimum of personally identifiable information should still be used

▶ staff should check, if possible, that a telephone caller is genuine and they are who they say they are. If at all unsure, tell the caller you will return their call and discuss with a senior manager

▶ there may be a procedure for recording information from telephone calls; any important information should be entered into an individual's care record. If you jot something down on a pad during a phone call, those jottings also need to be disposed of securely.

Your assessment criteria:

2.2 Demonstrate practices that ensure security when storing and accessing information

Discuss

Who might you need to share information with about people in your care? What procedures does your workplace have for sharing information with outside agencies, such as doctors or social workers?

General security practice

There are also general practices which normally need to be followed to ensure the security of information. These might include:

- ▶ wearing building passes or other **ID** issued to staff, and encouraging others to do so
- ▶ checking that any strangers in the work area have a right to be there
- ▶ knowing whom to tell if there are concerns about suspicious behaviour, or about information that may have gone missing
- ▶ ensuring there is a safe system for transfer of information, such as files going to another location, and a tracking system to ensure their safe and timely return
- ▶ ensuring that any visiting workers who wish to access records have the right to do so
- ▶ ensuring that anyone from an outside body, such as a charity or voluntary organisation, who might wish to access or use information, understands and is bound by the same strictness of practice around information security.

Case study

Terry is a health care assistant at a respite centre. The centre has recently admitted Mrs Singh for the first time: she lives at home with her husband, but the social services' referral letter mentions that he has had difficulty coping with her increasing medical problems and possible dementia. During a case conference, the social worker then confides that Mrs Singh may have to be taken into permanent care as there are questions of deliberate neglect and abuse by the husband, to be investigated but not yet proved. Mrs Singh does not seem very happy to see her husband when he visits, but gets very distressed after he leaves, so that at times it is difficult to carry out care.

How much information about Mrs Singh should Terry share with:

- ▶ another health care assistant who also cares for Mrs Singh?
- ▶ another health care assistant who knows her but does not carry out direct care with her?
- ▶ the activities assistant who attempts to engage Mrs Singh in various activities?
- ▶ the lady who serves the lunches every day?

Practical Assessment Task   2.2

1. Demonstrate to your assessor, using the files or other information on two individuals you care for, how you are following the correct procedures regarding physical security of information, both in paper and electronic files.

2. Demonstrate to your assessor, using the files or other information on two further individuals you care for, how you are following the correct procedures regarding security of information within individuals' files, both in paper and electronic forms.

3. Demonstrate to your assessor that you can make or receive a telephone call concerning an individual, or conduct a conversation about their care, following the correct procedures regarding security and confidentiality.

Your assessment criteria:

2.3 Maintain records that are up-to-date, complete, accurate and legible.

Making and maintaining good records

As well as knowing the procedures in your workplace, you will need to make sure that you always follow them when you are dealing with people's confidential records. To show that you have effective and competent information-handling skills you will need to make sure that service users' records are:

▶ up-to-date and complete

▶ accurate and legible

▶ stored safely

▶ shared appropriately.

Ensuring records are up-to-date

Tasks such as writing in someone's care file, recording medication given, or making notes about conversations with families, should be done as soon as possible. It is easy to forget important details, or get information mixed up, if you do not do this. Completing records only at the end of a shift is not ideal; talk to your workplace supervisor about your concerns if you are asked to work in this way. Any entry you make, in writing or on a computer, should normally be signed and dated; with some records, such as medication, the time of day may also be important. Entries should be consecutive – in other words, they should follow in strict date and time order. Also, make sure that any documents coming from outside the workplace, such as professional reports, are filed correctly so that it is easy to find the most recent one. Check with individuals and senior staff, if necessary, that any post and email addresses and phone numbers of family, friends or other professionals are up-to-date.

Discuss

'Good care records need to be up-to-date, complete, accurate, legible if handwritten, and stored, accessed and shared safely'.

▶ What aspects of this best practice do you find difficult in your day-to-day work?

▶ Do you feel you have sufficient support from senior staff to ensure best practice?

▶ Could you suggest any changes to practices in your workplace that would make achieving best practice easier?

Ensuring records are complete

Make sure you know the rules in your workplace about when, and how often, you need to record information in a person's file. Do not put off recording something until the next shift or the next day/week: it might get forgotten and there would be a gap in the records. Never make up information to fill a gap! Always speak to a senior member of staff if there is a problem because you or someone else has omitted to complete the records. You may be asked to contact an outside professional, for example a physiotherapist, if records from them appear to be missing.

Ensuring records are accurate

Making records up-to-date and complete is a large part of ensuring their accuracy. However, the individual entries that you make in someone's records must also be correct in the details. Only record what you have done yourself, and sign for yourself. If another staff member asks you to record something, it should be made clear who has done what. If a family member, for example, asks you to put something in an individual's record then you should record the name of the person who gave you that information – you may not know if it is accurate or not. Be extremely careful with recording numbers and quantities: it could make a huge difference if someone is to take 5mg or 50mg of a medicine, for example.

Ensuring records are legible

Your own handwriting must be clear and easy to read, neither too large nor too small, and not too 'flowery': you may need to practise a simpler style of handwriting for using in people's records. Don't crowd words or sentences too close together: in some workplaces you may have to leave a blank or scored line between every new entry. It is best not to use abbreviations (e.g. 'JR' for the John Radcliffe hospital) unless you can be quite sure that everyone will know what they mean. Some workplaces insert a sheet into people's files for recording common abbreviations and their meanings. Whether writing by hand or using the computer, make sure your spelling is correct. Computer spell checkers will not always know the correct spelling of surnames, for example.

Ensuring records are stored safely

Always put files or other paperwork back as soon as you have used it. Don't leave files or other information lying about, even in the office. Check that files are correctly placed if they are kept in alphabetical order. If you unlock a locked cabinet, lock it again as soon as possible and return the key straight away to its safe place. Don't allow members of the public (including relatives) to be left unsupervised in places like the office. If using files or records on the computer, change your password as often as you can and don't let anyone else use it. Make sure that you regularly save any document you are working on at a computer, and ask senior staff if there is any back-up for computer files in case of computer problems.

Sharing information appropriately

Information must only be given to those who really need to know it, but equally it is important to make sure that essential information is passed on when it is needed. This includes passing on information you have gained from someone you care for about their needs or preferences, especially if these have changed. Staff or visitors who do not know individuals as well as you do may need brief information about their likes and dislikes; for example, what name they wish to be called. Any change in an individual that worries you should be reported, in as private a way as possible, to a member of staff who could help or advise. In the same way any new information about a person – for example, from a district nurse – should be recorded and also shared with a senior member of staff rather than just filed as a report. Any apparent problems with people's behaviour, in particular, must be shared and recorded in a completely **objective** way which does not criticise or demean that person.

Your assessment criteria:

2.3 Maintain records that are up-to-date, complete, accurate and legible.

Key terms

Objective: applies to something described in a purely factual, non-emotional way

Reflect

Think back over the past week or so.

- ▶ With whom have you shared information about patients or clients, both within and outside your place of work?
- ▶ Do you think you shared that information appropriately in every case, and if not, what would you do differently in a similar situation in the future?

Care workers should ensure that records are out of sight and stored safely

Practical Assessment Task   2.3

1. Choose the records of two individuals in your workplace for whom you care. Ideally, one set of records should be written and one set should be electronic (created on a computer).

   a) Demonstrate how you *record* typical daily entries to these records during or just after a working shift, showing that they are up-to-date and legible following the guidelines above.

   b) Demonstrate how you *store* these records securely after daily use.

2. Choose the records of two individuals (the same or different ones from those you used before). During or just after a working shift carry out the following:

   a) Demonstrate that you have been *recording* accurately and completely in all the records that you are responsible for.

   b) Show, if appropriate, where you think there are gaps in the record which might cause a problem.

3. Choose one individual for whom you care and show how the rules on *sharing* information apply to your care for that person.

Your assessment criteria:

3.1 Support others to understand the need for secure handling of information.

Key terms

Appraisal: a formal meeting between an individual worker and a senior staff member, to monitor the worker's progress and discuss any concerns

How do you handle information securely?

Every health and social care workplace should have written policies and procedures relating to the way information should be handled. You should support staff, or others for whom you are responsible (e.g. students), to know:

▶ where to find this information

▶ what it says about information handling procedures

▶ how this affects their work role.

If the policies and procedures are very detailed or technical it is best to identify which parts are relevant for different people to see, depending on the needs of their role. It is advisable to demonstrate in a practical way how these procedures work, as well as showing the policies or telling people about them. New workers, students or volunteers in the work setting should be introduced to the main points about information security and confidentiality before, or as soon as possible after, they arrive in the workplace. They will probably be required to sign an agreement regarding their understanding of security and confidentiality in their workplace.

It can be useful, particularly for new staff, to include procedures and issues related to safe handling of information as an agenda item during staff meetings and **appraisals**. Whether it is a regular topic for a meeting or not, staff should never feel reluctant to ask or check what the correct procedure is in any particular case. Your workplace should offer training in handling information: it is important that workers do not skip these sessions, as they will help them understand in more detail how information governance rules determine access to and use of information.

Correct handling of information

Most people learn best by watching others, so you must make sure that your own handling of information is always done correctly and that you do not convey by your behaviour that sloppy practices are acceptable.

Remember that any breach of confidentiality, inappropriate use of health or social care records, or any abuse of secure computer systems, may lead to disciplinary measures for yourself or others. If the breach is severe it could bring into question any professional registration, result in legal proceedings and/or result in suspension or dismissal from work. Staff and others must always be encouraged to report any possible or actual breaches of security or confidentiality, no matter how senior the people involved, and be made aware of local procedures for reporting if these lapses have taken place.

Investigate

To whom do you report on a day-to-day basis? To whom do you report if that person is not around? Are these people senior enough to give you advice about using people's information? If not, who should you ask? Who is responsible for providing initial or updated training around information issues? If anyone reports to you, including unqualified or unpaid staff or volunteers, are they aware that they can and should come to you with queries about information handling?

Case study

Ayesha is a new carer in a mental health unit. She reports to you and you both share a senior manager. She has been shown where the paper files are kept, and has been given a computer password so she can send emails within the organisation. She can also fill in assessment forms on the computer.

1. What does Ayesha, as a new worker, need to know straight away regarding information handling?
2. What would you say to her if she mentions that some staff are writing up care records in the patients' lounge? What else might you do?
3. When could Ayesha bring up any other questions or concerns about handling information in the unit?

The importance of understanding the rules of access to and use of information can be discussed at staff meetings and appraisals

Supporting others to understand and contribute to records

All staff must be aware of the basic requirements of information security and confidentiality as it applies to accessing records; staff allowed to make entries in records also need to be clear about security and confidentiality requirements when doing so. Senior staff are responsible for the correct practice of new or junior staff, and so should ensure that these individuals have adequate induction and on-going training as well as adequate supervision. Staff should be encouraged to ask if they are unsure about their practice or the reasons for certain rules.

Sourcing, recording and sharing information

Some staff may have valuable contributions to make to someone's care by sharing information in meetings or case conferences. If they are not themselves allowed to make entries in care records – if they are students, for example – then their contribution should be noted and written up by another staff member, naming them as the source of the information (it is advisable to put 'Student', 'Volunteer' etc. after their name if they are not likely to be a permanent staff member). Family and friends of cared-for individuals may give new or relevant information to staff verbally: the important points of this information should be recorded in the appropriate place as soon as possible so that all staff are aware of it.

Making expectations clear

If staff or others are new or inexperienced it is advisable to start by showing them the various types and sections of care records before they are asked to make any entries. They should be shown examples in the records of entries that are:

▶ up-to-date

▶ complete

▶ accurate

▶ legible.

They should also be shown examples of where information has been:

▶ stored safely

▶ shared appropriately.

Your assessment criteria:

3.2 Support others to understand and contribute to records.

Reflect

What did you find difficult or confusing when you were first asked to start contributing to care records? How might you use this experience to show or explain to newer staff more clearly how to contribute to people's records?

Building experience

At appropriate times junior staff can then be given small opportunities to record details in the case records, always under supervision, gradually building up the amount and variety of entries they can write until they are deemed to be safe to do so alone. Any entries by very junior staff, students or volunteers, may need to be countersigned by the supervising staff member.

Keeping information up to date

Staff and others should be encouraged to report any changes in an individual's personal details, preferences, condition or care needs that they become aware of during the course of their work. While they might do this verbally to their colleagues, particularly if they feel the information is urgent, they should be encouraged to make entries in the individual's care record if allowed or to inform more senior staff who can do this.

Practical Assessment Task   3.1   3.2

1. Demonstrate, using one set of care records in detail, that you can explain to a new or more junior staff member the security and confidentiality aspects of handling the records and the information within them.

2. Demonstrate how you can support a new or more junior member of staff to enter information into a set of care records during, or just after, a working shift. Show that you are making them aware of the importance of ensuring the records are safely accessed and stored, and that the information entered into them is up-to-date, complete, accurate and legible.

Care workers should report any changes in personal information or care needs and records should be updated

Are you ready for assessment?

AC	What do you know now?	Assessment task	✓
1.1	Identify legislation and codes of practice that relate to handling information in health and social care	Page 263	
1.2	The main points of legal requirements and codes of practice for handling information in health and social care	Page 263	

AC	What can you do now?	Assessment task	✓
2.1	Describe features of manual and electronic systems that help ensure security	Page 271	
2.2	Demonstrate practices that ensure security when storing and accessing information	Page 273	
2.3	Maintain records that are up-to-date, complete, accurate and legible	Page 277	
3.1	Support others to understand the need for secure handling of information	Page 281	
3.2	Support others to understand and contribute to records	Page 281	

10 | Understand mental health problems (CMH 302)

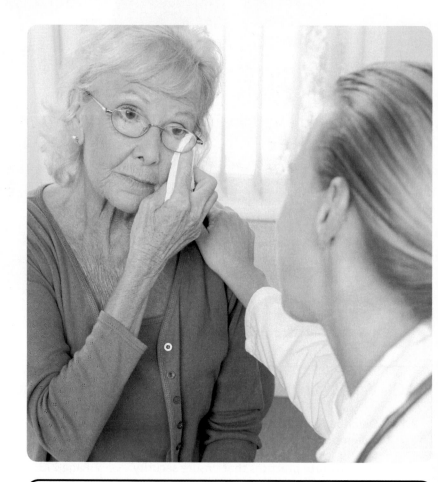

Assessment of this unit

This unit introduces the main forms of mental health problems. You will be expected to know the strengths and limitations of the main psychiatric classifications systems and have a working knowledge of alternative frameworks for understanding mental distress. The unit also looks at the ways that mental health problems affect the individual and others in their social network, and considers the benefits of early intervention in promoting mental health and wellbeing. You will need to:

▶ know the main forms of mental illness

▶ consider the impact of mental ill health on individuals and others in their social network.

The assessment of this unit is entirely knowledge-based. To successfully complete this unit, you will need to produce evidence of your knowledge as shown in the table opposite. Your tutor or assessor will help you to prepare for your assessment. The tasks suggested in the unit will help you to create the evidence you need.

CHAPTER 10

AC   What you need to know

1.1	Describe the main types of mental ill health according to the psychiatric (DSM/ICD) classification system: mood disorders, personality disorders, anxiety disorders, psychotic disorders, substance-related disorders, eating disorders, cognitive disorders
1.2	Explain the key strengths and limitations of the psychiatric classification systems
1.3	Explain two alternative frameworks for understanding mental distress
1.4	Explain how mental ill health may be indicated through an individual's emotions, thinking and behaviour
2.1	Explain how individuals experience discrimination due to misinformation, assumptions and stereotypes about mental ill health
2.2	Explain how mental ill health may have an impact on the individual, including: • psychological and emotional • practical and financial • the impact of using services • social exclusion • positive impacts
2.3	Explain how mental ill health may have an impact on those in the individual's familial, social or work network, including: • psychological and emotional • practical and financial • the impact of using services • social exclusion • positive impacts
2.4	Explain the benefits of early intervention in promoting mental health and wellbeing

This unit also links to some of the other units:

DEM 301	Understand the process and experience of dementia
DEM 312	Understand and enable interaction and communication with individuals who have dementia
DEM 304	Enable rights and choices of individuals with dementia whilst minimising risk

Some of your learning will be repeated in these units and will give you the chance to review your knowledge and understanding.

What are the main forms of mental ill health?

Experiencing 'mental illness'

Mental illness is a disorder of the mind that affects how individuals think and feel. It can change how those individuals behave. The problems associated with mental illness can extend to how an individual forms relationships, and how that individual interacts with the wider community.

People diagnosed with mental health problems can be **socially excluded** from normal activities and resources due to the **stigma** of the illness. **Discrimination** based on the wider community's perception of mental illness compounds the difficulties faced by individuals with mental health problems. Learning about mental health problems will help you understand these difficulties. Better understanding of mental illness will help you to:

▶ become more aware of the need to provide support for people who have been diagnosed with a mental illness

▶ learn the difference between an individual's needs when they are mentally healthy and when they are mentally ill

▶ learn about how health and social care practices support individuals with mental illness.

Key terms

Mental illness: a psychiatric term used to define disorders of the mind

Socially excluded: the condition of being isolated, left out and denied access to social activities

Stigma: a mark of social disgrace; the effect of negative impacts upon an individual's identity

Discrimination: the unfair treatment of an individual or group on the basis of prejudice

Mental health problems can be very isolating and cause people to be stigmatised by others

How does mental illness affect people?

Mental illness can affect the individual's relationships, their work, and their quality of life. Having a mental illness is difficult, not only for the person concerned, but also for their family and friends. Mental disorders can affect anyone of any age.

What are 'mental health' and 'mental illness'?

Mental illness is very common. According to MIND (2009), a mental health charity, about one in four people in Britain will receive this diagnosis at some point in their life. At any one time up to one in six people have a mental health problem (Department for Health, 2011). Despite this, there is a great deal of controversy about what 'mental illness' is, what causes it, and how people can be helped to recover from it. People who are experiencing mental or emotional distress are often very reluctant to see their experiences as 'mental illness' and sometimes reject or avoid a diagnosis of their condition. Most of us would prefer to think that we are 'mentally healthy' most of the time.

The World Health Organization defines 'mental health', in a report on promoting mental health, as:

> 'a state of wellbeing in which the individual realizes his or her own potential, can cope with the normal stresses of life, can work productively and fruitfully, and is able to make a contribution to her or his community' (WHO, 2005)

In contrast, mental illness is associated with abnormal psychological and emotional experiences and behaviour that is not recognised as being either a part of normal individual development or the cultural norms of a given society. A number of other terms are also used to describe 'mental illness', including:

▶ mental disorder

▶ mental health problems

▶ mental distress

▶ mental ill health.

Mental illness is divided into a range of disorders within **psychiatric** systems of classification. As we shall see, these psychiatric systems have both strengths and weaknesses.

Reflect

Reflect on the way you currently think about 'mental illness'. How is a 'mentally ill' person different to a, mentally well, person?

Reflect

How do people in your work setting refer to mental ill health? Are local or slang terms sometimes used to describe people's experiences of mental ill health? Are these negative about or critical of the person's experience?

Investigate

What is the Mental Health Act 2007? Find out using the internet or information available in your workplace.

Key terms

Psychiatric: the branch of medicine dealing with the diagnosis and treatment of mental illness

Classifications of mental illness

The two main systems for the classification of mental illness are:

▶ the Diagnostic and Statistical Manual of Mental Disorders (**DSM**)

▶ the International Classification of Diseases and Related Health Problems (**ICD**).

The DSM is published by the American Psychiatric Association and covers all mental health conditions for children and adults. It lists the known causes, prognoses and treatments for all known mental illnesses. The ICD classification is published by the World Health Organization and identifies the signs, symptoms, abnormal findings, social circumstances and external causes of a broad range of mental illnesses. According to the DSM and the ICD, mental illness or disorder can be classified and diagnosed in the same way that we classify and diagnose physical illnesses.

There are many different kinds of mental illness classified in the DSM and ICD. You are required to have a working knowledge of the disorders identified in figure 10.1 Health and social care practitioners frequently provide care and support for people experiencing one or more of these types of mental ill health.

According to the DSM and ICD systems of classification, individuals with mental disorders will experience and present with certain combinations of signs and symptoms that are not usually found in mentally healthy individuals. Medical and mental health practitioners diagnose a person's mental illness according to the combination of signs and symptoms they report or are observed to have.

Mood disorders

Mood disorders can be divided into illnesses that depress mood and illnesses that produce episodes of elated mood, or mania. Some illnesses, such as bipolar disorder, combine both types of mood disorder. Depression is the most common form of mood disorder. The signs and symptoms of depression include extreme or enduring sadness, loss of interest in life, sleep disturbance, appetite changes and tearfulness.

Personality disorder

This is a term used to describe the disordered inner experiences and the often challenging or anti social behaviour of people that frequently lead them into conflict with family, friends and the wider community or which lead them to have poor coping skills. An individual with a personality disorder may find it difficult to form proper relationships, can appear manipulative, may self-harm and can be thought of by others as 'attention-seeking'.

Key terms

DSM: abbreviation for the Diagnostic and Statistical Manual of Mental Disorders

ICD: abbreviation for the International Classification of Diseases

Classifications of mental illness are widely used by psychiatrists and other medical practitioners to make diagnoses

Reflect

What do you think of when you hear or read about 'hallucinations' and 'delusions'? Why might a person who experiencing these things be distressed by them?

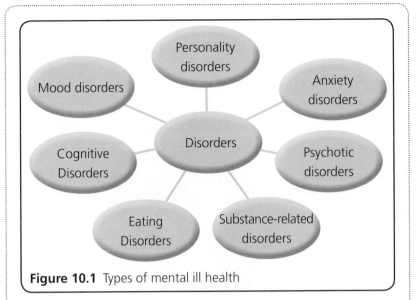

Figure 10.1 Types of mental ill health

Anxiety disorders

Conditions classified as anxiety disorders generally cause a person to be worried, unusually afraid or anxious most of the time or in particular circumstances. The source of anxiety can be unspecified or may be phobia-based. Examples of phobia-based anxieties are agoraphobia (fear of leaving familiar surroundings) and social phobia (fear of other people).

Psychotic disorders

Psychotic disorders are a group of serious mental illnesses that cause sufferers to periodically or permanently lose contact with reality. These disorders can be characterised by: **hallucinations**, **delusions**, and thought disorders. Hallucinations are sensory perceptions without external stimuli – hearing voices or seeing things that aren't there, for example. Delusions are strongly held false beliefs that run counter to evidence, common sense and widely agreed-upon fact. Characterised by rambling and disordered speech patterning, a thought disorder is the condition by which an individual's thinking is disrupted, blocked or repeated. Examples of thought disorder include: echolalia, where thoughts and speech are repeated like an echo; thought block, where thoughts are interrupted or stopped; and flight of ideas, where the person speaking moves rapidly from one unrelated subject to the next. One of the most common psychotic disorders is **schizophrenia**. An individual with schizophrenia may experience all three psychotic characteristics – hallucinations, delusionary thinking and thought disorders – as well as appearing unmotivated, lethargic and depressed.

Key terms

Psychotic disorder: a type of mental illness that causes the individual to periodically or permanently lose contact with reality

Hallucination: a sensory perception without external stimuli – hearing voices, for example

Delusion: a strongly held false belief

Schizophrenia: a mental illness characterised by delusions, hallucinations, thought and speech incoherence and physical agitation

Substance-related disorders

This category of conditions is used to classify and describe the behaviour and experiences of people who become dependent on drugs, alcohol or other addictive substances. Substance-related disorders can cause mental and physical health problems for individuals affected by them. They may also exacerbate or make worse other mental disorders. Dual diagnosis is the term for diagnosis of co-existing mental health and substance misuse problems.

Eating disorders

The most common eating disorders are anorexia nervosa and bulimia. Individuals with anorexia tend to over-exercise, under-eat, and will make themselves sick to control their weight. Disordered body-image perceptions and disordered thinking about food and appearance typically cause people with anorexia nervosa to become extremely underweight and malnourished. People with bulimia nervosa tend to over-eat by bingeing on food, and then cause themselves to vomit as a way of restricting their calorie intake. Many people with bulimia say that they think about controlling their weight most of the time. Individuals with either condition can exhibit delusional perceptions of their body shape.

Cognitive disorders

Cognitive disorders are conditions that affect a person's ability to think or use their memory. Though it is a rare condition, amnesia is a well-known example of a cognitive disorder. The most commonly occurring form of cognitive disorder is dementia, particularly Alzheimer's disease, which is mainly experienced by older people.

Discuss

Mental ill health is linked to poor physical health. Discuss with a friend or colleague how mental illness may affect an individual's physical health.

Case study

Jane is 17 years old and started work in a hairdresser's salon as a trainee a year ago. The girls she works with, Charley and Sam, always tell Jane how nice and slim she looks. Last Friday they asked Jane whether she would like to go to the pub with them after work for a meal. They explained that this was to celebrate Sam's 18th birthday. Jane very quickly said that she wouldn't be able to go, and made up a story about meeting her cousin that evening. This week Charley heard Jane vomiting in the salon toilets just after she had finished her lunch. Charley is now concerned and thinks Jane may be ill. After talking about it with Sam, Charley has realised that she has never seen Jane eat and that she seems very preoccupied with her appearance.

1. What pattern of behaviour or signs and symptoms suggest Jane may have a form of mental illness?
2. Which category of mental illness should Jane's apparent problem be classified under?
3. Why might Jane be reluctant to have her behaviour described as 'mental illness'?

Knowledge Assessment Task 1.1

Practitioners working in health and social care settings need to have an understanding of the main types of mental ill health. In this activity you are required to produce a four-page leaflet, suitable for a new member of staff, that:

▶ describes the main forms of mental ill health according to the DSM/ICD classification systems.

Keep the leaflet that you produce as evidence towards your assessment.

Investigate

What kinds of information and policies are there in your work place relating to mental ill health? Find out what is available and review what it says about the ways mental ill health can affect the people for whom you provide care or support.

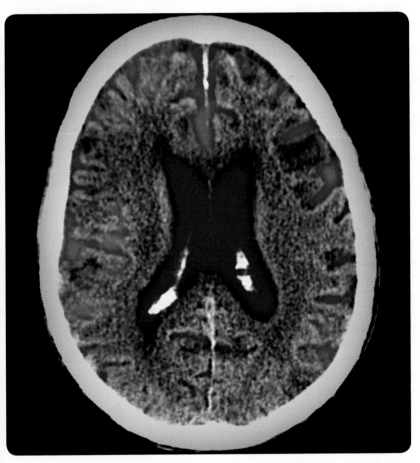

A brain scan of a patient with Alzheimer's disease

Psychiatric classification systems

The two main psychiatric classification systems used in health and social care settings in the UK, the DSM and the ICD, each have strengths and limitations in terms of understanding mental distress and diagnosing mental illness.

Strengths of the classification systems

The strengths of the two psychiatric classification systems are that they:

▶ provide a way for clinicians, particularly psychiatrists, to identify and make sense of disordered thinking, mood and behaviour

▶ identify and group symptoms in ways that help psychiatrists make a diagnosis of a recognised mental illness

▶ provide guidance on how to treat the person's mental distress

▶ help clinicians to exclude other possible causes of distress, of bizarre behaviour and/or experiences – drug taking, for example.

Case study

Mansell, a 22 year-old man, is seen running around the town centre and shouting. He looks very upset and worried. After a while two policemen arrive and take him away in their car. At the police station he continues to shout and the police think he might be mentally ill. They call a psychiatrist who interviews him. The psychiatrist finds out that Mansell thinks he is being followed by secret agents who want to harm him. He explains that he knows this because a voice in his head tells him that he must shout out to draw attention to himself and so stop the secret agents killing him in public. The psychiatrist also discovers that Mansell has other odd ideas about being a member of the royal family and that he will one day inherit millions of pounds and be made a duke.

1. What signs lead the psychiatrist to think that Mansell has a mental illness?

2. How does a classification system help the psychiatrist make a diagnosis?

3. What kind of mental illness diagnosis would you expect a psychiatrist who has seen and spoken to Mansell to make?

Limitations of the classification systems

Psychiatric classification systems are controversial and have been criticised by some health and social care practitioners, people who use mental health services and their families, for a number of reasons. Both the DSM and ICD classification systems are seen to have significant limitations.

Your assessment criteria:

1.2 Explain the key strengths and limitations of the psychiatric classification system

Discuss

How might the psychiatric classification systems that you have been reading about be beneficial to care practice in your work setting? Are there also drawbacks or reasons not to use formal psychiatric classification systems when individuals for whom you provide care or support become mentally distressed? Discuss your thoughts and ideas with a colleague or your supervisor.

Key terms

Reliable diagnosis: a diagnosis supported by peer diagnoses relating to the same case

Labelling: defining or describing a person in terms of a label, such as a diagnosis (e.g 'the depressed woman') rather than seeing them as an individual

Reliability

A psychiatric classification system that is **reliable** should provide those who use it with a consistent, dependable way of diagnosing the signs and symptoms of mental ill health. Several different practitioners using the same classification system should diagnose the signs and symptoms of an individual in the same way if the system is, in fact, reliable. However, people who are experiencing mental distress don't always behave in the same way or give exactly the same information when they are being assessed by more than one person. Reliability therefore depends on the practitioner asking appropriate questions to gather important information on which to base their diagnosis.

Inflexibility

Sometimes an individual's reckless or extreme behaviour can be mistaken for a mental illness simply because that behaviour fits an aspect of the psychiatric classification system. For instance, a keen cyclist might cycle a hundred miles in a day, which to some is not 'normal behaviour'. It could, in fact, be mistaken for a sign of mania or overactivity in an individual who has previously been diagnosed with bipolar disorder. However, it could also be that the person just enjoys long cycle rides and does this to keep fit. It is always important, therefore, to consider the meaning and purpose of an individual's behaviour before concluding that it is a symptom of 'mental illness'.

Accuracy

The system of classifying mental illnesses according to specific signs and symptoms creates some 'blind spots' where some behaviour that may have other, non-mental health causes, is seen as an indication of mental distress. For example, an individual may show signs of depression, but actually suffers from an allergy to wheat. Because some of the symptoms overlap, using a psychiatric classification system to make sense of the person's symptoms could result in an inaccurate diagnosis of depression. There are also situations where a person's symptoms could result in more than one possible diagnosis (see chapter 10 for discussion of dementia and depression symptoms, for example), making the use of the ICD and DSM classification systems questionable for accurate diagnosis.

Labelling

The use of psychiatric classification systems to make sense of 'out of character' behaviour and unusual experiences can lead to individuals being **labelled** as having a 'mental illness' when there may be other reasons for this. A 'mental illness' diagnosis can in turn lead to the person being stigmatised and discriminated against. For example, having a 'mental illness' diagnosis can mean that the person has to provide evidence from a doctor that they are fit to travel to some other countries. People who are open about their mental ill health and the diagnoses they have also complain that they are often discriminated against when applying for jobs or seeking promotion at work.

Knowledge Assessment Task 1.2

The psychiatric classification system has strengths and limitations which it is necessary to be aware of when working in health and social care settings. In this task you need to demonstrate your understanding of these strengths and limitations. Imagine that the manager of your work setting has sent an email to all members of staff asking for everyone's views on the way 'mental illness' and the mental distress of service users is discussed and referred to in your workplace. You manager is wondering whether it would be beneficial to start using a formal psychiatric classification system such as the ICD or DSM systems in your work setting.

You are asked to write an email to your manager in which you identify and explain what you think the strengths and drawbacks of using a formal psychiatric classification system in your work setting would be. You should ensure that you explain the key strengths and limitations of psychiatric classification systems in your email.

Keep a copy of the work that you produce as evidence towards your assessment

Alternative frameworks for understanding mental illness

Psychiatric approaches to mental illness tend to locate the source of a person's problems within the individual themselves. They don't take into account the influence of external social, economic and cultural factors such as poverty, social inequality or experiences of unfair discrimination. **Social model** explanations suggest that external factors such as poverty, inequality, the circumstances people live in and negative life events are significant causes of mental illness. Similarly, where the psychiatric model concentrates on treating the illness itself through physiological methods such as medication or electro-convulsive therapy, alternative approaches tend to see solutions in changing the person's environment or supporting their physical and spiritual wellbeing. The **holistic model**, for example, concentrates on the 'whole person', by considering the way an individual's physical, mental and emotional wellbeing work together to create 'health' and wellness

The holistic model

The holistic model for understanding mental illness accounts for factors beyond the individual's thoughts, feelings and behaviour. It examines all aspects of the individual's state of being. These include:

▶ physical aspects, including the person's appetite, sleep and the amount of exercise they do

▶ psychological aspects, including self-perception, **self-esteem** and identity

▶ emotional aspects – for example, anger, sadness, fear, disgust and happiness

▶ spiritual aspects – the individual's belief system

▶ social aspects, including personal relationships, activities and social network.

Your assessment criteria:

1.3 Explain two alternative frameworks for understanding mental distress

Key terms

Social model: an approach that views mental health problems as symptoms or consequences of larger social problems and as being caused by social factors such as poverty, discrimination and inequality in society

Holistic model: an approach which views mental health problems as a consequence of dysfunction or a lack of overall balance within the body and 'spirit', as well as the mind/brain

Self-esteem: the individual's sense of self-worth; general usage refers to low or high self-esteem

Case study

Anna feels tired much of the time. She has recently been made redundant from the florist shop where she has worked since her partner was sacked from his job after allegations of theft. Anna and her partner have two small children. The threat of a court case hangs over them. Anna feels she is letting the children down. She is tearful much of the time. Life doesn't seem worth living. She feels isolated, withdrawn, and does not want to meet her friends.

1. What aspects of the holistic model for understanding mental illness do you think would explain Anna's mental ill health?

2. What aspects of Anna's behaviour would be considered in a psychiatric classification system?

3. What diagnosis might you give her if you were a doctor?

The social model

The social model views an individual's position and experiences within society as the root cause of their mental health problems. The effects of stigma, social exclusion and low self-esteem cause high levels of stress that eventually lead to mental distress. The social model proposes that:

▶ mental illness is more like a form of disability than a physical illness

▶ poverty, inequality, personal circumstances and negative life events are significant causes or 'triggers' of mental illness

▶ social stigma and social exclusion become significant factors in prolonging and maintaining mental ill health

▶ society's institutions – its mental health services in particular – are an on-going factor in maintaining an individual's mental distress

▶ a person's recovery from mental illness depends on them having the opportunity to participate fully in society.

Interventions for the social model of disability

Mental health services based on a psychiatric approach have in the past treated mental illness with a combination of medication (drugs) and talking treatments (counselling). The social model of disability relies on new forms of intervention that seek to tackle the causes as well as the symptoms of mental illness. These interventions include changing aspects of the physical environment associated with mental ill health (such as overcrowded, poor quality housing, for example), improving the social networks and level of social support available to people who experience mental illness and challenging discrimination, stigma and negative attitudes towards mental illness.

> **Discuss**
>
> Speak to colleagues and make notes on how the holistic model is used for the treatment of mental health problems in your workplace. Which other approaches are used, and how?

Knowledge Assessment Task   1.3

Psychiatric classification systems don't take account of the influence on mental health of external social, economic and cultural factors such as poverty, social inequality or experiences of unfair discrimination. In this knowledge assessment task you are asked to explain two alternative frameworks to the psychiatric classification system that take a broader approach to understanding mental distress.

1. Write a letter to the relatives of a service user in which you two alternative ways of understanding mental illness other than the psychiatric classification system.

2. In your letter identify the key features of each alternative approach and explain how they differ from the DSM/ICD psychiatric classification systems.

Keep your written work as evidence for your assessment.

The signs and symptoms of mental illness

An individual's emotions, thinking and behaviour may indicate mental ill health. The indicators of mental ill health are usually described as the 'signs and symptoms'. Signs are what an observer can see and symptoms are what the individual experiences. A sign, for example, might be an individual apparently talking to him/herself; the symptom would be the individual's experience of an imaginary person with whom they are conversing.

Emotions

Emotions are about how people feel and are important in mental health. In fact, while mental ill health or mental illness is often thought of as being concerned with how the brain works, often it is the individual's emotions which are unsettled or upset. Experiencing very strong emotions can be a sign of mental ill health, for example. Strong emotions displayed by individuals when they are mentally distressed can include anger, fear, sadness, frustration and over-excitement. A person with depression might be tearful. A person with schizophrenia may not show any emotions at all, and may be what mental health professionals call emotionally 'flat'. However, another person might be 'labile' – meaning they experience rapid change in their emotions, such as from joy one moment to sorrow the next. Consistently negative emotions, or in-congruent emotions that do not reflect what is happening, are indications that a person may be experiencing mental ill health or is at risk of doing so.

Thinking

We all think, and take our ability to think for granted. However, thinking can be disturbed when a person is mentally unwell. Mental illnesses tend to disrupt the thinking process. The disruption can be mild, as in some forms of depression, where the individual is likely to have negative thoughts and not expect anything good to happen. The disruption can also be severe, as in a psychotic disorder such as schizophrenia. A person who experiences delusions, for example, can have frightening thoughts that other people find difficult to understand. With schizophrenia, thought patterns are so disrupted they are described as deluded or disordered – for example, an individual may believe the television is the 'voice of a god' or that there is a plot to harm or even kill them. Many mental illnesses also affect an individual's ability to think sequentially and to remember and recall information. This can disrupt an individual's ability to carry out apparently simple activities and perform everyday living skills – such as dressing or cooking – effectively.

People with enduring mental health problems can experience a lack of motivation and may slip into an unhealthy lifestyle as a way of coping with their symptoms

Investigate

Find the website of an organisation like MIND or the Mental Health Foundation and research the symptoms and impact of 'schizophrenia' on individuals' lives. Try to find out how this conditions affects people's thinking in everyday situations.

Behaviour

Behaviour is what we do, and how we act. It is the most objective sign of mental health and mental illness. When a mental health assessment is carried out, practitioners will often observe the behaviour of the individual and make an assessment of mental state based on what they see the person doing. An individual may at times act strangely or they might take extreme risks. On some occasions a mentally unwell person might behave in an unpredictable, aggressive, disinhibited or avoidant way. Other behavioural indicators of mental ill health are an exaggeration of or disruption in what is normal behaviour for a person, such as them becoming overactive or significantly less active than usual.

Figure 10.2 How mental illness shows itself

Discuss

What is the difference between mental illness and eccentricity? Discuss this question with a friend or work colleague.

Emotionally:

1. Frequent changes of mood

2. Persistent, unchanging mood

3. Feeling very low or very elated

4. Feeling 'numb': not feeling anything

5. Being unable to identify or empathise with feelings of others

Cognitively:

1. Poor concentration

2. Confused/muddled thinking

3. Interrupted thoughts

4. Bizarre thoughts

5. Repetitive, unwanted thoughts

Behaviourally:

1. Erratic and culturally inappropriate behaviour

2. Agitation

3. Withdrawal

4. Aggression/violence to others

5. Self-harm

Physiologically:

1. Poor/broken sleep

2. Changes in appetite

3. Changes in energy levels

4. Loss of sexual interest/energy

5. Physical tension

6. Unexplained headaches

Knowledge Assessment Task   **1.4**

Imagine that you have been asked to prepare a group information session for relatives of people recently diagnosed with mental illness. You have been asked by your manager to develop handouts explaining what 'mental illness' is and how mental ill health can be indicated by an individual's emotions, thinking and behaviour. You should assume that the group who will read your handouts have no previous knowledge of mental illness and are keen to understand what they should look out for in future.

Keep a copy of the work that you produce as evidence towards your assessment.

Experiencing discrimination

Mental ill health may not just affect the individual who experiences it. It can affect others in their social network as well because of discrimination and stigma. People who become mentally unwell will also often experience discrimination because of misinformation, negative assumptions and **stereotypes** about mental ill health. This means that the person may be treated less favourably, or even with hostility, because of their mental health problems or because they have a history of mental ill health. People with mental health problems are often discriminated against on the basis that they are perceived as being dangerous, contagious and a 'drain on society'.

What is stigma?

A stigma is an attribute, behaviour or reputation that is socially discrediting in some way. The stigma of 'mental illness' tends to lead to people taking an unfavourable view of someone who declares their experience or status of 'mental illness'. Individuals with mental ill health often say that they are treated differently and less favourably than other people because of their stigmatised status. Stigma and discrimination can affect people associated with the 'mentally ill' individual, such as their family and friends, as well as the individual themselves. This is because there is a common assumption that mental illness is partly inherited – thereby making relatives 'suspect' as either the source of 'defective genes' or as carriers of them.

Your assessment criteria:

2.1 Explain how individuals experience discrimination due to misinformation, assumptions and stereotypes about mental ill health

Key terms

Stereotypes: commonly held but simplified and over-generalised beliefs about individuals or groups in society

Reflect

Have you ever felt discriminated against – perhaps because of your age, appearance, gender or ethnicity? Reflect on how this made you feel and the impact of it on your relationship with the person or people who you felt was discriminating against you.

What does 'normal' mean? Are people who behave unusually mentally ill or just different from the majority?

Case study

Abel is new to the area having been allocated a flat after leaving the mental health unit where he had been treated for schizophrenia. He wants to buy cigarettes so goes to the local newsagent's. As he enters the shop he hears a voice in his head talking to him. As he is used to doing, Abel talks back to the voice. The newsagent looks at him very suspiciously, and when he sees him talking to himself says that he doesn't want his sort in his shop because it will frighten his other customers away. He then tells Abel that he knows all about people like him, that they all belong in an institution and that he won't serve him. The next customer comes into the shop as Abel leaves. The newsagent say to him that he has heard all about what people like Abel get up to and there is a disturbing report of an incident involving an individual with mental problems in the paper.

1. How is Abel discriminated against in this scenario?

2. What assumptions and stereotypes is the discrimination based on?

3. Why do you think the shopkeeper is discriminating against Abel?

Knowledge Assessment Task   2.1

Health and social care practitioners need an understanding of the impact of mental ill health on individuals and others in their social network. In particular, they need to understand that individuals are affected by societal attitudes as well as the mental illness itself. In this knowledge assessment task you are required to:

▶ design a poster explaining the impact of stereotyping, discrimination and stigma on people experiencing mental ill health.

Keep a copy of the work that you produce as evidence for your assessment. You should also be prepared to discuss the contents of your poster with your assessor.

Reflect

How do you and your colleagues think about and refer to the mental ill health of service users? Can you think of ways of challenging stereotypes and stigma about mental ill health in your workplace?

The effects of mental illness on the individual

Mental ill health may affect the individual in both positive and negative ways. These can be summarised in terms of psychological and emotional effects, the financial and practical impact on the individual, the impact of using services on the individual, the risk of being socially excluded and also the various positive impacts that can result from an episode of mental ill health. Figure 10.3 summarises these various impacts.

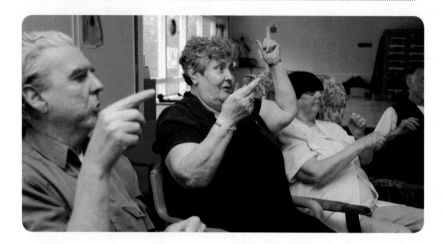

Key terms

Sectioned: Compulsorily admitted to hospital as the consequence of a mental health problem

Investigate

Using the internet, investigate famous people who have been said to have had a mental illness. Were there any positive aspects of their condition?

Case study

Phil and Kate live together in a one-bedroom flat. Phil paints pictures much of the time and likes to exhibit them at the MIND Centre where he and Kate go as regular members. He receives a great deal of praise for his paintings and is thought of as a talented artist. Kate gets a lot of headaches and often goes to the doctor's about them. The doctor thinks that the headaches are due to her depression and says things like: they will go when she feels more cheerful. Phil and Kate both want to go to the coast for a day but as they do not work they cannot afford the train fare. Kate thinks the fresh air would be good for her headaches and Phil wants to paint some seascapes. A friend at the MIND centre has noted a coach trip to the coast and told Phil about it. As a surprise for Kate he tries to book two seats but the coach company only accepts payments using a credit card which neither Phil or Kate have.

Explain how Phil and Kate's mental ill health has affected them:

a. psychologically and emotionally
b. financially and practically
c. in their use of services
d. socially
e. positively

Figure 10.3 Possible impacts of mental ill health on the individual

Type of impact	Examples
Psychological and emotional	• Mental illness can have a traumatic effect on the individual, with feelings of shame, anger, denial and fear. • Individuals with dementia may feel that they are losing their mind and feel afraid because they do not know what is happening to them. • Depression can lead to relationship difficulties and the individual may be tearful and sad a lot of the time. • An individual with an eating disorder may feel that their body is the wrong shape and that they are fat even when they really are quite slim.
Financial and practical	• The individual may need time off work to help them recover from an episode of mental ill health, or may even be sacked for poor work performance. This can cause financial pressures that in some cases make the mental ill health worse. • Practical effects of mental ill health include not feeling well enough to take the children to school or to go shopping, for example. Studying can be hard if the person is unable to concentrate or focus on what they need to do. • In more serious cases the individual might need hospitalisation in a psychiatric unit resulting in disruption to normal routines and relationships. Some people are sectioned under the Mental health Act 2007 and detained and treated against their will.
Using services	• People with mental ill health often say that they do not feel able to use the same services as everyone else. They might want to go to see their GP for a physical problem but have this misunderstood as a sign of mental ill health because they carry the 'label' of mental illness. When they feel ill, with a headache or backache, for instance, they may be directed to the psychiatric system as a matter of course.
Social exclusion	• Social exclusion occurs when groups or individuals are unable to gain access to the usual resources, services and institutions, which prevents them from taking part in normal life or experiencing an acceptable quality of life. Some people with mental health problems avoid using community services like leisure centres and swimming baths because of the stigma associated with 'mental illness' and the discriminatory behaviour that they experience. Such people can feel socially excluded from normal everyday services as a result.
Positive impacts	• Seeing an episode of mental ill health as a positive experience can be difficult for those who are suffering distressing symptoms. However, over time some people do believe that their past experiences of mental ill health have had a positive outcome for them in the end. For example, going through the distress of a relationship or personal breakdown may change a person's life for the better if they escape an abusive, unfulfilling or destructive relationship by doing so. Some people also say they feel more creative when they are experiencing mental ill health. They might dance, sing, write or paint more, for example. A number or celebrities, such as Stephen Fry, have 'come out' about their mental health problems and often link them to their success.

How does mental ill health affect others?

Mental ill health can also affect an individual's family, social relations and their networks of friends and colleagues at work. The impact of an individual's mental ill health on people close to them is likely to be different to the impact that the illness has on the person themselves (see figure 10.4).

Reflect

Why do you think that the friends and relatives of individuals with mental health problems might feel guilt, loss or anger?

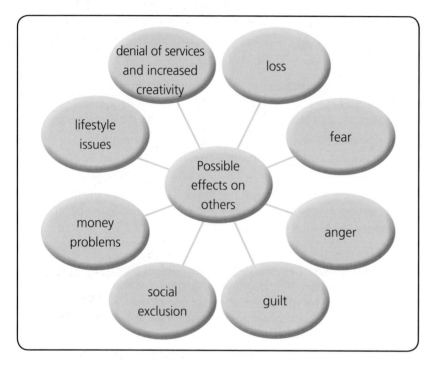

Figure 10.4 The possible effects of mental health on others

Type of impact	Possible effects on others
Psychological and emotional	• Psychological and emotional effects can include feelings of loss, anger, fear and guilt. The relatives, partners and friends of people who develop schizophrenia sometimes describe the impact as like losing the individual, even though they are still there. People with schizophrenia can become unemotional, have problems with their thinking and may behave in odd, out-of-character ways. • An individual with a substance-related problem might steal money from other family members or friends to buy drugs or alcohol, causing a great deal of upset and anger. • People with personality disorders can cause upset to family and friends because they may not be good at saying what they want. They might do things without thinking about what the consequences are. This can cause worry to others, especially if the individual keeps harming or threatening to hurt themselves.

continued...

Type of impact	Possible effects on others
	• Parents, in particular, feel guilt if a child develops mental health problems, believing that they are somehow responsible.
	• A family member who colludes in the detention or enforced treatment of their relative under the Mental Health Act 2007 may feel guilty about their involvement.
Financial and practical	The partner of an individual with a substance-related disorder might find that the household income is taken up buying alcohol or drugs with insufficient money then available for food, children's clothing or rent. The practical effects of this are very damaging if a partner is worried about eviction from the house or flat, or unable to send the children to school properly dressed.
Using services	The friends and relatives of people with mental ill health may find it more difficult to access public services. An older man whose wife has dementia may have difficulty using services for himself. Instead, all his attention and efforts go into helping his wife use services. He might have to focus on getting the doctor to visit to treat a bad cough, or the chiropodist to cut her toe nails. Often, in these situations, the wife or husband forgets about their own problems and focuses on the problems that their partner has.
Social exclusion	Social exclusion does not just affect the individual with mental ill health, but can also affect their friends and relatives. There might be gossip about a depressed woman's partner, suggesting that he is the cause of her depression. In this way, family can also be socially excluded from taking part in normal everyday events and using everyday services.

As a result of lack of time, the extra effort required and the associated stigma, friends and relatives of mentally ill individuals may stop participating in communal and social functions. Whole families self-isolate. |
| Positive impacts | Many people who care for a family member or friend with a mental health problem say it helps bring out their caring side and they become closer to their friend or relative. As the individual with mental ill health can become more creative, family and others can find their own creative skills and appreciate their friend or relative's creativity. |

Knowledge Assessment Task   2.2   2.3

Mental ill health can have significant effects on the individual and on members of their family as well as others in the individual's social or work network. You have been asked by your manager to produce a leaflet or poster as part of an awareness campaign to highlight the impact that mental ill health can have on an individual's life and on the lives of those close to or closely involved with them. Your leaflet or poster should explain the range of possible effects of mental ill health on individuals and members of their familial, social or work networks, using the following headings or categories:

▶ psychological and emotional
▶ practical and financial
▶ using services
▶ social exclusion
▶ positive impacts.

Keep the written work that you produce as evidence towards your assessment.

What are the benefits of early intervention?

Early intervention can be very helpful in promoting mental health and wellbeing. This is because early interventions can:

▶ prevent some mental illnesses developing

▶ promote good mental health and wellbeing

In the case of psychotic disorders early intervention is particularly important. When the mental illness is first detected it should be reported so a doctor can treat it because:

▶ it can ease distress to the individual and their friends and family

▶ it lowers the risk of relapse

▶ it improves the long-term prospects of the indvidual.

Early intervention in a psychotic disorder can be in the form of a holistic care approach that works with family and friends as part of the treatment programme. Services can offer a range of interventions including family therapy, cognitive behaviour therapy and medication.

Your assessment criteria:

2.4 Explain the benefits of early intervention in promoting an individual's mental health and wellbeing

Reflect

Why do you think it is helpful to involve an individual's family in early interventions when signs of mental illness are first noticed?

Investigate

Using the internet investigate psychiatric treatments. How is medication used? What types of talking therapies are there? What can you find out about electroconvulsive therapy (ECT)?

Case study

Andy is 19. His parents are very worried about him because he has stopped going to college and spends all his time alone in his bedroom. Most of the time he seems to be asleep or lying in bed, but sometimes at night they can hear him talking and laughing. After speaking to their own family doctor an arrangement is made for a psychiatrist to visit. The psychiatrist diagnoses a psychotic disorder and prescribes some tablets. Andy takes the tablets after a lot of persuasion. The psychiatrist also arranges for Andy's parents to go to classes on mental illness for carers. At the classes they learn about different kinds of mental ill health and how different conditions are treated. After a few days Andy stops talking to himself and spends more time out of his room with the rest of his family. The psychiatrist says the future for Andy looks good as long as he continues to take the prescribed tablets.

1. What interventions helped Andy and his family?

2. Explain the benefits of early intervention for Andy and his family.

3. Why is it important that Andy's parents understand more about mental ill health?

Carers' classes can help families of individuals with mental health problems to understand the benefits of interventions

How can early interventions promote wellbeing?

Early interventions can help people work towards their goals. An individual with depression can be helped to solve some of their problems and thereby reduce some of the causes of the depression.

Case study

Malcolm is diagnosed with depression after a failed attempt at taking his own life. He is offered a type of counselling called **CBT** (cognitive behavioural therapy) which helps him sort through his problems and deal with them one at a time. One of Malcolm's problems is debt. When he was depressed he drank a lot and now he owes a lot of money in rent arrears and hasn't paid his council tax bill. He tells his CBT therapist that he wants to retrain to be a plasterer and work with his brother. This has been an ambition since he was at school. The outcome of the CBT is that Malcolm realises he would feel a lot better if he starts his plasterer course. It would mean he can pay off his debts and bills one at a time. After a few months Malcolm has paid off his debts and is now saving for a new van.

Talking treatments can help individuals to work through their problems

1. How does CBT help Malcolm?
2. Explain how the early intervention promoted Malcolm's mental health and wellbeing.
3. What other treatment might Malcolm be offered?

Knowledge Assessment Task   2.4

Early interventions can be an effective way of treating many mental health problems. Appropriate early intervention can prevent an individual's mental health problems from developing further and can also be used to promote good mental health. Imagine that a reporter from a local newspaper has contacted your work setting. The reporter has asked whether somebody could write a short article of between 250 and 500 words on the benefits of early intervention in promoting an individual's mental health and wellbeing. The manager of your work setting has asked you to write the article, giving an example of an early intervention relevant to people who use your work setting.

Are you ready for assessment?

AC	What do you know now?	Assessment task	✓
1.1	Describe the main types of mental ill health according to the psychiatric (DSM/ICD) classification system: mood disorders, personality disorders, anxiety disorders, psychotic disorders, substance-related disorders, eating disorders, cognitive disorders	Page 291	
1.2	Explain the key strengths and limitations of the psychiatric classification systems	Page 293	
1.3	Explain the two alternative frameworks for understanding mental distress	Page 295	
1.4	Explain how mental ill health may be indicated through an individual's emotions, thinking and behaviour	Page 297	
2.1	Explain how individuals experience discrimination due to misinformation, assumptions and stereotypes about mental ill health	Page 299	
2.2	Explain how mental ill health may have an impact on the individual including: • psychological and emotional • practical and financial • the impact of using services • social exclusion • positive impacts	Page 303	
2.3	Explain how mental ill health may have an impact on those in the individual's familial, social or work network including: • psychological and emotional • practical and financial • the impact of using services • social exclusion • positive impacts	Page 303	
2.4	Explain the benefits of early intervention in promoting an individual's mental health and wellbeing	Page 305	

11 | The principles of infection prevention and control (ICO 1)

Assessment of this unit

This unit will help you understand the importance of infection prevention and control when working in health and social care. It outlines employer and employee roles and responsibilities, as well as the relevant legislation and national and local policies. You will learn about the potential impact of infection and the way systems, procedures and risk assessment can help minimise this. The unit explains how good personal hygiene – particularly hand washing – and the correct use of personal protective equipment (PPE), are vital in reducing the spread of infection. You will need to understand the importance of the following in the prevention and control of infections:

► roles and responsibilities

► legislation and policies

► systems and procedures

► risk assessment

► using Personal Protective Equipment (PPE)

► good personal hygiene.

The assessment of this unit is entirely knowledge-based. The table below outlines what you need to know to meet each of the assessment criteria for the unit.

AC	What you need to know
1.1	Explain employees' roles and responsibilities in relation to the prevention and control of infection
1.2	Explain employers' responsibilities in relation to the prevention and control of infection
2.1	Outline current legislation and regulatory body standards which are relevant to the prevention and control of infection
2.2	Describe local and organisational policies relevant to the prevention and control of infection
3.1	Describe procedures and systems relevant to the prevention and control of infection
3.2	Explain the potential impact of an outbreak of infection on the individual and the organisation
4.1	Define the term 'risk'

4.2	Outline potential risks of infection within the workplace
4.3	Describe the process of carrying out a risk assessment
4.4	Explain the importance of carrying out a risk assessment
5.1	Demonstrate correct use of personal protective equipment (PPE)
5.2	Describe different types of PPE
5.3	Explain the reasons for use of PPE
5.4	State current relevant regulations and legislation relating to PPE
5.5	Describe employees' responsibilities regarding the use of PPE
5.6	Describe employers' responsibilities regarding the use of PPE
5.7	Describe the correct practice in the application and removal of PPE
5.8	Describe the correct procedure for disposal of used PPE
6.1	Describe the key principles of good personal hygiene
6.2	Demonstrate good hand washing technique
6.3	Describe the correct sequence for hand washing
6.4	Explain when and why hand washing should be carried out
6.5	Describe the types of products that should be used for hand washing
6.6	Describe correct procedures that relate to skincare

This unit also links to some of the other units:

| HSC 037 | Promote and implement health and safety in health and social care |
| HSC 2028 | Move and position individuals in accordance with their plan of care |

Some of your learning will be repeated in these units and will give you the chance to review your knowledge and understanding.

Understanding roles and responsibilities in the prevention and control of infection

Roles and responsibilities

Everyone working in a health and social care setting is responsible for preventing infection. Health and social care practitioners must avoid getting and passing on pathogens, such as bacteria and viruses that cause illness. Employees and employers working in health and social care settings have particular roles and responsibilities for preventing infection.

Employees' roles and responsibilities

As a health or social care practitioners you should:

▶ maintain high standards of personal health and hygiene

▶ be aware of the infection control policies and procedures that are used in your workplace

▶ follow best practice in infection prevention and control

▶ maintain a clean and hygienic environment

▶ report infection risks to your employer

▶ attend training days relating to infection prevention and control.

Roles and responsibilities of the employer

Your employer must make sure all laws and legal regulations concerning infection prevention and control are followed in the workplace and should:

▶ undertake risk assessment and management to identify and minimise the impact of infection hazards

▶ produce infection prevention and control policies and procedure

▶ provide relevant equipment to enable you to prevent and control infection

▶ identify and distribute relevant information about infection hazards and prevention and control methods

▶ provide training and supervision in aspects of infection and control relevant to your work setting

▶ keep records relating to infection prevention and control in your workplace.

Your assessment criteria:

1.1 Explain employees' roles and responsibilities in relation to the prevention and control of infection

1.2 Explain employers' roles and responsibilities in relation to the prevention and control of infection

Health and Safety Law
What you need to know

All workers have a right to work in places where risks to their health and safety are properly controlled. Health and safety is about stopping you getting hurt at work or ill through work. Your employer is responsible for health and safety, but you must help.

What employers must do for you

1 Decide what could harm you in your job and the precautions to stop it. This is part of risk assessment.

2 In a way you can understand, explain how risks will be controlled and tell you who is responsible for this.

3 Consult and work with you and your health and safety representatives in protecting everyone from harm in the workplace.

4 Free of charge, give you the health and safety training you need to do your job.

5 Free of charge, provide you with any equipment and protective clothing you need, and ensure it is properly looked after.

6 Provide toilets, washing facilities and drinking water.

7 Provide adequate first-aid facilities.

8 Report injuries, diseases and dangerous incidents at work to our Incident Contact Centre: **0845 300 9923**

9 Have insurance that covers you in case you get hurt at work or ill through work. Display a hard copy or electronic copy of the current insurance certificate where you can easily read it.

10 Work with any other employers or contractors sharing the workplace or providing employees (such as agency workers), so that everyone's health and safety is protected.

What you must do

1 Follow the training you have received when using any work items your employer has given you.

2 Take reasonable care of your own and other people's health and safety.

3 Co-operate with your employer on health and safety.

4 Tell someone (your employer, supervisor, or health and safety representative) if you think the work or inadequate precautions are putting anyone's health and safety at serious risk.

If there's a problem

1 If you are worried about health and safety in your workplace, talk to your employer, supervisor, or health and safety representative.

2 You can also look at our website for general information about health and safety at work.

3 If, after talking with your employer, you are still worried, phone our Infoline. We can put you in touch with the local enforcing authority for health and safety and the Employment Medical Advisory Service. You don't have to give your name.

HSE Infoline: **0845 345 0055**
HSE website: **www.hse.gov.uk**

Fire safety
You can get advice on fire safety from the Fire and Rescue Services or your workplace fire officer.

Employment rights
Find out more about your employment rights at:
www.direct.gov.uk

Your health and safety representatives:

Other health and safety contacts:

 HSE

Health and Safety Executive

Employers must display this poster outlining British health and safety law in the workplace, or provide it in pocket card format to workforce

Case study

Fatimah, a community support worker, visited Mrs Yates at home to help her wash and dress this morning. During today's visit, Fatimah used the last of the plastic aprons and also noticed there was only one pair of disposable gloves left. Mrs Yates's husband, who is also her main carer, said he thought that throwing these items away after one use seemed wasteful. He also suggested that he and Fatimah should use (and share) cloth aprons and washing up gloves to provide personal care for Mrs Yates in future.

1. Who is responsible for ensuring that aprons and gloves are provided and replenished in this kind of care situation?
2. What role and responsibilities does Fatimah have regarding infection prevention and control in this situation?
3. What could Fatimah say to Mr Yates to explain why disposable rather than reusable aprons and gloves are used to provide care for his wife?

Knowledge Assessment Task   1.1   1.2

Infection prevention and control should be a high priority in all health and social care settings. Health and social care practitioners should receive clear information about their own and their employer's role and responsibilities for preventing and controlling infection.

You have been asked to produce a concise and clear information leaflet for your workplace that:

▶ explains the employee's role and responsibilities in relation to the prevention and control of infection

▶ explains the employer's role and responsibilities in relation to the prevention and control of infection.

Keep the written work that you produce for this activity as evidence towards your assessment.

Discuss

With a colleague or your supervisor, talk about how you could respond to a colleague who failed to keep to guidelines about infection prevention and control in your workplace. How could you draw this to their attention and what would you tell them about their infection prevention and control role and responsibilities?

Reflect

What do you do to prevent infection (to yourself and others) while at work? Do you remember to wash your hands, wipe surfaces and use gloves when delivering care?

Key terms

Infection: an invasion of disease-causing micro organisms that multiply in the body and cause illness

Pathogen: a micro organism such as bacterium or a virus that causes disease

Bacterium: types of micro-organism that can carry disease

Virus: a micro-organism containing genetic material that replicates within a host's cell causing illness

Legislation, standards and policies for infection prevention and control

In the UK, laws, legal regulations and standards relating to infection prevention and control cover a number of different issues that are relevant to health and social care practice. These include health and safety at work, public health issues, environmental safety and food safety.

Figure 11.1 Laws relating to infection prevention and control

Law	How does it affect care practice?
Health and Safety at Work Act 1974	Sets standards to prevent infection occurring and spreading
Public Health (Control of Disease) Act 1984	Sets standards for sanitation, water supply and disposal of rubbish
Food Safety Act 1990	Concerns food production and consumption
Environmental Protection Act 1990	Ensures the safe management (handling, transfer, disposal) of controlled waste
Management of Health and Safety at Work Act 1999	Introduced risk assessment

Your assessment criteria:

2.1 Outline current legislation and regulatory body standards which are relevant to the prevention and control of infection

2.2 Describe local and organisational policies relevant to the prevention and control of infection

---

GUIDANCE TO THE FOOD SAFETY ACT 1995

ALL STAFF PLEASE NOTE:

Always wash your hands before handling food and after using the toilet.

• •

Tell your boss at once of any skin, nose, throat or bowel trouble.

• •

Ensure cuts and sores are covered with waterproof dressings.

• •

Keep yourself clean and wear clean clothing.

• •

Do not smoke in a food room it is illegal and dangerous. Never cough or sneeze over food.

• •

Clean as you go. Keep all equipment and surfaces clean.

• •

Prepare raw and cooked food in separate areas. USE COLOUR CODED CHOPPING BOARDS AND KNIVES to avoid cross contamination.

• •

Ensure food is at correct temperature at all times. READ COOK CHILL GUIDELINES.

• •

Keep your hands off food as far as possible.

• •

Ensure waste food is disposed of properly. Keep the lid on the dustbin and wash your hands after putting waste in it.

• •

Deliveries of food to your premises should be checked to ensure they are at correct temperature on receipt. IF IN DOUBT ADVISE YOUR SUPERVISOR.

• •

Tell your supervisor if you cannot follw the rules. Do not break the law.

This notice gives guidance only and should not be treated as a complete and authoritative statement of law. For more information contact the environmental health officer at your local council.

Figure 11.2 Regulations relating to infection prevention and control

Legal regulations	How does it affect care practice?
Personal Protective Equipment (PPE) at Work Regulations 1992	Employers must supply and employees must use appropriate protective clothes and equipment (see page 292)
Food Safety (General Food Hygiene) Regulations 1995	Introduced safe hygiene practices to prevent pathogen **contamination** during handling and storage of food
Reporting of Injuries, Diseases and Dangerous Occurrences (RIDDOR) 1995	Ensures that work-related infection from handling **body fluids** and highly infectious diseases are reported
The Control of Substances Hazardous to Health (COSHH) 2002	Regulates storage and use of chemicals (e.g. cleaning solutions) that pose a danger. All workplaces must have a COSHH information file available for workers
Hazardous Waste Regulations 2005	Concerns the disposal of sharps and **clinical waste**, which pose a particular infection hazard
Code of Practice for the Prevention and Control of Healthcare Associated Infection (HCAI); Regulation 12; 2010	Provides guidance on ways to reduce the incidence of **HCAI**

COSHH warning symbols

Regulatory body standards

Health and social care professions produce standards which describe the skills, knowledge and understanding needed by a practitioner in order to demonstrate competence and protect the public from harm. Some examples of regulatory body standards which concern infection prevention and control include:

▶ National Occupational Standards (NOS) for health workers produced by Skills for Health.

▶ guidance for NHS and local authorities produced by the National Institute for Health and Clinical Excellence (NICE).

▶ *Essential Standards of Quality and Safety*, 2010, including eight cleanliness and infection control measures, produced by The Care Quality Commission (CQC).

Health and social care practitioners should also be aware of other sources of guidance about standards, such as those provided by the Department of Health and the Royal College of Nursing (RCN).

Infection control policies

The infection control policies developed for your workplace should incorporate all of the current laws, regulations and standards relating to infection prevention and control. If you put these policies into practice through the way you provide care, you should always stay within the law, uphold the conditions of your work contract and protect yourself and others from the risk of infection. The infection prevention and control policies used in your work setting must:

▶ be seen and read by all members of the care team (you may be asked to sign to show that you have done this)

▶ provide enough information for care workers to practice safely

▶ set out step-by-step guidance for using the infection prevention and control systems and procedures that operate in your work setting

▶ be available to visitors or family members of people receiving care.

Reflect

How do you use the infection prevention and control policies written for your workplace?

Which elements are most relevant to your work role?

Investigate

Think about ways to improve the information about infection control issues given to visitors to your workplace. Talk with your manager about the possibility of developing a simple questionnaire to check visitors' understanding about such issues as washing hands, use of hand gel and not visiting when feeling unwell.

Case study

Davina has just started working at a care home and has been given the infection prevention and control policy to read over. This isn't what Davina hoped to be doing on her first day at work. Shortly after starting to read through the infection prevention and control policy and procedures file, Davina gives up and starts playing a game on her mobile phone instead.

1. Why should Davina read the infection prevention and control policy?

2. What risks does Davina take by not reading the policy?

3. What could you say to Davina to help her recognise the benefits of knowing how to work within policy guidelines?

Knowledge Assessment Task   2.1   2.2

Infection prevention and control is a very important issue for all health and social care practitioners. However, the legal and regulatory framework relating to this issue can seem complex and isn't always well understood by practitioners. Consequently, the manager of your work setting has asked you to produce a summary, ideally in an easy to read table format, of:

▶ current legislation and regulatory body standards that are relevant to the prevention and control of infection in health and social care settings

▶ the local and organisational policies and procedures relating to the prevention and control of infection in your work setting.

The work that you produce should be factually correct, concise and useful to your colleagues. Keep a copy of your written work to use as evidence for your assessment.

Discuss

Talk together with colleagues, other learners and your manager or tutor about ideas to make and improve links between infection control policy and working practice. Perhaps there are issues which could be addressed by a training session for staff which you could help to run?

Standard precautions

Standard precautions or 'universal' precautions, as they are sometimes called, recognise that all individuals pose a potential infection risk to you and that you pose a potential infection risk to others. It is not always possible to know when a person is infectious, so it is best to treat everyone as if they are contaminated, including yourself. To apply standard precautions in practice you should:

▶ risk-assess all potential infection hazards in your day-to-day work

▶ wash your hands using correct procedure (see page 301) at appropriate times

▶ use personal protective equipment (see page 292) to create a barrier against pathogens

▶ clean and disinfect items and areas at appropriate times and with appropriate chemicals for the job

▶ dispose of waste, including sharps, safely.

Procedures and systems

A range of infection prevention and control systems and procedures are used in health and social care settings. These relate to food hygiene, disposal of waste, cleaning and laundry.

Food hygiene

Food hygiene is an important focus for infection prevention and control because food provides an environment suitable for pathogens to multiply and eating provides a route for infection to enter the body. Food poisoning causes vomiting and diarrhoea. This can lead to dehydration and, in severe cases, is sometimes fatal. Contamination of food can occur during the preparation, cooking, serving or storage of food. To avoid **cross-contamination** and **cross-infection** when dealing with food, pay particular attention to:

▶ personal hygiene – keep hands clean, wear PPE, and do not work if unwel

▶ kitchen and dining environment – keep surfaces and cooking equipment clean

▶ safe food practices – including thorough thawing, heating and cooking of food; correct food storage; preparing meat and fish separately to avoid contaminating foods that are eaten raw.

Disposal of waste

Rubbish and other waste products provide a perfect environment for harbouring pathogens and spreading infection. If left lying

Key terms

Standard precautions: a set of guidelines to minimise the spread of infection between individuals

Cross-infection: the spread of infection from one person to another

Cross-contamination: the transfer of pathogens from one person, object or area to another

Avoid cross contamination by using different coloured chopping boards to prepare different food types

around rubbish also attracts vermin, such as rats, which carry disease. The way waste is disposed on depends on the:

▶ type of waste involved

▶ risk the waste poses to people

▶ risk the waste poses to the environment.

You need to understand the waste disposal arrangements and procedures for your work area. Figure 11.3 outlines methods for disposing of **healthcare waste**. You should also be aware that different local authorities have different waste disposal arrangements for other forms of waste.

Key terms

Healthcare waste: any waste produced as a result of healthcare activities in hospital or community settings

Reflect

How many times in a day do you take measures to reduce or remove the potential for infection? Could (or should) you do this more frequently?

Figure 11.3 Disposal of healthcare waste

Category of waste	Example	Colour-coded waste stream	Method of disposal
Hazardous waste: infectious, dangerous or toxic			
1. Clinical waste: items soiled with infected body fluids, such as blood	• catheter bags • dressings	Yellow or orange bag	Incineration
2. Sharps: used to take blood, perform surgery, give injections	• needles, razors, scalpels	Rigid yellow receptacle, marked with a fill-to line – different coloured lids indicate content	Incineration
Drugs: medicines and tablets	• discarded medicines • toxic chemicals	Yellow receptacle with blue lid	Specialist disposal
Non-hazardous: also called domestic waste, which can be safely recycled or will compost	• packaging • food waste • vacuum cleaner dust	Black or clear bags	Recycle: (paper, glass, tin, cardboard, plastic) Compost: (vegetable and fruit peelings) Landfill: the rest
Offensive hygiene waste: non-infectious and non-hazardous, but may be unpleasant if individuals come into contact with it	• nappies • incontinence pads • sanitary wear	Yellow bag with a black stripe to alert handlers to content Picked up by arrangement with local authority	Landfill

Disposal of sharps

'Sharps' include needles, razors and scalpels. These pose a serious risk, because they may be contaminated with infected blood and can cause a penetrating wound, taking infection into the body.

Seriously harmful pathogens, such as HIV and Hepatitis B and C, can be transmitted directly into a person's blood stream through a sharps injury. When dealing with sharps you should:

▶ bring the disposal box to the used sharps, not the other way round

▶ never fill the disposal box beyond the mark indicated (approximately two thirds)

▶ keep handling of sharps to a minimum

▶ avoid passing items directly from hand to hand

▶ never recap, bend or break sharps or separate a needle from its syringe

▶ report all sharps incidents, in line with RIDDOR.

Investigate

Find out about the ways different types of healthcare waste are managed in your work setting. Include hazardous waste (clinical waste and sharps), offensive hygiene (incontinence products) and check how the colour-coded waste streams operate in your workplace.

Case study

Tilak is a personal care assistant visiting Mr Jenkins for the first time. While Mr Jenkins is in the toilet, Tilak finds used incontinence pads tied up in carrier bags under the bed. When asked about this Mr Jenkins explains that he is embarrassed to tell his daughter about his incontinence. He orders pads over the internet, but she sorts his rubbish on bin collection day, so getting rid of them has been a problem. Every few weeks Mr Jenkins removes the bags of pads from beneath his bed and burns them in the lounge fireplace.

1. What category of waste do incontinence pads fall into?
2. How is Mr Jenkins's behaviour increasing his risk of infection?
3. Explain how Mr Jenkins's incontinence pads should be disposed of to minimise infection risks.

Decontamination procedures

There are three levels of **decontamination**:

1. Cleaning: using soap-based products to remove surface dirt and odour. This must take place before disinfection or sterilisation takes place.

2. Disinfection: using chemicals to kill pathogens.

3. Sterilisation: removing all pathogens and the conditions in which they survive. This is used for high risk items, such as surgical instruments.

Regular cleaning with appropriate cleaning products is necessary to create hygienic surroundings.

Key terms

Decontamination: the process of making a person, object or environment free from pathogens

Cleaning

Disinfection

Sterilisation

Figure 11.4 Reasons for cleaning

Reasons:
- Removes surface dirt
- Removes conditions for pathogens to grow
- Fulfils health and safety requirements
- Helps to maintain equipment in good working order
- Reduces likelihood of cross-contamination
- Prevents odours

Cleaning policy

Healthcare settings must have an environmental cleaning policy which provides guidance about the use of cleaning equipment and chemicals, and cleaning regimes. Chemicals must be handled with care, used in the correct concentrations, and stored and disposed of safely in accordance with COSHH. Equipment such as mops and cloths should be colour-coded to indicate the area they are intended for. This prevents cross-contamination. Mops and cloths must always be cleaned after use, left to dry in the air and replaced as necessary. A cleaning timetable ensures all areas are cleaned regularly. For example, in a healthcare setting, floors will be cleaned daily, but windows less frequently.

Due to the risk of body fluids carrying infection, healthcare settings usually have a specific procedure for dealing with spillages of blood, vomit, urine or faeces:

▶ the person on the spot should deal with the spillage immediately and must *never* leave it for a cleaner

▶ do an immediate risk assessment to check if the area needs to be cordoned off

▶ use appropriate equipment to deal with the spillage

▶ use appropriate PPE, such as gloves and aprons

▶ sanitiser granules can be sprinkled over the spillage to absorb the fluid and prevent it spreading

▶ use paper towels to absorb spillage

▶ dispose of using correct clinical waste stream

▶ clean area with disinfectant

▶ wash your hands thoroughly after all cleaning tasks.

Discuss

With colleagues or your assessor, talk over some common procedures to do with meal-times, waste disposal, care of soiled laundry and cleaning, which you carry out regularly, perhaps many times a day. Try to pinpoint the aspects of the task that have the most potential for cross-infection to occur and link these to infection control precautions that need to be taken.

Reflect

It is easy for 'bad habits' to creep in to working practice, almost without noticing.

Think about the potential for this to happen in your working practice and decide what measures you can take to ensure infection control is not jeopardised.

Laundry procedures

Soiled laundry is a potential source of infection when it has been contaminated with body fluids. For this reason, you should:

▶ always wear personal protective equipment (PPE) when dealing with soiled laundry

▶ place soiled items directly in the correct type of laundry bag. In some work settings specific bags for soiled laundry which dissolve on contact with hot water are used.

▶ bring the laundry bag to the bedside to minimise cross-infection risks – don't carry soiled laundry around!

▶ remove and flush any solid faeces down the toilet.

Knowledge Assessment Task
3.1

Procedures and systems to prevent and control infection when dealing with food, disposal of waste, cleaning and laundry must be followed in your working practice. Think about one task associated with each of these areas which you carry out regularly, and describe the ways in which your actions follow the infection control procedures and systems at your place of work.

Keep your notes as evidence towards your assessment.

The potential impact of an outbreak of infection on the individual and the organisation

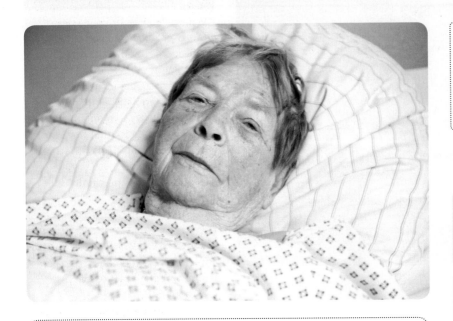

Key terms

Localised infection: an infection that is limited to a particular part of the body

Systemic infection: an infection that affects the whole body

Signs and symptoms: evidence indicating that a person is unwell

Impact of infection on the individual

Infections range from mild to very serious, and can be fatal. They can be **localised** or **systemic** and are identified by **signs and symptoms**. An infection can have a significant impact on an individual's life (see Figure 11.5).

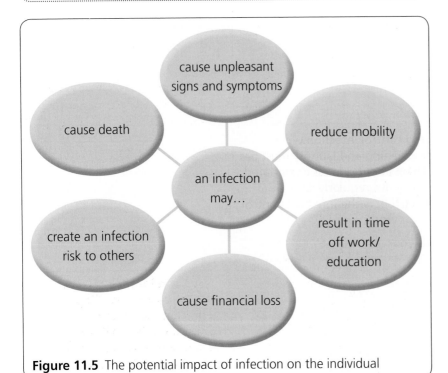

Figure 11.5 The potential impact of infection on the individual

Signs and symptoms of infection

The signs and symptoms of an infection will differ according to whether it is **localised** or **systemic**. Localised infections can spread to become systemic.

Figure 11.6 Signs and symptoms of infection

Localised infection	Systemic infection
Inflammation causing redness	Raised body temperature
Heat	Aching joints
Pain	Enlarged lymph glands
Swelling	Loss of appetite
Formation of pus	Listlessness and apathy

Adults vulnerable to infection

A number of adult groups are more vulnerable to infection than the average person. These include:

- ▶ older people
- ▶ people with chronic illnesses or disabilities
- ▶ people who have had surgery
- ▶ people who are being looked after in a hospital.

Older people and those with medical conditions may have reduced immunity. If this is the case, then it is easier for an infection to be picked up, and it is harder to fight the infection. Immobility due to frailty or illness means the lungs don't breathe as deeply and body systems are more sluggish, giving pathogens greater opportunity to invade. Surgical operations provide additional routes for infection to get into the body, such as through a wound, or at the site of an intravenous infusion or catheter.

Reflect

What signs and symptoms did you have the last time you were ill with an infection?

Investigate

Using internet or library sources find out about septicaemia (blood poisoning) which is one of the most serious affects of systemic infection.

Discuss

With colleagues, talk together about service users you have looked after who were more vulnerable to infection. Identify the reasons for this and the ways in which it impacted on their life.

Key terms

Immunity: the body's natural defence against infection provided by the immune system

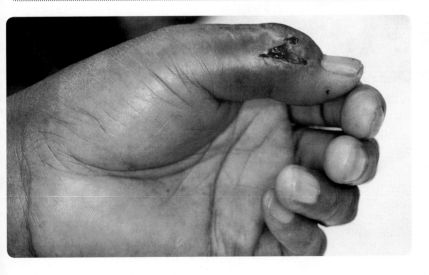

Localised infection of the thumb causes swelling, inflammation and pus formation, but without treatment this could spread via the blood stream to cause potentially fatal systemic infection.

Impact of infection on the organisation

Healthcare settings are particularly vulnerable to outbreaks of infection because sick people frequently carry pathogens. With many older, less mobile and vulnerable people gathered in one place the potential for cross-infection increases dramatically.

Health Care Associated Infection (HCAI)

Health Care Associated Infections (HCAI) are infections that originate from a healthcare environment. If a person develops an infection during their stay in a healthcare setting, or within three days of their arrival or discharge, it is classed as an HCAI. One complication of HCAI is that many of the infections do not get better with common **antibiotics**. This **antibiotic resistance** has given these pathogens the nickname 'superbugs'. One common HCAI is caused by **Methicillan Resistant Staphlococco Aureus (MRSA)**. Many people carry MRSA in or on their bodies without it causing infection. However, **carriers** can also transfer pathogens to others, who do develop infection. Without testing, it is not possible to know who carries MRSA.

Your assessment criteria:

3.2 Explain the potential impact of an outbreak of infection on the individual and the organisation

Key terms

Antibiotics: treatments used for infections caused by bacteria

Antibiotic resistance: the ability of some bacteria to thrive despite antibiotics

Methicillin Resistant Staphylococcus Aureus (MRSA): a staphylococcus bacterium that has developed resistance to the usual antibiotics and is a widespread HCAI

Carrier: a person who carries pathogens on or in their body without becoming ill

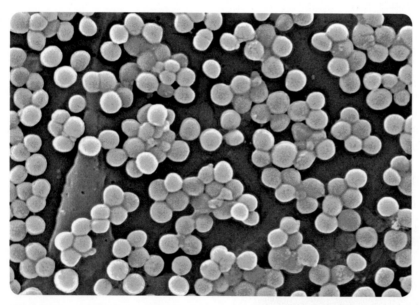

MRSA bacteria cells, magnified many thousands of times.

Case study

Mr Renfrew has dementia and attends a day hospital. This gives his wife respite and provides Mr Renfrew with a hot meal, interest and company. Before this, Mr Renfrew used to wander outside whenever his wife moved into another room. He continuously asked the same questions, and had episodes of frustration sometimes resulting in aggression towards his wife. However, Mr Renfrew has not been able to attend the day hospital since developing a chest infection, is now more confused, and has a cough which wakes him at night.

1. What factors make Mr Renfrew vulnerable to acquiring an infection?

2. What are the negative effects of acquiring an infection for Mr Renfrew?

3. How might this impact on him and his wife?

Investigate

Using newspapers, the internet and the library, find out about a recent epidemic of infection (swine flu, for example), or the increasing incidence of an infectious disease (measles, for example) in the population. What has to happen for an infection to be classed as an epidemic, or even a pandemic? What procedures are put in place in the event of an epidemic?

Key terms

Pandemic: an epidemic spread over a wide geographical area and affecting a high percentage of the population

Knowledge Assessment Task   3.2

When you work in health and safety settings there is always a risk of an outbreak of infection. Make an information poster that explains how infection can affect individuals and impact on an organisation.

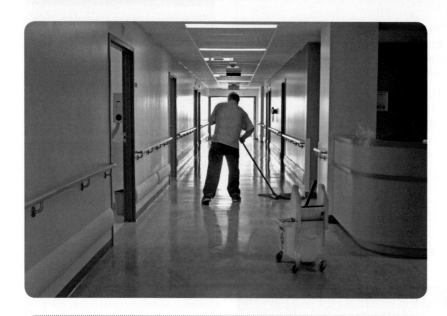

Key terms

Infection hazard: any situation that could spread pathogens

Host body: the person or animal which accommodates a virus or parasite

Cell division: the way in which bacteria reproduce and multiply

Managing the risk of infection in the workplace

In every work setting there will be potential **infection hazards** that pose a risk to those you care for, their families, your colleagues and yourself. Some of these risks can be removed, whilst others can be reduced to an acceptable level.

The meaning of 'risk'

Pathogens can be present anywhere. Being microscopic, it is impossible to know which area, objects or people are contaminated. Risk, or the chance of infection developing, is higher where the conditions are suitable for pathogens to multiply and be transmitted to others. A virus, for example, needs a **host body** in order to multiply, and cannot survive for long outside the body it invades. Similarly, bacteria need the following conditions to flourish:

▶ nutrients (broken down from deceased animals, plants, excreta, soil)

▶ moist conditions

▶ warmth

▶ oxygen, or no oxygen – depending on type of bacteria

▶ time – for **cell division** to take place

Infection hazards in the workplace

Infection hazards can be found in the work environment as well as being associated with the activities that commonly take place in a care setting.

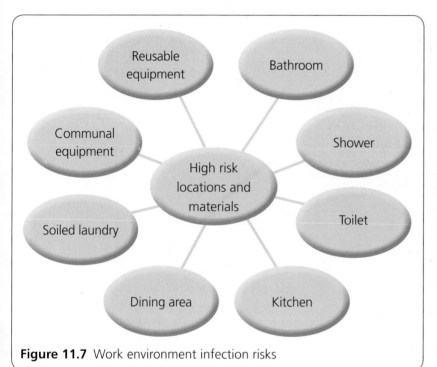

Figure 11.7 Work environment infection risks

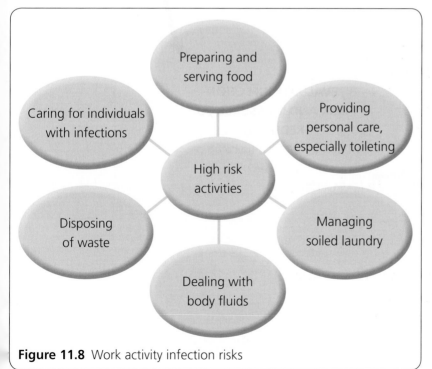

Figure 11.8 Work activity infection risks

Investigate

Using local resources and the internet, research MRSA, finding out when it was first identified, the conditions in which it develops and how it is treated and managed.

Reflect

What environmental and work-related infection hazards do you face in your work setting?

Why is risk assessment important and how is it done?

The risk assessment process

Risk assessment is a legal requirement and is central to providing infection-free work environments and working practices in health and social care settings. The steps involved in a risk assessment process relating to infection control are outlined in figure 11.9.

Your assessment criteria:

4.3 Describe the process of carrying out a risk assessment

4.4 Explain the importance of carrying out a risk assessment

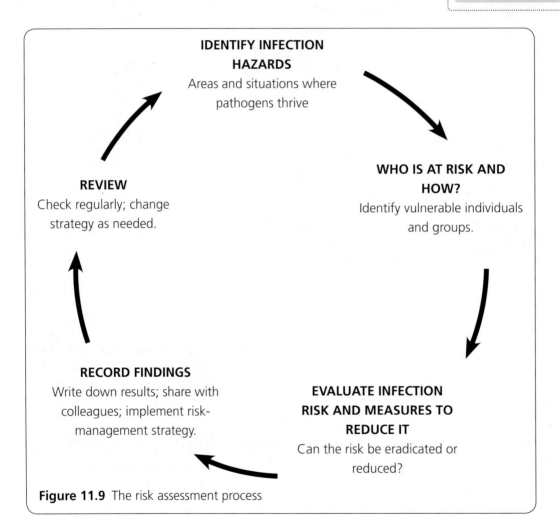

IDENTIFY INFECTION HAZARDS
Areas and situations where pathogens thrive

WHO IS AT RISK AND HOW?
Identify vulnerable individuals and groups.

EVALUATE INFECTION RISK AND MEASURES TO REDUCE IT
Can the risk be eradicated or reduced?

RECORD FINDINGS
Write down results; share with colleagues; implement risk-management strategy.

REVIEW
Check regularly; change strategy as needed.

Figure 11.9 The risk assessment process

Monitoring and reviewing risk assessments

Risk assessment is an on-going process that needs continuous review until the hazard has been eliminated or reduced to an acceptable level. Risk assessment reviews should consider:

▶ any changes in conditions that have occurred in the work setting since the last risk assessment

▶ whether the different individuals present different infection risks

▶ whether there are any new potential hazards arising.

Infection risk assessments are important because they provide an audit of infection hazards, draw attention to high risk activities and behaviours, indicate measures to reduce or remove risk, identify areas for staff training, and can be used to inform policy.

Key terms

Risk assessment: the process of identifying hazards and taking measures to reduce risk to an acceptable level

Case study

Enid Wright, aged 85, is an insulin-dependent diabetic and Precious is her carer. When helping Enid have a bath Precious notices one of Enid's toes looks red. Enid thinks it is just a mark from her shoes, as it doesn't hurt. Precious is concerned because she knows diabetics are more susceptible to infection and that diabetes can affect blood flow and cause nerve damage to the feet. She tells her manager, who advises her to carry out a risk assessment for infection.

1. What are the risks for Enid?

2. Why is it important for Precious to carry out a risk assessment on Enid?

3. What should Precious do at each stage of the risk assessment process?

Reflect

Do you think your colleagues and service users are aware of common infection hazards that exist in your work setting? Could anything be done to improve this situation?

Knowledge Assessment Task   4.1   4.2   4.3   4.4

There are likely to be a number of potential infection risks related to your workplace and the activities that take place there. Plan a teaching session to inform staff about the importance of the risk assessment process. You must include:

▶ a definition of risk

▶ an outline of the potential risks of infection within your workplace

▶ an example that describes the process of carrying out a risk assessment for infection

▶ an explanation of why risk assessment is important.

Keep the work that you produce as evidence towards your assessment.

Investigate

Talk to your manager and relevant staff members about ways to improve your understanding of infection prevention and control. Are there any local training courses or sources of information you could use to develop your knowledge further?

What are the correct ways to use personal protective equipment?

In adult health and social care settings **personal protective clothing (PPE)** creates a barrier between care practitioners and service users, protecting both parties from acquiring and transmitting pathogens.

PPE only remains an effective barrier when it is used correctly. Most items are disposable and designed for single use. If you repeatedly use the same item of PPE, it will become an infection hazard, and cease to protect against infection. PPE is used to cover areas of the body that can be both routes for pathogens to enter the body and cause infection, as well as routes for pathogens to exit the body to spread infection to others. PPE also protects against pathogens that are present in the air, on skin, on objects and in fluids, and which can be passed from person to person and from person to objects.

These are the main steps for correct use of PPE:

- ▶ wash your hands before using PPE
- ▶ select the appropriate type of PPE for the task
- ▶ make sure PPE is intact and undamaged
- ▶ make sure PPE fully covers the area intended
- ▶ remove PPE immediately following use
- ▶ dispose of PPE into the appropriate waste stream
- ▶ wash your hands after disposing of PPE.

Your assessment criteria:

5.1 Demonstrate correct use of personal protective equipment (PPE)

5.2 Describe different types of PPE

5.3 Explain the reasons for use of PPE

Key terms

Personal Protective Equipment (PPE): equipment and clothing, such as disposable gloves and aprons, that are used to create a barrier against pathogens that cause disease

Mucosa: skin that lines areas inside of the body, such as inside the mouth

Sterile: free from pathogens

Reflect

Consider the types of PPE that you use at work on a regular basis. Do you know the occasions when these should be worn? Do you know how to dispose of them correctly?

Using different types of personal protective equipment

A range of PPE items is commonly used in health and social care settings. These are set out in Figure 11.10, along with the reasons for their use.

Figure 11.10 Types of PPE and their uses

Type of PPE	Reason for use	Occasions to use
Plastic aprons	Cover clothes or uniform. Made from slippery plastic, it is harder for pathogens to stick. Suitable to protect from body fluids and to be worn during other tasks that hold a risk of bringing you into contact with pathogens	**1.** Helping service users with: • toileting • washing **2.** Contact with **mucosa**: • giving oral care • administering suppositories • doing dressings
Plastic or latex gloves	Protection for hands and nails, which are the main way pathogens are transmitted	**3.** Preparing and serving food **4.** Dealing with body fluids: • cleaning spillages • obtaining specimens • emptying catheter bags **5.** Disposing of rubbish
Paper masks	To cover mouth and nose, which are key sources of pathogens, as well as routes for pathogens to gain entry into the body	**1.** Tasks bringing you in close proximity to a source of infection, such as a wound
Cloth or paper gowns (sometimes fluid repellent)	Provide a complete covering for the body and can be used with plastic aprons on top	**2.** In areas where there is a need for **sterile** conditions, such as operating theatres
Plastic over-shoes	Worn over normal shoes to prevent pathogens from outside being brought into clean areas	**3.** Where there is the likelihood of splashing with body fluids, such as when assisting with childbirth
Paper hair-cover	Covers head to prevent stray hairs escaping	Handling, preparing, cooking and serving food
Plastic goggles	Completely cover eyes, including fitting over glasses	Used where there is particular risk of body fluid splashes, such as to protect dentists and hygienists

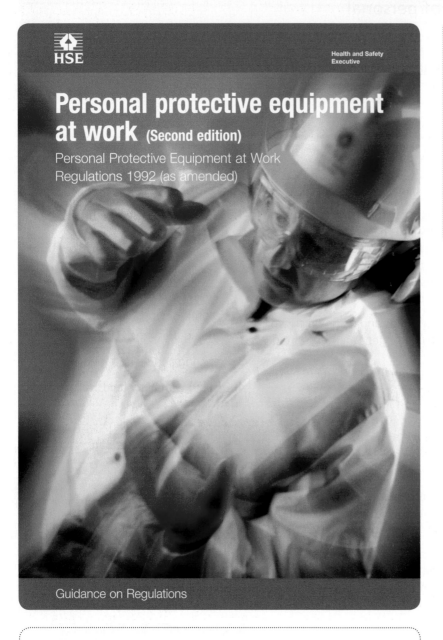

HSE

Health and Safety Executive

Personal protective equipment at work (Second edition)

Personal Protective Equipment at Work Regulations 1992 (as amended)

Guidance on Regulations

Legal regulations

Employers must manage the workplace and their workforce to satisfy the law regarding PPE, and employees must follow the guidance set out in organisational policy and procedures. The Personal Protective Equipment (PPE) at Work Regulations set out these responsibilities; European legislation means PPE must carry the **CE marking**.

Key terms

CE marking: the marking on an item of equipment that shows the product conforms to European standards to do with consumer safety, health or environmental requirements

Figure 11.11 Employer and employee roles and responsibilities

Your manager must:	You must:
• supply appropriate PPE	• use PPE at appropriate times
• maintain and store PPE correctly	• report if PPE is faulty or stocks are low
• provide training, instruction and notices about PPE	• attend training and follow instructions about using PPE
• carry out risk assessments to inform decisions about appropriate PPE	• carry out and follow risk assessments about appropriate PPE for task
• ensure PPE is being used and used properly	• use PPE on all appropriate occasions, and never cut corners.
	• dispose of PPE appropriately

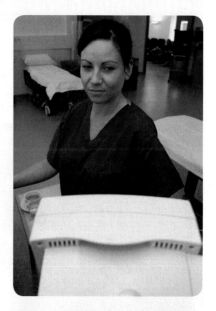

Knowledge Assessment Task   5.4   5.5   5.6

Case study

Maria is a new healthcare assistant working in an orthopaedic rehabilitation ward. She has recently returned to work after having a family and remarks that a lot has changed in the last ten years, especially the frequent use of plastic aprons and gloves. She feels the aprons look cheap and spoil the look of her uniform and the gloves get in the way when she is doing tasks. She says she cannot understand why their employer bothers.

1. Which current legislation and regulations relating to PPE does Maria need to know about?

2. Describe employee responsibilities regarding the use of PPE that Maria needs to be aware of.

3. What does Maria need to know about her employer's responsibilities regarding the use of PPE?

Keep the work that you produce as evidence towards your assessment.

Reflect

Do you or your colleagues ever 'cut corners' or avoid using PPE when providing care? Do you think stocks of PPE, such as aprons and gloves, are placed in the right places to remind practitioners in your setting to use and change equipment at the appropriate times?

Investigate

Using your local library, the internet and work sources, find out about training materials regarding PPE, and look at ways of adapting these to create an information poster relevant to your place of work.

Applying and removing personal protective equipment and disposing of used PPE

How to apply, remove and dispose of PPE correctly

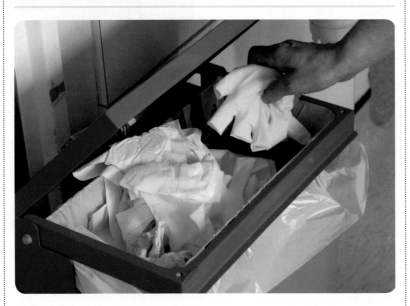

PPE must be applied, removed, and disposed of correctly, or it will become an infection control hazard rather than a means of protecting individuals from infection.

Reflect

Are there ever occasions when you may need to use PPE other than gloves and aprons? Perhaps paper masks, goggles, over-shoes. If this is the case, find out from your manager or other colleagues the correct ways to use these.

Figure 11.12 Correct application, removal, and disposal of PPE

PPE items	How to apply	How to remove	How to dispose of
Gloves and aprons	1. Wash hands before use. 2. Put on gloves and apron before starting the procedure. 3. Change gloves and aprons between caring for different service users and between different care tasks for the same service user.	1. Remove as soon as the procedure is complete. 2. Take off carefully and in such a way that your hands and clothes/uniform do not have contact with any substances contaminating the glove or apron surface.	1. Gloves are for single use only and must be disposed of after removing. 2. Dispose of as clinical waste. 3. Do not touch the bin with contaminated gloves or hands – where possible operate with a foot pedal. 4. Wash hands with soap as soon as gloves/aprons are disposed of.

Knowledge Assessment Task | 5.1 | 5.2 | 5.3 | 5.7 | 5.8

Personal Protective Equipment is an important element of infection prevention and control. Complete a table like the one below with an overview of each different item of PPE used in your work environment.

Description of type of PPE	Explanation of why it is used	How to apply, use, remove and dispose of

Keep the work that you produce for this activity as evidence towards your assessment.

The key principles of good hygiene

Personal hygiene is a private matter, but when you work in a care setting you have a professional responsibility to maintain a *regulated* standard of personal hygiene which is set out in a personal hygiene or infection control policy.

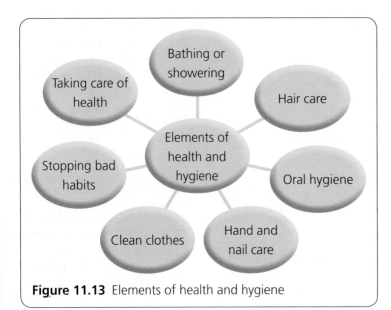

Figure 11.13 Elements of health and hygiene

Bathing and showering

Regular bathing or showering prevents the spread of bacteria, and reduces body odour.

Hair care

Regular hair washing prevents the spread of bacteria. Long hair will need to be tied back. Some care environments bring you into contact with head lice which infest clean hair as readily as dirty hair. Regular combing with a fine-toothed comb will help prevent this, but in the event of an infestation, ask your pharmacist for advice about treatment.

Oral hygiene

Good oral hygiene and six monthly visits to the dentist will prevent the build-up of bacteria and reduce halitosis (bad breath). It is especially important to brush following meals or after smoking.

Hand and nail care

Hand and nail care is vital in preventing and controlling the spread of infection. It is discussed in detail on page 300.

It is discussed in detail on page 300.

Your assessment criteria:

6.1 Describe the key principles of good personal hygiene

Key terms

Hygiene: a set of practices to achieve cleanliness and maintain health

Good personal hygiene standards are an important aspect of infection prevention and control

Clean clothes

Clean work clothes are an important aspect of personal hygiene, and should be changed daily, even when covered by plastic aprons while working. Uniforms are made of hard-wearing materials that launder at high temperatures to remove most pathogens.

Cutting out certain habits

Some habits that affect personal hygiene include:

▶ smoking, which involves putting your hand to your mouth and increases the likelihood of coughing

▶ touching the face, especially nose, mouth and ears, which are routes for infection

▶ nail biting, which can produce sores and risks spreading infection

▶ sneezing and coughing without covering the mouth; not disposing of tissues properly; and not washing hands afterwards.

Taking care of health

Good personal hygiene practice is bolstered by a healthy lifestyle, which helps both avoid and fight off infection. Sleep refreshes and renews your body. Good nutrition keeps your body and brain processes working well. Fluids help to rid you of toxic waste products. If unwell stay away from work to prevent spreading infection.

Reflect

Think about the standards you keep regarding your personal health and hygiene. Do you think you do enough?

Investigate

Using a library and the internet, look up information about a number of different infection epidemics within care services – such as outbreaks of winter vomiting in care homes. What procedures are put in place when outbreaks occur? What are the effects and the outcome of outbreaks of infection?

Reflect

Staff members going off sick can pose a difficult problem for managers in a care environment. Many care workers report feeling pressurised to go into work when unwell because of staff shortages. Talk about ways to deal with this problem and improve the health of staff.

Case study

Anya works at a forensic day centre for adults who have committed serious crimes while mentally unwell. She notices most of the patients and staff smoke and have a high sickness rate, with frequent colds and chest infections.

1. How does smoking impact on standards of personal hygiene?
2. What is the connection between other bad habits and reduced standards of personal hygiene?
3. Why is it important to maintain a high standard of personal hygiene at work?

Knowledge Assessment Task 6.1

For this activity you need to produce a set of personal hygiene guidelines aimed at new staff coming to work, volunteer or undertake work experience in your workplace. You can decide how you present this, as a poster, a leaflet or a booklet, but it must include a description of the key principles of good personal hygiene and the ways this relates to infection prevention and control.

Keep your notes as evidence towards your assessment.

Demonstrating good hand washing technique

Good hand washing technique

Hands are the most common means of transmitting pathogens and spreading infection. Hand washing following correct procedure and carried out in the right sequence at appropriate times is the single most effective way of preventing and controlling infection. There are three stages to a good hand washing technique: preparation; washing and rinsing; drying.

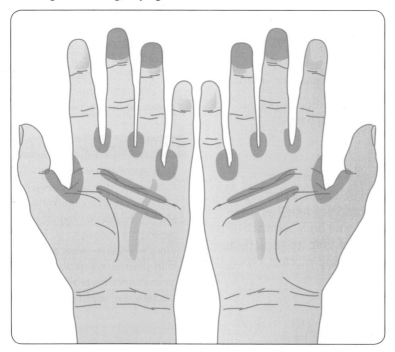

Most frequently missed areas in hand washing

Preparation

You need to carry out a number of preparations before washing your hands:

1. Check sink and taps to ensure these are clean before use.

2. Check equipment to ensure there is soap, towels or a hand drier available.

3. Remove jewellery, which harbours pathogens and may prevent you washing thoroughly for fear of damaging them.

4. Roll sleeves up to expose wrists and forearms.

5. Run water to a warm temperature as uncomfortable temperatures reduces time spent washing hands.

. Lather hands with soap

2. Rub both palms together

3. Rub each fingers and between fingers

. Rub palms with finger nails

5. Rub back of hand with finger nails

6. Wash thoroughly and towel dry

The stages of hand washing

Washing and rinsing

There are a number of important factors to consider when washing and rinsing your hands:

1. Preferably use running water.

2. Wet hands thoroughly before using soap.

3. Soap hands, making sure the solution comes into contact with all areas.

4. Rub hands together vigorously for a minimum of 10–15 seconds, paying particular attention to the tips of the fingers, the thumbs and the areas between the fingers.

5. Rinse hands thoroughly.

Drying

It is vital that hands are dried thoroughly. Ideally use a hot air drier, and continue using until your hands are totally dry. Alternatively, use paper towels, discarding them without touching the bin with your hands.

Knowledge Assessment Task   6.2   6.3

You have been asked to demonstrate the proper technique for thorough hand washing to Shilpa, a student on placement. Provide a detailed description of good hand-washing technique, including the correct sequence for each stage of the process. This will provide Shilpa with a written reminder of your demonstration.

Keep your notes as evidence towards your assessment.

When and why should hand washing be carried out?

Your assessment criteria:

6.4 Explain when and why hand washing should be carried out

Sometimes it is obvious when your hands need washing, because there is visible dirt, but at other times you must wash your hands even if they do not look dirty.

Figure 11.14 When and why to wash your hands

When	Why
Whenever hands are sticky or soiled with visible dirt	To remove surface dirt
After going to the toilet, touching mouth or nose	To remove pathogens present in body fluids and so remove possible contamination
Before and after direct contact with service users	To protect the service users from your pathogens and you from theirs
Between different care activities for the same service user	Some activities are cleaner than others and cross-contamination can take place between different areas of a person's body
Before putting on and after removing disposable gloves	You do not wear gloves as an alternative to washing your hands – gloves are just for higher risk activities
After any contact with body fluids	Body fluids provide a suitable environment for pathogens to multiply
Before and after handling, cooking, serving and eating food	Food is an environment where pathogens multiply; eating provides a route into the body, where infection can occur
After all cleaning tasks	To remove contamination transferred to your hands after cleaning dirty areas
After dealing with rubbish and soiled laundry	Waste and soiled laundry are environments where pathogens can multiply
After feeding and handling pets	Animals harbour pathogens that can spread to humans

Investigate

Use the internet, library or your workplace to find out as much as you can about the 'Cleanyourhands' campaign and the World Health Organization's (WHO) *Five Moments for Hand Hygiene*.

Discuss

Share ideas with colleagues for running a local hand hygiene campaign. Use the information you researched from the 'Cleanyourhands' campaign to make the campaign relevant to your workplace.

Knowledge Assessment Task   6.4

Read through the list, below, of Esther's duties, and indicate the occasions when she should wash her hands. Give reasons for your decisions.

Esther's first job of the day is to serve breakfast to all the residents. Part way through his porridge, Mr Lassiter needs to go to the toilet so Esther assists him and then helps him finish his breakfast. She makes three beds, one of which is soiled. She dispenses the medications, runs the newspaper group and goes to a supervision session with the deputy manager before going for lunch.

Keep your notes as evidence towards your assessment.

Hand washing products

There are two main types of hand washing products:

▶ soap-based for areas where there is a lower risk of infection

▶ antimicrobial products for use in high risk areas.

Ideally, soap dispensers should be used because these are more hygienic than bar soap. Bar soap is handled by a number of people and pathogens can survive on it, plus soap that has dried out to cracking point is not effective. If you are working in a service user's own home and using their facilities, it may be appropriate to request soap in a dispenser. However, there is less chance of cross-infection in a private home than in a healthcare environment.

Alcohol based hand-rub

If it is difficult to get access to running water and soap, and hands are not visibly soiled, it is acceptable to use alcohol hand-rub (gel or foam) instead. The solution must come into contact with all surfaces of the hand, and hands rubbed together vigorously, paying particular attention to the frequently missed areas (see page 300). Many care workers carry a bottle of hand-rub gel around with them.

Your assessment criteria:

6.5 Describe the types of products that should be used for hand washing

6.6 Describe correct procedures that relate to skincare

Key terms

Antimicrobial: a substance to kill or inhibit the growth of microorganisms, including bacteria and fungi

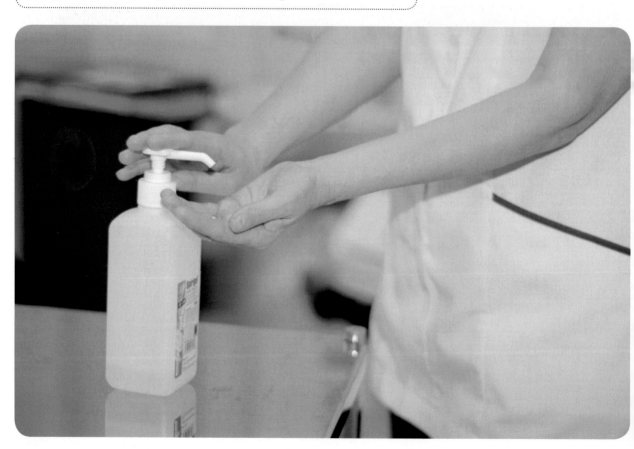

Skincare

Prevent your hands from becoming dry and sore, where abrasions can provide both a route and source of infection. Cleansing products that are gentle on the skin are recommended, also **hypo-allergenic** disposable gloves. If allergy problems arise see your doctor or ask to be referred to occupational health services.

Key terms

Hypo-allergenic: describes materials/chemicals free of substances that commonly cause allergies

Case study

Maxine works as a healthcare assistant and her hands are in and out of water all day. She carries a miniature bottle of alcohol hand-rub and hand cream, both of which she uses frequently. In the past couple of days Maxine has noticed a red rash on both hands made up of tiny raised pimples. It is inflamed, sore and itchy.

1. What might be happening to Maxine?
2. What implications does Maxine's skin condition have for carrying out her role as a healthcare assistant?
3. What would you do if you were Maxine?

Reflect

Think about the number of times you are required to wash your hands. It is no wonder they can become chapped and sore. How do you look after your hands to prevent the skin becoming damaged from hand washing?

Knowledge Assessment Task 6.5 6.6

Micah is on work experience and you have been asked to work alongside him. He is very keen and asks lots of questions. Read through these and give your answers, which must include full descriptions.

1. Why is soap from a dispenser used, rather than bar soap?
2. Why are visitors to the area asked to apply antiseptic hand gel?
3. Why do some of the care practitioners carry antiseptic hand gel in their pocket?
4. What are the correct procedures to care for skin when you work in a care environment?

Keep your notes as evidence towards your assessment.

Investigate

Find out if it is possible to hire a hand contamination box. This might be available through the infection prevention and control team based at your local hospital. This uses a particular light to show up areas of contamination – even after hands have been washed.

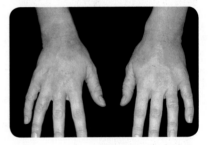

Hands affected by dermatitis, inflammation of the outer layer of skin

Are you ready for assessment?

AC	What do you know now?	Assessment task	✓
1.1	Explain employees' roles and responsibilities in relation to the prevention and control of infection	Page 311	
1.2	Explain employers' responsibilities in relation to the prevention and control of infection	Page 311	
2.1	Outline current legislation and regulatory body standards which are relevant to the prevention and control of infection	Page 315	
2.2	Describe local and organisational policies relevant to the prevention and control of infection	Page 315	
3.1	Describe procedures and systems relevant to the prevention and control of infection	Page 321	
3.2	Explain the potential impact of an outbreak of infection on the individual and the organisation	Page 325	
4.1	Define the term 'risk'	Page 329	
4.2	Outline potential risks of infection within the workplace	Page 329	
4.3	Describe the process of carrying out a risk assessment	Page 329	
4.4	Explain the importance of carrying out a risk assessment	Page 329	
5.1	Demonstrate correct use of personal protective equipment (PPE)	Page 335	
5.2	Describe different types of PPE	Page 335	
5.3	Explain the reasons for use of PPE	Page 335	
5.4	State current relevant regulations and legislation relating to PPE	Page 333	
5.5	Describe employees' responsibilities regarding the use of PPE	Page 333	
5.6	Describe employers' responsibilities regarding the use of PPE	Page 333	
5.7	Describe the correct practice in the application and removal of PPE	Page 335	
5.8	Describe the correct procedure for disposal of used PPE	Page 335	
6.1	Describe the key principles of good personal hygiene	Page 337	
6.2	Demonstrate good hand washing technique	Page 339	
6.3	Describe the correct sequence for hand washing	Page 339	
6.4	Explain when and why hand washing should be carried out	Page 341	
6.5	Describe the types of products that should be used for hand washing	Page 343	
6.6	Describe correct procedures that relate to skincare	Page 343	

12 | Provide support to maintain and develop skills for everyday life (HSC 3003)

Assessment of this unit

This unit provides the knowledge and skills required to work with individuals who need to retain, regain and develop skills for everyday life. The unit is relevant to work in a wide range of health and social care roles and work settings. You will need to demonstrate that you:

1. Understand the context of supporting skills for everyday life.

2. Are able to support individuals to plan for maintaining and developing skills for everyday life.

3. Can support individuals to retain, regain and develop skills for everyday life.

4. Are able to evaluate support for developing or maintaining skills for everyday life.

To complete this unit successfully you will need to produce evidence of your knowledge as shown in the 'What you need to know' chart opposite. You also need to produce evidence of your practical ability as shown in the 'What you need to do' chart. The 'What you need to do' criteria must be assessed in a real work environment by a vocationally competent assessor. Your tutor or assessor will help you to prepare for your assessment and the tasks suggested in this chapter will help you to create the evidence you need.

CHAPTER 12

AC   What you need to know

1.1	Compare methods for developing and maintaining skills for everyday life
1.2	Analyse the reasons why individuals may need support to maintain, regain or develop skills for everyday life
1.3	Explain how maintaining, regaining or developing skills can benefit individuals

AC   What you need to do

2.1	Work with an individual and others to identify skills for everyday life that need to be supported
2.2	Agree with the individual a plan for developing or maintaining the skills identified
2.3	Analyse possible sources of conflict that may arise when planning and ways to resolve them
2.4	Support the individual to understand the plan and any processes, procedures or equipment needed to implement or monitor it
3.1	Provide agreed support to develop or maintain skills, in a way that promotes active participation
3.2	Give positive and constructive feedback to the individual during activities to develop or maintain their skills
3.3	Describe actions to take if an individual becomes distressed or unable to continue
4.1	Work with an individual and others to agree criteria and processes for evaluating support
4.2	Carry out agreed role to evaluate progress towards goals and the effectiveness of methods used
4.3	Agree revisions to the plan
4.4	Record and report in line with agreed ways of working

The assessment criteria 2.1 – 4.4 must be assessed in a real work environment.

This unit is designed to develop your working practice, which is relevant to every chapter of this book, but has particular links to other mandatory units:

HSC 3013	Support individuals to access and use facilities and services
HSC 3020	Facilitate person-centred assessment, planning, implementation and review
HSC 3004	Support individuals in learning or development activities

Some of your learning will be repeated in these units and will give you the chance to review your knowledge and understanding.

How are skills for everyday life developed and maintained?

Skills for everyday life allow people do to the things that meet their daily needs. These are also known as **activities of daily living** that have a direct affect on any individual's health and well-being, as shown in Figure 12.1.

Doing things *with* individuals

It is often thought that care workers look after people by doing things for them. Another approach is to do things with people. Today care workers should work in **partnership** with individuals and groups of individuals. Partnership is about working together as equals in order to:

▶ support the individual to make as many decisions about their care as possible

▶ support the individual to do as much for themselves as possible.

Your assessment criteria:

1.1 Compare methods for developing and maintaining skills for everyday life.

Key terms

Activities of daily living: skills that directly affect an individual's everyday health and well-being

Partnership: working together as equals

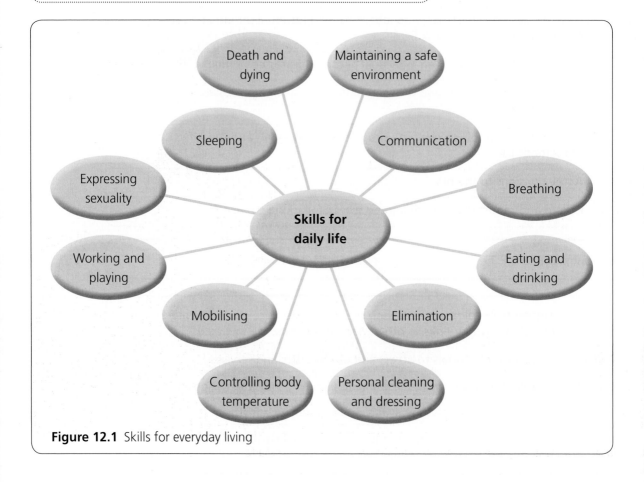

Figure 12.1 Skills for everyday living

Case study

Charlie is admitted to Hillcrest mental health unit after he is found living on the streets and drunk. He has a long history of mental health problems. A few weeks previously he ran away from the hostel where he had been living.

On admission his care plan is drawn up with his key nurse. In it they agree that Charlie would decide how long he would stay in the unit, be able to visit the hostel again and would prepare his own food and wash his own clothes. He would also attend occupational therapy to pursue his hobby of wood carving and take part in classes about the effects of alcohol on physical and mental health.

At the end of his stay at Hillcrest the care workers at the hostel comment that the support Charlie received at the mental health unit has helped him retain and regain his everyday living skills. Charlie says it makes him feel better about himself knowing that he has actively participated in his own care.

1. How does Charlie's key nurse support Charlie in actively participating in his own care?
2. What are the benefits for Charlie?
3. How has using his everyday living skills affected Charlie's self esteem?

Working in partnership can maintain and develop individual skills

Doing things *for* individuals

Providing too much care can make people's problems worse:

▶ Individuals can lose skills they once used

▶ Individuals do not learn new skills

▶ Individuals do not regain skills they have lost.

Reflect

Is it easier to learn a new skill than to regain a lost skill? Reflect on your own experience of trying to learn skills.

Case study

Mandy is a new care worker at the supported living centre for people with learning disabilities. She feels sorry for Tim when he comes to the centre because his mother who usually looks after him is going into hospital for an operation. She knows that Tim is worried and doesn't understand why he is brought to the centre today. Afterwards he is going to stay with another family he has only met once before until his mother is able to look after him again.

Tim's care plan says that he is to do as much for himself as he is able to and that he should be supported to use his daily living skills. Mandy, though, decides to do things for Tim instead. She takes his coat and hangs it up in the corridor, gets him a hot drink, and at lunch time makes some beans on toast for him instead of supporting him to prepare a meal.

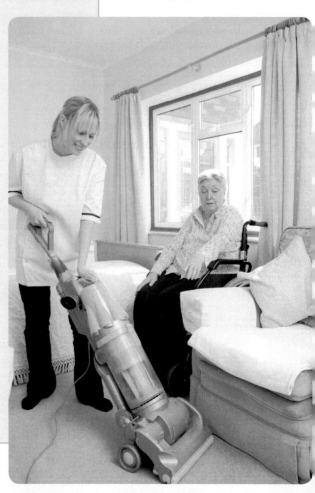

Care workers consider individual needs when maintaining skills *for* everyday life

1. To what extent is Mandy working in partnership with Tim?

2. Does she help him:

   a) retain skills in every day living?

   b) regain skills in everyday living?

   c) learn new skills in everyday living?

3. Why do you think care workers sometimes decide to do tasks for individuals rather than support and encourage them to do these tasks for themselves?

Knowledge Assessment Task   1.1

Health and social care practitioners need to understand how best to support individuals who need to develop or maintain their skills for every day life. With reference to your own care practice, produce a poster or a table that compares methods for developing and maintaining individual's skills for everyday life. Your poster or table should take account of:

a) doing things for individuals

b) doing things with individuals.

Discuss your poster with your assessor, making sure you use a specific example of an individual who requires support to learn a new skill, retain an existing skill or regain a lost skill.

Keep a copy of any written work that you produce as evidence for your assessment.

Investigate

What policy documents are available in your work area for encouraging active participation in everyday activities and using skills in everyday life? Try to find and review these, noting how active participation is or isn't encouraged.

Discuss

What do your friends and colleagues say are the benefits of partnership working with individuals? Discuss this issue, sharing ideas and experiences to extend your knowledge.

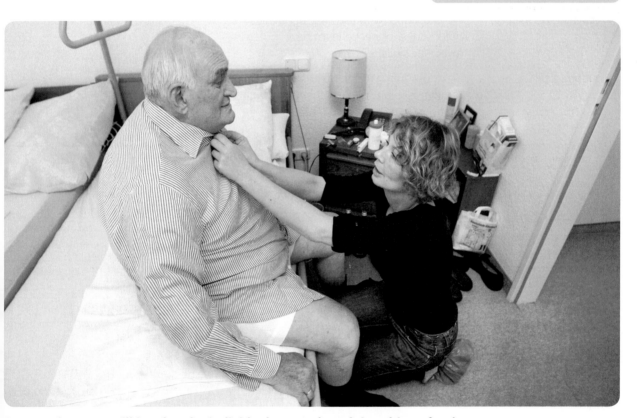

Care workers can still involve the individual even when doing things _for_ them

Why do individuals need support to maintain, regain, or develop skills?

At different stages of life individuals might have different health problems that affect their skills for everyday life, as shown in Figure 12.2. Being aware of the activities of daily living helps care workers understand the problems that individuals might have.

Figure 12.2 Problems with everyday living skills

Problem	An example of the effect on everyday living skills
Physical health	Feeling unwell such as with a fever leads to tiredness and inability to carry on with the usual activities of daily living.
Learning disabilities	An individual with learning disabilities might take longer to learn new everyday skills.
Mental health	An individual with mental health problems might neglect themselves so they do not eat and drink.
Frailty	Older frail people may not be strong enough to dress themselves or prepare their own meals.
Physical disability	Some physical disabilities prevent individuals going shopping unsupported.
Social isolation	An individual who is lonely is less likely to communicate with others.

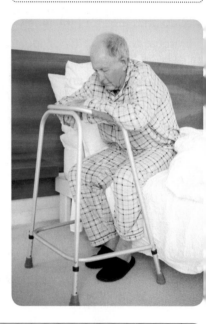

What happens if an individual cannot use everyday skills?

If a condition prevents an individual from using skills of everyday life, the result can have a significant impact on the person's quality of life, as outlined in Figure 12.3.

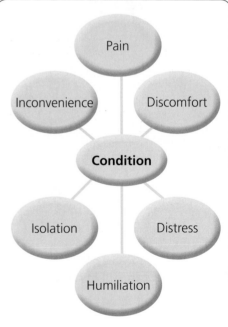

Figure 12.3 The effect of conditions on everyday skills

Case study

Aled lives alone in an apartment. He has a temporary physical disability resulting from a virus that affects his heart. It has left him very weak and unable to look after himself. There are skills in everyday living that people take for granted until they cannot use them, his nurse explains.

Aled hasn't thought about this before, but now he understands. As he lies on the sofa watching daytime TV programmes he thinks about the skills he has stopped using. It is a more than a week since he left the apartment, and he has hardly spoken to anybody for a couple of days. His meals are delivered and his laundry piles up. He now wishes that he had accepted the offer of support from one of the home help agencies the nurse suggested.

He continues to lie there thinking about what it would be like if his heart condition was permanent. It would be difficult to maintain all his everyday living skills. How long will his weakness last, and will it be difficult to regain the skills he is not using such as socialising, cooking and working for a living?

1. What everyday living skills does Aled not use when he is ill?

2. What is the effect of not using everyday living skills for Aled?

3. Reflect on your own experience of illness. What skills did you stop using?

Knowledge Assessment Task   1.2

With reference to individuals you have provided care or support for (and bearing confidentiality issues in mind) write a brief report or care study that analyses reasons why individuals may need support to maintain, regain or develop skills for everyday life.

Keep a copy of the written work that you produce for this activity as evidence for your assessment.

Reflect

Why might individuals need support to maintain skills for everyday living? You might want to think about one or two of the people with whom you work as a way of reflecting on this issue.

Investigate

What information is available on the Internet about how individuals can regain skills in everyday life? Carry out a search, identifying useful sites provided by government, voluntary organisations and support groups.

Discuss

What do your friends and colleagues say about how an individual's skills for everyday life can be developed if they have a mental or physical health problem? Share your thoughts, ideas and experiences and think about how you can use what you learn to develop your practice.

Care workers can develop their understanding of an individual's condition and how best to work in partnership to maintain, regain and develop their skills

Your assessment criteria:

1.3 Explain how maintaining, regaining or developing skills can benefit individuals.

Investigate

What groups, clubs and societies are in your local area where individuals might maintain, regain or develop everyday skills?

How can maintaining, regaining and developing skills benefit individuals?

Maintaining, regaining and developing everyday skills can benefit individuals' wellbeing in a range of ways, as shown in Figure 12.4.

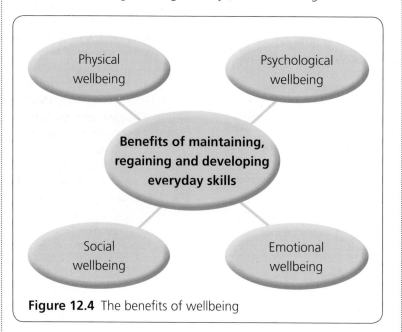

Figure 12.4 The benefits of wellbeing

What is wellbeing?

Wellbeing is being happy, healthy and prosperous, as outlined in Figure 12.5 opposite. The aim of health and social care work is to protect and promote the wellbeing of individuals. Care workers should assist individuals and groups of individuals with their everyday living needs, and thereby promote their wellbeing.

Key terms

Guided discovery: used by therapists to help individuals reflect on alternative ways of thinking, leading to changes in perceptions and behaviours

Wellbeing: being healthy, happy and prosperous

Figure 12.5 Benefits from promoting the wellbeing of individuals

Wellbeing	What it includes	How it benefits individuals
Physical	Eating, drinking, cleaning and washing, dressing, exercising and using toilet facilities.	Individuals are freed from hunger and thirst, they look clean and presentable to others, and risk of infections and disease is lowered.
Psychological	Self esteem, being happy and thinking clearly.	Individuals can be more confident and have a good opinion of themselves.
Emotional	Feeling happy and stable.	Individuals are able to avoid emotional distresses such as frequent tearfulness and sadness.
Social	Communicating with others and socialising.	Individuals are able to be part of a community with a sense of belonging, avoiding isolation and loneliness.

Case study

Petra has a liver condition as a result of years of alcohol misuse. She stopped drinking several years ago after her doctor explained the severity of the condition to her. She has been told that even though she is only in her late twenties, that to start drinking again would end in her premature death. She was referred to a counsellor who helped her understand through guided discovery that one of the reasons she drank heavily is because she does not have other interests.

Today Petra pursues a range of activities and interests, but also continues to gain support from a small group of individuals who have also misused alcohol in the past. They talk about life and its problems, but also socialise together. Among these individuals is Grant, a man nearly twice her age, but with whom she gets on very well. They both belong to the same local ramblers' club. One day Grant asked Petra if she was happy. The question was unexpected, and at first Petra didn't know what to say. After thinking about it a while, though, she confidently said she was and hugged him.

1. In what way does the small support group help Petra in maintaining skills in everyday life?

2. What physical, psychological, emotional and social benefits has Petra regained since abstaining from alcohol?

3. To what extent do the benefits of membership of the local ramblers' club contribute to Petra developing new skills?

Reflect

How do individuals where you work maintain skills in everyday life? Reflect on the ways in which different people do (or don't do) this and think about your role in supporting this aspect of people's functioning.

Discuss

How can people who are users of health and social care services develop new skills? Discuss with a colleague or your supervisor the different ways in which the people who use your care setting (or other settings that you know of) are enabled to develop new skills for everyday living.

Knowledge Assessment Task 1.3

You have been asked to contribute a short article to the newsletter of your care organisation. The newsletter is aimed at both service users and their relatives. Your manager has asked you to write up to 500 words explaining how maintaining, regaining or developing skills can benefit individuals. You should focus on the ways in which individuals receiving care or support in your work place are encouraged and enabled to maintain, regain or develop everyday living skills and the reasons for this.

Keep a copy of any written work that you produce as evidence for your assessment.

Be able to support individuals to plan for maintaining and developing skills for everyday life

Your assessment criteria:

2.1 Work with an individual and others to identify skills for everyday life that need to be supported.

2.2 Agree with the individual a plan for developing or maintaining the skills identified.

How can individuals be supported to identify and plan for everyday skills?

Individuals can be supported with identifying skills that need to be maintained, regained or developed. Others might work with you, including those shown in Figure 12.6.

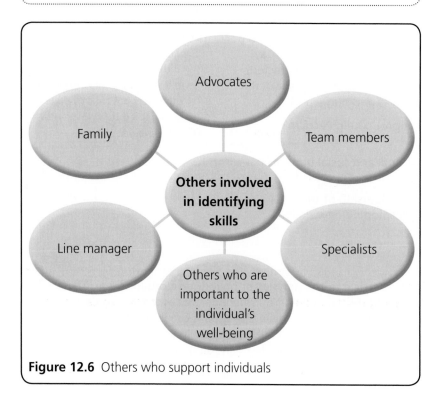

Figure 12.6 Others who support individuals

How are everyday skills identified?

Individuals might identify their own everyday skills that need to be supported, or you might identify them in partnership with the individual and others. This means working with the individual to make sure that support is provided as needed, as a result of:

▶ discussions with the individual

▶ discussions with others involved

▶ a previous care plan or health and social care history

▶ observation and new assessment of the individual.

Discussion with others involved with the individual can help identify and plan for everyday skills

Agree a plan for developing skills

When an everyday skills need is identified a plan should be made that aims to address the need, as shown in Figure 12.7.

Your assessment criteria:

2.1 Work with an individual and others to identify skills for everyday life that need to be supported.

2.2 Agree with the individual a plan for developing or maintaining the skills identified.

Figure 12.7 Examples of plans for everyday skills needs

Everyday living skill	Identified everyday need	Plan to meet the identified everyday need
Communication	Tom, who has Asperger's syndrome, is unable to communicate with people he does not know very well.	To gradually increase the number of people Tom can talk with.
Expressing sexuality	Miranda, who has a learning disability, is over-familiar with strangers and is at risk of sexual exploitation.	To be accompanied when she goes to public places.
Eating and drinking	Reggie, who has had depression since his wife died, is unable to cook for himself.	To be offered treatment for his depression and domestic skills classes.
Elimination	Carter has dementia and is incontinent.	To be supported in washing, cleaning and dressing.
Mobility	Dympna has **ME** and finds it difficult to walk.	To assess and facilitate the use of the most appropriate mobility aid.

Key terms

ME or **myalgic encephalomyelitis:** a syndrome with tiredness, muscle pain and reduced ability to exercise following a viral infection

Discuss

Identify individuals in your care setting and with your line manager or supervisor discuss their short, medium and long-term goals. To what extent are they different?

Case study

Terry has rheumatoid arthritis, a chronic condition that is painful and which has resulted in him falling in his home. When he stands up he loses balance and has fallen over furniture. On one occasion he fell and knocked a hole through the wall plaster with his head. Pain keeps him awake at night so he is very tired, and there is a risk if he gets up in the night to use the toilet. At his next doctor's appointment, after a long discussion of how the condition has affected Terry's life a plan is agreed. In the short term he is to be given stronger analgesic tablets to dull the pain, and reduce the risk of falling at night. In the medium term Terry's needs for a mobility aid, a walking frame, and help around the home are reviewed, and referrals are made to an occupational therapist, social worker and to a consultant rheumatologist. The referral letters outline how the condition affects Terry's everyday skills, including: mobility, maintaining a safe environment, eating and drinking and sleeping. It is agreed that each professional would be responsible for their specialist long term goals, but would communicate at regular intervals to monitor the plan and ensure the best long term care for Terry.

1. How are Terry's skills in everyday life affected by his condition?

2. To what extent are the short, medium and long-term goals likely to affect the type and level of support Terry receives?

3. In what ways might support from different professionals benefit Terry in maintaining his everyday life skills?

Key terms

Rheumatoid arthritis: a long-term disease that leads to inflammation of the joints

Short-term goals are often about reducing or removing risk to the individual, and should be addressed before longer-term plans are made

359

How can conflicts be resolved and plans followed?

Your assessment criteria:

2.3 Analyse possible sources of conflict that may arise when planning and ways to resolve them.

In health and social care individuals are encouraged to share decision-making and participate in their own care and care planning. Sometimes there is conflict between their wishes and preferences and what can be provided.

▶ you might try to carry out a care activity that the individual does not want

▶ the individual prefers an activity that is not going to benefit them.

This can result in risks to the individual and others.

What kind of situations might cause conflict?

Conflict can arise when there are a number of different situations, as outlined in Figure 12.8. Figure 12.9 shows you some factors that might be involved in the conflict.

Figure 12.8 Sources of conflict

Conflict	Example
Individual	On the ward where you work an individual is incontinent and needs a bath, but refuses because he denies being incontinent.
Family and friends	In the assisted living centre where you work an individual's family refuse to give permission for a relative to go out shopping for new clothes because they say the individual won't know the difference.
Colleagues	In the retirement home where you visit a co-worker wants to organise games for all residents, but you know that some are looking forward to watching a particular television programme.
Policies	In the older people's home where you work the policy says that all residents should be in bed by 10 p.m. because of night time staffing levels, but you think this is not treating them like adults.

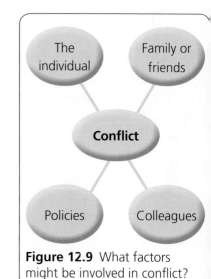

Figure 12.9 What factors might be involved in conflict?

How can conflict be resolved or avoided?

Conflict can be resolved or avoided by:

- ▶ developing a good relationship with the individual
- ▶ mutual respect
- ▶ good communication
- ▶ negotiating different ways to meet goals.

If you are still not able to resolve conflict with an individual you should seek the assistance of a senior worker.

Case study

Carmen has a mental health problem. For much of the time she is not aware of her appearance or how she presents herself to other people. She rarely washes or changes her clothes and is often dirty and untidy.

Lucy is a care worker on the mental health unit. Carmen has been admitted because she is a danger to herself due to self-neglect. Other patients on the unit complain that Carmen smells and they want the staff to make her have a bath and dress in clean clothes. Carmen is very resistant to the idea.

The situation causes conflict between Carmen's choice not to bathe and Lucy's plan to provide care.

Lucy decides the best way to act is to try to resolve the conflict between Carmen and others by getting to know Carmen a lot better. She treats her with respect, listens carefully to her and finally negotiates a way that meets Carmen's preferences.

Lucy finds out that Carmen was sexually exploited when she bathed when staying in a hostel. Carmen eventually has a bath when she is sure her needs for privacy and safety are listened to and respected.

1. Did Lucy try to overrule Carmen's decision not to bathe, or did she try to resolve the conflict between Carmen and others?
2. What steps did she take to resolve the conflict?
3. Reflect on your involvement with any resolutions of conflict. Was negotiation involved?

Reflect

Has any conflict of views arisen in your work area when implementing a care plan? What was the conflict about, and how was it resolved?

Investigate

Do any procedures or policies in your work area deal with conflict and how to respond to conflict? You can find this out by obtaining and reviewing the policies and procedures that apply in your work setting.

Discuss

Different people respond to conflict in different ways. How do your friends and colleagues respond to conflict at work? Share your ideas and experiences with an couple of colleagues or your supervisor and consider whether there are any new strategies that you could use in the future.

Your assessment criteria:

2.4 Support the individual to understand the plan and any processes, procedures or equipment needed to implement or monitor it.

Individuals may need support in understanding how to use equipment as part of their care plan

How can you support individuals to understand their plan?

Care plans should be discussed and agreed with the individual and others who provide support. It cannot, however, be taken for granted that individuals understand their care plan.

It is necessary in some situations that individuals are supported in understanding their care plan and any processes, procedures or equipment needed to implement or monitor it, as shown in Figures 12.10 and 12.11.

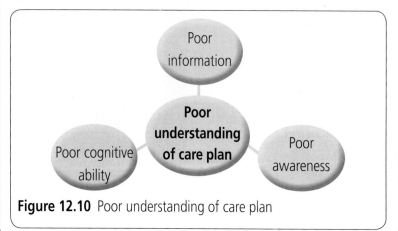

Figure 12.10 Poor understanding of care plan

Figure 12.11 Supporting individuals to understand the care plan

Poor understanding	Example	What is the process, procedure or equipment used?	How they are supported
Poor cognitive ability	Frank has dementia. He does not understand that he is staying at the residential home.	The procedure is that all residents are supported in settling into the residential home.	Care workers explain to Frank that he is staying at the home. They respect him as an individual, are patient with him and repeat the information as necessary.
Poor awareness	Carmen has a mental health problem. She is not aware of her appearance and how others see her.	The process is that care workers respect service users and treat them as individuals.	Care workers take the time to develop and maintain a relationship with Carmen, and negotiate how to improve her appearance and hygiene, and its effect on others.
Poor information	Julie has **MS (Multiple Sclerosis)**. She finds it painful and difficult to walk at times.	Equipment used includes a mobility scooter.	Julie is supported in choosing and learning to use the mobility scooter.

Practical Assessment Task | 2.1 | 2.2 | 2.3 | 2.4

Health and social care practitioners should be able to work in partnership with individuals to plan ways of maintaining and developing skills for everyday life. With the permission of your manager and an individual for whom you provide care or support, you need to show that you can:

▶ work with an individual and others to identify skills for everyday life that need to be supported
▶ make a record of any everyday skills that need supporting
▶ discuss ways that the identified skills can be supported and agree a plan for developing or maintaining the skills identified
▶ analyse possible sources of conflict that may arise when planning care for the individual and ways to resolve them
▶ support the person to understand the plan and any processes, procedures or equipment needed to implement or monitor it.

Your evidence for this task must be based on your practice in a real work environment and must be witnessed by or be in a format acceptable to your assessor.

Key terms

MS or **Multiple Sclerosis**: a progressive chronic disease of the nervous system

Your assessment criteria:

3.1 Provide agreed support to develop or maintain skills, in a way that promotes active participation.

3.2 Give positive and constructive feedback to the individual during activities to develop or maintain their skills.

How does feedback support active participation?

Sometimes it is necessary to provide support to develop or maintain everyday skills. This support should encourage the **active participation** of the individual. Active participation is a way of working that sees the individual as an active partner in their care with the following benefits:

▶ promoting independence

▶ promoting skills development

▶ increasing self esteem

▶ promoting choice.

The barriers shown in Figure 12.12 can prevent individuals from actively participating in their own care.

Key terms

Active participation: a way of working that sees the individual as an active partner in their care

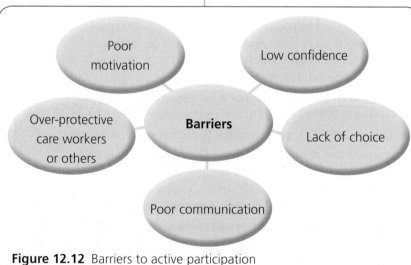

Figure 12.12 Barriers to active participation

What support should be given?

In order to support individuals' participation in their own care, care workers must think about the overall care plan, as outlined in Figure 12.13.

Reflect

What are the benefits of active participation for individuals? Are there any drawbacks to active participation?

Figure 12.13 Supporting the overall plan of care

Key stage	Explanation
Assessment	An up-to-date assessment must be made of what individuals can do for themselves, and what support they need.
Care plan	The care plan should be realistic and reviewed regularly.
Relationships	Care workers should get to know the individual as a person, including their likes and preferences.
Activities	Make sure activities are manageable taking into account the individual's condition.
Involvement	Individuals should be involved in their care as much as possible.
Encouragement	Give encouragement and positive and constructive feedback that builds on the individual's strengths.

Choose the words or phrases that the individual finds encouraging

Giving positive, constructive feedback

Positive and constructive feedback is a way to support individuals in their care that takes into account:

▶ relationships and communication

▶ capabilities and skills

▶ goals and skills development.

Positive and constructive feedback is given to encourage the active participation of individuals in their care, as outlined in Figure 12.14. It involves communicating what the individual does well and how the individual can improve on a skill.

Your assessment criteria:

3.1 Provide agreed support to develop or maintain skills, in a way that promotes active participation.

3.2 Give positive and constructive feedback to the individual during activities to develop or maintain their skills.

Investigate

Does care plan documentation in your work area indicate how positive and constructive feedback might be given? Obtain the advice and guidance on care plan feedback that is provided to practitioners in your work area and assess the extent to which helpful advice is provided on this issue.

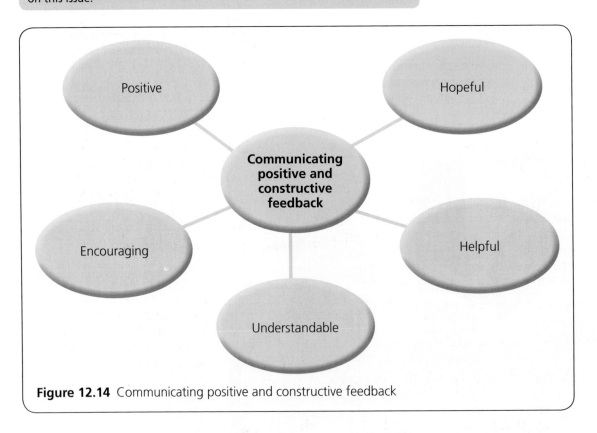

Figure 12.14 Communicating positive and constructive feedback

Case study

At the Resource Centre Steve is asked to work with Pete preparing lunch. This is one of the activities Steve likes doing because it gives him the chance to assess the progress Pete is making.

Pete has learning disabilities and has been learning to prepare simple meals so that in time he can live more independently from his parents. Steve knows that Pete is very capable of peeling potatoes but will try to get him to do it.

Before it is time to go into the kitchen Steve agrees with Pete what they are going to make. He listens to Pete's preferences and they agree on mashed potato and beans, one of his favourites.

Steve asks Pete what they will need, and reminds him about the peeler. Pete says he doesn't know how to use it, but Steve reminds him he used it when they cooked together before, and that he did a good job of the potatoes.

When they finish preparing the meal Steve says that soon Pete will be able to make a range of different meals. This pleases Pete and he says he wants to cook some sausages as well next time.

1. What support does Steve provide for Pete that promoted his active participation?

2. In what way did he give positive and constructive feedback to him?

3. Reflect on how positive and constructive feedback encourages you.

Discuss

How do your friends and colleagues give positive and constructive feedback? Share your ideas and experiences and consider what you can learn from other people about giving feedback.

367

What if an individual becomes distressed and unable to continue?

While performing everyday skills some individuals might become distressed or be unable to continue with the activity. This can be for a number of reasons, as shown in Figure 12.15.

Figure 12.15 Reasons for distress

What actions should care workers take?

Care workers can take a number of actions if an individual becomes distressed or unable to continue with their activity:

▶ offer reassurance that the person will not come to harm

▶ communicate that you understand their distress

▶ say how well the individual is doing with the everyday skill

▶ seek advice or assistance from a senior colleague

▶ make sure the individual remains safe

▶ suggest stopping the activity.

Stopping the activity should normally be an option after other options have been tried. The distress the individual experienced should be recorded and reported and the care plan reviewed.

Case study

Esther has agoraphobia and is being supported in using a bus to go to the shopping centre as part of her care plan. Tariq is familiar with the bus routes and the local area and has volunteered to accompany her.

When they are on the bus Esther begins to look distressed and anxious, and holds herself very tight. Tariq, who is sitting next to her, is aware of her discomfort and tries to reassure her, saying that it is only one more stop before they get off the bus. Even though the bus is moving Esther tries to get off. The bus driver tells her to get away from the door and then slows the bus down to a stop.

All the time Tariq talks to Esther, saying she will be all right and then holds her hands until they are able to get off the bus. When they are on the pavement Tariq helps Esther to a quiet place down the road.

1. What does Tariq do to continue to support Esther?
2. What other options can Tariq consider?
3. Reflect on activities that you have been unable to continue. Was this because they were not right for you at the time?

Practical Assessment Task   3.1   3.2   3.3

Health and social care practitioners need to be able to support individuals to retain, regain or develop skills for everyday life. To demonstrate that you are able to do this as part of your own work role, obtain the permission of your line manager or supervisor and with the consent of an individual:

▶ provide agreed support to develop or maintain skills in a way that promotes active participation

▶ give positive and constructive feedback to the individual during activities to develop or maintain their skills

▶ describe what actions you would take if the individual becomes distressed or is unable to continue with a skills-focused activity.

Your evidence for this task must be based on your practice in a real work environment and must be witnessed by or be in a format acceptable to your assessor.

Discuss

What actions might a friend or colleague take when an individual becomes distressed during an activity? Discuss this and share ideas and strategies for responding to individuals' distress in these circumstances.

Agreeing criteria and processes for evaluating support

Care workers need to work with service users and others to agree criteria and processes for evaluating support. The evaluation criteria depends on the aims and goals for the individual as set down in the care plan. Some examples are given in Figure 12.16.

Figure 12.16 Examples of evaluation criteria

Everyday skills need	Aim	Evaluation criteria
Following a stroke Marge is in need of support to eat and drink.	To be able to eat and drink independently.	That Marge can use a spoon to eat and hold a cup to her mouth.
Following a back injury Douglas cannot use toilet facilities independently.	Douglas to be shown how to use a bathroom appliance to use the toilet unsupported.	That Douglas can use the toilet unsupported.
Jason has autism and won't look at other people.	Jason to look at cards with peoples' faces.	That Jason can look at faces on cards without turning his head away.

Your assessment criteria:

4.1 Work with an individual and others to agree criteria and processes for evaluating support.

4.2 Carry out agreed role to evaluate progress towards goals and the effectiveness of methods used.

4.3 Agree revisions to the plan.

4.4 Record and report in line with agreed ways of working.

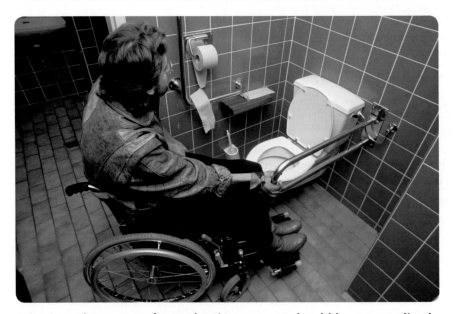

Criteria and processes for evaluating support should be personalised to each individual's needs and care plan

How do you agree evaluation with the individual and others?

Evaluation criteria are agreed with the individual and others at the time the care is discussed and planned. Evaluation criteria should based on:

▶ the individual's agreed needs

▶ the individual's aims and goals.

Processes are the way things are done. When agreeing how support is to be evaluated, the processes for agreeing support should also be confirmed. Some examples of processes for agreeing support are shown in Figure 12.17.

Figure 12.17 Examples of processes for agreeing support

Evaluating progress

The evaluation considers responses to the following questions:

▶ Has the goal been achieved?

▶ If not, how much progress has been made?

▶ How effective is the care to date?

▶ Are different forms of care needed?

How do you agree and record revisions?

After the plan has been evaluated, revisions to the plan should be agreed and they should be recorded in line with agreed ways of working.

Your assessment criteria:

4.1 Work with an individual and others to agree criteria and processes for evaluating support.

4.2 Carry out agreed role to evaluate progress towards goals and the effectiveness of methods used.

4.3 Agree revisions to the plan.

4.4 Record and report in line with agreed ways of working.

Case study

Jimmy lives in a secure unit for teenage boys. He has his liberty restricted to protect himself and others. Steve, a worker on the unit, has identified that budgeting is a problem for Jimmy. He spends his money as soon as he receives it. Jimmy then has no money for the rest of the week.

The local policies and procedures documents for managing service users' money state that in some circumstances staff can safeguard residents' money for short periods with the agreement of the resident. After consulting his manager, Steve asks Jimmy if he would like help with his budgeting. After another week without any money, Jimmy agrees.

Steve works with him and the other staff to make sure Jimmy is given enough money each day for one day, and the remainder of his weekly allowance is kept safe for him. Jimmy signs an agreement to try this new way of budgeting for three weeks. A date is set to evaluate the budgeting agreement, arranging that just Jimmy and Steve will be present for the evaluation process.

On evaluating the budgeting plan, they agree that it works as Jimmy has money for the week. Jimmy asks for it to be extended for another month. Steve records this in Jimmy's case file and reports the evaluation to other staff. Jimmy's care plan is amended to state that the budgeting plan is to be evaluated after a further four weeks.

1. In what ways are Jimmy and others involved in the plan?
2. What are the agreed criteria for evaluating the plan?
3. What is the process for evaluating the budgeting plan?

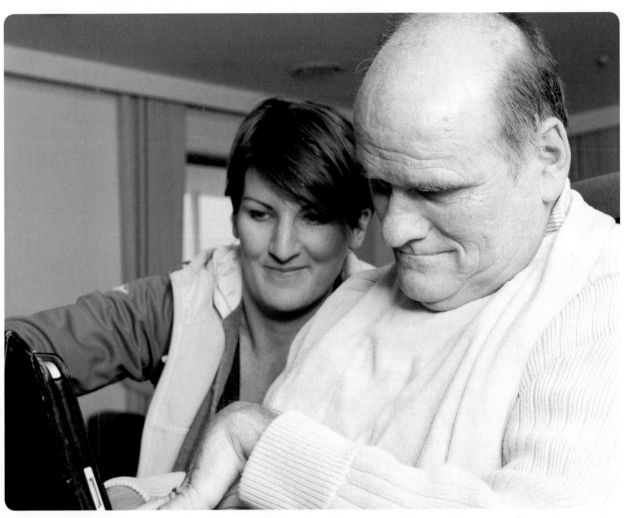

Work with individuals to agree how to evaluate the effectiveness of their care

Practical Assessment Task **4.1 4.2 4.3 4.4**

Evaluation is a key stage in the care planning process. It focuses on the effectiveness of the care plan in meeting an individual's need for support or other specific interventions. With the permission of your line manager or your supervisor, and the consent of an individual:

▶ work with an individual to agree criteria and the processes for evaluating the support they have received to develop or maintain everyday living skills

▶ contribute to the evaluation process by providing feedback on the extent to which the person has made progress towards goals and the effectiveness of the methods used

▶ agree any revisions to the plan with the individual and others

▶ record and report the evaluation feedback in line with agreed ways of working in your work setting.

Your evidence for this task must be based on your practice in a real work environment and must be witnessed by or be in a format acceptable to your assessor.

Are you ready for assessment?

AC	What do you know now?	Assessment task	✓
1.1	Compare methods for developing and maintaining skills for everyday life	Page 351	
1.2	Analyse the reasons why individuals may need support to maintain, regain or develop skills for everyday life	Page 353	
1.3	Explain how maintaining, regaining or developing skills can benefit individuals	Page 355	

AC	What can you do now?	Assessment task	✓
2.1	Work with an individual and others to identify skills for everyday life that need to be supported	Page 363	
2.2	Agree with the individual a plan for developing or maintaining the skills identified	Page 363	
2.3	Analyse possible sources of conflict that may arise when planning and ways to resolve them	Page 363	
2.4	Support the individual to understand the plan and any processes, procedures or equipment needed to implement or monitor it	Page 363	
3.1	Provide agreed support to develop or maintain skills, in a way that promotes active participation	Page 369	
3.2	Give positive and constructive feedback to the individual during activities to develop or maintain their skills	Page 369	
3.3	Describe actions to take if an individual becomes distressed or unable to continue	Page 369	
4.1	Work with an individual and others to agree criteria and processes for evaluating support	Page 373	
4.2	Carry out agreed role to evaluate progress towards goals and the effectiveness of methods used	Page 373	
4.3	Agree revisions to the plan	Page 373	
4.4	Record and report in line with agreed ways of working	Page 373	

13 | Facilitate person-centred assessment, planning, implementation and review (HSC 3020)

Assessment of this unit

This unit provides the knowledge and skills required to facilitate person-centred assessment, planning, implementation and review across a range of care settings. It focuses on the development of an individualised care or support plan and the various processes and stages involved in this. You will need to:

1. understand the principles of person-centred assessment and care planning

2. be able to facilitate person-centred assessment

3. be able to contribute to the planning of care or support

4. be able to support the implementation of care plans

5. be able to monitor care plans

6. be able to facilitate a review of care plans and their implementation.

The assessment of this unit is partly knowledge-based (things you need to know about) and partly competence-based (things you need to do in the real work environment). To successfully complete this unit, you will need to produce evidence of both your knowledge and your competence. The tables below and opposite outline what you need to know and do to meet each of the assessment criteria for the unit.

Your tutor or assessor will help you to prepare for your assessment and the tasks suggested in the unit will help you to create the evidence that you need.

AC	What you need to know
1.1	Explain the importance of a holistic approach to assessment and planning of care or support
1.2	Describe ways of supporting the individual to lead the assessment and planning process
1.3	Describe ways the assessment and planning process or documentation can be adapted to maximise an individual's ownership and control of it

AC	What you need to do
2.1	Establish with the individual a partnership approach to the assessment process
2.2	Establish with the individual how the process should be carried out and who else should be involved in the process
2.3	Agree with the individual and others the intended outcomes of the assessment process and care plan
2.4	Ensure that assessment takes account of the individual's strengths and aspirations as well as needs
2.5	Work with the individual and others to identify support requirements and preferences
3.1	Take account of factors that may influence the type and level of care or support to be provided
3.2	Work with the individual and others to explore options and resources for delivery of the plan
3.3	Contribute to agreement on how component parts of a plan will be delivered and by whom
3.4	Record the plan in a suitable format
4.1	Carry out assigned aspects of a care plan
4.2	Support others to carry out aspects of a care plan for which they are responsible
4.3	Adjust the plan in response to changing needs or circumstances
5.1	Agree methods for monitoring the way a care plan is delivered
5.2	Collate monitoring information from agreed sources
5.3	Record changes that affect the delivery of the care plan
6.1	Seek agreement with the individual and others about: • who should be involved in the review process • criteria to judge effectiveness of the care plan
6.2	Seek feedback from the individual and others about how the plan is working
6.3	Use feedback and monitoring/other information to evaluate whether the plan has achieved its objectives
6.4	Work with the individual and others to agree any revisions to the plan
6.5	Document the review process and revisions as required

Assessment criteria 2.1–2.5, 3.1–3.4, 4.1–4.3, 5.1–5.3 and 6.1–6.5 must be assessed in a real work environment.

This unit also links to the following units:

SHC 33	Promote equality and inclusion in health and social care
HSC 036	Promote person-centred approaches in health and social care
SS MU 3.1	Understand sensory loss

Some of your learning will be repeated in these units and will give you the chance to review your knowledge and understanding.

Why is a holistic approach important?

A holistic approach to assessment and planning of care or support is important because it:

▶ takes into account all aspects of a person's needs

▶ supports the whole person

▶ doesn't limit a person's needs to one health condition or social disability.

What is a holistic approach?

'Holism' means looking at the whole person. A holistic approach to care and support is one that takes into account all aspects of a person's life, as shown in Figure 13.1.

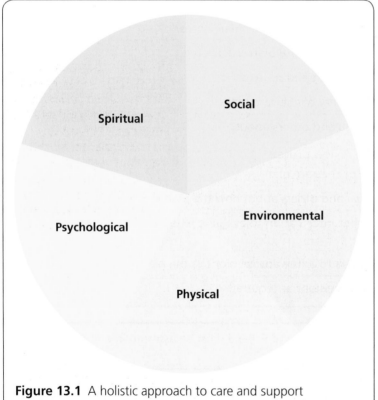

Figure 13.1 A holistic approach to care and support

A holistic approach to assessment and planning of care or support therefore aims to see the individual as more than just a person with asthma, social needs or a mental health problem. Figure 13.2 opposite outlines the aspects of holism.

Key terms

Holism: an approach that involves looking at the whole person – their needs, situation, wishes, preferences etc.

Reflect

To what extent would a holistic approach by workers affect the way they provide care?

Investigate

Using the internet, investigate how using a holistic approach benefits individuals with different health conditions or social disabilities.

Discuss

Discuss with a friend or colleague how a holistic approach might help in assessment and planning care or support.

Figure 13.2 Aspects of holism

Aspect of holism	Examples of what each aspect might involve	Questions to ask
Social	The relationships an individual has	Is the individual lonely or isolated?
Environmental	Where the person lives and wider environmental aspects such as the economic status of their family	Does the individual live in an area where there is no public transport and the family does not have a car?
Physical	Any health conditions that affect the individual	Is the individual healthy? What health condition does the individual have?
Psychological	An individual's self-esteem	Is the individual happy or sad most of the time? Do they feel respected by others?
Spiritual	The meaning life has for the individual	Does the individual have a faith?

Case study

Claris is a student social worker on placement with a care manager who is assessing a new client, Jacob, for a service. It has been arranged for Claris and the care manager to meet Jacob in the social services office so that she can carry out the assessment as part of her training. Jacob is late for the appointment. When he arrives he is coughing and seems breathless. After a while he recovers his breath and tells Claris that he has asthma and that he has had to run some of the way to the appointment. Claris asks him what he wants from social services. Jacob replies that he has had a cough for months, and that he was told by his doctor to make the appointment so that a social worker can help sort out his cough. Claris is not sure how she can treat Jacob's cough but says that she will see what can be done. They explore Jacob's circumstances and needs further using a holistic approach. Jacob is unemployed and lives alone in a small damp flat with mould on the walls, ceiling and windows. The nearest bus stop is half a mile away, but to get there he has to pass a playground where youths gather and mock him, so he goes the long way round. He doesn't think he has much of a life.

1. What aspects of a holistic approach should Claris look at in Jacob's case?
2. How might social services address Jacob's needs?
3. Reflect on the benefits of a holistic approach to assessing need.

Knowledge Assessment Task

1.1

A holistic approach to care planning is important because it enables care practitioners to take account of the individual as a whole and not just as someone with a health condition or disability. In this task you will demonstrate that you understand the principles of person-centred assessment and care planning.

1. Draw a pie chart with five segments: social, environmental, physical, psychological and spiritual. In each segment:
   a. identify two factors that can affect a holistic assessment of an individual
   b. identify what care or support you might offer.
2. Explain to your assessor the importance of a holistic approach to assessment and planning care and support, using the examples you identify on the pie chart.

How are individuals supported to lead the assessment and planning process?

A person-centred approach to assessment and planning of care requires the individual for whom the care plan is designed to be at the centre of all decisions made. This means that the individual should lead on carrying out the assessment and planning of their own care. In practice this involves:

▶ the individual identifying their own health and social care needs

▶ the individual expressing their own needs

▶ the individual planning how to meet their own needs.

What if the individual is unable to lead?

Sometimes in health and social care individuals are not able to lead on assessing and planning their own care because of their health condition or disability. In these situations individuals might need support to lead the assessment and planning of their own care.

Your assessment criteria:

1.2 Describe ways of supporting the individual to lead the assessment and planning process.

Reflect

Reflect on an occasion when you needed support to make a decision about your future.

Investigate

Investigate how individuals are supported in leading on assessment and planning of their own care in your workplace.

Discuss

Discuss with a friend or colleague how they have supported another person in assessing and planning.

Case study

Desmond has a severe learning disability. He is unable to communicate in words and has difficulty controlling his body movements. Apart from when he is asleep in bed, he spends most of his time in a special chair that is designed for his condition. It is known that from an early age Desmond liked swimming. It is part of his care plan to visit the local leisure centre where he is supported in the water.

The care home where Desmond lives is being taken over by a charitable trust which wants all its clients to actively participate in decisions about the care they receive. Each client is invited to a care review meeting to assess their care needs and plan future care. Maurice, a care worker, has known Desmond for several years and recognises when he wants to communicate. Maurice tries to explain to Desmond the purpose of the review meeting and says he will support Desmond in taking a lead on assessing and planning his care.

During the meeting Maurice sits next to Desmond. When it is time for Desmond to express his wishes Maurice supports him by asking questions and providing suggestions. By knowing Desmond well, Maurice knows when Desmond indicates 'yes' or 'no.'

1. To what extent do you think Desmond is able to lead on assessing and planning his own care?

2. How does Maurice hope to support Desmond?

3. Reflect on how you would support an individual who is unable to lead on assessing and planning their own care.

How can individuals be supported?

Individuals can be supported in leading the assessment and planning of their care by care workers and others such as family, friends, advocates or professionals as shown in Figure 13.3.

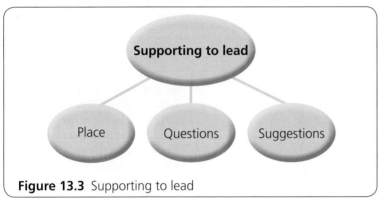

Figure 13.3 Supporting to lead

The place is the environment where the assessment and planning is carried out. It must be comfortable for the individual. Note how, in the case study on page 380 Maurice sits next to Desmond so that he feels supported.

Questions to ask in supporting the individual could include:

▶ What do you want to do?

▶ Have you tried to …?

▶ When was the last time you …?

▶ Do you find it difficult to …?

Workers and others can also make suggestions to support the individual, such as:

▶ You can do this because you are good at …

▶ You enjoyed it when we …

Family and friends can support an individual in their care plan, helping to identify and assess changing needs

Knowledge Assessment Task   1.2

A person-centred approach to assessment and planning of care requires the individual for whom the care plan is designed to be at the centre of all decisions made. This means that the individual being supported should lead on carrying out the assessment and planning of their own care. In this task you will demonstrate understanding of the principles of person-centred assessment and care planning.

1. Think of an individual and reflect on how you would support them to lead on the assessment and planning process.

2. Write a letter as if you were the individual and address it to yourself in which you:

   ▶ explain what you could do to ensure the environment is suitable

   ▶ outline questions you might ask

   ▶ outline suggestions you might make.

Discuss the contents of your letter with your assessor.

Maximising the individual's ownership of the assessment and planning process

In person-centred care the individual should be at the centre of all aspects of their own care. This includes ownership of the assessment and planning process and documentation. Ownership means that the individual:

▶ has control over their own care

▶ has control over the processes that support their care

▶ has control over the documentation that supports the processes.

What are processes?

Processes are when a care worker uses a routine, or established way of working, to achieve a goal. Examples of processes include arranging assessments of need and review meetings. Much of health and social care is carried out using processes which are also agreed ways of working.

Processes are used in:

▶ giving medication to patients

▶ organising a risk assessment

▶ involving relatives in discharge arrangements from hospital.

How can processes be adapted to maximise the individual's ownership?

Processes can be adapted to maximise ownership by involving the individual as an active participant in their own care, as outlined in Figure 13.4.

Figure 13.4 Maximising ownership through adapting processes

Process	Adaptation
Review	The individual can call a review of their care plan without needing to wait for a care worker to call a date for review.
Documentation	The individual keeps a copy of their own care plan in their home or personal space so that they have access to it without having to consult or ask a care worker.
Choosing the care team	The individual decides who should be involved in their own care and review meetings instead of being told who will be involved.
Preparation	The individual is supported in preparing for review meetings so that they can get ready for what they want to say or think about how they would like their needs met.
Advocacy	The individual can use the services of an independent advocate to maximise their ownership when they are not able to.

Reflect

Think about how individuals can be supported to maximise their ownership of approaches and documentation.

Investigate

Look at the documentation in your work place. How can it be adapted so that individuals can maximise their ownership and control of their care?

Discuss

Discuss with a friend or colleague how they support individuals to take control of their care.

How can documentation be adapted to maximise ownership?

There are ways that care workers can help individuals maximise their ownership of their own care records and documentation. One way of achieving this is to adapt records and documentation by:

▶ using simple terminology so that the individual understands, avoiding specialist language

▶ addressing the individual as 'you' instead of the service user, patient, resident or client. For example, 'How do you feel about the care you are receiving', in place of 'How does the client feel about the care they are receiving?'

▶ allowing the individual to make their own comments about their care in a prominent place on the documentation

▶ allowing space for the individual to express their opinions

▶ giving priority to the preferences and needs of the individual over the priorities of the service providers.

An individual can be supported in preparing for review meetings so they are ready for what they want to say and can take ownership

Case study

It is Tracey's care review meeting. Since she has been at the hostel for people recovering from mental health problems she has made good progress. She feels more confident and has developed many necessary skills for everyday living, such as cooking for herself and keeping her appearance presentable. At a pre-review discussion her key worker, Jason, has suggested to Tracey that she take more control over the review meeting and makes some suggestion on how this can be done. She agrees and decides whom to invite to the review, and what she would like to be talked about. At the meeting Jason lends her his pen and suggests she takes the notes and fills out some of the forms. At the end of the review record document Tracey is able to make comments on the care plans with which she has been supported. Tracey says she would like the next review to be within three months.

1. To what extent has Tracey been able to maximise her ownership of the process?

2. In what ways has Tracey been able to maximise her ownership of the documentation?

3. Why is it important that individuals have ownership of the process and documentation of their care?

Knowledge Assessment Task   1.3

Ownership of the assessment and planning process and documentation means that the individual has control over their own care, has control over the processes that support their care, and has control over the documentation that supports the processes. In this task you will demonstrate understanding of the principles of person-centred assessment and care planning.

Write a proposal to your manager in which you describe:

▶ the advantages of individuals maximising their ownership of the processes and documents about their own care

▶ how this can be achieved in your place of work or another care setting.

Discuss your proposal with your assessor.

Facilitate person-centred assessment

What is a partnership approach to assessment?

A partnership approach to person-centred assessment is a way of working that puts the individual at the centre of the process, but takes into account the views and roles of others. A partnership approach is important because it means that the individual is working with others to assess their needs. Others might include relatives, carers, professionals and advocates.

It is important that there are partners in care because:

▶ professionals have particular knowledge about health conditions

▶ workers know what care resources are available

▶ some responsibilities can be shared and others taken by individuals

▶ it allows people to work together towards a common goal

▶ the individual may not realise they have particular needs.

How can a partnership approach be established?

A partnership approach to the assessment process can be established by involving the individual and key others in the whole assessment process from the beginning. This entails making sure the individual understands:

▶ what the assessment aims to achieve

▶ how the assessment process works

▶ who will be involved

▶ where it will take place.

Reflect

What do you do to establish a partnership when carrying out assessments of need with individuals?

Investigate

Try to find out how a partnership approach is established in your workplace.

Discuss

Talk with a friend or colleague about ways that they establish a partnership approach to assessment.

Case study

Carla is Matt's key worker at the day centre where he is referred. She is responsible for making sure that he has an assessment of his needs and that arrangements are made to establish a partnership approach to the assessment. Following the agreed way of working she contacts Matt by letter to discuss with him the approach that the care service takes with new referrals and assessments. Carla writes that she will telephone him the following week and explains what the assessment will involve, how it will be carried out, who will take part, and where it is going to be held. She also asks him if he agrees to this approach and to make any suggestions for the assessment that fit his particular needs at that moment.

When Matt receives the letter from Carla he understands that the assessment is to find out what his care needs are, and that it will take the form of a conversation between him and care workers. A referral letter from his doctor will also be discussed. The assessment will take about an hour and will be held at the social services offices in the town centre. Matt wants his mother involved so he replies by telephone saying that she will accompany him.

1. How does Carla establish a partnership approach to the assessment process?

2. What does Matt understand about the assessment process?

3. Reflect on how, if you were in Matt's position, you would like to be involved in an assessment of your needs.

Practical Assessment Task   2.1   2.2

A partnership approach to person-centred assessment is a way of working that puts the individual at the centre of the process, but takes into account the views and roles of others. In this task you will demonstrate your ability to facilitate person-centred assessment.

With the permission of your manager or supervisor and the consent of an individual who is to assessed for care needs, you need to show that you can:

▶ establish with the individual a partnership approach to the assessment process

▶ establish with the individual how the process should be carried out and who else should be involved in the process.

Your evidence must be based on your practice in a real work environment and must be witnessed by or be in a format acceptable to your assessor.

How is the outcome of assessment agreed?

The intended outcomes of an individual's assessment are the needs that are identified and the ways that the needs are to be met. These should be agreed with the individual and others and incorporated into a care plan.

The assessment should take account of the individual's:

▶ strengths

▶ aspirations

▶ needs.

What else should be considered?

To meet the individual's needs the assessment should be developed into a care plan that meets the individual's support requirements and preferences.

Case study

Bill has a life-limiting illness. He knows that he is going to die. The doctor told him that he has about three weeks left to live. He has asked that his care be provided in his own home because that is where he would like to die. His wife, Marjorie, wants to do everything she can to make sure that his last few days are as comfortable as possible and that his wishes are met. She and Bill discuss the choices they have with the specialist visiting nurse. They assess Bill's strengths, aspirations and needs. They then work out, using a table like the one on page 387, how his wishes can be met.

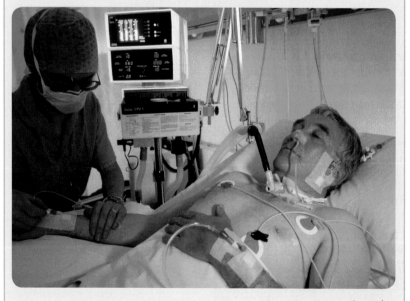

continued...

Your assessment criteria:

2.3 Agree with the individual and others the intended outcomes of the assessment process and care plan.

2.4 Ensure that assessment takes account of the individual's strengths and aspirations as well as needs.

2.5 Work with the individual and others to identify support requirements and preferences.

Reflect

What are your strengths and aspirations? To what extent do they compare with those of individuals in your care?

Investigate

Investigate how individuals' support requirements and preferences are met in your workplace.

Discuss

Discuss with a friend or colleague how they would use an individual's strengths in assessing and planning care.

Assessment	Support requirements	Preferences
Strengths: • He has a supportive wife. • He knows what he wants.	Marjorie requires help with his personal care and to lift him	Bill's preference is that Marjorie has help with the personal care as he doesn't want her overworked
Aspirations: • He wants to die at home.	To be assisted to stay in his own home	Not to be taken to hospital except as a last resort if Marjorie is unable to cope
Needs: • He needs end-of-life care.	End-of-life care including support with personal care, medication to relieve pain and someone to talk to	He wants to be seen by a member of the local church they attend

1. To what extent are Bill's strengths and preferences taken into account?
2. To what extent is his assessment and plan person-centred?
3. Reflect on how outcomes of assessments can be person-centred.

Practical Assessment Task   2.3   2.4   2.5

In this task you will demonstrate the ability to facilitate person-centred assessment. The intended outcomes of an individual's assessment are the identification of their care needs and agreement about the ways that the needs are to be met. With the permission of your manager or supervisor and the consent of an individual you need to show that you can:

▶ agree with the individual and others the intended outcomes of the assessment process and care plan
▶ ensure that assessment takes account of the individual's strengths and aspirations as well as needs
▶ work with the individual and others to identify their support requirements and preferences

Your evidence must be based on your practice in a real work environment and must be witnessed by or be in a format acceptable to your assessor.

Contribute to the planning of care and support

What factors are involved?

Care workers should take account of a range of factors that affect the type and level of support to be provided. These factors include:

- age
- illness
- dependence
- gender
- disability
- cognitive ability
- skills.

What do types and levels of care mean?

Types of care are the kinds of support provided, based on the individual's needs. Levels of care are often divided into high, medium and low, depending on the type of care and the individual's capacity.

Figure 13.5 Types and levels of care

Individual needs	Type of care	Level of care
Amy has severe dementia. She is not aware of where she is or who other people are. She cannot take care of herself.	Amy needs support with all the skills for everyday living, such as feeding, washing and using toilet facilities.	High
Jackson has broken his wrist playing rugby.	Jackson needs his wrist plastered and immobilised. In other respects he can take care of himself.	Low
Trudy has depression. She finds it difficult to sleep and take care of herself. She feels sad and doesn't want to talk to anyone.	Trudy needs encouragement to socialise. She needs support with her medication to raise her mood and to help her sleep.	Medium

How can workers support individuals to explore options and resources?

Care workers should work with the individual to explore options and resources based on the type and level of care that is needed. They can contribute, with the individual and others, to agreement on how component parts of a plan can be delivered.

This is based on:

- the individual's assessed needs
- the individual's strengths and aspirations
- availability of resources.

3.1 Take account of factors that may influence the type and level of care or support to be provided.

3.2 Work with the individual and others to explore options and resources for delivery of the plan.

3.3 Contribute to agreement on how component parts of a plan will be delivered and by whom.

3.4 Record the plan in a suitable format.

Reflect

Reflect on your practice when contributing to care plans. To what extent do you take into account the type and level of support that needs to be provided?

Investigate

Investigate care plans where you work. How do they take into account the individual's options and the resources available?

Discuss

Discuss with a friend or colleague how it is decided who will implement parts of the care plan. Is it agreed by the care team, and how much is agreed with the individual?

How are the component parts of a plan agreed?

Component parts of the care plan should be agreed between the individual and those planning and delivering care. Others, such as family members, may also be consulted. The planning team will need to agree:

▶ the individual's assessed needs

▶ the aims and goals of the care plan

▶ how it will be implemented

▶ who will deliver the care

▶ how long it will last (the timescale)

▶ how it will be evaluated.

How is the plan recorded?

Care plans are usually recorded electronically, but can also be on paper. They usually consist of the assessed need, the aim of the plan (including any specific goals), the action or implementation to meet the aim, and a means of evaluating the action or implementation.

Component parts of a care plan should be agreed between the individual and those planning and delivering the care

Figure 13.6 Aspects of a care plan

Assessed need	Aim/goal	Actions	Evaluation or review
Byron has difficulties sleeping. He wakes throughout the night and would like to sleep the whole night through at least once a week.	That Byron sleeps for six consecutive hours at night	• Byron to be supported in a bedtime routine • Medication to be offered, if still awake at 1.00 a.m. • a sleep diary to be kept by Byron • Byron's sleep to be monitored by staff	To be evaluated after two weeks

Practical Assessment Task   3.1 3.2 3.3 3.4

It is important that when you contribute to the planning of care you take account of all the factors, options and resources that affect the type and level of care that can be provided. In this task you will demonstrate that you can make an appropriate and effective contribution to the planning of care or support. You will need to produce evidence based on your practice in a real work setting. The evidence must be witnessed by, or be in a format acceptable to, your assessor. You will need to show that you can:

▶ take account of factors that may influence the type and level of care or support to be provided

▶ work with the individual and others to explore options and resources for delivery of the plan

▶ contribute to agreement on how component parts of a plan will be delivered and by whom

▶ record the plan in a suitable format.

Support the implementation of care plans

Your assessment criteria:

4.1 Carry out assigned aspects of a care plan.

4.2 Support others to carry out aspects of a care plan for which they are responsible.

4.3 Adjust the plan in response to changing needs or circumstances.

Carrying out and supporting a care plan

It is a central part of care workers' roles to carry out the assigned actions of a care plan. Often they work with other staff, supporting them in carrying out care plan activities for which they are responsible. All care plans might, however, need adjusting at some point in response to the changing needs of the individual or changing circumstances.

Adjusting to changing needs or circumstances

The intended action in a care plan may no longer be appropriate because it:

▶ poses a risk to the individual

▶ is no longer required

▶ is replaced by another care plan activity

▶ is adjusted.

Reflect

Reflect on a time when you supported another care worker in carrying out a care plan activity. To what extent did you feel responsible for what you did?

Investigate

Investigate how care plans are adjusted in your workplace. Are they adjusted by one member of staff or as a team approach? To what extent is the individual involved in the decisions?

Discuss

Discuss with a friend or colleague examples of when they have been involved in adjusting care plans due to changing needs or changing circumstances.

Case study

Terry has mild learning disabilities and a mental health problem. He lives alone in a small flat. At times he has tried to harm himself. His brother, George, pops in regularly to see him. On Tuesday George visits Terry and finds him trying to strangle himself with a tie. After stopping Terry and talking to him about what he is doing, George phones the community mental health team which is in contact with Terry. It is decided that because Terry lives alone and is a danger to himself, he will be admitted to a mental health unit for observation and to make sure he remains safe.

He is admitted on Wednesday to the mental health unit where Stella, his key nurse, negotiates a care plan with Terry and George. The care plan focuses on the risks Terry poses to himself and on maintaining his skills in everyday life, including his personal hygiene. Terry is encouraged to bathe daily. As part of the preparation for the evening bath, Stella is helped by Jan, a support worker. Jan supports Stella in carrying out the risk aspect of the care plan, bearing in mind the risk of self-harm. Jan searches the bathroom for sharp objects before Terry is left alone. She starts to run the bath water and then leaves the room.

A short time later the care workers hear screams from the bathroom. On entering the bathroom Stella finds Terry standing in piping hot water.

1. How have Terry's needs and circumstances changed since Tuesday?

2. In what ways does his care plan need adjusting following in the incident in the bathroom?

3. Who should be involved in adjusting the care plan, and why?

Practical Assessment Task   4.1   4.2   4.3

Sometimes you may implement actions in a care plan, and sometimes you may be helped by another care practitioner or support another member of staff to carry out actions in a care plan. To complete this assessment task you will need to demonstrate you can carry out assigned aspects of a care plan, support others and adjust plans when necessary. You will need to demonstrate that you can:

▶ carry out assigned aspects of a care plan

▶ support others to carry out aspects of a care plan for which they are responsible

▶ adjust the plan in response to changing needs or circumstances.

Your evidence for this task must be based on your practice in a real work environment and must be witnessed by, or be in a format acceptable to, your assessor.

How do you monitor a care plan?

To make sure that care negotiated with the individual and others is delivered as planned, the actions taken should be monitored. Monitoring means keeping an eye on the care plan activities to find out if they are effective or not. Monitoring can result in the activity being implemented as planned, or the plan might be amended. This could be for a number of reasons:

▶ the individual's needs have changed so the activity is no longer appropriate

▶ not enough time has been allowed for the activity to be effective

▶ the activity is no longer required.

Collating information and recording changes

When the care plan is drawn up, the way it is to be monitored should be agreed. This usually involves one person taking responsibility for monitoring the activity. This is often the individual's key worker, who will:

▶ communicate with people involved in the care plan, including the individual

▶ collate information gathered from various sources, such as care records, attendance records, medication sheets and care plan evaluations

▶ record changes that affect the delivery of the care plan.

Your assessment criteria:

5.1 Agree methods for monitoring the way a care plan is delivered.

5.2 Collate monitoring information from agreed sources.

5.3 Record changes that affect the delivery of the care plan.

Reflect

Reflect on ways that care delivery can be monitored. Who might be involved? What sources might be used?

Investigate

Investigate how care delivery is monitored in your work setting.

Discuss

Discuss with a friend or colleague how they have monitored care delivery.

Case study

Anthony has Asperger's syndrome. He lives in a shared house with a small group of men who are recovering from mental health problems. He works in a supported community where he is responsible for ensuring that his fellow workers have access to refreshments. In most respects he is managing very well. Unfortunately, he has two particular problems which are associated with Asperger's syndrome. The first is that he likes to count out loud when he feels stressed or under pressure. The second problem is that he touches women who do not know him inappropriately (on the hair, arms or legs). Although he is not a danger to women his behaviour has brought him to the attention of the police and the criminal justice system. He has been placed on probation and his behaviour towards women is being monitored as part of his care plan.

Care plan activities should be monitored to find out how effective they are

Dave, Anthony's care worker, has been given responsibility for collating information as part of the process of monitoring Anthony's behaviour. He talks to Anthony, his employer, his landlord and the probation service. Only Anthony himself reports any changes. He says he had got a bit drunk at the weekend and shouted obscenities at a woman in the town centre. Apparently the woman was with a group of friends who were laughing at him.

1. What methods can Dave use for collating information about the way the care plan is delivered?

2. Are there any sources of information he does not use?

3. Are there any changes you would record that might affect the delivery of the care plan?

Practical Assessment Task   5.1   5.2   5.3

Care plans need to be monitored to ensure that they provide an appropriate and effective way of meeting an individual's needs. To complete this assessment task you will need to demonstrate you are able to monitor care plans. In particular you need to show that you can:

▶ agree methods for monitoring the way a care plan is delivered

▶ collate monitoring information from agreed sources

▶ record changes that affect the delivery of the care plan.

Your evidence for this task must be based on your practice in a real work environment and must be witnessed by, or in a format acceptable to, your assessor.

Review care plans and their implementation

What are the criteria for reviews?

When care plans are drawn up thought should be given to how they are to be reviewed, in particular:

▶ when the review should take place

▶ who will be involved

▶ what criteria will be used to judge the effectiveness of the care plan.

Who should be involved in the process?

Anyone involved with the individual should be included in the review process. In particular, the individual should be at the centre of the review process and decisions made. Others might be involved, although some people might be more involved than others depending on the nature of the individual's needs.

What criteria are used?

To review a care plan it is essential that you have criteria by which to review it. The table below illustrates SMART criteria used to judge the effectiveness of a care plan. It uses the example of Barbara, who is a resident in a home for older people. She has a raised temperature and is taking Paracetamol to reduce it.

S	Specific	Is the goal clear and unambiguous?	To reduce Barbara's temperature
M	Measurable	How can progress towards achievement of the goal be measured?	Barbara's temperature to be measured using a thermometer
A	Attainable	Is the goal achievable?	Barbara agrees to the use of an aural thermometer
R	Relevant	Does the goal match the individual's needs and preferences?	A lower temperature would be indicated by the use of a thermometer
T	Timely	What is the time frame for achieving the goal?	Barbara's temperature to be monitored every four hours until it returns to normal

Reflect

Reflect on how you can gain feedback at work. Is it just by talking to someone?

Investigate

Investigate the different people and agencies who are involved in the care of individuals where you work.

Discuss

Discuss with a friend or colleague the ways that criteria for reviews are agreed.

How do you obtain feedback on the plan?

Information for reviews is obtained from feedback given to the person facilitating the review. To enable this to happen, the person responsible needs to know who else is involved in the individual's care and their role in the care. The facilitator might have to contact each person involved in care to seek feedback. There are numerous ways feedback can be obtained – for example, letters, emails, verbal communication and case reports.

Case study

Diana, a social worker, is responsible for facilitating the care plan review of Pauline, who is diagnosed as having an anxiety disorder. Pauline's care plan was initially based around her anxiety and looked for ways to help her manage. It is now complicated because her partner recently left her, shortly after being accused of child abuse. Before he left their front window was broken by angry neighbours who shouted accusations about him being a paedophile. The care plan has therefore been extended to include the issue of child protection, and the involvement of the police, the housing department and social services. Diana therefore needs to seek feedback from a number or people across a range of agencies.

Her first step in arranging the review is to discuss it with Pauline. She explains the involvement of different agencies, their roles and the value of the feedback they can give. The criteria they will use to judge the effectiveness of the care plan has been decided. She next contacts each agency in turn and arranges a meeting that all can attend.

1. Why is it important to seek feedback from each person and agency involved?
2. Apart from managing anxiety what else would be in Pauline's care plan?
3. What do you think the criteria for judging the effectiveness of the care plan might be?

The individual should be at the centre of the review process and decisions made

Practical Assessment Task   6.1   6.2

When reviewing care plans it is essential that feedback from others is sought and that the criteria for judging the effectiveness of the care plan are agreed. With the permission of your manager or supervisor and the consent of an individual, facilitate a review of a care plan. You need to show that you can:

▶ seek agreement with the individual and others about:
  ▶ who should be involved in the review process
  ▶ criteria to judge effectiveness of the care plan.
▶ seek feedback from the individual and others about how the plan is working.

Your evidence for this task must be based on your practice in a real work environment and must be witnessed by or be in a format acceptable to your assessor.

Has the care plan achieved its objectives?

The purpose of care plans is to implement actions that deliver care to meet identified needs for an individual. The final stage is to find out if the actions delivered have been effective in meeting the identified needs.

Agreeing and documenting changes

The effectiveness of care is evaluated by monitoring and collecting feedback on the care delivered. Care workers collaborate with others, including the individual at the centre of the care. The evaluation process is shown in Figure 13.7.

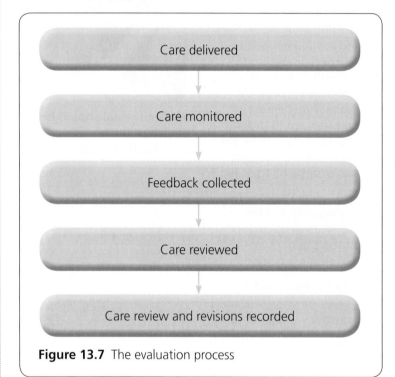

Care delivered

↓

Care monitored

↓

Feedback collected

↓

Care reviewed

↓

Care review and revisions recorded

Figure 13.7 The evaluation process

Your assessment criteria:

6.3 Use feedback and monitoring/other information to evaluate whether the plan has achieved its objectives.

6.4 Work with the individual and others to agree any revisions to the plan.

6.5 Document the review process and revisions as required.

Reflect

What would you do if the feedback on care you receive from a person or agency conflicts with feedback from the individual at the centre of the care package?

Investigate

Use the internet to investigate the Child Protection Register and how it is used.

Discuss

Discuss with a friend or colleague ways that monitoring information is gathered.

Care workers may need to collaborate with a range of agencies when reviewing and changing a care plan

Case study

Diana, a social worker, arranges the care review for Pauline who has been diagnosed with anxiety. Pauline has multiple problems: her partner who is accused of child abuse has gone missing and the front window has been smashed by angry neighbours. Diana has had to communicate with Pauline and a range of agencies in order to gain feedback on the care plan. The feedback is as follows.

▶ There is a letter from the council: the window has been repaired and the family have been referred, as a matter of urgency, for rehousing.

▶ A verbal report from the police states that her partner has not been traced. Two neighbours have received police cautions.

▶ A report from social services says that the children have been placed on the Child Protection Register, but that they can stay with their mother at the moment.

▶ The psychiatrist, in a confidential email, has reported that Pauline remains anxious and should be referred for counselling, and that she is likely to remain anxious while she has the other issues to deal with.

The original purpose of the care plan, that Pauline becomes able to manage her anxiety, has not been achieved. However, now that other agencies are involved, underlying problems can be tackled. She records the outcome of the review and files copies of each of the letters and reports.

1. Does Diana have enough information to evaluate the effectiveness of the care plan?

2. What revisions to the plan is Diana likely to make in consultation with others involved?

3. What priorities for Pauline and her family would you set?

Practical Assessment Task   6.3   6.4   6.5

In care work, feedback and other monitoring information is periodically gathered to evaluate the effectiveness of an individual's care plan. Usually more than one person or agency is involved. The review and any revisions must be recorded. With the permission of your manager or supervisor and with the consent of an individual:

▶ use feedback and monitoring/other information to evaluate whether an individual's care plan has achieved its objectives

▶ work with the individual and others to agree any revisions to the plan

▶ document the review process and revisions as required

Your evidence for this task must be based on your practice in a real work environment and must be witnessed by or be in a format acceptable to your assessor.

Are you ready for assessment?

AC	What do you know now?	Assessment task	✓
1.1	The importance of a holistic approach to assessment and planning of care or support	Page 379	
1.2	Ways of supporting the individual to lead the assessment and planning process	Page 381	
1.3	Ways the assessment and planning process or documentation can be adapted to maximise an individual's ownership and control of it	Page 383	

AC	What you can do now	Assessment task	✓
2.1	Establish with the individual a partnership approach to the assessment process	Page 385	
2.2	Establish with the individual how the process should be carried out and who else should be involved in the process	Page 385	
2.3	Agree with the individual and others the intended outcomes of the assessment process and care plan	Page 387	
2.4	Ensure that assessment takes account of the individual's strengths and aspirations as well as needs	Page 387	
2.5	Work with the individual and others to identify support requirements and preferences	Page 387	
3.1	Take account of factors that may influence the type and level of care or support to be provided	Page 389	
3.2	Work with the individual and others to explore options and resources for delivery of the plan	Page 389	
3.3	Contribute to agreement on how component parts of a plan will be delivered and by whom	Page 389	
3.4	Record the plan in a suitable format	Page 389	
4.1	Carry out assigned aspects of a care plan	Page 391	
4.2	Support others to carry out aspects of a care plan for which they are responsible	Page 391	
4.3	Adjust the plan in response to changing needs or circumstances	Page 391	
5.1	Agree methods for monitoring the way a care plan is delivered	Page 393	
5.2	Collate monitoring information from agreed sources	Page 393	
5.3	Record changes that affect the delivery of the care plan	Page 393	
6.1	Seek agreement with the individual and others about: • who should be involved in the review process • criteria to judge effectiveness of the care plan	Page 395	
6.2	Seek feedback from the individual and others about how the plan is working	Page 395	
6.3	Use feedback and monitoring/other information to evaluate whether the plan has achieved its objectives	Page 397	
6.4	Work with the individual and others to agree any revisions to the plan	Page 397	
6.5	Document the review process and revisions as required	Page 397	

14 | Understand sensory loss (SS MU 3.1)

Assessment of this unit

This unit provides you with the knowledge of what sensory loss is, how individuals may be affected by it and how to recognise that individuals may be having sensory problems. You will learn to show understanding of the factors that impact on people with sensory loss, and in particular how effective communication can help these individuals. The unit also provides information about how to act if there are concerns about sensory loss and how to identify sources of support for individuals. You will need to:

1. Understand the factors that impact on an individual with sensory loss.

2. Understand the importance of effective communication for individuals with sensory loss.

3. Understand the main causes and conditions of sensory loss.

4. Know how to recognise when an individual may be experiencing sight and/or hearing loss and actions that may be taken.

To complete this unit successfully you will need to produce evidence of your knowledge as shown in the 'What you need to know' chart opposite. There is no practical assessment for this unit but it is very important to be able to apply your knowledge practically in the real work environment or in your placement. Your tutor or assessor will help you to prepare for your assessment, and the tasks suggested in this chapter will help you to create the evidence you need.

AC	What you need to know
1.1	Analyse how a range of factors can impact on individuals with sensory loss
1.2	Analyse how societal attitudes and beliefs impact on individuals with sensory loss
1.3	Explore how a range of factors, societal attitudes and beliefs impact on service provision
2.1	Explain the methods of communication used by individuals with sight loss / hearing loss / deafblindness
2.2	Describe how the environment facilitates effective communication for people with sensory loss
2.3	Explain how effective communication may have a positive impact on the lives of individuals with sensory loss
3.1	Identify the main causes of sensory loss
3.2	Define congenital sensory loss and acquired sensory loss
3.3	Identify the demographic factors that influence the incidence of sensory loss in the population
4.1	Identify the indicators and signs of sight loss / hearing loss / deafblindness
4.2	Explain actions that should be taken if there are concerns about onset of sensory loss or changes in sensory status
4.3	Identify sources of support for those who may be experiencing onset of sensory loss

This unit also links to the following units:

HSC 3013	Support individuals to access and use facilities and services
SHC 33	Promote equality and inclusion in health and social care
HSC 036	Promote person-centred approaches in health and social care

Some of your learning will be repeated in these units and will give you the chance to review your knowledge and understanding.

How can a range of factors impact on individuals with sensory loss?

A person with **sensory loss** will have problems receiving or interpreting information coming to them through one or more of the five senses. They may or may not be able to compensate for this by the use of their other senses. Even a slight sensory loss can cause problems for an individual. For example, a problem with sight may cause them to fall more easily. Many factors that impact on individuals with sensory loss apply to all types of sensory loss. Others are particular to the type of loss(es) the individual is experiencing.

Figure 14.1 shows factors that might have an impact on individuals with sensory loss.

Your assessment criteria:

1.1 Analyse how a range of factors can impact on individuals with sensory loss.

Key terms

Loss: 'loss' of one or more senses may be complete or only partial. Loss may also be called impairment

Sensory: involving any of the five senses (sight, hearing, touch, smell, taste), most often sight or hearing

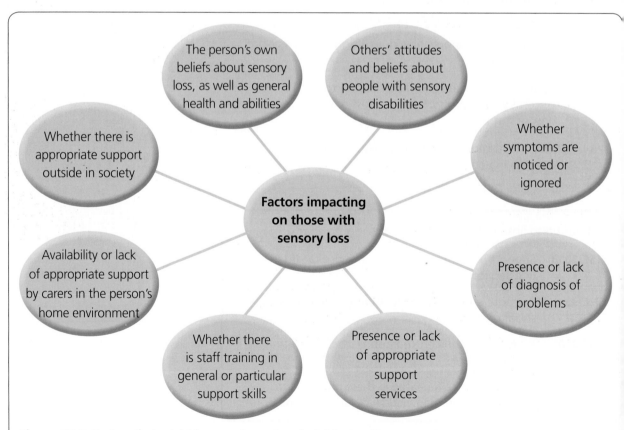

Figure 14.1 Factors that might have an impact on individuals with sensory loss

Positive and negative aspects and their impact

Many factors can have a *negative* impact on the person with a sensory loss and these can determine whether or not the person is well supported to remain active and involved in everyday life.

▶ Others may ignore, not notice or not support individuals' sensory needs for reasons similar to those given by the individual.

▶ The disabling belief may be different from any held the individual, so there are two obstacles to supporting the individual's needs. For example, an individual may feel they are too old to learn to use a hearing aid, whereas a carer or family member may feel they don't want to check and clean the aid.

▶ It may be upsetting for families or carers to admit that individuals are losing a sense such as hearing or sight.

▶ Some may be afraid that, with use of an aid, the individual might become more independent and not need them as much.

Although the negative factors affecting those with sensory loss can most often be due to the attitudes of others, the individual's own disabling beliefs can also have an impact as outlined below.

▶ 'I'm 82 you know, I can't learn new stuff any more'.

▶ 'I've been deaf for years, that's just the way I am'.

▶ 'I'm not clever enough to learn Braille'.

▶ 'If I have an eye test people will realise I've just been pretending to be able to read'.

▶ 'If people realise my sight and hearing are both going I won't be allowed to live alone any more'.

▶ 'I'm used to staying at home, if I get a white stick I'll be expected to go out and that's scary'.

▶ 'Nobody else in my care home uses Braille/sign language/tactile signs, and so I'll feel silly'.

Some people may also have tried something in the past and not realise that things have improved. For example, modern digital hearing aids are generally much better than the old body-worn type.

Positive factors affecting sensory loss are ones that enable the individual to be properly assessed, treated and supported in the way they need. This enables them to remain as independent as possible, avoid isolation and frustration, and potentially avoid further serious harm. Figure 14.2 outlines the potential impact from negative factors on individuals with sensory loss, and Figure 14.3 outlines the potential impact from positive factors (see pages 404–405).

Figure 14.2 The potential impact from negative factors on individuals with sensory loss

Negative factors	Potential impact on individuals with sensory loss
An attitude of **ageism/disablism**.	Sensory loss is expected and carers believe the condition won't improve so it is assumed to be an untreatable part of an existing condition. The individual may have lived with untreated loss for so long that they are unwilling to undergo assessment or treatment.
Lack of person-centred care.	Sensory loss is not noticed, or noticed but not properly diagnosed.
Seeing individuals only in terms of present or past conditions.	This is known as 'Diagnostic overshadowing' – a pre-existing condition such as mental illness leads to new symptoms being ignored, or an existing sensory loss may be known about but another loss develops that is missed or ignored. Also, a loss may be acknowledged but deterioration not noticed or admitted (by the individual or by the carers).
Ignorance of how sensory loss can affect individuals' behaviour.	Symptoms are put down to 'bad' or 'challenging' behaviour and not investigated.
Lack of knowledge of likely problems in the type of individuals being cared for (e.g. heavy ear-wax in the elderly). Diagnosis may be more difficult with certain people so it is not attempted at all (e.g. eye tests with people who can't reply verbally to the questions).	Individuals have to suffer needlessly as a result of their sensory loss not being diagnosed and helped. This may lead to further health or social problems such as depression.
The home environment is not conducive to living with a sensory loss. For example, floors are not kept free of clutter where there are partially sighted people, or rooms are noisy and echoing so cause difficulty for those with a hearing loss.	Individuals are likely to become less mobile or withdrawn or both, and to lose out on social interaction.
Carers are ignorant of how to use aids or keep them working (e.g. keeping glasses and hearing aids clean) or unwilling to learn new skills (e.g. sign language).	Help and support given by professionals are frustrated by lack of knowledge/skills on the part of the everyday carers of the individual.
Lack of available support from wider society (e.g. books or other information are not available in a suitable format for the blind, or equipment is not provided to enable partially-hearing people to use the telephone).	The individual may become depressed and isolated, and may miss out on vital information or social involvement.

Figure 14.3 The potential impact from positive factors on individuals with sensory loss

Positive factors	Potential impact on individuals with sensory loss
The individual/carers are alert to changes and ask questions, with a proper referral for a professional diagnosis. This is done even where the person has a long-standing condition (sensory or otherwise).	Timely and effective help and support is provided for the individual, and further deterioration may be minimised.
The individual is carefully prepared for any testing and the choices are explained where possible, rather than imposed.	The diagnosis is likely to be more accurate and the individual is more likely to understand and accept any support needed.
The carer is aware of likely problems even after diagnosis. For example, getting used to a hearing aid takes time and practice. Carers are trained generally in routine assistance with sensory aids (e.g. changing batteries on a hearing aid). Carers are given specific training to meet special needs of certain individuals (e.g. sign language).	The issues for the individual are understood in depth and specialist help is provided to meet the daily support they need.
A person-centred approach is taken at all times so that individuals' needs are met, rather than expecting all individuals to respond in the same way, or denying an individual support because they are the only one in a group with particular needs.	Each individual will be able to use their senses as well as they possibly can, even if the means to do so varies from person to person.
Environmental changes are made as necessary to support individuals (e.g. **tactile** methods of navigating around a care home for partially-sighted people).	Individuals with sensory needs will be more able to keep as active and as independent as possible, aiding both their physical and mental health. They will also be at less risk of other problems (e.g. having falls because of poor sight).

Reflect

Think about the impact on your life if your sight or hearing became badly impaired. What kind of daily activities would be affected? What kind of support might you need from other people?

Key terms

Ageism/disablism: treating someone less well simply because they are elderly or disabled

Tactile: using the sense of touch

The effort taken by society to include individuals with sensory loss impacts greatly on access to facilities many take for granted

Your assessment criteria:

1.2 Analyse how societal attitudes and beliefs impact on individuals with sensory loss.

Key terms

Stereotype: a view of everyone in a particular group, such as age or race, as being exactly the same. A stereotype can often be negative (e.g. all deaf people are stupid)

How can societal attitudes and beliefs impact on individuals with sensory loss?

Individuals with sensory loss can be affected by the attitudes and beliefs of groups and organisations in society, in addition to those of family or carers. These could include people keeping shops, administering theatres and churches, providing health or social services, running care homes, councils, facilities such as libraries or swimming pools, and public amenities such as roads and car parks. The effort taken to include and consider individuals with sensory loss impacts greatly on how much they can enjoy and access the facilities and services that many take for granted. Some organisations may make token gestures only, or ignore people with sensory loss. They may underestimate the number of people who could benefit from positive changes and the degree to which 'ordinary' members of the public can also benefit from changes such as clearer signs.

Disabling beliefs held by society

Some of the most common disabling beliefs held by society are outlined below.

▶ They consider that individuals with sensory loss are too old or too disabled to change.

▶ They are used to dealing with individuals in a certain way and don't want to change.

▶ They think that learning new skills to help individuals will be too difficult or a waste of time.

▶ They are afraid that admitting the extent of peoples' disability will mean they have to give more help, or spend more money.

Establishing positive approaches in society

The individual with sensory loss has the same human rights as anyone else to access good services and facilities, and to take an active part in the community as far as possible. Any disabling attitudes or beliefs held by society should be addressed by education on what is possible for people with sensory needs and the availability of specific types of support, with training similar to that provided in care homes or social services. Carers may need to challenge assumptions and **stereotypes** and show a positive example of what can be achieved. They may need to be an advocate on the individual's behalf, ensuring correct support is in place so the individual can take part in everyday activities without feeling left out or a burden to others.

Investigate

Conduct an informal interview with three people you know outside work, of different ages if possible. Ask them what they know and think about the sensory needs of the type of people you work with (you and they should not discuss or refer to any specific individuals). Do not tell them they are right or wrong: simply note their responses and thank them for their time. Afterwards, make some brief notes on the different types of response you got, and whether you think these showed positive or disabling attitudes and beliefs.

Discuss

Someone you are caring for is starting to lose their sight. The senior carer wants to have a basic eye test conducted at the home, followed by a referral to an eye clinic and other services as necessary. The individual seems happy about this, but their family who visit are not. They think the individual should be 'left in peace' and not have any tests. What might you say to them?

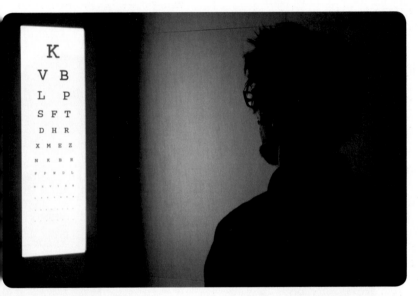

Individuals developing sensory loss should be supported to access tests and services

Knowledge Assessment Task 1.1 1.2

1. Describe five negative factors that might impact on an individual with, or developing, a sensory loss. Analyse why you think these factors happen, and what positive factors could replace them.

2. What are the main ways that societal attitudes and beliefs have an impact on those with sensory loss? Analyse why people in society might think this way, and suggest alternative attitudes.

How might a range of factors impact on service provision?

The negative or positive factors, societal attitudes and different peoples' beliefs about individuals with sensory loss can impact on service provision in three main ways:

1. The level of help and support provided to meet the needs of individuals in their everyday setting.

2. The extent of changes and modifications to everyday settings that help individuals function as independently and safely as possible, including provision of staff training.

3. The level of support to help individuals access community facilities and, where provision is not made or there is lack of awareness, the impact of advocacy for the individual with sensory loss.

Help and support for individuals in their everyday setting

Knowledge and awareness of individual needs

A good baseline knowledge is needed of each individual's care and medical needs, including current sensory needs. Ideally each individual's sight and hearing status should be known. Assessments should be arranged if they haven't taken place in the last year or so, to pick up any existing problems that may not be obvious.

There needs to be a questioning of any apparent problems, and a constant alertness to any changes in people's behaviour. For example, a hearing problem may become apparent by someone withdrawing from social groups, rather than an obvious lack of response in conversation.

It helps to be aware of needs in particular groups of people or cases, such as the high likelihood of hearing problems in someone with Down syndrome.

Your assessment criteria:

1.3 Explore how a range of factors, societal attitudes and beliefs impact on service provision.

Service providers need to be alert to sensory needs that may emerge from an existing condition, such as hearing loss with Down syndrome

Carers need to consider early on the possibility of sensory needs if behaviour changes, rather than assuming emotional or mental health causes. Changes are more likely to be noticed if the staff team around the person is stable and the key worker gets to know the person well.

Sensitive support if assessment or treatment is needed

Ongoing support may be required with daily needs (e.g. keeping hearing aids clean and functioning). Staff should be trained in the correct procedures as a matter of priority, in the same way they may be trained to give medication.

There must be adequate training around general or specific sensory needs in the person or people being cared for, and around any special techniques required.

Outside agencies may need to be involved, for example for assessment for suitability to have a guide dog.

Training, positive approaches and sharing of information with individuals

Carers and others must be willing to alter their behaviour where necessary (e.g. not speak to someone with hearing loss in a noisy room). Extra training may be required for sensory need awareness in addition to other required topics.

There should be a positive, non-ageist and non-disablist attitude shown by staff towards diagnosing and supporting the needs of an individual developing a sensory problem. It should be made clear to individuals that carers will do all they can and make any changes necessary to support the individual. People might benefit from being shown or told of examples of individuals who succeeded with particular support.

The individual should be given as much choice over the type of support they receive as possible. They should not be rushed into new kinds of support but introduced gradually with lots of help and encouragement. This may take extra staff time.

Carers need to support individuals in the way that is best for that person

Changes and modifications to everyday settings

People with sensory losses may need different adjustments to the settings where they live, spend leisure time and possibly work, to enable as much independent functioning as possible. Sometimes quite small changes can reduce an individual's reliance on someone else helping them, giving them more self-esteem, more privacy and enabling them to carry on with the activities they enjoy. Some changes can be carried out quite easily, for example by staff in a care home. Other changes may need to be discussed with or implemented by higher management, for example the owners of a group of care homes who set the budgets. Examples of changes and modifications can include the following.

Staff training in sensory loss

Staff should be trained in the basics of sight and hearing loss, how to spot when a problem may be starting or getting worse, and how to care for any special equipment.

They should also be trained in particular ways of communicating with individuals with sensory loss. This includes techniques that may currently apply just to one person (e.g. sign language), but also techniques that may be useful for many others (e.g. not having the TV on in the background while talking to people).

Your assessment criteria:

1.3 Explore how a range of factors, societal attitudes and beliefs impact on service provision.

Care workers should be trained so they can communicate with people with hearing loss

Familiar layouts and routines

The home or day setting can ensure use of clear, large-print notices wherever individuals need information. Simple clear pictures and easy symbols can also be helpful.

It may help many people to use clear, colour-coded areas for different parts of the setting. For example, all bedroom doors could be blue and all toilet doors white.

As well as using colour, the setting can use clear **visual** and also **auditory** ways of helping people find their way around and take part in everyday life. There could be a coloured strip on the wall leading from the day room to the dining room for those with poor vision, or a flashing light to indicate time for lunch for those who can't hear a dinner bell.

It is helpful to keep physical settings tidy – for example nothing on the floor that people could trip over. It is also helpful to keep the arrangement of furniture the same as far as possible.

Some people will benefit from daily routines remaining the same, including the same staff where possible. They can then predict when something will take place, rather than needing to constantly be told or taken by someone.

Senior management may need to review or implement policies around the support of people with sensory needs. They may need to approve, for example, money to be spent on installing a loop system to help the hard-of-hearing, or on training courses run by outside agencies specialising in sensory loss.

Key terms

Visual: to do with the sense of sight

Auditory: to do with the sense of hearing

A setting can be adapted to help individuals with sight loss find their way around and take part in everyday life

Case study

You have been helping to care for Mr Singh for some time in his own home, but he and his family are now looking at his moving into care. They have asked you to look at some possible homes with them and give your opinion. Mr Singh wears a hearing aid for a moderate hearing loss in one ear, and struggles to look after the aid himself. He is also developing cataracts in both eyes and they will not be operated on for some time.

1. What kind of things might you look for in the potential homes that would be helpful to Mr Singh, considering his sensory losses?

2. What kind of personal support might you have to enquire about for him?

Provision of transport can enable individuals with sensory loss to access community facilities safely

Your assessment criteria:

1.3 Explore how a range of factors, societal attitudes and beliefs impact on service provision.

Support for individuals to access community facilities

Enabling and encouraging people with sensory loss to access community facilities may affect service provision in several ways, including the following.

Supporting access and mobility in the community

Extra staff may be required at certain times. Some individuals may need one-to-one support to access facilities, for example to guide them physically or to describe the facilities so they can choose what they wish to do.

Carers may need to find services in the community that cater for individual needs, such as borrowing large-print books from the library. They may then need to encourage and enable individuals to use them.

The provision of good safe transport can enable individuals to make as much use of community facilities as they can, so they do not have to struggle to find bus stops or a taxi, or pay a lot of money in fares. However, a staff member needs to be available at appropriate times and ideally also be skilled in helping individuals when they arrive if necessary. If the home or day setting does not have its own transport there may be a local community transport scheme with volunteer drivers that could be used, although they may not be available at holiday times.

Accessing the community from home

Carers may need to encourage outside facilities or agencies to provide services in the person's own home or day setting, particularly where there are transport issues. For example, a 'talking book' service from the library might visit a care home on a regular basis. This should only be done if normal access to the service is difficult or dangerous, as the individual with sensory needs could effectively become housebound.

Widening support within the community

Carers may also be able to raise awareness of the needs of those with sensory loss, resulting in better facilities and support for individuals in the community. They might provide facilities and support for people with sensory needs coming in from outside the workplace to join those cared for within it. For example, they might run a group for those with sight loss where the individuals they work with can meet others like them from the community.

Knowledge Assessment Task   **1.3**

1. What are the three main ways that different factors, attitudes and beliefs can impact on service provision?
2. Give two examples of each of the three main ways.

Your assessment criteria:

2.1 Explain the methods of communication used by individuals with:
- sight loss
- hearing loss
- deafblindness.

Methods of communication used by individuals with sight loss, hearing loss or deafblindness

Carers should understand that all individuals can and do communicate, and it is the carers' responsibility to find out how to enable this to happen. Although some factors apply to specific groups, individuals within those groups are not all the same and their communication needs are specific to them. Communication can take several forms, and carers should develop the ability to receive and understand what others are communicating, as well as their own ability to communicate with each individual. If one sense is deficient then another sense may become even more important. For example, those with problems *hearing* need to use a more *visual* method of communication and those with *sight* problems may need to communicate using *touch*. The main ways of communicating are shown in Figure 14.4.

Key terms

Deafblind: an individual who has both hearing and sight loss. They may occur together from birth, or one sensory loss may be added to another later in life. The loss may not be complete but a degree of impairment from mild to severe

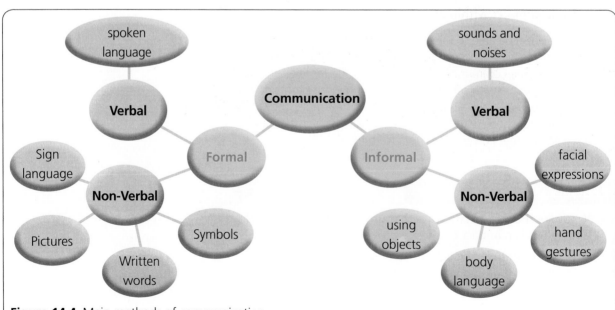

Figure 14.4 Main methods of communication

Effective communication

Informal communication is virtually all **non-verbal** rather than **verbal**. Some types of **informal communication** may be used alongside **formal communication**.

For example, someone with limited spoken language may convey a great deal through their body language. This may need careful interpretation by carers as to what it means for the individual.

The form of communication used by individuals with sensory needs may not be the same form of communication they find easiest used by others towards them. For example, an individual with a severe hearing loss may be able to hear normal speech quite well if it is amplified enough, but their own speech may be too distorted for others to understand easily and so they may need to write things down, point to pictures or use gestures and sign language.

As well as considering what type of communication the individual prefers, carers need to be aware of what they can do to encourage and support each individual's communication efforts.

Key terms

Formal communication: an organised system that enables different people to communicate more easily with each other, e.g. sign language

Informal communication: communication that is not part of a formal system and which may vary from person to person, e.g. gestures

Non-verbal: to do with other non-spoken ways of communicating, e.g. signs, symbols, objects

Verbal: to do with spoken language

Carers should encourage and support communication efforts and carefully interpret an individual's use of body language

Communication methods used with sight loss

Methods of reading

Some blind or partially sighted people use the **Braille** or **Moon** system to read, feeling raised dots or shapes on paper. Many who are blind or almost blind from birth will have learned the Braille system. Braille is more abstract than the Moon system so may be difficult for new or older learners.

Use of the Braille or Moon systems should be encouraged where available, for example with hymn books in church or with labels on drug packets and other products, so individuals are as independent as possible.

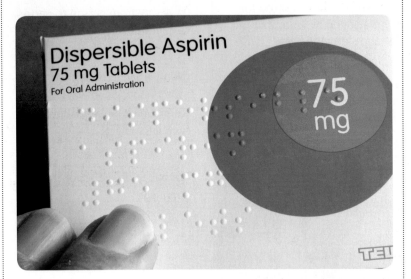

Many partially sighted people can read to some extent *if* the text is large and clear enough. The Scottish Sensory Centre (SSC) estimates that as many as 70% of people with eyesight problems could do this. It is therefore important for carers and organisations to communicate with people in large clear print wherever possible, as this will help the largest number of people.

Your assessment criteria:

2.1 Explain the methods of communication used by individuals with:
- sight loss
- hearing loss
- deafblindness.

Key terms

Braille/Moon: systems to enable those with sight loss to read using tactile dots or shapes

Use of equipment and objects

People who cannot use much or any print can benefit from the use of audiotapes or CDs, but may need practise in their use. Some people with sight loss, particularly if they have other disabilities, may be encouraged to use tactile objects to understand which activities they are going to take part in and to request activities themselves. For example, a small towel could be used to represent or request bath-time.

Support from note takers and companions

Some individuals benefit from having a note taker. For example, in a doctor's appointment the note taker would note down anything the individual may need and discuss it with them later. Some individuals can use a designated companion, sometimes called a Guide Help. This person goes around with them and describes what is happening and/or helps them with everyday activities.

Support from companions and note takers who may also provide notes in large clear print can help communication for individuals with sight loss so they can manage everyday activities

Case study

Laurence is a man of 60 who has had fairly poor sight all his life.

He understands and communicates well verbally and is able to read some print, though his standard of literacy is not high. He enjoys going on the bus to the bowling alley at the weekend, and doing a little personal shopping at the supermarket.

Now that he is getting older his sight is beginning to get worse.

1. What kind of support with reading might help him?
2. What kind of support with everyday tasks might be useful?
3. Are there any community activities that you think might help him?

Communication methods used with hearing loss

The majority of people with a degree of hearing loss still use and understand spoken language, but they may need support to do this. They may need others to speak a little louder, or always to face them when speaking (see page 425).

Use of hearing aids

Some individuals may use a hearing aid but this does not always enable the person to hear completely normally. Depending on the aid, the person may still struggle to hear clearly in a group or against any background noise.

Some buildings are fitted with an 'induction loop' system. By turning the aid to the 'T' setting, they can hear anyone whose voice is picked up by the special microphones. Hearing aids need regular cleaning and their batteries need changing. Some individuals may need help or reminding with this.

Use of lip reading and cued speech

Many individuals learn to lip read to help their understanding of others' speech. We all lip read to a surprisingly large extent, but a person with a significant hearing loss can benefit from learning how to do this very accurately.

A small number of people may use a method known as 'cued speech' where both speaker and 'listener' need to be trained in the system. The person speaking uses hand shapes near the mouth to indicate what type of speech sounds they are making, so that it becomes an enhanced kind of lip-reading.

Your assessment criteria:

2.1 Explain the methods of communication used by individuals with:
- sight loss
- hearing loss
- deafblindness.

AN INDUCTION LOOP IS PROVIDED FOR THE BENEFIT OF HEARING AID USERS. TO USE PLEASE SWITCH YOUR HEARING AID TO 'T'

Published by THE ROYAL NATIONAL INSTITUTE FOR THE DEAF 105 Gower Street London WC1E 6AH 01-387 8033

Use of notes

Some individuals, whether using a hearing aid or not, find it easier to write things down and/or have information in a written form for them to understand. This can be particularly important in, for example, the doctor's surgery, where communicating in writing can ensure that the person has understood what the doctor or nurse is asking or telling them. Not everyone is very literate, however, so use of very simple clear words and print along with simple pictures and symbols can be easier for everyone.

Use of sign language

Some individuals have learned to use a formal sign language, such as British Sign Language (BSL), if they have been deaf or very hard of hearing from a young age. They may be able to go to clubs or other meetings arranged by the deaf community where BSL is the normal method of communication among the members. Others communicating with them need to learn the basics of that language.

Other individuals who find it difficult to learn a complex sign language may use a simplified version of BSL known as Makaton. Although originally devised for those with learning disabilities, it is now used with other groups and may be particularly useful for those developing hearing loss in later life. This is because unlike BSL it uses normal English word order and fits in well with using normal signs and gestures.

Investigate

Have a look on the Makaton website (http://www.makaton.org.uk/) or a book of Makaton sign-language signs. Can you find three or four signs that could help you, alongside the spoken words, to convey something more clearly to someone with a hearing loss?

Carers may need to learn the basics of British Sign Language or Makaton to communicate effectively with individuals with hearing loss in their care

Case study

You are running a small activities group, in which you have two people with some sight loss and at least two people with some hearing loss. You normally sit around a table by the window in the kitchen, and play games such as Scrabble or card games. What could you do to make sure you are taking into account the communication needs of the people in your group who have sensory loss?

It's in our hands

sense
for deafblind people

A positive attitude and careful assessment by carers can enable deafblind individuals to access the support they need to communicate and succeed

Communication methods used with deafblindness

An individual with deafblindness has a dual sensory loss of both hearing and sight. The degree of sight and hearing impairment will vary from person to person.

Using and adapting methods used in either sight or hearing loss

Communication methods used in either sight or hearing loss may be used with people who are deafblind. These may vary depending on which sensory loss came first or is more severe or whether both types of loss have always been present.

Communication methods may also have to change or adapt if one or both of the sensory losses gets worse. For example, someone with hearing loss who uses sign language may need to change if their sight becomes too poor to clearly see hand movements. A blind or partially sighted person who uses speech to communicate may find it difficult to adjust to an alternative method of communication if they develop hearing loss, particularly if they are elderly. Careful assessment and a positive attitude by carers can enable them to continue communicating as well as possible.

Use of tactile support

A deafblind person is likely to need much more in the way of tactile support, both during one-to-one communication and for finding their way safely around the place they live. Using the sense of touch with objects and, as appropriate, with people will help the individual to feel less insecure about what is happening to them and encourage them to communicate as much as they can. In the home environment, having support such as tactile strips to guide them along corridors, along with tactile notices or signs, can encourage independence and involvement in activities, enabling them to have more to communicate about.

Some people can benefit from tactile signing, where sign language is adapted so that the signs are made on the person's hand or upper body. This may be particularly relevant for people with complex disabilities who are deafblind from an early age.

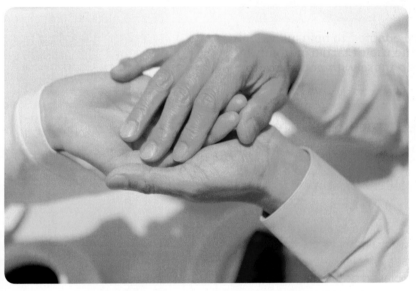

Individuals who are deafblind are likely to need much more in the way of tactile support and may use tactile sign language

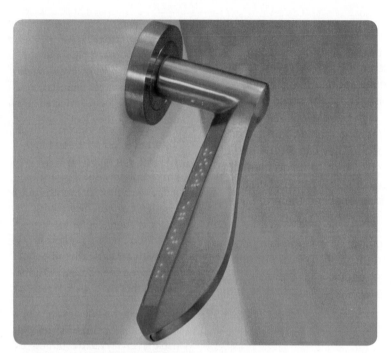

The physical environment can be adapted to help individuals with sensory loss, for example the use of tactile methods of communication on doors can help those with poor sight to understand where they are

How can the environment facilitate effective communication for people with sensory loss?

There are three main ways in which the environment can facilitate communication for people with sensory loss.

1. The physical environment can be modified or adapted to take account of the needs of people with sensory loss. Sometimes this requires minor adjustments but sometimes it requires major and expensive work. Where possible it is best to take their needs into account from the beginning when designing or laying out the area they will use.

2. People in the individual's environment can modify or adapt their behaviour to maximise the person's understanding and their ability to communicate.

3. Individuals can be given information in a way that is accessible and user-friendly to them and which they can also use, for example, in hospital clinics. This means they have a format they can use for giving and receiving information, so they are not disadvantaged socially or in respect of their health.

Facilitating communication by physical adaptations

The main adaptations that facilitate communication for people with sensory loss are shown in Figure 14.5.

Figure 14.5 The main physical adaptations that facilitate communication for people with sensory loss

Physical adaptation	How it helps those with sensory loss
Induction loop – either portable or built-in.	People with a hearing aid can enable their aid to pick up speech coming through the microphones which are part of the loop system.
Not too many thick carpets or curtains in rooms.	The sounds they can hear are not muffled by the soft furnishings in addition to their hearing loss.
Rooms not too bare and echoing (kitchens and bathrooms in particular).	People can hear as clearly as possible, without too much echo or amplification of noises as opposed to speech.
Good lighting, but not dazzling.	People will be able to see other people's faces better, and their hands if they are being signed to. They will be able to read and write better, in particular. Those who lip read also need good lighting that should not be behind the person speaking to them.
Good contrast, e.g. not using white china on a white table; putting contrast strips on the edge of steps.	People will be able to see better and avoid knocking things over or hurting themselves. This helps them to be involved in activities rather than avoid them.
Attention is paid to making steps and stairs safe, alongside awareness that many people with poor sight have poor depth perception so may not be safe on stairs at all.	People will avoid trips and falls on stairs or steps, but will still be able to move around freely.
Use of handrails, guardrails and guide lines.	These modifications can help a person move around more independently but can also be used to 'tell' the individual where they are or where they are going.
Limiting unnecessary background noise.	People will be able to hear speech more clearly, and will not have to shout.
Use of visual signs or objects to replace sounds, or add to them.	These can help people understand things in their daily routines which would normally use auditory signals, e.g. a dinner bell.
Large, clear printed signs.	These can help tell or remind people what to do, e.g. beside the emergency cord in the bathroom.
Use of simple pictures and symbols.	These can be used with or instead of words to make something even clearer.
Use of tactile methods (Braille/Moon systems or simpler methods) e.g. on cupboards or doors.	These can help those with poor sight to understand where things are or to follow instructions independently.
Use of colour-coding for different rooms or areas.	This helps people navigate confidently around different areas and conveys information to them about where they are.
Use of different floor patterns and textures (but not very shiny or slippery).	This helps those with both sight and hearing problems to recognise different rooms or areas without being told.

Facilitating communication for people with sight loss

Approaching the individual

It is always good practice to say someone's name when you wish to speak to them, so they can tell where the sound is coming from and tell if it is a familiar voice. If it is a first approach it is less startling for them if you also touch them lightly on the arm or shoulder when saying their name, so you do not seem to appear to out of nowhere and start speaking. It is polite to tell them your own name if you are not very familiar to them and it is good to face them at their eye level, especially if they have some sight.

You do not need to raise your voice unless you know they need this and try not to call to them from several feet away, as they may have trouble locating the direction of the sound.

Communicating with the individual

Always address the person directly, rather than a carer, even though they may appear to be looking past or through you. Some people will not realise they are doing this, and some people with additional hearing loss may need to turn their head to present their 'good' ear towards your voice. Stand still when speaking, so your voice is coming from the same place and does not get softer if you move your head around. Describe things as you speak to the person, especially to let them know where things and people are and if anything is being put in front of them. Do not move a person with sight loss (e.g. in a wheelchair) without giving them adequate warning, and never leave without telling the person you are doing so.

If their usual style of communication appears not to be working as well as before, consider whether they might need further assessment of their sight in case it is deteriorating.

Your assessment criteria:

2.2 Describe how the environment facilitates effective communication for people with sensory loss.

If a person has sight loss it is good practice to first speak their name so they can tell where the sound is coming from, and never to leave without telling the person you are doing so

Facilitating communication for people with hearing loss

Approaching the individual

As with partially sighted individuals, make sure you have the person's attention and say their name if necessary, before you start to speak. Try not to speak or call out from some distance away.

Communicating with the individual

It is even more important with individuals with hearing loss that you face the person when speaking, and don't cover your mouth, especially if the person depends on lip reading. Speak clearly, and slightly slower than usual, but don't over-exaggerate your lip movements as this can be confusing. Familiarise yourself with the particular hearing needs of the individual – ask them and the people who know them well. Notice if they need their hearing aid in before you try to speak to them, for example.

If you really need to raise your voice then do so, but don't shout – this can make you look angry and distorts the shape of your lip movements. Don't have a light behind you. This can make it difficult to see your face if the light is bright or casts a shadow on your face.

It is very important to reduce background noise, whether of others talking or the TV or radio playing, as people with even a mild hearing loss find it very hard to pick out speech from general noise. Move to a quieter place if necessary, though be aware that rooms that are very echoing, or full of heavy carpet and curtains, are equally difficult for people to hear clearly in.

Using equipment or sign language

If your workplace has an induction loop system installed, people with hearing aids can hear anyone whose voice can be picked up by the microphones by turning their aid to the 'T' position (up-to-date aids may do this automatically). Check if this applies in your workplace and, if so, exactly how it works. If the amplified sound comes through speakers, for example in a hall, this may also help others without a hearing aid.

Carer support for the individual's best method of communication is vital: if the person uses a system such as sign language, for example, the carers should be sufficiently fluent in it both to 'talk' to the individual and to understand what the individual may be 'saying' to them. This applies equally to an individual who may have a more informal way of communicating, for example making certain gestures or using eye-pointing to indicate what they want.

Remember that the individual's level of hearing may continue to change. People should be supported to have regular checks so that any extra support can be given when needed, such as changing the type of hearing aid.

Regular checks for individuals with hearing loss ensures the support they need is at the right level

Discuss

Think of three people with sensory loss who you have worked with. How have they benefited, or how might they benefit, from a specific approach or attitude to help them live with a sensory loss? What was done, or could be done?

Facilitating communication using accessible information

Most everyday information is spoken or written. This may need to be modified for a person with sensory loss, or another format or specific alternative used to enhance or replace it. When making information accessible to those with sensory loss, bear in mind the following.

▶ Accessibility can have wider benefits for everyone, e.g. the use of large, clear signs.

▶ In addition to ways of using print, think about the use of tapes, CDs, pictures, symbols, colours and objects which are also important.

▶ Make plans for how the individual will take advantage of access, as well as the format of access – e.g. large print books are only useful if the person can get hold of them, and other types of access issues may be involved.

▶ Consider that providing accessible information properly may take more time and money – e.g. using large print can involve a different format and more pages.

▶ Be aware that often, however good the accessibility of the information, some people with sensory needs may need the help of another person to enable them to make the most of it.

▶ People who speak languages other than English may have different levels of understanding or literacy in their different languages – their preferred language should always be used.

Accessible information formats for sight loss

Accessible information formats for sight loss are shown in Figure 14.6.

Your assessment criteria:

2.2 Describe how the environment facilitates effective communication for people with sensory loss.

The use of accessible information benefits those with sensory loss and can have wider benefits for everyone

Tactile support
e.g. different floor textures in different home areas, tactile 'signing', and using objects

Reading with Braille
This uses patterns of six dots, so is more abstract

Reading with Moon
This uses curved shapes closely resembling letters, so may be more suitable for new/older learners

Radio programmes
Also 'listen-again' on a computer (where accessible)

Accessible information formats for sight loss

Use of large clear print
Size at least at 14 point using black on a white or yellow background, allowing lots of space around the text

Audiotapes and CDs
Make sure the players are suitable for those with sight loss

Colour-coding
e.g. parts of a text or areas of a home

Use of simple symbols
if they are readily understood

Figure 14.6 Accessible information formats for sight loss

Accessible information formats for hearing loss

Accessible information formats for hearing loss are shown in Figure 14.7.

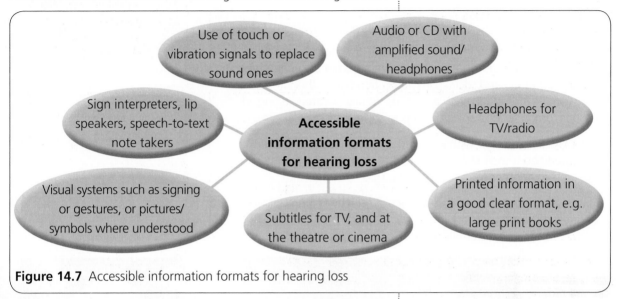

Figure 14.7 Accessible information formats for hearing loss

How may effective communication have a positive impact on the lives of individuals with sensory loss?

Effective communication includes not only the individual making their own needs, wishes and opinions known, but also benefiting from information and social communication from others. These may include individuals such as friends, family or carers, alongside groups, organisations or institutions in society.

For example, a person with impaired sight will be much better informed about their choice of vote if the candidates' leaflets are available in another format such as on CD.

Figure 14.8 shows the positive impact of effective communication on individuals with sensory loss.

Your assessment criteria:

2.3 Explain how effective communication may have a positive impact on the lives of individuals with sensory loss.

Effective communication involves individuals and engages them in a positive way

Figure 14.8 The positive impact of effective communication on individuals with sensory loss

Positive impact of effective communication	Because...
Less isolation	The person is not left out among others who can communicate easily
Less depression	The person does not feel useless or friendless
Maintenance of family and social friendships	The person can still communicate on an equal footing
The person can be treated more as an individual adult than a child who has things 'done' to them. They can take part in their own care, so it is more person-centred	The person can convey what they do and don't like, or do and don't want to do
The person may feel more confident in communicating in the way they need to	They can find support from others who communicate in a similar way to them, and those who enable this
The person can have a fuller and more involved life	They can get information on services, leisure facilities and so on, in a way that they can understand
The person can make a contribution to developing better health and social care	They can give their views and opinions to help shape services in a way that suits them
The person can take part as a citizen in the affairs of the community and country	They are enabled to take part in wider society if they wish to, e.g. council surveys, local or national voting

Discuss

Think of the main relationships you are part of and the activities you take part in.

► How do these involve communication?

► Can you imagine how a communication difficulty due to sensory loss might affect those relationships or activities?

► How might this help you to empathise with the needs and wishes of people in your care with sensory loss?

Knowledge Assessment Task   **2.3**

Explain three ways that effective communication can have a positive impact on people with sensory loss, giving one explanation for each of the below:

1. In one-to-one communication
2. With family, friends and carers
3. In wider society.

Understand the main causes and conditions of sensory loss

What are the main causes of sensory loss?

The main causes of sensory loss are due to **congenital** defects, inherited disorders, illness or injury. Some causes are sudden, while others come on slowly. A person may be born with one or more sensory losses, but then **acquire** others during the course of their life. For example, a person with Down syndrome is likely to be born with a degree of hearing loss but might later develop a problem with sight or touch. The parts of the ear are shown in Figure 14.9, with the most common hearing impairments following and shown in Figure 14.10. The parts of the eye are shown in Figure 14.12 (page 432) with the most common sight impairments following and shown in Figure 14.13. However, **congenital** or **acquired disorders** can also affect a person's ability to feel or interpret touch sensations, to smell or to taste (the latter two being closely linked). This is very common after some general illnesses or diseases, for example a stroke, or as part of a **degenerative** disease such as Parkinson's or multiple sclerosis.

Some main causes of hearing loss

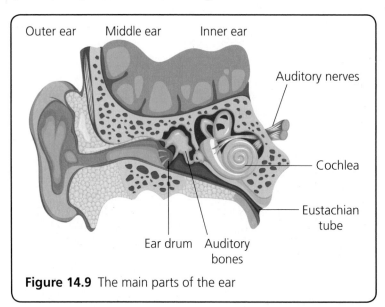

Outer ear   Middle ear   Inner ear

Auditory nerves

Cochlea

Eustachian tube

Ear drum   Auditory bones

Figure 14.9 The main parts of the ear

The outer ear can sometimes affect a person's hearing, for example by being too small to collect sound waves properly or by the ear canal being full of wax.

The middle ear is more often involved with both congenital and acquired hearing loss. The eardrum may become tough and not vibrate properly because of infections, or the eardrum may become perforated (pierced). The middle ear must have air in it for the small bones to vibrate and pass the sound waves on to the nerves in the inner ear. Normally the Eustachian tube, connecting the middle ear to the throat,

Your assessment criteria:

3.1 Identify the main causes of sensory loss.

Key terms

Acquired disorder: a condition that occurs sometime in life after birth

Amplified: made bigger, in this context sound that is boosted and made louder

Congenital disorder: a condition which is present at birth, caused either before or during birth, although it may or may not be obvious until later in life; if it shows itself later it may be referred to as being acquired

Degenerative: a condition that will always get progressively worse rather than better

Trauma: damage (in this case physical)

helps to do this, but it may get blocked or inflamed. The middle ear may also fill up with a kind of 'glue' after infections that cannot drain away properly.

Conductive hearing loss: the above types of hearing loss are known as 'conductive' because they affect sound being conducted through the outer and middle ear. However, the person may be able to hear quite well if the sound is conducted through the bones of the head straight to the inner ear, or if the sound is **amplified** enough. Because they can often hear their own voices this way, people with an acquired conductive loss tend to speak more quietly than before.

The inner ear turns the vibrations from the middle ear into impulses which travel along tiny hairs on the cochlea and from there become electrical nerve impulses going to the brain. Ultimately we 'hear' with the auditory part of our brains.

Hearing loss involving the nerves (nerve deafness) may not be helped by amplifying the sound if the nerves are too damaged to convey it to the brain. This type of hearing loss may be separate from, or occur along with, conductive loss, particularly in old age or after certain illnesses. People with this type of loss cannot hear their own voice properly so will tend to speak more loudly or shout.

Congenital and acquired hearing loss

Figure 14.10 outlines some factors in congenital hearing loss and Figure 14.11 some factors in acquired hearing loss.

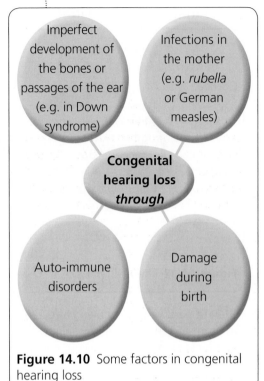

Figure 14.10 Some factors in congenital hearing loss

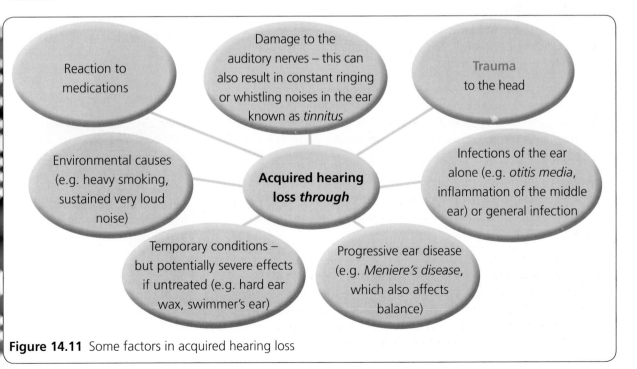

Figure 14.11 Some factors in acquired hearing loss

Some main causes of sight loss

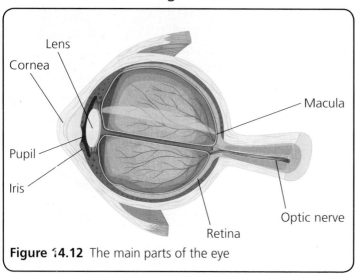

Figure 14.12 The main parts of the eye

Your assessment criteria:

3.1 Identify the main causes of sensory loss.

Different parts of the eye being affected will produce different symptoms when examined by an ophthalmologist (eye doctor), but the effects on people's behaviour may be similar.

The lens: if this is clouding over, light cannot be focussed properly. This is known as a cataract and may be successfully removed.

The cornea: if this gets thickened or inflamed it will affect sight but may be treated successfully if it is a result of infection.

The retina: the most acute problem with the retina at the back of the eye is for it to become detached. If this happens it must be assessed by an ophthalmologist urgently to prevent any permanent loss of sight.

The macula: if the macula in the centre of the retina begins to degenerate, the person will start to lose the sharp central vision needed for reading or driving.

Glaucoma is a common condition in older people and in some ethnic groups, caused by rising pressure inside the eye. This may cause no obvious symptoms until it is too late and much of the sight is permanently lost so regular eye tests should take place so it can be spotted.

Damage to the nerves, for example from the pressure of a tumour, will affect eyesight even if the eye itself is normal, since signals cannot get through properly to the visual part of the brain.

Congenital and acquired sight loss

Figure 14.13 outlines some factors in congenital sight loss and Figure 14.14 in acquired sight loss.

Investigate

Look into a source of information about a condition which some of the people you work with are likely to have, for example Down syndrome or Parkinson disease. What are the main congenital problems with sensory loss that such people may have, if any? What sensory problems might they acquire later on?

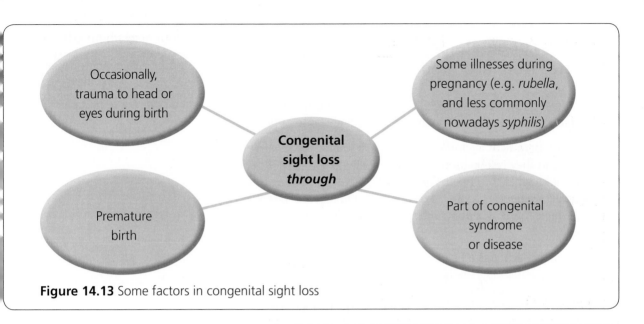

Figure 14.13 Some factors in congenital sight loss

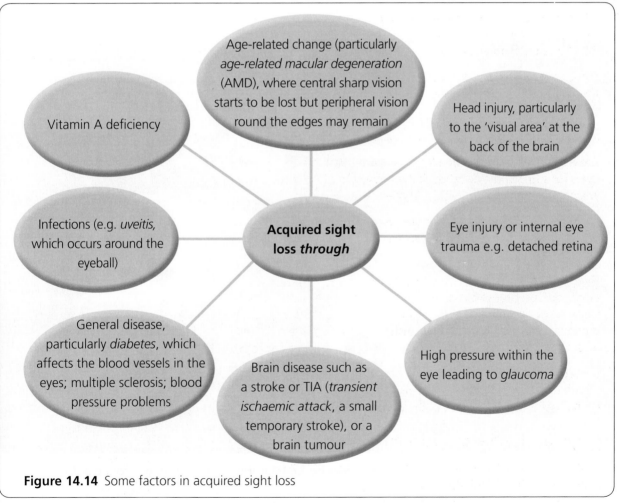

Figure 14.14 Some factors in acquired sight loss

What is congenital sensory loss and how does it differ from acquired sensory loss?

Your assessment criteria:

3.2 Define congenital sensory loss and acquired sensory loss.

The difference between a congenital sensory loss from birth and an acquired sensory loss as life progresses is not simply one of timing.

If a person born with a congenital sensory loss had appropriate help and support they will be used to their disability to some extent and familiar with what they need. For example, a person born deaf will probably have been brought up to use sign language or lip reading, and perhaps to use a hearing aid. Many of their friends may also be deaf.

A person who acquires a hearing problem in later life, however, may not want to admit they are going deaf or may find it hard to adjust to using an aid. Their friends may not have hearing problems and may find it difficult to adjust to someone using a hearing aid, or a new way of communicating.

An individual with congenital hearing loss may be familiar with sign language from childhood and many of their friends may also be deaf

Awareness of family and carers to congenital and acquired sensory loss

Another issue is the awareness of family and carers to the problems likely to be caused by an acquired as opposed to a congenital sensory loss. Assuming a person with a congenital loss has had a good and accurate diagnosis of their problems and the support needed, family and carers should be fairly clear about what they need to do to help and encourage the individual. If a person suddenly or gradually develops a sensory loss where none was suspected before, however, family or carers may not know what to do. In the case of someone with an existing sensory loss, the development of a new problem may not get the attention it deserves because family or carers are used to the individual's problems and assume that their situation will not change.

An individual with acquired hearing loss may need the attention of an expert team, and their families and carers may need guidance on how best to support the individual

Knowledge Assessment Task   3.1   3.2

1. Outline four different types of causes of sensory loss (hearing) and four different causes of sensory loss (sight).

2. Which of these causes is congenital and which is acquired? What does this mean, and what difference might this make to the individual and their carers?

Demographic factors that influence the incidence of sensory loss

There are various **demographic** factors that influence the number of people with sensory loss in the general population, where they live and what services they need. The most important current factor is the increasing number or **incidence** of elderly people living to a greater age with the increased risk of sight and hearing problems. This means there are increasing numbers of people with one or more sensory loss. The other significant factor is the number of babies being born and surviving with complex handicaps. Many of them will have sight or hearing problems from birth. As these individuals now live longer and age they may also acquire the typical sight or hearing problems that others in the general population develop in later life.

The impact of statistics on services

The figures for people suffering one or more sensory losses come mainly from government statistics, and also from charities concerned with the deaf, hard-of-hearing or blind/partially sighted, such as the RNID (Royal National Institute for Deaf People) and the RNIB (Royal National Institute of Blind People). Figures for people with sight or hearing losses are fairly easy to come by, but figures for people with touch, smell or taste problems are not usually recorded as such. Official figures tend to come from surveys or from registers such as the one of individuals registered as blind. Since not everyone can or wants to respond to surveys and some people don't want to be registered or don't know they can be, the numbers are likely to be underestimated. This has serious implications since social, health and care services tend to base their services around the number of people they actually know about with particular needs.

The incidence of hearing loss

In the year ending 31 March 2010, the RNID reported that the number of people registered through social services was as follows.

Deaf: 56,400 on the register – approximately 0.1% of the population and an increase of 24% since 1995. The largest increase was in the number of people over 75, which rose by 8%.

Hard of hearing: 156,500 on the register, approximately 0.3% of the population, also an increase of 24% since 15 years previously. The number of people aged over 75 in this category increased by only 1%, but overall they had become 69% of people on the register which was a much bigger proportion than previously.

Deafblind: this is the most common dual sensory loss, outlined on page 420.

Percentage of the population: the RNID estimate from their experience that there are over 2 million people with hearing loss

Key terms

Demographic: relating to the structure of a population

Incidence: how common something is

The increase of the elderly population is leading to a higher number of individuals with sensory loss

between the ages of 16 and 60, and over 6 million people with hearing loss over the age of 60, which would be nearly 15% of the population. They also believe that about 71% of people over the age of 70 have hearing loss – in other words the majority. Of this group, people may have a mild loss (over 26%), a moderate loss (nearly 37%), a severe loss (over 6%) or a profound loss (over 1%). The implication for carers is that they should assume an older person has some degree of hearing loss unless proved otherwise.

The incidence of sight loss

The RNIB reckons there are around 80 different eye conditions, though some such as short/long-sightedness and colour-blindness are fairly common in the general population. Those receiving care need to have regular eye tests to check for any possible medical conditions, and whether they need new or stronger glasses or contact lenses. RNIB research (2008) suggested that there were a total of 1.8 million adults with blindness or partial sight in the UK, or about 4% of the population. Research also suggests that in the next thirty years the number of such people will double to around 4 million.

The incidence of deafblindness

In 2008, there were 88,500 people registered as being blind/ partially sighted plus another disability. Of these 29%, i.e. nearly a third, had hearing loss as their additional impairment, giving a figure of around 23,000 deafblind people or 0.05% of the population. However, the results of a needs survey in 1991 suggested that many over 75 with both sight and hearing loss were not on any register, so had not been counted. Some deafblind people may already carry a red and white stick, as opposed to a plain white one, but many people don't know what this means. When a person is diagnosed as deafblind, this does not mean their condition will necessarily stay the same as when they were first registered.

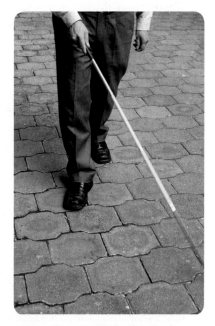

Around one-third of people registered blind/partially sighted also have hearing loss. Deafblindness can be signalled by use of a red and white stick

Case study

Simon is going to work at a new elderly care facility being set up in his area. The management are discussing with the new staff how they are setting up services for the residents. They are proposing various ideas for laying out the home and for social and other activities, but do not appear to have taken into account any sensory needs that residents might have or might develop.

1. What issues do you think Simon might raise with the management of the home?
2. What figures could he use to support his arguments?

Knowledge Assessment Task   3.3

What are the main demographic factors that influence the numbers of people with sensory loss in the population? If you were working with the elderly, what proportion or percentage of people might you expect to have some sensory loss?

What are the indicators and signs of sight loss, hearing loss and deafblindness?

The signs of sensory loss will vary according to whether the individual has always had a sight problem (or hearing problem, or both), has developed it in recent times, or is just starting to develop it. Some signs are very obvious, but others may be subtle or develop over such a long period that they are missed. For example, a person who suddenly cannot see, perhaps because of a detached retina, is likely to show verbally or by their distress that something has happened. The gradual loss of sight in glaucoma, on the other hand, may go unnoticed by carers, or they or the individual may assume it is an inevitable part of ageing. Some signs will be reported immediately by the individual; others may be attributed by the individual or carers to other causes. For example, a person who goes suddenly deaf because of a virus may be able to describe to a carer what has happened, but if they cannot then a sudden change in their behaviour may be attributed to personality, or a general illness, rather than the specific effect on their hearing.

Some typical signs of possible sensory loss

Figure 14.13 shows some typical signs of possible sight loss, and Figure 14.14 shows some typical signs of possible hearing loss.

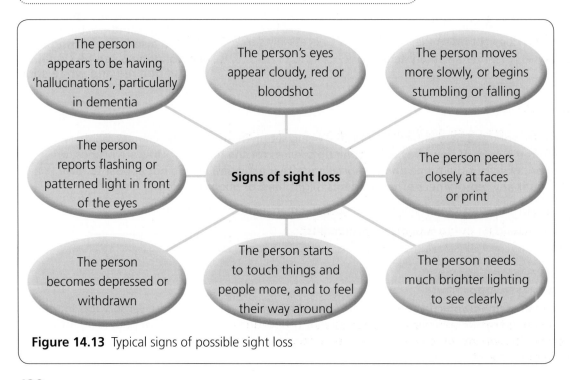

Figure 14.13 Typical signs of possible sight loss

The person appears to be having 'hallucinations', particularly in dementia

The person's eyes appear cloudy, red or bloodshot

The person moves more slowly, or begins stumbling or falling

The person reports flashing or patterned light in front of the eyes

Signs of sight loss

The person peers closely at faces or print

The person becomes depressed or withdrawn

The person starts to touch things and people more, and to feel their way around

The person needs much brighter lighting to see clearly

The person becomes withdrawn from social contact, or becomes irritable in social situations

The person starts to talk too loudly (nerve deafness) or too softly (conductive deafness)

The person cannot follow speech, especially in a group or where there is background noise

The person starts to rely more on touch, e.g. knowing the phone is ringing from vibration, not sound

Signs of hearing loss

The person looks more closely at faces, trying to lip read

The person turns up the TV or radio to a degree that annoys others

The person does not respond to their name or social greetings as before

The person frequently asks others to repeat what they have said

Figure 14.14 Typical signs of possible hearing loss

Case study

Rachida is a young woman who has been living in a supported living home for several years. Her carers are present overnight, in the early mornings and in the evenings, but during the day she attends activities at various day services. She wears strong glasses, which the carers remind her to put on every day.

Over a period of several weeks, Rachida starts not wanting to go to her day activities any more. The activities supervisor at one service reports that she does not take part in tabletop activities any more, and seems reluctant to make drinks in the kitchen as she did previously. She sits happily in social groups, but doesn't seem to talk to people as much as she did before.

1. What do you think may be happening to Rachida and why?
2. How could you start to find out whether her change in behaviour is due to:
   a) boredom or depression   b) increasing sight problems   c) hearing problems?

Deafblindness

Those who may be developing **deafblindness** may show any of the previous symptoms, depending on which sense is beginning to be affected. However they may find it more difficult to convey to carers what is happening to them, according to how good they are at communicating, and carers need to be alert that behaviour changes may be the first and possibly only indication that something is wrong. Some individuals may become withdrawn or apathetic, whereas others may become irritable or aggressive.

Knowledge Assessment Task   4.1

Describe the main indicators and signs of sight loss and of hearing loss. What other signs might there be in the case of a person developing deafblindness?

What actions might you take if you have concerns about onset of sensory loss in an individual, or changes in sensory status?

If you notice someone appears to have a sensory loss that has not been addressed, or appears to be developing one, you should speak first of all to your manager. Record in the person's notes that these issues have been raised. Find out if the individual's medical background may predispose them to certain kinds of sensory loss.

If professional staff such as a district nurse or psychologist visit the individual, discuss your concerns with them. They may have knowledge on particular issues likely to affect that person.

Record the results of any verbal conversation in the notes. If there is a case conference on the individual, make sure a copy of the minutes is filed in an appropriate place in the person's records.

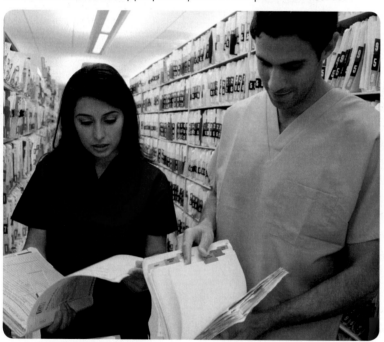

Concern about onset or change in sensory loss should be noted and placed in an individual's records

Speak to a manager as a matter of urgency if you feel the person is at risk of coming to harm, or if their sight or hearing appears to have failed suddenly. Sudden loss of sight, in particular, is usually a medical emergency and must be treated as such even if there is no pain or discomfort. The symptoms might only affect eyesight or they could be the result of something such as a stroke.

Further actions where sensory loss is suspected

Where sensory loss is suspected, take the further actions below.

1. Consider referring the individual for a basic hearing or sight test, or for further investigations, and consider what extra support they might need for this. Make sure any test results are entered in the notes, and discuss with your manager or the appropriate professional whether anything needs to be done next.

2. Make short, regular notes observing the individual's behaviour, so that you can explain if needed what they are doing and how their behaviour might have changed. Make sure that your notes are recorded and dated in an appropriate way in the records so that they could be useful later if necessary, for example at a hospital visit.

3. Always discuss tactfully with the person, if possible, what your concerns are and try to find out from them whether they feel they are having problems. If they deny that they are, they may not have noticed anything or they may in fact be very worried and need careful support.

4. Discuss your concerns with any others who are dealing with the individual, being careful about confidentiality, so that all information on the individual can be gathered together in a useful way. The person's key worker should be responsible for following up on any referrals or further actions until the problem is resolved as far as possible.

Short, regular notes from observing an individual's behaviour may be of use at a hospital visit, ensuring the person is given appropriate support

Knowledge Assessment Task   4.2

Explain what you would do, in the most professional way, if you had concerns about the onset of sensory loss in an individual or changes in their sensory status. When might you need to take action urgently?

Sources of support for people with sensory loss

Relevant organisations

The organisation you work for is the first place to look for extra support, as they may well have experience in supporting people with sensory loss. Modifications can be made to the individual's routines or everyday activities, which can be carried out by staff familiar with the effects of sensory loss. More major changes to support the individual, such as providing larger clearer signs around the home, may need discussion with senior management, especially if the physical fabric of the home requires modification or alteration. Further support can be sought from outside organisations, such as the local social services for aids to daily living, or specialist organisations for advice and training.

Training and assistance

The organisation you work for may also provide support for the individual by ensuring staff are well trained in appropriate methods of communication, for example. Your workplace may offer **in-service training** as an optional or mandatory part of your work. If you know you may be dealing with individuals with sensory loss such as the elderly, it is better to start training early so that you can help these individuals in the best way from the start.

Most local social services departments have staff who can help with queries or with assessment and training. For example most have a **sensory impairment team**, and some will have a team specialising in people with profound and severe sensory loss. They should help with obtaining aids for daily living (ADLs) such as phones that vibrate or microwaves with large buttons, or will know who to refer you to for the right help.

The individual's GP should be the first port of call if you feel a hearing or sight assessment is required for someone, and they or others at the practice may be able to signpost you to further help.

Key terms

In-service training: training for employees to help them develop skills that are relevant to the service they provide in their job

Sensory impairment team: a team consisting of specialists in different kinds of sensory impairment

Training sessions enable care workers to best support those who may be experiencing sensory loss

Specialist support for hearing loss

Several specialist organisations can help at a local or national level with advice, support, training and equipment for those with a degree of hearing loss. The RNID (Royal National Institute for the Deaf) is perhaps the best known, and there is also the BDA (British Deaf Association) as well as the NDCS (National Deaf Children's Society) that people may have known when younger.

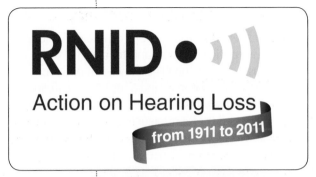

If needing to use sign language, courses are often offered in community education centres, taken by trained tutors. These are usually in BSL (British Sign Language). Those who might not cope with learning, in effect, a whole new language may benefit from learning the reduced version of BSL, known as Makaton. Unlike BSL this uses normal English word-order but does not sign every word, and can be used to support and enhance spoken language, rather than as a substitute for it as used by the profoundly deaf. Makaton tutors can generally be found through a local speech and language therapy department, or via the Makaton website. An organisation known as CACDP (Council for the Advancement of Communication with Deaf People) is responsible for awarding training certificates to those training in British (or Irish) sign language, and registers those who wish to work as interpreters for the signing or deafblind community, lipspeakers for those who can lip-read, and speech-to-text interpreters.

If an NHS hearing aid is needed following the person's assessment, a hearing therapist can advise on the suitability of different aids and on the procedure for learning to use the aid for maximum benefit. This advice is useful even if the person decides to buy an aid privately, as it could avoid costly mistakes.

Thriving support networks can be found for people who are deaf and have used sign language most of their life – look in local directories or local library information. For people with acquired hearing loss, there may need to be a more individual approach to finding support, for example finding a club for the elderly where the premises has a loop system installed. Social services and local council offices will probably be able to help with this.

It is always worth 'picking the brains' of any visiting health or social care professionals to your workplace, who often have a wide range of contacts in the local area. Out in the community, find out and look out for businesses and services which advertise that they have an induction loop fitted, to help those with hearing aids, or which can provide a sign-language interpreter.

Specialist support for sight loss

Several specialist organisations can help at a local or national level with advice, support and training for those with a degree of sight loss, such as the RNIB (Royal National Institute for the Blind), Action for Blind People, and Sense (for deafblind people). There is also SeeAbility for those with additional complex needs. Sense has published useful guidance on communicating with deafblind people, called *Making Contact* (www.sense.org.uk).

Large hospitals usually run Low Vision clinics, where an ophthalmologist (eye doctor) will assess an individual's needs, particularly where surgery is unlikely to succeed. The person may need to be seen by such a specialist to qualify for registering as partially sighted. This registration then entitles the individual to various types of support, such as the special card that they or a helper can put in the windscreen of a car to get free or more convenient parking.

The local optician can check the eyes but will need to refer on to the hospital if a problem is suspected. Opticians can also recommend whether glasses will be of use to the individual.

Some councils have rehabilitation workers for the partially-sighted, and also for the deafblind – contact your local council offices for advice.

Many local services or volunteers run 'Blind Clubs' which are typically for those with poor sight as well as the totally blind.

The local council is the place to go to find out about sign-language interpreters and Guide Helps (communicator guides). They will probably also have details about the Guide Dogs charity in the local area (many shops and other places will display a sign to indicate that guide dogs are welcome, even if normally dogs are not allowed.)

Out in the community, look for accessible information used by businesses and services, such as information in large print or on a CD. Places such as libraries may have such information on further services and support for the sight-impaired. Many shops and businesses now display a logo on their doors to indicate that the premises are user-friendly to those needs, including with sight or hearing problems.

Investigate

Have a look around your local community and see if you can find at least three different examples of places where people with sensory loss could expect to find support to carry out an activity: for example, an induction loop facility at the doctor's surgery, or a staff member who understands sign language available at a certain shop.

Case study

Ben and Anna are an older married couple living in assisted care. Ben has quite a severe hearing loss, while Anna has a mild hearing loss but is also developing rather poor sight. They wish to be as independent as possible, but are finding it difficult to deal with their various drugs, medical appointment letters and diet sheets. They also do not go out very much.

1. What accessible formats could you try to develop, or seek advice on developing, to help them both cope better?

2. What other assessment, advice or support could you consider offering or suggesting to them?

Knowledge Assessment Task   4.3

1. Give examples of three national organisations that you or an individual could contact at national or local level, for further information and support around sensory loss.

2. Suggest six examples of local people or services that might help you and/or an individual with advice and support around sensory loss (including sight loss, hearing loss and deafblindness).

Are you ready for assessment?

AC	What do you know now?	Assessment task	✓
1.1	Analyse how a range of factors can impact on individuals with sensory loss	Page 407	
1.2	Analyse how societal attitudes and beliefs impact on individuals with sensory loss	Page 407	
1.3	Explore how a range of factors, societal attitudes and beliefs impact on service provision	Page 413	
2.1	Explain the methods of communication used by individuals with: sight loss/hearing loss/ deafblindness	Page 427	
2.2	Describe how the environment facilitates effective communication for people with sensory loss	Page 427	
2.3	Explain how effective communication may have a positive impact on the lives of individuals with sensory loss	Page 429	

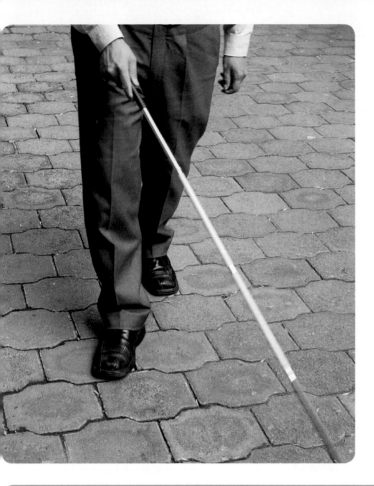

AC	What do you know now?	Assessment task	✓
3.1	Identify the main causes of sensory loss	Page 435	
3.2	Define congenital sensory loss and acquired sensory loss	Page 435	
3.3	Identify the demographic factors that influence the incidence of sensory loss in the population	Page 437	
4.1	Identify the indicators and signs of: sight loss/hearing loss/deafblindness	Page 439	
4.2	Explain actions that should be taken if there are concerns about onset of sensory loss or changes in sensory status	Page 441	
4.3	Identify sources of support for those who may be experiencing onset of sensory loss	Page 445	

Index

Acknowledgements

© Action for Blind People: 444

Alamy: 7, 8, 10, 13, 15, 17, 18, 20, 23, 24, 28, 38, 40, 45, 46, 55, 56, 60, 61, 62, 64, 66, 69, 72, 73, 76, 77, 79, 80, 84, 85, 87, 88, 90, 90, 91, 96, 106, 108, 110, 114, 120, 121, 122, 125, 126, 131, 133, 137, 146, 149, 152, 154, 155, 156, 157, 159, 167, 168, 171, 174, 175, 176, 178, 182, 184, 186, 188, 189, 190, 192, 193, 197, 198, 199, 200, 201, 212, 213, 214, 215, 216, 217, 218, 224, 226, 228, 230, 232, 233, 236, 239, 248, 258, 261, 262, 264, 266, 267, 271, 274, 275, 277, 279, 280, 284, 288, 291, 292, 294, 295, 296, 298, 299, 299, 300, 304, 308, 314, 315, 316, 318, 319, 319, 320, 321, 323, 324, 326, 329, 330, 334, 336, 340, 341, 342, 349, 351, 354, 357, 359, 362, 364, 365, 367, 368, 370, 371, 372, 376, 381, 383, 385, 389, 390, 393, 396, 400, 403, 403, 406, 408, 409, 410, 411, 413, 415, 416, 417, 418, 421, 424, 425, 428, 434, 436, 440, 442

British Deaf Association: 443

© Crown copyright: 128, 235, 310, 312, 332

iStock: 2, 29, 32, 36, 42, 51, 58, 82, 83, 90, 104, 106, 112, 116, 135, 142, 144, 150, 162, 166, 195, 195, 195, 195, 203, 206, 211, 220, 225, 230, 234, 241, 242, 246, 247, 256, 263, 268, 269, 270, 273, 278, 281, 286, 290, 305, 322, 325, 327, 346, 350, 353, 356, 360, 361, 373, 395, 419, 435, 437, 441, 445

© Royal National Institute of Blind People: 444

© Royal National Institute for Deaf People: 443

Science Photo Library: 26, 27, 227, 338, 343, 386

© Sense: 412, 414, 420, 422, 426

Shutterstock: 30, 48, 100, 102, 123, 139, 145, 209, 221, 229, 244, 245, 251, 253, 276, 301, 313, 319, 327, 335, 352, 407, 430, 432

Notes

Z960074

Health and Social Care

Level 3 Diploma Candidate Handbook

Mark Walsh • Ann Mitchell • Elaine Millar • John Rowe
Lois Greenhalgh • Eleanor Langridge • Richard Chaloner

Published by Collins Education
An imprint of HarperCollins Publishers
77-85 Fulham Palace Rd
Hammersmith
London
W6 8JB

Browse the complete Collins Education catalogue at
www.collinseducation.com

10 9 8 7 6 5 4 3

ISBN 978-0-00-743053-6

Mark Walsh, Eleanor Langridge, John Rowe, Ann Mitchell, Elaine Millar,
Richard Chaloner and Lois Greenhalgh assert their moral rights to be
identified as the authors of this work.

British Library Cataloguing in Publication Data. A Catalogue record for this
publication is available from the British Library.

Commissioned by Charlie Evans
Edited by Shirley Wakley
Picture research by Erdinch Yigitce and Matthew Hammond
Design and typesetting by Q2A Media
Cover design by Angela English

Index by Robert Spicer

Printed and bound by Printing Express, Hong Kong

MIX
Paper from
responsible sources

FSC
www.fsc.org
FSC™ C007454